AF361473

CANADIAN ECOPOLITICS

CANADIAN ECOPOLITICS

Rosalind Warner | Peter Stoett | Will Greaves

UNIVERSITY OF TORONTO PRESS
Toronto Buffalo London

© University of Toronto Press 2025
Toronto Buffalo London
utppublishing.com
Printed in Canada

ISBN 978-1-4875-0816-6 (cloth)   ISBN 978-1-4875-3767-8 (EPUB)
ISBN 978-1-4875-2570-5 (paper)   ISBN 978-1-4875-3766-1 (PDF)

Library and Archives Canada Cataloguing in Publication

Title: Canadian ecopolitics / Rosalind Warner, Peter Stoett, and Will Greaves.
Names: Warner, Rosalind, 1964– author | Stoett, Peter J. (Peter John), 1965– author | Greaves, Wilfrid, 1984– author
Description: Includes bibliographical references and index.
Identifiers: Canadiana (print) 20250159767 | Canadiana (ebook) 20250159783 | ISBN 9781487508166 (cloth) | ISBN 9781487525705 (paper) | ISBN 9781487537678 (EPUB) | ISBN 9781487537661 (PDF)
Subjects: LCSH: Political ecology – Canada. | LCSH: Environmental policy – Canada. | LCSH: Natural resources – Canada – Management. | LCSH: Canada – Environmental conditions.
Classification: LCC JA75.8 .W37 2025 | DDC 333.70971 – dc23

Cover design: Liz Harasymczuk
Cover image: iStock.com/Halfpoint; Nalidsa/Shutterstock.com

We welcome comments and suggestions regarding any aspect of our publications – please feel free to contact us at news@utorontopress.com or visit us at utorontopress.com.

Every effort has been made to contact copyright holders; in the event of an error or omission, please notify the publisher.

We wish to acknowledge the land on which the University of Toronto Press operates. This land is the traditional territory of the Wendat, the Anishnaabeg, the Haudenosaunee, the Métis, and the Mississaugas of the Credit First Nation.

University of Toronto Press acknowledges the financial support of the Government of Canada and the Ontario Arts Council, an agency of the Government of Ontario, for its publishing activities.

Contents

7 Freshwater and Canadian Ecopolitics 155

8 Oceans   179

9 Climate Ecopolitics   210

10 Biosecurity and Health   229

Illustrations

Table

Boxes and Case Studies

Preface

As this book goes to print in early 2025, the field of ecopolitics is attracting the steadfast attention it so clearly deserves, if for rather gloomy reasons. Donald Trump's re-election to a second term as president of the United States has sent shock waves across Canada as he muses aloud about a Canadian "fifty-first state" and threatens massive tariffs on cross-border trade. Equally remarkable is his full-scale intent to diminish the environmental protections and clean energy investments made by his predecessors, particularly Joe Biden. To most observers, Trump's ruminations about seizing parts or all of Canada, Greenland, and Panama point to one thing: the hunger to acquire resources – including critical minerals, fresh water, and strategic waterways – that those countries possess. How the Canadian public and political elite respond to these statements will play a key part in determining how these events unfold.

Prime Minister Justin Trudeau has announced his intention to retire as prime minister, motivated by public opinion polls showing him trailing the Conservative Party, which has made political gold out of criticizing the carbon tax the Liberal government passed into law in 2018. Indeed, both leading contenders for Trudeau's job as leader of the Liberal Party have declared their intention to scrap the consumer carbon tax if elected. Meanwhile, the Canadian government announced a new $20 billion loan to the Trans Mountain Pipeline Expansion (TMX), bringing the total spent on this project to around $50 billion. In 2024, TMX began operation to transport diluted bitumen from Alberta to terminals in British Columbia; the pipeline (approved prior to Trump's re-election) has been praised by the oil and gas sector, rationalized by the federal government, and condemned by environmentalists on the grounds that pipelines leak when they fail and contribute to climate change when they succeed. Members of Indigenous communities remain divided over the impacts and benefits of this carboniferous infrastructure. Many British Columbians remain fiercely opposed to transporting diluted bitumen to their beloved Pacific Coast, yet BC continues to subsidize and grow its own new liquified natural gas sector, including pipelines that run through Indigenous territories, for export to Asia.

Other ecopolitical events too recent to be covered in this book are also in the news. Unseasonal fires recently devastated large swathes of Los Angeles, California, and the "fire season" has become a "fire year" in some parts of Canada, as so-called zombie fires continue to burn through the winter in British Columbia and Alberta. The North Atlantic right whale continues along the path to extinction, joined by many other mammals, insects, plants, and other forms of biodiversity native to Canadian soil and waters. Negotiations for a global plastic treaty failed to reach a conclusion despite a high-stakes conference in South Korea, though there is sufficient political energy to continue the talks into late 2025. The increased incidence of avian flu is raising the price of eggs and poultry across North America and poses a sincere threat to biosecurity. Indeed, all the issues discussed in this book continue to capture the public imagination as the triple planetary crisis of climate change, biodiversity loss, and pollution continues to threaten Canadian landscapes, urban and rural communities, and coasts.

Our intention with *Canadian Ecopolitics* is to provide the reader with a sound, historically challenging, issues-based journey into a topic that changes constantly but is rooted in some perennial truths about competition over natural resources, the creation of political narratives, and the severe consequences of living beyond the limits afforded by Earth's diminishing ecosystem services. No matter how much turmoil Canadians face, they will be more resilient and better able to plan ahead if they have a firm grounding in the fundamental ecopolitical context that has been the canvas on which the idea of Canadian statehood – with its idiosyncratic mix of coloniality, extractivism, and envious social, economic, and political achievements – has been painted. As we enter what is, arguably, one of the most uncertain half-decades of Canadian history, amid worsening ecological and geopolitical conditions, it is more vital than ever to be equipped with such knowledge. Just as important, we must challenge the ways we think about our current circumstances and future possibilities, guided by the ethical light of environmental justice. Ecopolitics is the stuff of historical trajectories, but it is also, we argue, the real politics of our world that is constantly evolving. It demonstrates both peril and promise in this precarious age.

Rosalind Warner, Kelowna
Peter Stoett, Oshawa and Montreal
Will Greaves, Victoria

Acknowledgements

This book would not have been possible without the support of many people, over several years, including during the COVID-19 pandemic. We are grateful for all the help and encouragement we've received, from far too many people to list, throughout our careers in academia and beyond, including thousands of students who have demonstrated their curiosity about things ecopolitical.

Rosalind wishes to thank Okanagan College research assistants who helped write and research parts of the work: Joshua Anson Lee, Lindsey Jones, Caroline Araujo Pinheiro Da Costa, Nallely Wong Perales, and Randolph Ramos. She also wishes to acknowledge the inspiration of her advisor at York University, David V.J. Bell, and her family, spouse Paul and son Justin, for their love and support. Peter thanks all his kids (Ally, Giuliana, and Gianluca) and his superstar wife, Cristina Romanelli. Will thanks his wife, Carolyn, daughter, Eleanor, and neighbours on southern Vancouver Island for being a source of support and inspiration in the pursuit of a more sustainable future.

We extend a special note of appreciation to Dr. Shane Mulligan for his assistance in researching and writing sections of the book, and to Matt General for contributing a case study.

We also extend our sincere appreciation and thanks to the many people who contributed at University of Toronto Press, including but not limited to Leanne Rancourt, Janice Evans, and Rebecca Duce, and to anonymous reviewers for reading and commenting on the draft.

Finally, we thank the Canadian Defence and Security Network (CDSN) and the North American and Arctic Defence and Security Network (NAADSN) for their financial support of this work.

CHAPTER ONE

The Canadian Ecopolitical Landscape

LEARNING OBJECTIVES

1. Describe the concept of Canadian ecopolitics and its significance in addressing contemporary environmental challenges.
2. Analyze the key themes and common issues in Canadian ecopolitics, including the role of Indigenous Peoples, climate change, biodiversity loss, product life cycles, security, and environmental ethics.
3. Evaluate the role of multilevel adaptive governance in addressing Canadian ecopolitical challenges.

INTRODUCTION: WHAT IS CANADIAN ECOPOLITICS?

This book was written as several overlapping global crises permeate the thinking of citizens and policymakers alike: climate change, biodiversity loss, military conflict, zoonotic disease and pandemic, rising food prices, and pressure from mass migration. This occurs as other massive changes are swirling around us, including accelerating technological advancement, political waves of populism and persistent authoritarianism, democratic backsliding in many jurisdictions, and continued social conflict in activist politics and social media. It is, to put it mildly, a complex and confusing decade, and Canada is not immune to any of these circumstances. Indeed, in many ways Canada exemplifies many of them, and Canadian policy responses will be shaped at least partly by the context in which Canadian decision making takes place.

Indeed, decisions made today – by politicians, investors, citizens, teachers, students – in short, by all Canadians – will have a profound impact on the range of options future citizens will have as they seek to ensure their own survival and advance their quality of life. And a very important aspect of this creation of future conditions will be the actions taken today that will shape the natural world in the future, just as actions taken decades ago are having their impacts now. One need not be a dedicated existentialist to accept this proposition: The decisions taken today will influence those that must be made tomorrow in profound ways.

This book is designed primarily to provide readers with the necessary background to begin to understand what we are broadly referring to as **Canadian ecopolitics**. To be fair, no one could possibly understand Canadian ecopolitics entirely – it is far too vast a subject to be grasped as a whole, full of interdisciplinary subfields, historical twists and turns, and ongoing and fluid developments. Our more modest aim is to introduce readers to some of the main approaches and issues currently framing the Canadian ecopolitical landscape. The complexity of the subject should not preclude efforts to understand where, when, how, and why the everyday lives of people living within the borders of the contemporary Canadian state are profoundly affected by environmental changes and political and legal efforts that respond to those changes – or changes that are likely to come soon.

And these changes are indeed profound. Climate change is literally transforming the lives of Canadians right across the country, from those directly impacted by a fast-warming Arctic, to those living near flooding rivers and lakes or burning forests, to those living in overheated urban centres.[1] A process now known as *Arctic* or *polar amplification* has resulted in the warming of the Arctic at a rate four times faster than the global average since 1979 (Rantanen et al., 2022; see also Zubrow et al., 2019). Scientists believe that both the catastrophic floods from "atmospheric rivers" and the hundreds of deaths caused by a sustained "heat dome" over parts of British Columbia in 2021 would probably not have occurred in the absence of climate change (Weber, 2022). Agricultural output is as threatened as biodiversity. Invasive species are changing local ecologies across the country, and the climate change–induced migration of species threatens Canadians with new diseases (see Chapter Ten). Unprecedented forest fires in recent years have caused billions of dollars in damage; displaced small communities and mid-sized cities in eastern, western, and northern Canada; and harmed the health of humans and wildlife alike. The shift from climate change as a future threat to climate change as the context of contemporary ecopolitics has occurred with alarming rapidity.

Canadians should not be surprised by these developments. Despite misinformation campaigns that have proliferated over the past few decades, fairly high levels of awareness of serious environmental problems date back at least to the 1960s. Air and water pollution, acid rain, deforestation, overfishing and whaling, endangered species, dumping of waste – all of these environmental "problems" (though, arguably, the real problem is unsustainable human activities) were on the public agenda long before we were openly concerned with climate change or, even, stratospheric ozone layer depletion (see Dwivedi et al., 2001, for discussion). Along with millions of Americans, many Canadians also read Rachel Carson's groundbreaking book *Silent Spring*, which described the chemical pollution destroying habitat in the United States when it was published in the early 1960s (Carson, 1962). Environmental commentators such as David Suzuki have helped keep Canadians informed through television programs like *The Nature of Things*. Politically, the Canadian–American relationship has been as deeply rooted in shared environmental issues, such as managing transboundary pollution in the Great Lakes, as it has been about trade and military alliances (see LePrestre & Stoett, 2006). The world-famous non-governmental organization Greenpeace was founded in Canada in 1971, and Canadian leadership was visible at the first global summit on environmental issues, the United Nations Conference on the Human Environment in Stockholm in 1972, and the first high-level global conference on climate change held in Toronto in 1988. Yet the sheer scope of the environmental problems faced by Canadians today can still come as a bit of a shock to the uninitiated.

There are even serious questions about the survival of humankind amid all these environmental challenges. It is common today to refer to three interrelated "global crises," including climate change, biodiversity loss, and pollution (also known as the "triple planetary crisis"). No doubt, many other environmental problems also affect Canada and all of humanity, but most can be placed one way or another into these three categories. For example, overfishing of the oceans reduces biodiversity and makes marine ecosystems more susceptible to the vagaries of pollutants and climate change, including ocean acidification and sea-level rise (see Chapter Eight). Though globally significant, ocean issues are particularly relevant for Canada; given its immense size (it is the second-largest country by land area, after Russia) it is easy to forget that Canada is surrounded on three sides by ocean water.

All of these environmental threats to the basis of human survival are a steady feature of what has been popularly termed the **Anthropocene**. On the one hand, the Anthropocene is a term employed to describe our present geologic epoch in which the impact of humankind on the planet has become so transformative and indelible that it can be considered dominant. Put differently, in the Anthropocene humanity has become a geological force in its own right. On the other hand,

> In general, the Anthropocene, as a guiding concept, has come from a rather bad place: it stands as formal recognition not just of the tremendous impact of human ingenuity, but of ecological, economic, and cultural imperialism, the folly of a utilitarian approach to nature, and other forms of both empirical and epistemological violence visited upon the earth; and it is characterized by the distinct threat of an unprecedented mass extinction that could easily include our own species … It is certainly an immediately political, and not just geological, term, inseparably linked with the thematic anxiety of a crisis peculiarly forged by modernity. (Stoett & Dalby, 2022, p. 203; see also Grove, 2019; Todd, 2015; Hamilton et al., 2015)

Contemporary "ecopolitics" involves the intersection of environmental issues with distinct patterns of conflict and cooperation in the Anthropocene: It is a social space where ecology and politics become inseparable (see Box 1.1). It views ecological outcomes as products of underlying power relations between human communities and the non-human world. Studies of Canadian environmental issues have used an ecopolitical framework to examine bilateral ecopolitics between the United States and Canada (Le Prestre & Stoett, 2007) and also to focus on the local–global dimension of Canadian environmental issues (Bernstein & Cashore, 2002; Bernstein, 2008; Gore & Stoett, 2009). The framework ideas of ecopolitics have, as well, been used in the context of area studies, including Latin America (Gudynas, 2017), Brazil (Barbosa, 2000; Guimarães, 1991), China (Harrington, 2017), and the Soviet Union (Rezun, 1996). Arguably, the study of global environmental governance has been an important incubator for a broader approach to ecopolitics (Le Prestre, 2017; Stoett, 2016, 2013). The field has helped develop richly explanatory concepts such as the Anthropocene, complexity, and multilevel adaptive governance. Canada has a complex and varied ecological history, has extensive interlinkages among the global and local levels, and is a site of increasingly contentious and vital environmental debates. It represents an important subject for ecopolitical analysis, rife with the environmental conflict and democratic tensions described in the work of Laurie Adkin and others (see Adkin, 2009).

BOX 1.1. Defining Ecopolitics

The prefix "eco" derives from the Greek term *oikos*, meaning household. It has been widely adopted by ecology – the study of the relationships between organisms and their environment. Political ecology, meanwhile, refers to a "critical research field within anthropology and related disciplines that examines how and why economic structures and power relations drive environmental change in an increasingly interconnected world" (Roberts, 2020). Politics is also from a Greek term (Πολιτικά, *politiká*, or "affairs of the cities") and relates to decision making and power relations between decision makers (thus we have terms such as democracy – rule of "the people" – and autocracy – "rule by one"). Another popular discipline is known as environmental ethics, or the "study of ethical questions raised by human relationships with the nonhuman environment," which emerged as an "important subfield of philosophy in the 1970s" (Palmer et al., 2014), giving rise to traditions such as ecofeminism and environmental pragmatism and creating room for the academic study of Indigenous and local knowledge (ILK).

The term "ecopolitics" was probably first used by political scientist Dennis Pirages nearly 50 years ago. He defined it as the study of "the cluster of economic, ecological, and ethical issues" that animated a "new assessment of remaining resource-intensive growth possibilities in a finite world" (1978, p. 30). This perspective itself was spurred by the famous Club of Rome Report entitled *Limits to Growth* (Meadows et al., 1972). Ecopolitics "takes place at the intersection of ecology and politics" and is characterized by "the centrality of collective action problems, the wide range of actors, the technological and scientific challenges and opportunities, and the need for both leadership and widespread legitimacy" (Stoett, 2019, pp. 3, 9). **Agency** is therefore a major element of ecopolitics: What deliberate actions do people take that impact the environment, for better or worse, while acting within social structures that limit their influence? And how does the positionality of the actor – their political efficacy and power, wealth, prestige, cultural capital, collective solidarity, and other factors – affect their impact?

Several disciplines beyond political science cover much of the same ground. For example, ecological geopolitics has emerged as a popular field among geographers (see O'Lear & Dalby, 2016). International studies has often focused on global environmental politics and governance; for example, Stoett and Laferriere (2006) referred to "international ecopolitical theory" in one of several efforts to synthesize critical theories of international relations with environmental politics. Ecopolitics can also be applied at numerous levels of analysis, from households to cities to countries to the entire planetary system. We are focusing mainly on the national level in this text, but the impact of both subnational and international levels will be a constant feature.

In this book, we frame ecological challenges as *those issues demanding multilevel adaptive governance in the midst of rapid change and uncertainty.* Though power structures are relatively stable over time, and Canada's social context, position in the global economy, and political system retain their main characteristics, the only true constant is change. The term "ecopolitics" encompasses all the fields discussed above, focusing most explicitly on the political structures and processes and ethical dilemmas that shape the governance of issues related to the environment, including natural resources, wildlife conservation, pollution control, and the environmental impact of industry, war, development, and other human activities.

Questions

1. When it comes to Canadian ecopolitics, what does it mean to say that "the only true constant is change"? What would be a good example of this?
2. What academic disciplines help to shape the synthetic field of ecopolitics?

The academic literature on Canadian environmental policy covers specific issue areas such as fisheries, oil and gas production, mining, agriculture, pollution, forestry, biodiversity, and species protection (Adkin, 2009; Boardman & VanNijnatten, 2002, 2009; Boyd, 2003; Greenbaum & Wellington, 2010;

Hessing et al., 2007; Muldoon et al., 2009; Olive, 2019; Paehlke, 2000; Van-Nijnatten, 2016). On the political side, many works also discuss social and economic schisms, environmental social movements, class relationships, regional differences, federal politics, and bureaucratic politics (Hessing et al., 2007; Van-Nijnatten, 2016; VanNijnatten & Boardman, 2009). Core texts in the field have focused on environmental agency, including the influence of science, media, social movements, interest groups, businesses, and Indigenous Peoples on environmental politics and policy (Olive, 2019). As environmental issues have moved closer to the core concerns of the Canadian state, research has emphasized the impact of activism and administrative growth for environmental politics. Canadian environmental assessment, monitoring, regulatory arrangements, federalism, party and electoral politics, regional and bilateral relationships, and levels of government are often the subjects of analysis, with topical issues of climate policy and resource management occupying thematic space.

As described by John Barry (2011), an ecopolitical approach advances three key and unique ethical concerns. The first is a longer time scale that accounts for the needs and interests of future generations by incorporating a future-oriented viewpoint. We discuss intergenerational environmental rights and security at greater length below and in subsequent chapters, but they are clearly central to our approach: Ecopolitics today reflects ecopolitics of the past and will shape the options future generations have at their disposal to respond to threats to their own survival.

The second principal ethical concern of ecopolitics is a global perspective that looks beyond the borders of sovereign nation-states while viewing projects of capitalist globalization from a critical vantage that recognizes the inherently unequal nature of human relationships and ecological impacts. We centre the discussions of Canada to follow in a broader context by explicitly addressing the continental and international dimensions of ecopolitics in Chapter Three. This global perspective appreciates the importance of multilevel adaptive governance systems that can work across and between institutional levels, governance that can be anticipatory and work to prevent problems before they occur or worsen and can be responsive to public input and not beholden to any specific set of interests. Power structures intervene here, of course: The history of Canadian ecopolitics is exemplary of the domination of natural resource industries, for example. But this does not consign us to that future scenario.

Third, Barry (2011) notes that an ecopolitical viewpoint is fundamentally concerned with the ethical basis of human–non-human relationships and the necessity of coming to terms with the changing characteristics of this relationship in the context of the Anthropocene (see also Lamalle & Stoett, 2023). The emphasis we place on the dramatic issue of biodiversity loss throughout this text reflects this concern: To various degrees, Canadians now know what is happening to the natural world and can no longer claim ignorance. Indeed, many Indigenous Peoples contend that they have known this all along; as McGregor and Sritharan observe, "dramatic and devastating environmental change is not new to Indigenous peoples, but can be understood as a continuation of the challenges many had to overcome as a result of colonialism" (2023, p. 71).

This moves ecopolitical analysis toward interdisciplinary approaches that bridge the natural and social sciences, recognize multiple levels of governance, and address the complexity of human–nature relationships, including the need to recognize and respect ecological limits. The concept of planetary boundaries (see Figure 1.1) reflects the widespread concern that humans are altering earth's surface, polluting its atmosphere and water, and extracting its resources at clearly unsustainable levels. Admittedly, these boundaries are arbitrary, but their placement reflects the most advanced scientific material. The list of categories was first developed by Swedish scientist Johan Rockström and colleagues in 2009. The framework calls for measurements of these key categories to ascertain how far we are, collectively, from exceeding the "**safe operating space**" they provide for human existence (Rockström et al., 2009).

We return to this planetary boundary framework in Chapter Two, as it has arguably been instrumental in encouraging natural scientists to think in terms of planetary health (see Haines & Frumkin, 2021). Climate change and biospheric integrity are core earth system processes that cut across all others (we adopt a similar approach in this text: Climate change and biodiversity loss are two of our most prominent common themes; see also Chapters Three, Nine, and Ten). Other earth system processes at risk of or already exceeding their "safe" boundaries include stratospheric ozone depletion, atmospheric aerosol loading, ocean acidification (see Chapter Eight), phosphorus and nitrogen cycles (known also as biogeochemical flows), land-system change (see Chapter Five), global freshwater use (see Chapter Seven); and "novel entities," which mainly includes forms of pollution such as persistent organic pollutants, plastics, endocrine disruptors, and nuclear waste.

The planetary boundaries approach is imperfect, and there are other ways of measuring things. For example, the Intergovernmental Science-Policy Platform on Ecosystem Services and Biodiversity (IPBES), the Intergovernmental

Figure 1.1. The Nine Planetary Boundaries, 2023

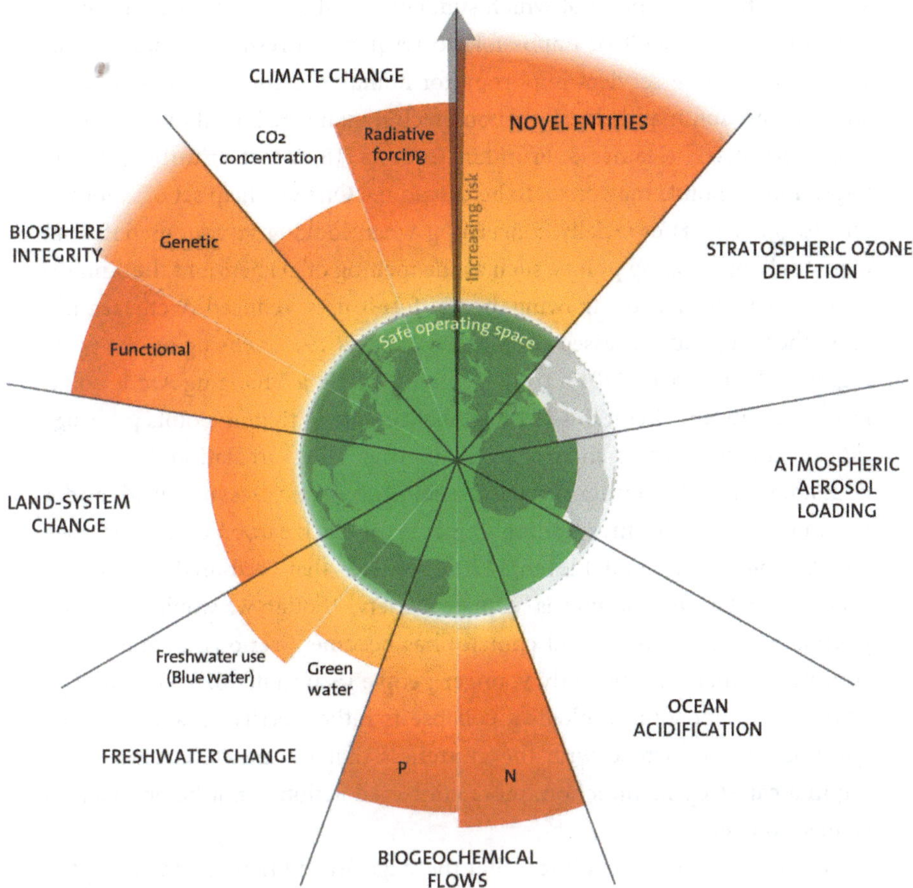

Source: Azote for Stockholm Resilience Centre, based on analysis in Richardson et al., 2023. Licensed under CC BY-NC-ND 3.0.

Panel on Climate Change (IPCC), and the Global Environmental Outlook (GEO) all have their own frameworks, which change periodically to reflect shifting priorities and the perceived needs of governments.[2] We mention these alternatives throughout the book as well, but they all point in the same direction: Despite improvements in some categories, such as a reduction of air pollution in some regions and the partial recovery of the stratospheric ozone layer from chemical assault, global environmental conditions are getting worse, not better. Canadian ecopolitics is embedded within this stark realization, which has indeed permeated scientific, if not always policy, knowledge for several decades.

Importantly, scientists are worried about **tipping points** in these earth systems, which is "a point at which sudden, non-linear, shifts may occur … which may be difficult or impossible to reverse and result in major reductions in ecosystem services important for human societies … Some of these shifts are predominantly local phenomena but many are linked to underlying global processes" (Haines & Frumkin, 2021, p. 18). Most disturbingly, perhaps, tipping points may prove to be cascading: One will help set off another, and so on. This is especially concerning when looking at various potential climate change tipping points, such as the melting of glaciers and the Antarctic ice sheet, permafrost thawing, boreal forest fires, reduced Arctic sea ice, and other ongoing processes (see Lenton et al., 2019). Focusing on the polar regions, Mark Roberts (2019, p. 39) reminds us that a "changing Arctic could lead to significant alterations in the global climate as tipping points pose significant threats, such as changes to the thermohaline circulation, [methane] emissions from the tundra permafrost and the Arctic Ocean seabed, and a rise in the number of fires leading to increased black carbon emissions" (see also Chapters Nine and Eleven). Little wonder that "eco-anxiety" (sometimes also referred to simply as "climate anxiety," though we would argue the phenomenon extends beyond climate) has become a serious mental health concern for many, particularly younger people (Schmidt, 2023). Knowledge of possibly impending ecological collapse is rather terrifying and begs the question of why, armed with the awareness that we are collectively moving in a catastrophic direction, more concerted action is not being taken to change course.

And that is where ecopolitics enter the stage. In addition to addressing the conflict and cooperation that occurs among actors, institutions, and agendas (the "politics" of ecopolitics), we need to look at how political and governance systems incorporate ecological ethics, values, and concerns into their functioning, and evaluate their effectiveness in achieving ecological outcomes (the "eco" of ecopolitics). While there are ideational factors that influence everything we do – and we discuss these at some length in Chapter Two – it is relevant to stress the impact of structural power in the political realm, as well as the need to analyze ecopolitics in terms of multilevel adaptive governance. The tensions and intersections between the local and global levels of human interaction and community are evident throughout the case studies we present in this book.

Political theorist Antonio Gramsci is an important figure in the conceptualization of the political process employed in this book and other accounts of Canadian environmental politics. For example, Laurie Adkin mentions "the need to connect both normative conceptualizations of environmental citizenship and green (deliberative) democratic theory to an understanding of politics that foregrounds power relationships and hegemonic struggle" in the introduction to her excellent edited volume titled *Environmental Conflict and Democracy in Canada* (2009, p. xi). Gramsci held that ideas are as important as guns and bank vaults; indeed, the best way to measure who has power in any society is to gauge the dominant ideas of the day. Arguably, we are at a crossroads in Canada and elsewhere, since the ideas that held industrialization and economic growth as the pinnacles of human achievement (forcing all other forms, from art to education to technological innovation, into a largely subservient role) have been slowly, though unsurely, challenged by the realization that they have also proven self-destructive at a collective level. In Adkin's words, "once certain ecological parameters are established as 'nonnegotiable,' conflict between capitalist accumulation, on the one hand, and societal and ecological interests, on the other, becomes inevitable" (Adkin, 2009, p. 9). Power, specifically the power of ideas, has always been at the forefront of the Canadian national narrative – the historical arc that shapes the creation and evolution of the Canadian state as an ongoing idea that is itself in motion – since it evolved as a colony embedded in the most powerful geopolitical empire of the eighteenth and nineteenth centuries and imposed this political reality onto the inhabitants of the geographic space that would eventually constitute a sovereign state. As such, Canadian ecopolitics is inseparable from Canada's historical and contemporary relationships to empire, settler-colonialism, and an economic system of Euro-American-dominated global capitalism.

CANADIAN POLITICAL BASICS

There are several important political parameters that readers should bear in mind before proceeding with any discussion of Canadian ecopolitics. Though we expand on this in Chapter Four, it is important to briefly introduce the complexities of Canadian federalism. Importantly, areas of what is now known as the sovereign state of Canada have been ruled by French and then British kings and queens since 1534. Although British monarchs, in particular, played an important role in Canada's early historical development – notably through quasi-constitutional documents such as the *Royal Proclamation of 1763* that established nation-to-nation relationships between the Crown and Indigenous Peoples – Canada is now a constitutional monarchy, meaning that the government is still referred to in legal settings as the Crown, even if the actual human wearer of a crown in England has little direct influence on Canadian affairs. The *Constitution Act, 1982* (which largely superseded the *British North America Act, 1867*) divides formal political powers and responsibilities between the federal and provincial orders of government, and the democratic and liberal (as in the rights and liberties of individual citizens) nature of the system is enshrined in the *Charter of Rights and Freedoms*.

Legislators are elected to the House of Commons in Ottawa and to various provincial legislatures (though it is worth noting that elections for mayors in Canada's large cities are, arguably, as important for sustainable development). Since 1867, the division of powers between the federal and provincial governments has been axiomatic, with most responsibilities related to resources and the environment falling under provincial jurisdiction (along with health and education). Little gets done in Canadian politics outside the box of this jurisdictional friction, which extends downward into the municipalities. Indeed, fragmented governance of environmental issues may reflect a certain type of democracy, but it also, arguably, precludes a more integrated, concerted approach across the country (see Case Study 1.1). All levels of government boast powerful bureaucratic apparatuses, and though bureaucratic entities such as Environment and Climate Change Canada (ECCC) exist at the federal level, no observer would be foolish enough to assume Canada is a technocracy run in Ottawa, despite the considerable spending power and access to other resources wielded by the national government. Political parties have dominated the political process throughout Canadian history, helping to rotate political elites while the machinery of actual governance was administering the exigencies of colonial power, including the enclosure of the commons and spread of capitalism as the dominant mode of production. And as in most liberal democracies, the courts play a substantial role in forging environmental law, and in some cases are the main arbiters of ecopolitical outcomes (see Case Study 1.1).

CASE STUDY 1.1. Accounting for the Cumulative Impact of Development across Turtle Island[3]

A recent court decision in British Columbia, known now as the *Yahey* decision, will be hard to ignore by any judge in the future. Prevailing Indigenous and academic legal thought holds that when Crown representatives made certain promises to maintain the hunting, fishing, and trapping rights of Indigenous Peoples and protect them from interference in the future, the Crown undertook a serious binding and legally enforceable obligation. This means that governments (federal and provincial) were, are, and remain indefinitely bound to ensure that there is always a sufficient amount of land of adequate quality to maintain the resources necessary to ensure hunting, fishing, and harvesting rights; in turn, these resources depend on healthy, functioning ecosystems.

Federal and provincial governments do consult First Nations to determine whether a given project or activity might infringe or impact their "Aboriginal" and Treaty rights; however, governments generally focus on the direct effects or footprint of a project such as a forestry cut block, an oil well site, a gas plant, or an access road or facility. Using this narrow window approach, governments often reach the conclusion that there is zero or limited effect on the environment or on Indigenous rights. But Indigenous Peoples (and supportive civil society groups) have challenged governments on this high stakes shell game, arguing that the pertinent issue is not the individual project but the hundreds to thousands of these projects approved, decade after decade, with their attendant impacts and other anthropogenic stressors acting on ecosystems, landscapes, and the territories of Indigenous Peoples. After years of frustration, several Indigenous governments in western Canada have opted to bring the matter before the courts. It is noteworthy that much of the legal action initiated has occurred in Canada's Western Sedimentary Basin, where thousands of square kilometres have been impacted by oil and gas facilities, a vast network of roads and linear disturbances, large-scale industrial forestry, and agricultural clearing.

The first case emerged in northeastern Alberta, where Indigenous traditional territory encompasses the Athabasca oil sands producing area. In 2008, the Beaver Lake Cree Nation (BLCN) took the governments of Canada and Alberta to court over the cumulative impact of development on their Treaty #6 rights. Government lawyers have used every procedural lever available within the law to try to have the case dismissed and to drag out proceedings for well over a decade. Alberta's war of attrition approach was intended to force the BLCN to abandon the case. But the BLCN has fought this tactic by bringing an application to the courts to oblige Canada and Alberta to pay for court costs so that it could make its case before the Supreme Court of Canada, which responded by broadening the strict tests courts apply to such matters given the dire funding constraints faced by the community.

The Blueberry River First Nation (BBRFN) of northeastern British Columbia followed suit and brought an action against the Government of BC over infringement of its Treaty #8 rights. Since the signing of the Treaty in 1899, the BBRFN's traditional territory has essentially been overrun by agricultural, oil and gas, forestry, and road development. For decades, community members had made government representatives aware of how it was simply impossible for them to succeed on their traditional hunting grounds as prior generations did. The *Narwhal* magazine reports that by 2016 more than 110,000 linear kilometres of roads, pipelines, transmission, and seismic lines had been cut or placed across less than 40,000 square kilometres of land, much of it in traditional BBRFN territory (Pollon, 2018).

On June 29, 2021, the BC Provincial Court released a significant decision that confirmed much of what Indigenous Peoples had been asserting for years (*Yahey v. British Columbia*, 2021 BCSC 1287 [*Yahey*]). In summary, the judge issued a declaration prohibiting the province from authorizing further activities that infringe on BBRFN's rights, ruling that

- the Province's power to take up lands under the Treaty must be exercised in a way that upholds the Treaty's promises.
- the test for treaty infringement is whether a First Nation's rights have been significantly diminished.
- the Province had taken up so much land that the exercise of rights was no longer meaningful.
- the existing regulatory processes for authorizing industrial development do not adequately account for cumulative effects or ensure that Treaty rights are protected (Pinder, 2021).

Subsequently, the parties reached a comprehensive agreement that has the potential to vastly alter natural resource decision making and Crown–Indigenous relations in Canada (Hall, 2023).[4]

However, *Yahey* was a lower court decision and is not binding on the Government of Alberta or other provinces. The Duncan's First Nation (DFN) of northwestern Alberta has filed a similar treaty infringement action and joined the Beaver Lake Cree Nation in arguing that its traditional territory and Treaty rights, culture, and way of life have been affected by the cumulative impact of development. The case will require and involve the weighing and testing of complementary Indigenous Knowledge and Science and complex cumulative impact assessment landscape modelling and simulations (Unrau, 2022).

In the long run, all Canadians will benefit if a sustainable balance between ecology and development is found to be a requirement already embedded in treaties with Indigenous Peoples, which constitute some of the highest and oldest foundational laws of the country. And this balance will certainly be sought in any ongoing or future land claim treaty processes.

Critical Thinking Questions

1. Does the federal structure of Canada's government limit how Indigenous Peoples' claims can impact environmental policies?
2. When it comes to cumulative impacts of development on the Canadian environment, which is more important: political negotiation or court decisions?

Equally important, arguably, is Canada's position – and corresponding image – on the world stage. There are two dominant themes beyond Canada's colonial history and membership in both the British Commonwealth (now known simply as the Commonwealth of Nations) and la Francophonie: one is the Canada–United States relationship, and the other concerns Canada's relations with the rest of the world.

Given its proximity to the United States, it is understandable that this relationship is often at the forefront of debates over Canada's long-term future, national security, economic growth, and political autonomy. It has also helped define the Canadian ecopolitical landscape in many ways (see Le Prestre & Stoett, 2007). Of course, borders began as colonial and then legal abstractions; the shared continental wealth of resources in North America means that Canada and the United States are irrevocably entwined in ecosystems, watersheds, and shared coasts alike. Efforts to institutionalize this mutual dependency on shared resources have met with limited success. For example, the International Joint Commission (focused largely on the Great Lakes) and the North American Environmental Commission (focused largely on justifying a trilateral free trade agreement) have well-established pedigrees and have certainly contributed to conservation measures, alongside bilateral agreements on acid rain, fisheries, and other measures. It would be incorrect to conclude that the United States always gets "its way" on environmental matters, and the fact that there has been some development of pan-continental bureaucratic or even technocratic governance is testament to the perseverance of economic over nationalist sensibilities (see Temby & Stoett, 2017). But the shadow of American politics looms large on Canadian ecopolitics, as the shifts on environmental policy between the Obama, Trump, and then Biden Administrations has demonstrated.

And it would also be parochial to ignore the larger stage involved in ecopolitics – the global stage – with which we engage in Chapter Three of this text. At the United Nations and elsewhere, Canada's reputation on environmental matters has oscillated between liberal internationalist promises and isolationist climate change denialism but seems most comfortable somewhere in between. A good song and dance routine is occasionally spoiled by harsh reminders that extracting oil, habitual overfishing, and old growth clearcutting have been integral parts, by design, of the evolution of the Canadian economy. In this light, Canada's public commitment to the UN 2030 Sustainable Development Goals (SDGs), and attendant demands on Canada's national reporting and accountability processes leading up to 2030, are interesting topics that we will explore in this book (see also Boyd, 2017; Marvier, 2012). Other international developments and collective actions, such as the adoption of a Global Biodiversity Framework in Montreal in late 2022, the Sendai Framework on Disaster Reduction, the Paris Agreement on Climate Change, an embryonic treaty on plastic pollution negotiated partially in Ottawa, and many others, will test not only Canada's level of commitment but our political boundaries and diplomatic skill sets both within and outside of the country. Indeed, the international commitments that often flow from high-profile summitry have proven lightning rods in the domestic national politics in both Canada and the United States, and there is no evidence to suggest this will be any different in the future, regardless of how serious the ecological threats have become.

COMMON THEMES

There are several common themes that are as intrinsic to ecopolitics in Canada as they are unavoidable. Rather than feature extensive chapters on each of them, we have ensured that we cover them in the issue-area chapters that structure the remainder of this text. These broad common themes include the fundamental role of Indigenous Peoples, climate change, biodiversity loss, product life cycles, security, and environmental ethics. Each of the chapters to follow will touch on each of these themes in different ways, so it is important to introduce them briefly now. We have opted to include the themes within chapters rather than attempt to assemble individual chapters for each, believing this stresses their significance in the ecopolitical landscape today in more forceful fashion.

It is, simply put, impossible to separate the existence and history of the **Indigenous Peoples** of North America from what they often refer to as Turtle Island, namely, the land itself. As discussed in Chapter Four, diverse people existed in the Americas long before the arrival of Europeans – according to recent archaeological discovery, much longer than previously thought. Cree-Métis archaeologist Paulette Steeves believes there is ample evidence that, contrary to Eurocentric anthropological and archaeological assumptions that date human activity in North America to the last 12,000 years, the actual dates could go back as far as 50,000 years ago (Steeves, 2021). In the past 500 years, Indigenous Peoples and their knowledge of local ecosystems enabled settlers to colonize the Americas in so many ways it would be impossible to summarize them adequately here. That this is largely a narrative replete with violence and even genocide is not lost on the most casual observer of Canadian ecopolitics; discoveries of what appear to be mass graves at former residential schools remind us on an almost monthly basis of the shameful coordinated efforts to assimilate Indigenous children and the systemic neglect and abuse that accompanied that effort. Less discussed, however, is the process of enclosure that accompanied the construction of the Canadian and American nation-states. Of course, First Nations groups had their own territorial limitations (and engaged in sometimes violent conflicts related to them), but the advent of colonialism thrust private property and the enclosure of the commons upon Indigenous communities across the continent, even into the great expanses of the circumpolar regions.

It's a narrative that continues today, since enclosure of the commons is an integral feature of the spread of western capitalism begun in the imperial ages of the 1700s. As Donna Harrison explains in her essay on the west coast Ahousaht First Nation (the largest of the 14 Nuu-chah-nulth tribal nations located on the west coast of Vancouver Island), which initially opposed salmon farms but later partnered with a subsidiary of the Norwegian company Mainstream, "the process of 'modern enclosure,' which is much more subtle but still involves dispossession from political power and still generates resistance, continues today" (Harrison, 2009). In the same edited volume, Martha Stiegman suggests that "First Nations are well versed in the art of deciphering the double-speak used by the federal government to avoid genuine power transfer … Many commentators have noted the paternalistic approach and continued agenda of assimilation and rights extinguishment that make Canada's post-colonial age difficult to distinguish from its colonial past" (Stiegman, 2009, p. 71). The characteristics of the highly diverse community of First Nations in Canada should not be generalized, but their sustained physical and cultural struggle to survive the exigencies of colonialism and the present threats to their environmental security are an obvious commonality (McGregor & Srithara, 2023). Indeed, Indigenous Peoples across Turtle Island continue to take steps to have their inherent Indigenous title, rights, and Treaty rights recognized and enforced. The passage of the United Nations Declaration on the Rights of Indigenous People (UNDRIP) represents an important shift in the international sphere of the recognition of Indigenous governments as title holders and the rightful stewards (and decision makers) of their ancient lands and territories. Indigenous Peoples of Turtle Island have also been active in having their inherent and Treaty rights enforced through Canada's domestic legal system (see Case Study 1.1).

One of the greatest threats to Indigenous communities today, without doubt, is the continuation of **climate change**, which is indeed reshaping the natural landscape of all continents and oceans. Of course, it is obvious that climate change mitigation, adaptation, policy, regulation, and law – in short, climate governance – is such a dominant theme in Canadian ecopolitics today that it necessitates a chapter of its own (see Chapter Nine). But each chapter to follow will also cover climate change (or its shadow) to some degree, since it is such a pervasive subject today. Not only does it impact the daily lives of all Canadian and First Nation citizens, but it will also shape their future options and the broader global context as well. If the Cold War affected everyone, climate change is affecting everything, living and inanimate. Every level of government, every public institution, every corporation, and almost all interest groups, political parties, and religious organizations have had to respond to what has been aptly termed the "climate crisis." Each of the chapters to follow will invariably deal with climate change at some length, but this book as a whole certainly reflects the urgency presented by the climate crisis, which in turn permeates ecopolitics today.

Another threat to both human and non-human life that extends across Canada and Turtle Island is the rapid **loss of biodiversity**. As discussed in Chapter Three, this is indeed a global problem; some of the biodiversity and biota that is being exploited and driven to extinction is located in areas beyond national jurisdiction in the oceans (see Chapter Eight), but much of it falls within the territory of legal nation-states. The main drivers of biodiversity loss, identified by the IPBES global assessment in 2019 (a report approved by the vast majority of governments), are land and sea use change (which often entails the destruction of habitat), the direct exploitation of organisms (over-hunting, overfishing, overharvesting), climate change, pollution, and invasive non-native (alien) species (IPBES, 2019). We will cover these drivers in various places; suffice it to say here that Canadian policies and regulatory efforts have sought to stem the tide of biodiversity loss with varying levels of success. The SARA (*Species at Risk Act*) took many long years of political wrangling (in comparison with the *Endangered Species Act* in the United States, at least) before it came into effect in 2003, and it has been criticized for its spotty coverage of Canadian land, conceptual ambiguity, lack of inclusion of Indigenous knowledge, and the use of a subjective (i.e., easily politicized) methodology for prioritizing species protection (Turcotte et al., 2021). There is a robust body of literature on biodiversity loss and related policies in Canada (Bocking, 2009, 2000; Boyd, 2017; Foster, 1998; Marvier, 2012; Neave & Branch, 2002; Olive, 2014). The chapters to follow will all touch on the theme to some extent, and Chapter Ten in particular focuses on the issue of providing biosecurity in the Canadian context.

Pollution is not only a driver of biodiversity loss, but it is also a contributor to climate change and an ongoing threat to human health. Indeed, each stage of the agricultural and industrial production process creates immense challenges to biodiversity and contributes to climate change; the **product life cycle** ranges from raw resource extraction to commodity production to product distribution to the end-of-life waste that permeates the landscape today. Agricultural production – essentially, the growth and distribution of food products – entails massive usage of nutrients and pesticides, emissions of greenhouse gases, and other environmental costs, and yet approximately a third of all food produced in North America goes to waste. (This is an unimaginable amount, given the persistence of world hunger and the resultant 193 million tonnes of greenhouse gas (GHG) emissions of carbon dioxide equivalent, over 17.6 billion cubic metres (m^3) of wasted water, 22.1 million hectares (ha) of cropland, and nearly 4 million tonnes of fertilizer used, among other costs; see CEC, 2017.) Industrial production is characterized by the use of chemicals, and the often-unanswered question of how to effectively and safely dispose of waste products remains a major issue today. Plastic pollution (especially in marine ecosystems) has risen in prominence on the environmentalist agenda on a rocket trajectory, and recycling programs have proven to be the source of very false comfort as the vast majority of plastic waste ends up in landfills or, worse, is shipped overseas to lower-income countries for burning (legally and, often, illegally). The UN's SDG 12 draws attention to the need for responsible production and consumption. There is an urgent need for the reduction of waste in food, water, and resource consumption, as well as the sustainable management of toxic wastes and pollutants (United Nations, 2017). There are points all along the product life cycle where environmental justice issues can be easily identified (Bullard, 1994; Bullard & Johnson, 2000; Stoett, 2022): Quite simply, not everyone suffers the same exposure to environmental risks associated with contemporary global capitalism, risks that are still considered "externalities" by many corporations and economists today despite the popularity of ecological economics (Daly & Farley, 2004; Princen et al., 2002).

Another common theme that will permeate subsequent chapters is that of **security**, which can be defined in many ways by many people for many reasons, but we will use it here in four main, closely intertwined ways:

- **National security** – the protection of the Canadian state from foreign attack (military, economic, reputational)
- **Human security** – the protection of individuals and communities from harm, be it physical, emotional, or cultural
- **Environmental security** – the protection of the biosphere and ecosystems from deliberate or incidental harm or destruction
- **Biosecurity** – the protection of all life from threats to all of the above, covered at length in Chapter Ten

National security is considered one of the fundamental imperatives of Canadian state policy, but the provision of security is more complex and multidimensional when viewed through an ecological perspective. The political, economic, environmental, and social/cultural dimensions of defence and security policy, especially its gender dimensions, are often neglected aspects of the national security discussion. A shift in focus toward environmental security broadens the timescale perspective toward a longer-term and wider definition of security and threats (Hardt, 2017; Stoett, 1999); for example, we fear nuclear war not because it could lead to defeat, but because it would invariably ecompromise the health of the vast majority of people across the globe, since radioactive contamination would not be contained to local areas (see Robock & Toon, 2010). Even a purely regional nuclear conflict, if such a thing were possible, would threaten food security everywhere (the Russian invasion of Ukraine in 2022 gave us a glimpse of what disrupted global food chains would look like – see Case Study 11.1).

Human security, meanwhile, has its own pedigree as a concept that emerged to some extent to counterbalance the hegemonic dominance of the national security narrative, but it also reflects the importance of human rights as an emerging theme in the past several centuries. Canada was a vocal proponent of a human security approach at the United Nations and elsewhere in the 1990s, prompted partly by the ethical paroxysms that followed the bitter civil conflict in the former Yugoslavia and the brutal genocide in Rwanda. It has come in and out of focus over the ensuing years; hopes that it was on the verge of more permanent footing were dashed against the hard realities of the terrorist attacks against the United States in 2001, the American invasion of Iraq, and the Russian invasion(s) of Ukraine. But, like a stubborn second actor, it will not go away, since the human individual and their community is still the centre of movements to promote and protect human rights, Indigenous Peoples, local community survival, equality, and even democracy itself. And without environmental security and biosecurity, none of this will matter.

Finally, **environmental ethics** are foundational to the study of ecopolitics, though this is less often acknowledged than we might desire. We deal with this fairly extensively in Chapter Two on ecopolitical worldviews, but each chapter to follow also covers conflicts and controversies that reflect competing visions of what might be broadly termed "the right thing to do." Which brings us to what many would consider the heart of the matter: Ecopolitics is about ethical positions in real-time conflict. As authors, we make no futile effort to hide our own positions: We are insistent that an environmental ethic that embraces both contemporary and intergenerational and environmental justice along with gender and racial equality should permeate any discussion of an ecopolitical future. We recognize that a shift in how humans conceive the non-human biota and ecosystems that sustain them is as necessary as it is desirable from an ethical viewpoint. A consequent shift away from retrospective, short- and medium-term political analysis toward more holistic, future-oriented systemic analyses of ecopolitics as a distinct realm or domain of conflict and cooperation follows. Thinking globally demands that we situate ourselves within the context of global environmental change and planetary health today, but it does not diminish the analytical or ethical significance of the local politics (conflicts as well as collaborations), as many of the case studies used in this book demonstrate. We proceed in our analysis with this in mind. The need to merge ecological concerns with ethical considerations, transformation, inequality, sustainability, complexity, and adaptability, and the political issues of achieving security, sovereignty, prosperity, and stability at various levels of governance helps guide us in this journey.

Assembled as a framework, the chapters that follow together provide a grounding in case studies and explanations based on recent events, while keeping the focus on the themes described above.

STRUCTURE OF THE BOOK

This book is designed to survey historical and contemporary patterns in a select series of ecopolitical issue-areas. Chapter organization is designed to balance and focus each issue-area with an awareness of the interlinkages among them and to address the distinctly Canadian context while developing the themes described above in greater detail. Each chapter will overview the nature of ecopolitical challenges and describe differing economic, political, social, and environmental dynamics, including the key ways in which the global intersects with other levels of governance, and conclude with an evaluation of existing arrangements, governance gaps, and promising routes for transformation.

Chapter Two sets the ideational foundation for the rest of the book with an explicit discussion of what we term "ecopolitical worldviews." Worldviews organize information and help people make sense of the world and their place in it. The recognition and rising influence of the concept of the Anthropocene has contributed to an evolving planetary imaginary, which is characterized by longer and deeper timescales and a wider range of ethical questions regarding human–nature relationships. The chapter will analyze four key debates: The first concerns whether Canada can sustain economic growth in the face of ecological limits; the second asks whether the transformation of nature by humans necessitates changes in the way nature is valued; the third questions whether society can transform quickly enough to meet ecological challenges; and finally, the last key debate raises the issue of whether calls for ecojustice can be realized within the context of Canadian democracy. These debates build on the key themes of the book by pointing to worldviews as the key arbiters of ecological issues, especially biodiversity loss, climate change, and the need to preserve security. More specifically, the chapter analyzes how worldviews evolve in response to each other, shaping the emergence of new concepts such as ecological modernization (Warner, 2010), critical political ecology (Biro, 2015; Luke, 1997; Stoett & Laferrière, 2006; Wiebe, 2017), the ecological footprint (Rees, 2002), and ecosystem services, as well as degrowth, planetary, ecofeminist, and First Nations thought.

Chapter Three will introduce the concept of the commons and the global context in which the Canadian state operates. The governance of common resources and public goods constitutes a particular set of challenges for Canadian ecopolitics because of the unique patterns of conflict and cooperation these problems engender. After defining the concept of "the commons," the chapter explains the related concepts of carrying capacity, public goods, and the mechanisms of "open-access" systems. Case studies focus on Canada's role in the ozone regime and the Convention on Biological Diversity. We feel the twinned concepts of the commons and the global context are so fundamental to an understanding of Canadian ecopolitics that this chapter should precede more detailed analysis and case studies.

Chapter Four describes a small slice of the **ecopolitical history** of what is now known as Canada. Beginning with pre-history, the chapter traces changes in ecopolitics through the pre- and post-Confederation eras, including the development of Staples Theory in the 1930s, the constitutional implications of federalism, relations with the United States, and the growth of modern environmental movements (1950s to the present). Focusing on the origins of current ecopolitics today, the chapter identifies key historical touchpoints, including the changing system of Indigenous–colonial relationships, the challenge of growing US power, and the drive for "province building." Along the way, the chapter recounts the development of agriculture, forestry, tourism, and industries to fuel prosperity and growth. The chapter also recounts the history and growth of Canadian environmental movements and activism, with a focus on the ethical interplay of instrumentalist and intrinsic notions of nature and the non-human in ecopolitical discourse. The chapter brings the story up to the twenty-first century with a discussion of the Truth and Reconciliation Commission and Canada's role on the global stage as an environmental actor, setting the stage for the chapters that follow.

Chapter Five focuses on three integral aspects of the development of the Canadian state: people, products, and planning. Canada is a capitalist country, meaning that most decisions about resources and investment are made outside of the range of government by private capital investors interested in maximizing their returns. The pursuit of capital accumulation has shaped how and where people live, how and where goods and services are provided, and how resources are allocated and extracted. The first section analyzes how human movement, demographic changes, and urbanization impact environmental sustainability in Canada, while the second elaborates on the environmental ramifications of production and consumption patterns, including the life cycle impacts of products. In the last section, the chapter looks at urban planning, land management, and development projects in Canadian communities. Even as plastics and toxins infiltrate the environment and affect health and wellbeing, companies sometimes hesitate to take action without regulation. The chapter covers a few illustrative cases: tourism, urbanization, mining, free trade, agriculture, forestry, and municipal land use planning. A key theme is the way in which "everyday" ecopolitics is related to how governments at all levels adapt and plan for changes in the future. Governments need to anticipate rather than just react. They also need to (or be seen to) create equitable outcomes for a highly unequal and uneven system of economic provision in a capitalist society.

In Chapter Six, the book moves on to examine a key area of ecopolitics that is important and often divisive: **energy**. The UN's SDG 7 calls for affordable and clean energy, drawing attention to the need for fair energy access as well as the need to develop renewables to reduce emissions from fossil fuels (United Nations, 2017). Through the lens of ecopolitics, energy appears as a fundamental long-term process of ecosystem functioning, with patterns of entropy and exchange, transformation and consumption that span the generations and have ethical implications for the future. The question of timescales, from prehistoric to modern eras, brings the risks of excessive fossil fuel energy consumption into sharp relief. To what degree can the employment needs of resource workers be addressed in an age of energy transition? What kinds of energy options make sense in the Anthropocene?

Moving to Chapter Seven, the book discusses the importance of **freshwater**. If Canada's international reputation exceeds its characterization of a rather chilly place full of snow and ice, it is probably for its immense volume of freshwater. The Great Lakes, themselves forged by melting glaciers 20,000 years ago, are an especially evocative aspect of the Canadian identity, as are key river basins such as the St. Lawrence (one of the most voluminous in the world), the Mackenzie River (which, at over 4,200 kilometres, is the longest in Canada), the Fraser River, and the Ottawa River. Despite this abundance, governance and policy priorities work to ensure that water remains a highly contested issue, not only in terms of its potential commercialization (note: it's already commercialized) but also its uneven distribution, where some areas have been without drinkable water for decades, some areas are heavily polluted (oil sands rivers), and some areas are being drained. Finally, this chapter will conclude with the point that solutions for cleaner, healthier water must take account of the concerns of inequality and marginalization, as illustrated by the crisis of water quality on First Nations reserves.

Yet freshwater is only part of the story: Canada is a coastal state. Chapter Eight incorporates the concerns of SDG 14 with **oceans**. Canada has tremendous water assets, both in terms of its coastal EEZs (exclusive economic zones) and the vast Arctic region, and its coasts are physically linked to those of the economically larger United States. The impacts of climate change on marine environments are clearly disastrous. The political, economic, social, and ecological importance of oceans, transboundary freshwater, and the Arctic in relation to local and global factors are key subjects of analysis in this chapter. Case studies include discussions of marine pollution, aquatic invasive species, fish farming effects and controversies, effects of ocean acidification, plastic pollution, overfishing, and the role of the Law of the Sea (McDorman & Chircop, 2012; Rothwell & VanderZwaag, 2006).

Chapter Nine zooms in on the topic of climate ecopolitics. As mentioned above, climate change has become a ubiquitous theme in Canadian ecopolitics today, and political conflict over what exactly to do about it is rife and loud. Governance issues permeate any treatment of climate because it forces very difficult decisions on governments, corporations, and citizens alike. Chapter Nine discusses the influence of local and global climate action movements on politics and policy, and especially the dynamic of Canadian domestic and international stances on climate over time. The chapter looks at and develops the idea of climate as a commons, with many of the same features of collective action problems discussed in Chapter Three. As climate-affected disasters have increased in magnitude and frequency, Canada has taken action over the years to reduce emissions. For the most part, these efforts have failed to have an appreciable effect on national carbon emissions. Ecopolitics can help explain how and why these efforts have run into roadblocks. Part of the reason lies in the complex interplay between federal and provincial governments in addressing climate change, including tensions around carbon pricing and emissions reduction targets. The chapter concludes with a discussion of prospects for Canada's climate plans into the future (Barnsley, 2006; Bernstein, 2008; Chater, 2018; Drexhage, 2010; Harris, 2016).

In Chapter Ten, the book turns to the compelling issues of biosecurity and health. In the wake of COVID-19, the Canadian public finally began to realize what many observers had been pointing out for decades: Biosecurity – the protection of natural and human community health – is a vital public policy issue-area. This came at a time when some of the broader appeals for a conceptualization of planetary health (one that put ecological and human characteristics together) is becoming more popular (Haines & Frumkin, 2021). SDG 3 concerns good health and wellbeing and includes considerations of inequality as well as mental health and wellness. Recent studies of ecological wellbeing have developed sophisticated analyses of the link between environmental quality and health (Boyd, 2015; WHO-CBD, 2015). Health professionals are increasingly looking at the link between climate change and public health risks, including the impact of insect migration, the emergence and spread of new diseases, and the impact of air, water, and chemical contamination (Ostry et al., 2010; US EPA, 2006). Mental health benefits of exposure to biodiversity are well researched and suggest many compound benefits of improved biodiversity protection (Louv, 2008).

Chapter Eleven examines the Arctic, also known as the Far North, which occupies a special place in the hearts and minds of Canadians. It is indeed hard to imagine the country without it. Importantly, other countries are also involved: Members of the Arctic Council include Canada, Denmark, Finland, Iceland, Norway, the Russian Federation, Sweden, and the United States (thanks to Alaska). Of course, it is often forgotten that people actually live there; according to the Council, some 4 million people now live within the international circumpolar circle, and approximately 10 per cent of them are Indigenous Peoples, including the Aleut, Athabaskan, Gwich'in, Saami, and Inuit, as well as several other groups living in Russian territory. If there are geographic locations where physical change is evolving more rapidly than human communities can reasonably adjust, they are the islands being submerged by sea level rise and the circumpolar regions facing melting permafrost, migrating biodiversity, and the vicissitudes of chronically unseasonal weather.

Finally, Chapter Twelve ends the book with a reiteration of the key issues and concerns discussed throughout, especially the concepts of expanded timescales, multilevel adaptive governance as an analytical and normative category, and an overview of potential governance gaps. The chapter reiterates the ethical basis of an ecopolitical approach, including a concern with transformation, inequality, sustainability, and adaptability, and includes an evaluation of the impact of ecological ideas on the traditional political concerns of sovereignty, stability, security, and prosperity. The chapter critically assesses Canada's progress and shortcomings in addressing major environmental challenges like climate change, biodiversity loss, and pollution. A shift in the representation of the relationships between human and non-human worlds constitutes an important potential axis of transformative change. Tracking the origins and trajectory of this cultural shift, from a view of nature as an instrumental resource toward a view of nature as a subject of law with intrinsic value, is also a focus. Using the idea of ecological citizenship, the chapter reviews the importance of ethics as a focus of ecopolitical discussion and the necessity to confront ethical questions that underlie Canadian politics and policy. For example, how might "business as usual" be transformed to improve the ecological sustainability, equity, and adaptability of Canada? What kind of ethical basis is there to prompt policy changes, improve cooperation, and formulate innovative ways to solve ecological problems?

CONCLUSION: PUTTING ON THE ECOPOLITICAL LENSES

It is our hope that, upon reading this book, readers will be able to recognize Canadian ecopolitics as a multilevel governance phenomenon that focuses on economic, political, social, and environmental dimensions of wellbeing. They will be able to identify specific examples that illustrate how global currents, such as the UN's adoption of the Sustainable Development Goals, a global pandemic, or the onset of a major military conflict, intersect with Canadian ecopolitics. Again, understanding the importance of multilevel, adaptive governance is important, and as our case study in this chapter illustrates the role of the Canadian legal system and court decisions will also have an ongoing impact on future decision making.

We hope that our readers will be inclined to use and apply a critical analysis and ecopolitical lens on Canadian issues that emphasizes the need for urgent action to address problems equitably and sustainably and to evaluate areas of governance and policy gaps and the potential for multiscale adaptive governance to address them (Biermann, 2014, p. 41). If we are genuinely concerned with the fate of future generations, it behooves us to evaluate contemporary trends in Canadian ecopolitics in terms not only of their ecological implications, but in terms of their potential for transformative change. The challenges moving ahead will be severe, and it is a consistent, if understandable, disservice of political discourse to understate them. Biodiversity loss is not just about losing species – it is a serious threat to human existence. Climate change threatens entire populations, human and non-human alike. Cultural identities and self-knowledge are also at stake. Global environmental change is local in its manifestations, and adapting to it will hurt, demanding sacrifices from many; to pretend this is not the case is either wishful thinking or, worse, purposefully distracting political theatre.

Yet we do not wish to close this introductory chapter on a gloomy note. This book is ultimately an optimistic look at the possibilities emerging for creative and innovative ecopolitical change, as well as a call to action for citizens and governments alike to engage further with the ecopolitical challenges of our time. There can be no doubt that our actions need to be taken in the context of a vivid awareness of planetary boundaries; that with the advent of the Anthropocene comes great responsibilities that, arguably, have been with us all along but have never been so at the front of urgent thinking about our very survival into the next century.

NOTES

1 The forest fires in 2023 alone forced 232,000 people to evacuate northern towns and Indigenous communities, and cumulatively released three times as much greenhouse gas emissions as Canadian industry that year (*The Economist*, 2023a, p. 67).
2 These assessment processes are intensive and involve international scientific expertise. For example, one of the co-authors of this book, Peter Stoett, co-chaired the recently concluded IPBES Assessment on Invasive Alien Species and Their Control, which involved over 90 experts from 35 different countries and was subject to review by hundreds of other experts and accredited observer organizations as well as the nearly 150 country Parties of IPBES. See www.ipbes.net /invasive-alien-species-experts-2019.
3 Special thanks to Matthew General, Manager of Indigenous Advisory Services, JFKLaw LP, for providing material for this case study.
4 Watch a short video on the decision produced by the BBRFN here: https:// blueberryfn.com/where-happiness-dwells.

CHAPTER TWO

Ecopolitical Worldviews

LEARNING OBJECTIVES

1. Compare and contrast the four main ecopolitical worldviews: resource extractivism, sustainable development, critical political ecology, and deep ecology.
2. Assess the evolution of environmental thinking in Canada from a national to a planetary imaginary.
3. Analyze the key debates within ecopolitical thought, including growth versus limits, human–nature ethics, timeframes for change, and ecopolitical ethics.

INTRODUCTION: IDEAS IN CANADIAN ECOPOLITICS

Thinking about and acting on ecopolitics is never done in a vacuum. Ideas have material impacts on the possibilities for action. Ideas about ecopolitics have become highly diverse over time as more voices have brought their attitudes, values, and cultural perspectives to bear on the Canadian system of governance. As with many political issues, navigating the range of ideas can pose a challenge for those looking for solutions, since the pathways are often complex and conflictual. People come to ecopolitical relationships from their own standpoints and experiences, reflective of the power relationships that prevail at a given time and place. To help navigate the ecopolitical ideas that are most salient to the situations we encounter in the study of Canadian ecopolitics, this chapter will analyze and organize a wide variety of ecopolitical ideas in terms of "worldviews." Worldviews organize information and help people make sense of sometimes confusing and contradictory arguments. In the Canadian context, there are a wide range of actors and organizations working to influence public opinion on ecopolitical issues, and the resulting cacophony can be daunting and confusing. Understanding the conceptual "lay of the land" can help improve our critical thinking and judgment about ecopolitical issues by prompting us to think systematically about where ecopolitical ideas come from and how they impact politics and policy. When considering the role of ideas in the study of Canadian ecopolitics, it helps to ask, where did a worldview come from, and what effect has it had on the institutions and policies designed to address problems?

After a brief discussion of the term "ecopolitical worldview," we focus explicitly on four of them: resource extractivism, sustainable development, critical political ecology, and deep ecology. Each of these worldviews have played important roles in the evolution of Canadian ecopolitics; there are others that we have not included, and there are many subvariants of each of these as well. We've landed on these four as largely representative, however, and trust they will help form an idea of the conceptual landscape. Examining these worldviews will also help to clarify the relationships of power that affect how problems are identified, defined, and addressed. Later in the chapter we will examine how these worldviews encounter each other, how they compare, and the ways in which conflicts between worldviews sometimes play out in specific cases from history.

ECOPOLITICAL WORLDVIEWS

A worldview is a way in which people make sense of the world and their place within it. It is composed of ideas, attitudes, and framings that help to "construct meanings and relationships, help define common sense and legitimate knowledge" (Dryzek, 2013, pp. 9–10). The term "worldview" is widely used within the social sciences and can be considered similar to other terms such as "ideology," "attitude," "values," "perceptions," and "beliefs" (Chuang et al., 2020). When people discuss, form groups, and protest against environmental degradation, they are using a shared worldview to frame the issues they care about. Studying worldviews helps students of ecopolitics understand the ways in which ideas are expressed through language. It also helps us understand how new concepts have developed and the ways in which these have shaped policy responses to problems.

Ecopolitical worldviews help to identify relevant issues and define the limits of political debate and the discussion of alternative courses of action (see Litfin, 1994). Worldviews display some consistency and stability over time, and they capture widespread thinking about the environment in distinct eras and contexts. As environmental problems have become more complex, worldviews articulating ecopolitical issues have evolved in relation to one another, having varying impacts on politics and policy. We could even say that worldviews are in constant dialogue with each other, enriching but also blurring the edges of the realm of ecopolitics.

FROM A NATIONAL TO A PLANETARY IMAGINARY

As discussed in the opening chapter, environmental ethics are foundational to the study of ecopolitics. Given the vagaries of daily headlines, the ecopolitical agenda can be affected as much by political polling (and trolling) as by expert knowledge and opinion. One way to help us understand how and why worldviews clash is by considering that worldviews are set against the backdrop of a wider "social imaginary," a concept developed by the renowned Canadian philosopher Charles Taylor. A social imaginary is neither "theories nor ideologies," but implicit "backgrounds" that visualize and map space and normalize a particular sense of time. Social imaginaries form from the everyday "prototypes, framings and metaphors" that enable us to make sense of the world and our place in it, thus providing the bedrock on which social discourses and practices rest and a widely shared sense of their legitimacy (Patomaki & Steger, 2010, p. 1057).

In much of Canadian history, the social imaginary of the national state has been dominant. For many of the early decision makers in Canada, and many still today, the goal of national economic, social, and political development has dominated other considerations. In Canada, the social imaginary of the national state has been shaped by the history of colonialism, the struggle for territorial consolidation across the continent, the growth of an open economy based on resource extraction and global trade, and Canada's historical geographic proximity to the United States. All this occurred while capitalist accumulation, transported with violence from Europe, spread across the continent. The subsequent development of Canada into what many consider a model liberal democracy does not supersede this story of extractive capitalist development. As democratic theorist John Dryzek suggests, today's liberal democracies must "operate in the context of a capitalist market system [and they are] greatly constrained in terms of the kinds of policies [they] can pursue. Policies that … are even perceived as likely to damage … profitability … are automatically punished by the recoil of the market" (Dryzek, 1995, p. 112; also quoted in Adkin, 2009).

The crosscutting tendencies of integration, separation, and multilevel governance have come into play over time as worldviews have clashed. The traditional national drive to achieve security, prosperity, and stability of the nation-state persists and remains strong. However, these overriding concerns are joined by newer issues that foreground a different value set organized around a competing ethics of transformation, sustainability, democracy, and adaptability (see Adkin, 2009). As Simon Dalby argues, the globalization of the economy and technology are also accompanied by a globalization and acceleration of biogeophysical processes, including climate change, that are important to geopolitical realities and identities (Dalby, 2019). In particular, the increasing awareness of the complexity of interdependent relationships (or ecosystem thinking) is an important trend in the changing landscape of worldviews. The push and pull of local, regional, national, and global forces continue to exert influence on the new social imaginaries in the twenty-first century.

Starting in the 1960s, the national imaginary was joined by a planetary imaginary. As the global nature of environmental problems and the threat of global nuclear Armageddon became evident, a turning point was reached when we were able to look back from space and see a fragile blue marble floating in a seemingly endless void. This "planetary imaginary" was expressed in the environmental movement's use of metaphors like "spaceship earth," "planet," "globe," and "humanity." The idea of "spaceship earth" was popularized by environmentalists in the 1960s to represent a holistic approach to the biosphere (Stevis, 2005, p. 326). The first images of the earth from the moon, which encapsulated both the unity and fragility of the planet, were instrumental in shaping the popular imagination and contributed to the emergence of a planetary imaginary in the 1960s and 1970s (see Box 2.1 for more).

Also building on a planetary imaginary was the publication in 1972 of the Club of Rome report *Limits to Growth* (Meadows et al., 1972). This report was among the first to use modern technologies of computer modelling to project trends of natural resource use into the future, in the process emphasizing the scarcity of these natural resources and the resultant potential for social disruption and political breakdown. Harold and Margaret Sprout (1971) published an influential text in 1971 calling for a "politics of the planet earth," and

BOX 2.1. The Earthrise Photograph and Apollo 8

Figure 2.1. The Earthrise Photograph

Source: NASA and the Lunar and Planetary Institute. Reprinted with permission.

On December 21, 1968, the crew of the Apollo 8 mission, after orbiting the moon for three days, photographed the rising of the earth over the moon's horizon (see Figure 2.1). The mission also included two live broadcasts, with the second one being seen in 64 countries by approximately 1 billion people.

The discovery of the earth from space through this colour photograph, captured by astronaut William Anders while orbiting the moon, contributed to a "planetary imaginary" in which humans seemed insignificant in the larger universe. In many ways, the vision of the planet illustrated for many not only the shrinking of time and space through increasing economic and technological globalization, but also the need for global political cooperation. The "space race" – of which the Apollo program was a central part – took place against the backdrop of the ever-growing competition of the Cold War and the deepening fear of mutual nuclear annihilation. The Earthrise photo spoke to this growing insecurity by highlighting the fragility of the earth and the power of human technological developments. As well, the image sparked a change in collective consciousness as people could appreciate the beauty and isolation of our planet. In the four years following the publication of the photo, widespread popular movements culminated in the first Earth Day, the establishment of the Environmental Protection Agency in the United States, the formation of Canada's Department of Environment, and the convening of the first major United Nations Conference on the Human Environment in Stockholm, in 1972. The Earthrise photo raised awareness of the planet as a whole and the common nature of problems such as "diseases, health inequalities, grotesque biodiversity losses, climate change, environmental degradation, resource depletion, spread of ultra-processed foods, overconsumption, incivility, and social injustices" (Logan et al., 2020). As NASA's Artemis project begins preparations to circle the moon yet again with a Canadian astronaut on board, the planetary imaginary continues to influence thinking in interesting ways.

today researchers engaged with the Earth Systems Governance Project pursue a similar goal (Biermann, 2014). Arguably, the Anthropocene – the idea that human effects on the planet are so substantial that they are now equivalent to that of a geological force or epoch – arises from the growth of a planetary imaginary (see Chapter One; Steffen et al., 2011; Stoett & Dalby, 2022). While it should be recognized that a planetary imaginary may take different forms and have different framings with implications for ecopolitics (Stevis, 2005), the planetary imaginary is also apparent in Canadian ecopolitical worldviews. The commitment of successive Canadian governments to multilateral environmental negotiations, such as the Stockholm Conference on the Human Environment (1972), the United Nations Earth Summit (1982), and the United Nations Conference on Sustainable Development (2012), is an example of a planetary imaginary at work with a corresponding emphasis on multilevel governance. Canadian foreign policy has often reflected this planetary social imaginary when it comes to environmental issues, even if the reality of corresponding domestic policy has been quite different (see Stoett, 2016).

In sum, then, worldviews influence ecopolitical agendas by shaping how individuals and societies perceive and interact with the environment, which in turn determines the types of policies and practices that are prioritized. These worldviews guide decision making, as they affect the interpretation of social and environmental issues and the solutions deemed viable. Broader social imaginaries underlie ecopolitical worldviews. In recent times, the overriding dominant social imaginary of nation building and capitalist development has been challenged by a competing ethic guided by ecological concerns that focus on the need to value interdependence and sustainability. National and planetary imaginaries embody different and competing ethical values: The national imaginary focuses on the growth of a secure and stable Canadian community, while the planetary imaginary prioritizes adaptability and sustainability.

COMPARING WORLDVIEWS

As mentioned in the introduction to this chapter, we are highlighting four broad worldviews to illustrate the range of ideas in Canadian ecopolitics. As described in Table 2.1, these worldviews are resource extractivism, sustainable development, critical political ecology, and deep ecology. There are, of course, many other ways to categorize these perspectives; we have chosen these four as the main representative ecopolitical worldviews in Canada today, but they are rough categories indeed and encompass many other ways of thinking about the same human-caused environmental problems. Table 2.1 compares the key concepts, timescales, ethics, and action plans of each one. Strands are variations of the worldviews. Key concepts represent terms that have salience and meaning within the worldview. Ethics are described as either anthropocentric (human focused) or ecocentric (nature focused). The table also draws on the ideas discussed below in an overview of the four key debates within ecopolitics in Canada. While many of these issues are not unique to the Canadian context, their characteristics have changed over time in response to historical developments. Each worldview, and the interaction between them, has had various degrees of impact on Canadian ecopolitics. Nevertheless, it is not accurate to say that this is a "level playing field," since the dominant worldviews that influence policy and institutional governance have remained consistent throughout Canadian history.

Table 2.1. Comparative Summary of Worldviews in Canadian Ecopolitics

Worldview	Key Concepts	Timescale	Action Plans	Human–Nature Ethics	Strands
Resource Extractivism	Frontier economics	Short	Responsible resource development	Anthropocentric	Free market liberalism Resource nationalism
Sustainable Development	Ecological footprint Decoupling	Medium	Industrial development Green growth	Anthropocentric	Ecological modernization Institutionalism Resource conservation
Critical Political Ecology	Ecojustice decolonization Environmental racism	Medium	Doughnut economics Degrowth	Anthropocentric	Ecofeminism Environmental rights Staples theory
Deep Ecology	Ecological integrity Ecosystem services	Longer	Nature protection	Ecocentric	Indigenous ecological knowledge Nature rights

It would be an exaggeration to claim that the Anthropocene and the planetary imaginary have driven practical decisions and policymaking at any level in Canada. Rather, the national imaginary has dominated, propelled chiefly by the worldview of **resource extractivism**. In this worldview, the image of Canada is one of a "vast hinterland with a superabundance of resources" that are naturally available for use. In this worldview, it is necessary for human survival to extract such resources on a growing scale (Kraushaar-Friesen & Busch, 2020, p. 6). The worldview is well illustrated by the attitudes of early settlers, who viewed the forests as "frightening places with wild animals such as bears and wolves and wild men whom they viewed as savages. From European folklore and literature, they had learned to view forests as eerie, awful places, places where the sound of the wind and the shadows cast by trees played tricks with the imagination" (Macdowell, 2012, p. 46). The view that the forests were a source of threat as well as opportunity made it imperative (in the settlers' view) to clear the forest for building, fuel, and eventually the milling and export of wood. This worldview was also influenced by the religious doctrines of Christianity, which drew from the Book of Genesis to imagine settlement and clearing as a process of creating a "Garden of Eden" out of the untamed, uncivilized wilderness. As well, this worldview was influenced by the assumptions of frontier economics and neoclassical free market thinking. Market liberals tend to embrace policies of free trade, secure property rights, and the use of market forces to determine exchange values. Based on a market liberal approach, frontier economics postulated that natural resources were so abundant and easily accessible that they were less valuable than technology, capital, or labour as inputs to production.

Extractivism can also be traced back to the philosophical roots of western European culture (discussed further in Chapter Three) and a utilitarian perspective on the environment. The most influential progenitor of thought on these topics was perhaps John Locke. Locke viewed the process of development of nature as virtually a moral imperative, and to leave land uncultivated or unproductive was wasteful and therefore morally wrong. As he stated: "a thousand acres will yield the needy and wretched inhabitants as many conveniencies [*sic*] of life as ten acres of equally fertile land in Devonshire where they are well cultivated" (quoted in Cahn & O'Brien, 1996, p. 81). Despite their adherence to a superficial norm of efficient use, settlers were often exceedingly wasteful and burned and removed trees without much thought. As Dalby argues, the Canadian national identity (i.e., its national imaginary) is closely tied to the priority of territorial consolidation of sovereignty and the leverage of resources to achieve security and prosperity in a competitive global economy (Dalby, 2019). It should also be mentioned that the worldview of extractivism is not only about the unfettered or unmanaged use of resources, but also about the application of scientific knowledge and technological innovation to resource use. In an extractivist worldview, efficient use of resources to aid consumption and growth is the best means of securing prosperity. This worldview has recently been demonstrated in both the Harper Conservative's promotion of Canada as an "energy superpower" and the efforts of the Trudeau Liberals to tie the construction of the Trans Mountain Pipeline to the fate of the nation (Kraushaar-Friesen & Busch, 2020, p. 7). Despite growing concerns about the impacts of climate change, the Harper government focused on the need for "responsible resource development" that would facilitate extraction of resources and growth of the economy (especially that of the oil and gas industry). Similarly, in 2017 Justin Trudeau stated: "No country would find 173 billion barrels of oil in the ground and just leave them there" (*Maclean's*, 2017).

Sustainable development as a worldview challenges extractivism and promotes a move away from free market–based extraction and economic development. As first set down in the Brundtland Commission Report of

1987 (United Nations World Commission on Environment and Development, 1987), it melds the recognition of planetary limits with the necessity of growth to alleviate poverty and meet social needs in the present world. In this view, sustainable development charts a moderate pathway between state-led economic development and social programs on the one hand, and market-led growth and ecological efficiency on the other. Sustainable development as a worldview also brings forward the need to "think globally" and "act locally" to realize environmental goals. Canadians were active participants in the preparation of the Brundtland Commission Report, which toured Canada and held public consultations across the country from 1986 to 1987. The most widely quoted definition of sustainable development, put forward in the report, refers to a system that would meet the needs of the present without compromising those of future generations. This view considers economic growth and environmental protection to be complementary (Dryzek, 2013, p. 16). As described in the report, sustainable development was growth-positive, although mitigated by the belief that wealthy countries had a stronger obligation than poor countries to limit their growth in line with the earth's ability to sustain life.

Sustainability as a concept has become mainstream, and at times it has become so generalized as to risk being trivialized and rendered meaningless. As an overarching guide for action, sustainability has come to represent a family of approaches focused on regulatory reform, corporate social responsibility, individual actions, environmental citizenship, and natural resource conservation. Sustainability encourages a focus on economic growth, anthropocentric ethics, and gradual reform-based changes to existing institutions, policies, and processes. Within the worldview of sustainable development there are differences, especially concerning the appropriate roles for government and business: Market environmentalists argue for a minimal role for government and administrative regulation, while institutionalists respond with a focus on regulation, tax policies, and procurement and investment policies led by governments. Institutionalists agree with many of the main assumptions of market liberals while also arguing that strong state capacities are needed to counterbalance inequalities and address market failures (Clapp & Dauvergne, 2011, pp. 7–8). They tend to focus on the need to establish cooperative political institutions (referred to as "regimes" in the international relations literature; see Chapter Three) to solve collective action problems. It's safe to say that much of the Canadian political agenda, both nationally and internationally, has been driven primarily by a combination of extractivism and sustainable development worldviews; when these do clash, the former is usually, but not always, the stronger.

Critical political ecology questions the logic of economic growth and is skeptical of sustainable development plans that rely on continued industrial development to finance ecological policies and programs. Critical political ecology challenges the necessity of resource extraction and questions its basis in Canadian institutions, history, and law. In general, critical political ecology promotes the need for a transformation of economic thinking in line with the need to respect planetary boundaries and ecojustice. It focuses on the unequal effects of conventional forms of capitalist and extractivist economic development on disadvantaged groups, including women, Indigenous Peoples, and ethnic and racial minorities. For example, ecofeminist thought compares the oppression of women to the degradation of nature, tracing both back to common origins in European modern philosophical thought. In these philosophies, ecofeminists argue that both women and nature were considered to be little more than resources available for use (Plumwood, 2003). Ecofeminists argue that it is no accident that the destruction of nature by industrial capitalism is also characterized by male domination. Within ecofeminism there are differences over the degree to which women might be considered "closer" to nature, nevertheless the gendered categories of "nature" versus "culture," or "anthropocentric" versus "ecocentric" worlds are highly questioned (Plumwood, 2003).

Ethically, critical political ecology is focused on the social and political injustices that arise from unfettered capitalist development, and as a worldview it would point out that environmental and social injustices have common origins. The inequitable distribution of environmental harms is often a consequence of deliberate political decision-making structures that reflect the power and wealth inequalities prevalent in Canadian society. The practical outcome is that waste dumps, chemical and industrial works, and polluting factories are more often located close to racial minority and Indigenous communities. This reflects a larger pattern of **environmental racism** that is structurally embedded in local, regional, and national economic development planning. In this way, critical political ecology stands in contrast to resource extractivism and even some schools of sustainable development. Critical political ecology has many branches but, arguably, shares a common, Marxist root. As John Vogler suggests, because "Marxist analysis seeks explanation through the ways in which an ever-changing system of capital accumulation determines economic activity that is fundamentally responsible for excessive resource use, loss of habitats and rising levels of pollution, it provides a powerful account of the global ecological predicament" (Vogler, 2022, p. 38; see also Paterson, 2001; Laferrière & Stoett, 1999). The essential point made is that it is not humans *per se* who harm nature, but rather a small group of elites that do most of the harm, and the system itself promotes this harm as part of a standard of living worth striving for, not one to avoid. This is an important observation regarding the unequal world we live in. The argument that oppressive societies "naturalize" exploitation and harm to both humans and nature is central to "eco-anarchist" thinking such as that of Murray Bookchin, who believes that the conception of hierarchy as a natural phenomenon is based on groundless assertions mirroring the creation of hierarchies to establish social control and dominance (see Bookchin, 1990). Another key concept is offered by the Italian Marxist Antonio Gramsci, who wrote of *hegemony*, or "the persistence of specific social and economic structures that systematically advantage certain groups" (Levy & Newell, 2002, p. 86). Critical political ecologists agree that, in order to overcome the environmental problems we face, the current hegemony (and system of patriarchy) must be superseded and replaced.

Deep ecologists would certainly agree with the latter point; they would have us focus on the need to deepen understanding and appreciation for nature, drawing on an older *preservationist* view that appreciates the non-material benefits of wilderness protection and that inspired many movements for the creation of national parks. In the 1980s, a philosophical movement toward deep ecology led by thinker Arne Naess (2005) argued for an appreciation for the intrinsic value of nature rather than an instrumental view of nature as little more than a resource to be used and consumed. Deep ecology is distinguished from critical political ecology by its explicitly ecocentric focus. Deep ecology also draws from the historical movements for animal rights, animal welfare, and anti-speciesism, which have their origins in the mid-Industrial Revolution period in England. Animal rights are in some ways extensions of the movements for human rights that emerged in response to industrial abuses like child labour and the emergence of occupational diseases. Deep ecologists tend to argue that nature is a source of spirituality and almost religious inspiration rather than an exploitable resource. The reverence that Canadians share for the works of the famous artists that made up the Group of Seven and the popularity of camping, hiking, and fishing is emblematic of a Canadian "love" of nature and wilderness that has cultural and national significance. The principles of nature protection live on in the drive to preserve natural areas in federal and provincial legislation, park systems for recreation and tourism, and in the burgeoning system of marine protected areas designed to preserve biodiversity and **ecological integrity**. But we are nowhere close to the vision of living in harmony with nature extolled by the deep ecologists.

In terms of ethics, deep ecology has a close affinity with approaches that promote the incorporation of Indigenous ecological knowledge into environmental policies and programs. Both approaches share a conviction that the environmental crisis we face is a symptom of a more profound disconnect in the human–nature relationship, and that a change in the way human societies view and value nature is needed to address systemic problems. These ideas are not new. The works of Aldo Leopold, John Muir, and Thomas Berry have previously articulated the need for an ethical realignment of the human–nature relationship and a radical revaluation of the natural world in light of threats from human economic development and industrial pollution. Such ideas spurred the establishment of national parks and protected areas in Canada and the United States. More recently, Robin Wall Kimmerer's (2013) book *Braiding Sweetgrass: Indigenous Wisdom, Scientific Knowledge and the Teachings of Plants* has sold 2 million copies globally and reached the top of Canadian bestseller lists since its publication in 2013. A prominent theme in Kimmerer's work is the need for reciprocity, respect, and gratitude for nature's gifts, as reflected in Indigenous wisdom and modern scientific knowledge. To extend these teachings to human governance systems, Naess sums up deep ecology as a worldview that concerns itself with "principles of diversity, complexity, autonomy, decentralization, symbiosis, egalitarianism, and classlessness" (Naess, 2005, p. 1).

FOUR KEY DEBATES WITHIN ECOPOLITICAL THOUGHT

The ongoing dialogue between ecology and politics with which this book is concerned has undergone a series of iterations, with particular issues coming to the fore at different times. One way to organize the plethora of ecopolitical ideas is to consider the debates that have emerged and the ways in which worldviews have shaped and been shaped by those issues. The key debates we will discuss are as follows:

1. *Growth versus limits* – The question of economic growth and the sustainability of prosperity given planetary ecological limits
2. *Human–nature ethics* – The broad question of humans' ethical and moral relationship with the non-human world

3. *Timeframes* – The timeframes for ecopolitical change and human agency within them
4. *Ecojustice* – The role and form of social and economic ecojustice

With respect to the first debate, Canadian environmental thinking has undergone radical changes over the course of the country's history. As discussed above, early thinking by government officials, historians, teachers, churches, and the general public about the Canadian environment viewed the country largely in terms of realized or potential natural resource extraction and use. With an overwhelming focus on economic and business development, politicians and institutions in early Canadian history imagined the country as a limitless frontier, open and available for development, with the only limitation being the need for capital investment and technology to efficiently use the available resources. These tendencies persist in Canada as a result of the urban concentration of the population, the distribution of the population along the southern border and their distance from the sites of resource development, and the "Canadian experience" of battling the harsh elements and climate to achieve security. In this setting, **frontier economics**, in which the natural world is viewed as a vast, infinite resource and unlimited sink for human wastes (see Liboiron, 2021), transitioned from a paradigm of colonialism to being ingrained in Canadian resource development policies and practices (Hessing et al., 2007, pp. 13–15). While difficult to describe this idea as "environmental," as a worldview it has influenced national economic policies and continues to cast its shadow on everything from pipeline planning to forestry to fisheries to suburban development, even if the undeniably finite capacity of nature to provide these resources is recognized and part of the planning process. The principle that most natural resources are essentially limitless, or that limitations can be overcome by technological fixes, is also central to an extractivist worldview.

A more critical school of thought (related to critical political ecology) emerged around **staples theory**, originally developed in the 1930s by Harold Innis to explain Canada's continued reliance on natural resource development and the pattern of exploitive relations between the Canadian heartland (the industrial zones of southern Ontario and Quebec) and its hinterland (northern, western, and coastal zones of resource extraction). Staples theory argues that this relationship produces a political economy leveraged around resource extraction that is unsustainable and inequitable. Staples theory contains an implicit critique of the extractivist worldview, building on the pragmatic recognition that Canada's economic and political historical development pathway has been overly constrained by extractivism (Innis, 1930, 1940; see also Watkins, 1963). This became further developed with rising concerns in the post–World War II period that many Canadian natural resources were owned by non-Canadian companies profiting from export-led extraction without paying back into the Canadian economy and social system.[1]

Despite its centrality in Canadian environmental decision making, and as suggested by staples theory, the extractivist view has not gone unchallenged. Indeed, contestation over natural resource extraction has now become a central component of Canadian ecopolitics, impacting a wide range of sectors, levels of government, actors, and institutions. Starting in the 1960s, conventional extractivist views of economic development were challenged by more critical perspectives arising from different levels of governance and growing environmental movements, including the assertion of Indigenous sovereignty closely tied to a non-extractivist worldview. These movements will be examined in greater detail in Chapter Four, but for now a brief overview of the various strands of thinking that helped define the ecopolitical issues will provide a basis for understanding how the different worldviews emerged. Some approaches, for example sustainable development, emphasized the need to move away from "business as usual" models to a more cautionary approach that focused on sustainability in the longer term, while not rejecting growth entirely. **Ecological modernization theory** recognized the need to respect planetary boundaries but argued that sustainability could be achieved by using modern industrial methods of production to improve efficiencies and reduce environmental impacts (Warner, 2010). In general, ecological modernization theory suggested that economic growth (in GDP) could be decoupled from energy use such that the negative effects of growth on the environment would be mitigated over time. Ecological modernization also informed many proposals for **green growth** – a term meant to convey the synergies between economic growth and environmental sustainability, particularly at the local level. The focus on environmental limits to growth inspired a strand of environmental thinking that would develop new concepts for understanding and analyzing human impacts on the environment. For example, the idea of an **ecological footprint** was developed in 1990 by Mathis Wackernagel and William Rees at the University of British Columbia (Global Footprint Network, 2021). The footprint is a way of measuring and quantifying the human impact on a given environment based on limits defined by the biocapacity of that environment. At the same time, a legalist tradition emerged that sought greater legal rights for the environment, as well as to ensure that access to a healthy environment was a Canadian human right. Again, there were links here to Indigenous laws that pre-dated colonization. For example, "Mi'kmaq law is rooted in ecological relationships, extending legal personality to animals, plants, insects, and rocks, and imposing legal obligations on Mi'kmaq persons" (Boyd, 2012, p. 15; see also Borrows, 2010).

Developments in science and ecological knowledge broadly in line with critical political ecology also impacted the mainstream view of natural resource development. Around the turn of the twenty-first century the idea of the Anthropocene brought the concern with ecological limits to growth together with longer timescales. The Anthropocene idea emphasizes the growing human impact on the earth's ecosystems (or more generally, the biosphere) as its key organizing principle. Building on these ideas, the academic study of humanities, physical sciences, and traditional ecological knowledge has deepened and developed an awareness of how ecological limits impact human civilization. Whereas neoclassical market-based economics understood the economy and the environment as distinct and separate, **ecological economics** began to understand that economic activity takes place within the context of ecological limits. Unlike neoclassical economics, ecological approaches focus on the awareness of planetary limits within which economies operate. For example, GDP (gross domestic product) occupies a central place in the popular and political discussion about the Canadian economy. **GDP** measures the total value of all the goods and services produced in Canada in a given year. GDP increases are often viewed as positive signals for the national economy. However, the measure of GDP has been subjected to a sustained critique over the last few years. Because GDP only measures economic activities that involve the exchange of money, GDP not only ignores a lot of economic activity that contributes to the good of the society (like household maintenance, child home care, and beach cleanups by volunteers), it also tends to paint environmentally destructive activities in a positive light (oil spills actually increase GDP by requiring the paid work of oil cleanup professionals). GDP has also been criticized because it devalues many alternative social goods that people want and that increase their security, health, and wellbeing, including biodiversity and ecosystem services (see Case Study 12.2 for more).

Building on the broad critique of GDP-based policies focused on economic growth, a plethora of literature has explored alternatives of degrowth. **Degrowth** draws on critical political ecology to critique the idea that economies can continue to grow while externalizing their environmental costs or impacts. As stated by Lorenz Keyszer (2021), "a key point of degrowth is that we can secure livelihoods and access to the goods and services people need no matter what happens to GDP if we change how our economy functions and what things we prioritize." In this view, growth moves from being an end in itself and becomes a means by which societies can achieve wellbeing. As Barry (2021) argues, economic growth has become much like Achilles' spear, a myth that the spear can heal the wounds it inflicts. Accordingly, a lot of environmental defences of the need for economic growth assume that the fruits of growth would be invested in the clean-up of the problems created by the growth itself. Barry points out this is a fallacy, because the technological innovation required to, for example, reduce greenhouse gas emissions requires a level of decoupling of economic growth from the material effects on the environment. While some decoupling can be achieved in certain sectors, broad macroeconomic decoupling is undermined by the tendency of growth to increase the rebound effect, where efficiency gains lead to higher levels of overall consumption. Degrowth calls for a reduction in consumption in some areas with increases in others to allow for growth in sectors and areas where it can be used as an instrument to create a social justice floor.

Drawing on the arguments of degrowth, planetary boundaries, and the Sustainable Development Goals (SDGs), Kate Raworth developed the idea of **doughnut economics**. Doughnut economics uses the 12 dimensions of planetary boundaries (see Chapter One) and nine social boundaries defined in the SDGs to describe and measure the **safe operating space** of humanity beyond economic growth: "The social foundation forms an inner boundary, below which are many dimensions of human deprivation. The environmental ceiling forms an outer boundary, beyond which are many dimensions of environmental degradation. Between the two boundaries lies an area – shaped like a doughnut – which represents an environmentally safe and socially just space for humanity to thrive in. It is also the space in which inclusive and sustainable economic development takes place" (Raworth, 2012). These studies have sought to transcend disciplinary boundaries between economics, politics, and society, and between the hard and soft (social) sciences. They have sought to think in more integrated ways about how sustainable societies might function within ecological limits, rather than being reliant on unlimited growth. These approaches still remain outside the mainstream economic models, which continue to use measures like GDP to encourage a focus on growth, often without taking environmental effects into account.

In addition to an ongoing dialogue about the role of growth versus limits within ecopolitical thinking, another debate has focused on the ethical relationship between humans and the natural world. This debate is similarly a key component of environmental thinking and has found various iterations in different places and decades. On the one hand, anthropocentric (human-centred) approaches tend to focus on the challenge of meeting human needs in the face of environmental challenges, while on the other hand, ecocentric approaches focus on the necessity of maintaining the intrinsic value of nature and ecological integrity. Some of these approaches are in alignment with deep ecology traditions and worldviews, while some variants focus on the need for a spiritual approach that "fosters compassion for non-human others by reintroducing a sense of sacredness and reverence for all interactions making up the planet's intricate ecology" (Blewitt, 2008, p. 28). Principles of **Indigenous ecological knowledge** emphasize the co-dependency and equality of human and natural worlds, focusing on the obligations that human societies have toward nature and the need for long timescales to evaluate and incorporate the interests of future generations into current decision making. Deep approaches to environmental problems use an **ecocentric** approach to pollution, natural resources, cultural diversity, and ethics that are highly critical of industrial society and call for fundamental structural and cultural changes to politics and policy. **Anthropocentric** approaches argue that human needs and welfare are appropriate drivers for ethical and environmental decision making, and that such considerations are not necessarily at odds with achieving a healthy environment. The key question in this debate is, are humanity's needs and interests reconcilable with those of nature, and how can value systems reflect both moving forward?

A third debate within ecopolitical thought concerns the rate and scale of change required to meet ecological and social sustainability goals. Critical political ecology has focused on the need for deep structural transformative changes in the face of rapid ecological change, while sustainable development approaches have focused on the need for gradual, longer timescale reform processes that move policies and procedures in more sustainable directions at a progressive rate. For example, environmental thought on ecological modernization has focused on the many ways in which the existing industrial systems can be modified without fundamental or radical changes to their basic institutional structures. In contrast, critical political ecologists argue for rapid and more fundamental transformational changes capable of moving away from extractive industrial structures. The key question in this debate is, are modern industrial societies capable of responding to ecological challenges and limits rapidly enough to cope with the looming crisis that they are producing? Furthermore, will modern industrial societies be able to adapt, or are deeper, more transformational responses needed to respond to growing risks and threats? Are social change agents, such as the famous environmentalist group Greenpeace (see Case Study 2.1), able to lead the way with counterhegemonic discourse, civil disobedience, and other efforts, or will a more profound social change movement need to arise to change the very basis of the social imaginary?

CASE STUDY 2.1. The Establishment of Greenpeace

The rise of environmental movements beginning in the 1960s was a cultural, economic, and political phenomena. It corresponded with the rise of **post-materialist values** in western culture, characterized by an increasing concern with political issues of social equity, identity, and wellbeing. Post-material culture also brought a rising interest in movements to protect the natural world, anti-nuclearism, anti-racism, and feminism. Prompted by the increasing awareness of the effects of extractivist and wasteful consumerism, environmentalism was spurred by headlines about chemical contamination, oil spills, and other environmental disasters (Santese, 2020). Greenpeace has maintained its status as one of the largest global civil society groups in the world, virtually the "brand name" of environmentalism (Harter, 2004).

Greenpeace emerged just over 50 years ago in response to US plans to begin large-scale underground nuclear testing in the north, which had potentially negative consequences for humans and nature alike. The title "Greenpeace" was first published as a headline in Vancouver's *Georgia Straight* newsmagazine, heralding the plans of the "Don't Make a Wave Committee" (DMWC) to protest a series of nuclear tests in Amchitka, Alaska, which was close to the Alaskan Wildlife Refuge (Harter, 2004, p. 87). One of the immediate concerns was a probable earthquake or tsunami derived from the underground tests that could affect the surrounding territories (Zelko, 2004, p. 320). The DMWC planned to protest the pending tests by taking a fishing boat, the *Phyllis Cormack*, to intervene in the place of action (Zelko, 2004, p. 321). Even though it was not possible for the explosion to be stopped, Greenpeace counted it as a win since the United States never used the site again (Harter, 2004, p. 88). For the first time in the organization's history, the media coverage strategy gave the expected results and diffusion needed to establish the group's bona fides. In the 1970s, the newly formed World Greenpeace Foundation continued its anti-nuclear campaign in the Pacific Islands, protesting French nuclear testing, which had continued long past the point when other countries had abandoned above-ground tests. The sinking of the Greenpeace ship *Rainbow Warrior* in an ill-conceived "black ops" plot by French commandos ended in loss of life and was a huge embarrassment for that country, with the publicity eventually leading to the ending of their nuclear testing program (Montgomery, 2015).

Paul Watson and David Garrick launched the first Greenpeace anti-sealing campaign in the spring of 1976, at first directed only against the large Norwegian commercial sealing outfits but later directed against all facets of the seal hunt. Seal hunting had been a staple activity in Newfoundland and Labrador by both settlers and Inuit since the seventeenth century, with the seal oil industry forming a major export in the eighteenth century (Harter, 2004). Greenpeace exercised its international muscles by lobbying the European Economic Community (EEC) to ban the importation of harp seal fur (Zelko, 2004, p. 332). The combination of anti-fur, anti-cruelty, and anti-hunting movements would reach a nadir in the 1980s, leading to a worldwide shift in views aimed at eliminating animal abuses, especially if committed for apparently trivial reasons such as fashion or entertainment. While the brutal clubbing of baby seals on open ice was difficult for sealers to defend from an animal rights' perspective, a more nuanced narrative of the seal hunt would emerge years later, in conjunction with the collapse of the cod fishery that decimated the seal population. More recently, attitudes toward Inuit and Indigenous Peoples' hunting practices have been moderated by education around the role of hunting in Indigenous culture. Nevertheless, Greenpeace was unrelenting in its attacks on all forms of seal hunting, and the campaign was a huge success for the organization. Paul Watson would go on to form his own splinter group, the Sea Shepherd Society, known for taking direct physical action against whalers and other extractivist operations.

The Greenpeace environmental movement is known worldwide, with offices in over 40 countries and almost 3 million supporters (Montgomery, 2015). In its more than 50 years of history, Greenpeace has become one of the largest non-governmental organizations, demonstrating that political **scalability** can be reached. Operating within the realm of "world civic politics" (Wapner, 1996), Greenpeace set out to deliberately span multiple levels of governance, from local to national to global (Zelko, 2004, p. 319). Even though its tactics are debatable and have often prompted strong reactions (which

Figure 2.2. The *Arctic Sunrise* at Sea

Source: © Bente Stachowske / Greenpeace.

may be part of its strategic goals), the organization has created heightened awareness of environmental issues, and its media campaigns have influenced the public environmental agenda worldwide.

Critical Thinking Questions

1. Greenpeace has long refused government financial support for its activities. What are the pros and cons of taking this position? What is the political impact of Greenpeace's methodology to inform the world's community about its protests?
2. Do you agree with Greenpeace's anti–seal hunt campaign? What factors do you think have led to the worldwide influence of anti-hunting movements?

Another important debate in Canadian ecopolitics concerns ecological or environmental justice. While not always in consensus, **ecofeminists** have long argued that environmental degradation is a symptom of a patriarchal colonial

Canadian society that devalues both women and nature. Ecofeminist critiques have joined up with movements seeking to decolonize and resist domination by the Canadian state (and the corresponding national imaginary). Ecofeminism stresses the importance of intersectionality in understanding environmental issues, recognizing how race, class, and other social factors intersect with gender and ecology. Ecofeminists note the patriarchal roots of extractivist worldviews and policies, which disproportionately impact women because of their roles as caregivers and in social reproduction (Berman, 1993). This "logic of domination has created a situation where women, non-European races, children, the elderly, and nature are considered inferior and available for exploitation" (Harvester & Blenkinsop, 2010, p. 124). As a result, the violence inflicted against people based on racial, class, and gender differences is inseparable from the degradation of the natural environment; indeed, it is woven into the very fabric of thought that privileges masculinity as well as extractivism (this is often referred to as "epistemic violence").

Ecofeminist and decolonial thinkers are also critical of mainstream environmental approaches because they neglect questions of social justice. Historically, environmental movements in Canada have been led by urban, white, middle classes whose exclusive focus on wilderness and nature protection has allowed environmental racism to become institutionally established in government policies and structures. The effects of environmental racism are evident in the continued marginalization of First Nations voices in resource development project decisions. It is also demonstrated in processes of local government planning and zoning that consistently impose higher environmental costs on racial minority communities (see Case Study 12.2). Often, the ecojustice critique is in the form of advocacy for **environmental rights**, emphasizing the necessity of addressing institutional and legal inequities alongside policy measures to reduce environmental degradation. Similarly, concerns about violence associated with environmental destruction accompanying human–human exploitation can also be viewed as part of the pursuit of environmental justice (see Stoett, 2013; Stoett & Omrow, 2022).

CONCLUSION: INESCAPABLE COMPLEXITIES

This broad overview of ecopolitical worldviews is not meant to be exhaustive, but rather to provide a schema for understanding how environmental ideas in Canada have emerged, been defined, evolved, and contested the issues of

Canadian ecopolitics. Worldviews help to make sense of the complex interactions, new players, and institutional changes that have impacted Canadian ecopolitics over time and continue to shape it today. The four main worldviews of extractivism, sustainable development, critical political ecology, and deep ecology represent nodes of contestation and competition over the essential issues of Canadian ecopolitics. As noted above, however, these worldviews are also grounded in people's experiences, cultural backgrounds, and lifeways. As people are not equal, ideas are also not equal. Canadian ecopolitics has consistently given greater weight to extractivist worldviews with some incorporation of sustainable development, while ignoring, containing, and even limiting critical political and deep ecology approaches. As we will see, the various strands, action plans, and imaginaries (see Table 2.1) associated with ecopolitical worldviews form a landscape of ideas that have important effects on Canadian political institutions and policies. The Canadian ecopolitical debates over economic growth, the need for respect for planetary limits, the ethical value of nature, and the necessity of integrating social and environmental justice continue to evolve today. This leaves us with some key critical thinking questions to consider: Are there ecological limits to growth, and how do we know they exist? What are the ethical implications of thinking of nature as a resource? What alternatives exist for thinking of nature in ways that respect environmental values? What are the promises and pitfalls of changing worldviews, and how do these impact Canadian ecopolitics?

NOTE

1 Innis ultimately offered a deep critique of Canadian development: "He blamed the coercive and anti-democratic institutions of Canadian life on the dominant presence of monopolies, the practices of the commercial state, and the influence of the branch-plants which had prospered and grown in influence … In his mind the power of monopolies was linked to the erosion of individual and collective rights both within Canada and without. His preoccupation with these central issues made Innis into a nationalist, a critic of incremental growth, an opponent of continentalism, and an agnostic about the viability of the liberal tradition itself" (Drache, 1982, p. 52).

CHAPTER THREE

The Global Commons and Global Issues

LEARNING OBJECTIVES

1. Explain Canada's role in addressing global environmental issues and managing the global commons.
2. Analyze the challenges and successes of international environmental agreements using the examples of ozone depletion and biodiversity protection.
3. Evaluate the tensions between Canada's domestic policies and its international environmental commitments.

INTRODUCTION: CANADA IN THE WORLD

As discussed in Chapter One of this book, Canada's formal relationship with the rest of the world has been characterized by a mix of liberal international-ism (and even idealism) punctuated by periods of disengagement and isolationist tendencies. In terms of ecopolitical worldviews, the dominance of an extractivist worldview, with its focus on an open economy and market-based relationships, has been tempered at times by Canada's active participation in projects designed to advance sustainable development, particularly regarding the Global South. As part of key leadership groups like the G7, the G20, and the United Nations, Canada has sought to play the role of a "middle power," capable of "punching above our weight" on the world stage. On the other hand, Canada's historical treatment of Indigenous Peoples and racial minorities has not made it particularly well suited to be an environmental justice champion. The expansion and consolidation of the Canadian state has come at the expense of the country's natural resources, biodiversity, and freshwater, and Canada's share of the global production of pollutants and waste, including greenhouse gases, is substantial. This chapter will illuminate the roots and implications of Canada's global role as a state citizen of the international community, as well as a steward of a large proportion of the planet. By examining two examples of Canadian involvement in global issues, the chapter will identify key characteristics arising from Canada's international position, its role in the management of common resources, and its responsibilities as an environmental citizen in the current era of the Anthropocene.

Any discussion of Canada's global ecopolitical role should recognize its historical roots as a white settler society. Historically, as encounters between Europeans and Indigenous Peoples increased, so did the struggles over rule that were to have profound effects on the relations among peoples to this day, a process that was repeated throughout the continents (with the only exception being Antarctica; Ryser, 2012). In general, any country that is not a good steward of lands and waters within its own sovereign jurisdiction will find it difficult to preach responsible environmental decision making to others. Inconsistencies abound in Canada's foreign policy decision making on transnational pollution, toxic chemicals, carbon emissions, and biodiversity protection, to name a few. Having said that, Canada is a relatively minor power on the world stage, and global issues have generally had little impact on Canadian ecopolitics domestically. There is little electoral/political incentive for Canadian decision makers to be bold in their environmental advocacy around the world, as Canadian public opinion tends to prioritize politics "at home." The muddy waters of Canadian federalism have also often presented challenges for any federal government hoping to bring provinces together to back international agreements, as was shown through Canada's participation and then withdrawal from the Kyoto Protocol of the United Nations Framework Convention on Climate Change (UNFCCC, discussed in Chapters Four and Nine).

Successive Canadian governments have tried to cultivate an image of a compromising "middle power," a supporter of the international order based on the rule of law. Environmental issues have often provided rich opportunities for Canada to develop its persona and to profile its commitment to multilateralism and international organizations. In Chapter Four you will read more about Canada's historical role in international initiatives like the 1972 United Nations Conference on the Human Environment (the Stockholm Convention), the 1992 UN Conference on Environment and Development (the Earth Summit), and more. Before we get to that, in this chapter we want to address the unique problems of "the commons" as distinct dilemmas at the intersection of state sovereignty and global cooperation. Managing the global commons means confronting ethical dilemmas around sharing resources, the role of future generations, and the structures of international law that deserve examination on their own terms. While the specific arrangements and agreements to govern the global commons are often filled with impressive language and pay lip service to important principles like the precautionary principle and the polluter pays principle, often such high expectations are dashed when it comes to implementation and enforcement.

As with many other questions, the global commons dilemma shows how the global ecopolitical system, including the system of international law, operates in unequal and discriminatory ways. International law and diplomacy has sought to protect the global commons through a variety of means. However, remote frontiers, the open ocean, the Arctic and Antarctic, the atmosphere, and even the moon and other planets present particular problems. To the extent that such areas contain natural resources, economic theory has sometimes labelled them as "common property" or open-access systems, governed by the state but accessible, in theory, to all (McKenzie, 2002, p. 131). When state sovereignty reaches its limits and an area is beyond the reach of any one given state, it is governed by international law. To the extent such open regions become the subjects of international law, they are jointly governed by the international community. For example, the United Nations Convention on the Law of the Sea (UNCLOS; see Chapter Eight) dictates that countries may claim up to 200 nautical miles of coastline as an "exclusive economic zone" suitable for fishing and other economic activities, but anything beyond that is governed by international laws and agreements. Antarctica – the only continent on earth without native human populations – is governed by a group of claim-staking states (this is known as the Antarctic Treaty System), though some argue it should also be considered part of the commons and subject to United Nations governance.

At the international level, Canada participates in a wide variety of governance forums designed to resolve issues that have wide-ranging implications for environmental sustainability, justice, and ecological integrity. Some of the earliest international agreements on environmental issues signed by

Canada (or Britain) were around common issues such as migratory birds (1917, with the United States), fisheries management (1909 Boundary Waters Treaty), and even a treaty governing the exploration and use of outer space (1967; McKenzie, 2002, p. 243). Today, the Arctic Council, the UNFCCC, the UNCLOS, and the Stockholm Convention on Persistent Organic Pollutants are some of the leading international bodies that govern global issues. A key feature many of these share is that they concern lands or waters that are otherwise considered outside of states' prevailing territorial claims and sovereignty: In other words, they are "unclaimed" or "common."

Canada is also a "steward" of large parts of the planet whose management and treatment affects the health, prosperity, and futures of many other people and ecosystems around the world. For example, Canada contains a large part of the boreal forest, an important planetary repository of biodiversity as well as being a carbon recycler for the planet. The now-epic forest fires in the autumn of 2023, which raged "from the Atlantic Coast to the Pacific and from the southern border to the Arctic's Beaufort Sea," affected more than 180,000 square kilometres of forest and produced 1,800 metric tonnes of carbon dioxide, "three times Canada's industrial greenhouse gas emissions that year" (*The Economist*, 2023a, p. 67). This release of greenhouse gas emissions affected the carbon budget of the entire planet. Canada governs large swaths of land in the Arctic, and as much as 20 per cent of the world's supply of freshwater. These facts mean that Canada has both rights and responsibilities as a member of the international society of states and is obligated and constrained by the interests of the international community as a whole. Canada is also, increasingly, a global actor itself. Canada is a source of major international capital investments in natural resource extraction around the world. As much as 75 per cent of the world's mining companies are headquartered in Canada, and Toronto is a financial centre for the mining industry: As of 2016, around 80 per cent of the world's equity trades in mining stocks took place in Toronto's markets (Block, 2017).

THE COMMONS AND GLOBAL ISSUES

The time has long passed when Canadians were unaware of Canada's interdependence with the rest of the world. No one with an even minimal understanding of climate change, for example, can consider that Canada is insulated from challenges that face the world as a whole. The outbreak of the COVID-19 pandemic in March 2020 demonstrated the innate vulnerability of Canadians to the emergence of infectious diseases, the dependence on global supply chains for vital goods and services, and the overall embeddedness of Canadian life in a planetary ecosystem. It also demonstrated the interdependence of economic, social, and environmental issues for the achievement of *national* stability, security, and development.

This chapter focuses on Canada's engagement with the commons in its economic, social, and political dimensions and explores cases where Canada has engaged with global issues of ecopolitics. Here, we will sample two examples of global issues, comparing and contrasting Canada's role in international ecopolitical governance: the problems of ozone layer depletion and biodiversity protection. Climate change is discussed separately in Chapter Nine. For now, it is important to address the structure of global issues through specific examples to determine whether Canada has acted as a "good global citizen" in addressing these common problems.

Global issues are usually viewed as collective action problems that cannot be solved by any single country acting on its own but instead transcend bilateral or cross-national environmental challenges. Transnational environmental problems may require coordination across borders between one or two or even a small group of countries within a region, but **global issues** demand common action across many or all of the countries of the world in order to be addressed. On the world stage, the structure of relationships and the patterns of conflict and cooperation are loosely governed by laws, institutions, and norms that are rooted in state sovereignty. State sovereignty, which is widely accepted as an international norm, is the mutual recognition of countries' independence and autonomy from external interference in processes of governance. The foundational norm of state sovereignty is recognized in international environmental law, institutions, and practices designed to address global problems.

As the degree of international coordination has expanded, so have the number and range of civil society actors, business organizations, multilateral organizations, and international regimes that are involved in governance. The term "regime" has been developed in the literature to describe how informal arrangements can spring up to create new structures for international order. A regime is defined as the set of norms, institutions, and practices around which actors' expectations converge in a particular issue-area (Keohane, 1989; Krasner, 1982, 1991). Regimes develop around ecopolitical global issues like environment and trade, intellectual property rights, pollution, climate, and species protection. Canada has been an active partner in supporting and building international regimes around biodiversity, climate change, chemical pollution, and international development. For example, Canada was the first country to sign the Convention on Biological Diversity and continues to house its secretariat, and Canada has played a key role in developing the Montreal Protocol on Substances That Deplete the Ozone Layer (discussed below).

Global environmental regimes often emerge around areas of governance that are called "open-access" systems. Open-access systems are ones where the availability of common goods is relatively unregulated and free. While a "commons" (some schools of thought use the term "common pool resources") may be jointly owned and collectively managed, either by law or norms, an open-access system refers to broader portions of the global environment that are not property (Greer, 2012; Ostrom, 1990). Some examples include the open ocean, clean breathable air, and parks and other protected areas. The oceans have constituted a system of open access due to the ease with which states are able to extend their activities beyond their own sovereign borders with little cost or effort. For example, the free availability of large numbers of cod stocks off the east coast of the North American continent allowed for the easy extraction of fish from the open ocean by competing powers (see Chapter Eight). Despite efforts to create and enforce an international fishing regime, competition among fishers created conflicts as cod stocks began to decline. Eventually, the stock of cod available for fishing collapsed in the 1980s due to overexploitation. In part, the inability of the international community to agree on and enforce common rules around ocean fishing contributed to this collapse, which had severe consequences for Atlantic fishers and for the regional economy as a whole, and a similar situation arose just a few years later with turbot, another commercially important species of fish (see Stoett, 2001).

The governance of such open-access resources and public goods locally and globally constitutes a particular set of issues and challenges for Canadian ecopolitics because of the unique structure and patterns of conflict and cooperation these problems engender. **Public goods** are resources that tend to be provided or governed by states because their use is non-rival and non-excludable. A good (something that people value) is considered to be non-rival when its consumption by one user does not compromise its consumption by another user. A good is considered to be non-excludable when it is too costly or even impossible for one user to exclude others from enjoying the good. This is distinct from private goods, where supply is affected by each user's level of consumption and it is easier for users to exclude others from consuming that good. Unlike private goods, public goods are vulnerable to **free riding**, meaning that consumers of the good can easily benefit from its provision without contributing to the costs of producing the good.

Environmental regimes and public goods are also related to the similar concept of a "commons." A commons is a public good that is available for the use of many, such as a common grazing ground for animals or a national park. Examples of a global commons include the open seas (including the ocean floor), space, the atmosphere, and even, potentially, a technological or scientific discovery that can be considered the common heritage of human-kind, such as a genetic sequence or a vaccine. Notably, efforts have been made to privatize all of these things in various ways, and though we have related international conventions (such as the Nagoya Protocol on Access to Genetic Resources and the Fair and Equitable Sharing of Benefits Arising from Their Utilization to the Convention on Biological Diversity) designed to guard against this, much of the commons has effectively been enclosed by private ownership.

Governing a global commons provokes ethical issues of access, equity, sus-tainability, and the limits of natural **carrying capacity**. The "Tragedy of the Commons" could be considered an ancient phrase, but its modern use dates to a widely influential article by Garrett Hardin written in 1968 that refers to the "population problem" (Hardin, 1968). Hardin argued that the "tragedy" results from a "situation in which the rational choices of individuals, acting independently and solely in their own self-interest, collide with the interests and needs of the larger community, resulting in the depletion of resources against the long-term interests of both individuals and the group" (Cochran, 2020). For example, Hardin's article argued that a common grazing area that has a limited carrying capacity will inevitably be overgrazed and degraded because of the tendency for users to add more cows for their own benefit until the commons itself is degraded for all. Hardin depicted the problem as aris-ing from unrestricted rational self-interest, which would lead individuals to prioritize their own self-benefit at the expense of the common good (Cahn & O'Brien, 1996, p. 135).

While Hardin was pessimistic about finding solutions to the tragedy, his argument was sometimes used to advocate for enclosure of the commons – in other words, the elimination of the commons through the privatization of its resources and management by property owners. This in turn is often traced back to John Locke, who described the distinction between property, which was enclosed, and the "wild woods and uncultivated waste of America, left to nature, without any improvement, tillage, or husbandry" (quoted in Greer, 2012, p. 367). Locke's idea of property was intimately tied up with the idea of the state of nature. For Locke, although nature was communal, this was not the preferred or even the correct way to view it, since "it cannot be supposed he (i.e., God) meant it should always remain common and uncultivated" (Locke, 1996). Locke argued that since nature was given for the benefit of humans, and the rational and industrious would demonstrate their right to ownership through the application of their labour, then enclosure (or colonization) was justified for the good of all as long as it led to improvement (Cahn & O'Brien, 1996, pp. 77–79). Locke's defence of property and enclosure of such "wild woods" was a justification for the violent European colonization of the lands of Indigenous Peoples in North America, Africa, and elsewhere.

The prospects for governing the commons have often been treated with pessimism. Indeed, for a long time the consensus that the commons would inevitably be overused if left unregulated was entrenched and persistent. However, others (in particular Nobel Laureate Elinor Ostrom) have systematically "debunked" the claims of commons pessimists by demonstrating that commons do not have to be "managed" per se but can be highly ordered spaces in which limits on growth are respected over time. Ostrom's work demonstrated that commons do not have to be subsumed into private property or strict rules of enforcement to be orderly, and that such "third way" solutions are in fact fairly regular and everyday occurrences. Commons could, in fact, be ruled through collective action (Nordman, 2021, p. 4). Indeed, the international community, including Canada, has persistently and progressively worked to improve collective action for the commons in the absence of any overarching system of enforcement. Such efforts would presumably not be evident were the prospects for governing the commons so bleak.

The two examples discussed below, ozone depletion and biodiversity protection, demonstrate the particularly thorny problems of public goods, open-access systems, and global issues for Canadian ecopolitics. These issues differ from many others in that they require higher levels of coordination and cooperation to solve, they tend to have weaker systems of enforcement and ruling arrangements to prevent abuses, and they often have ill-defined territorial and environmental borderlines between areas of sovereign jurisdiction. The incentive to achieve more sustainable, ethical, and beneficial practices is often weaker because of the unequal distribution of costs and benefits and the blurry lines of accountability and control. Importantly, governments are often only one of a set of numerous actors who must be rallied to engage in problem solving, since global issues and protection of the commons involve large numbers of civil society groups, private companies, subnational institutions, and multilateral organizations. Diving into the commons problems described below illustrates how the larger number of parties complicates efforts to achieve success and makes for a challenging set of governance problems for Canadian ecopolitics. While progress has been made, with multiple jurisdictions, cultures, economies, and interests, the governments of the world are not yet at a point of thinking about issues as planetary in scope. A sense of shared "enlightened interest" remains elusive for global ecopolitics and undermines attempts to move human societies toward a common planetary vision of a greener, more equitable and sustainable world.

OZONE DEPLETION

In the 1920s and 1930s refrigeration became widespread in Canada, allowing for huge improvements in food safety, health, and convenience. To keep things cool, refrigerators used methyl chloride, which was highly toxic and caused a series of household deaths. In the 1950s, scientists discovered a way to replace methyl chloride with chlorofluorocarbons (CFCs), believed to be inert in the atmosphere, which also found wider uses in air conditioners and as a propellant for things like hair sprays and fire extinguishers. In 1974, an article in the widely read journal *Nature* noted that CFCs did not dissipate in the atmosphere but were destroyed by exposure to sunlight, which produced a chemical reaction that damaged ozone in the stratosphere (Molina & Rowland, 1974). Ozone is important for life because it absorbs harmful ultraviolet rays from the sun that cause eye damage, cancers, and obstruction of photosynthesis. It wasn't until 1984 that scientists discovered that the ozone layer over the Antarctic had thinned by about one-third, and by 1985 the hole was imaged by NASA (Scott, 2022). Although the problem was identified quickly, the thinning observed by this time was the result of CFCs manufactured many years or decades earlier because of the delay from the time of production to release, to the time to be cycled into the stratosphere (Meadows et al., 2005, p. 188).

The debate over the potential for thinning ozone had actually been going on for several years in the scientific literature, while at the same time chemical manufacturers like DuPont had actively resisted efforts to move toward regulation of CFCs because of their wide usage. Traditionally, air pollution had been considered a transnational issue. The effects of acid rain, smog, and mercury poisoning were usually regional or transboundary in nature. However, the effects of CFCs in the atmosphere were different – they were global in nature. Reducing emissions in one area would likely be insufficient to affect the whole problem, so only global action would work to solve it (Peloso, 2010, p. 306). The United Nations Environment Programme (UNEP) convened the International Conference on the Ozone Layer in 1977, which began to lay the groundwork for an international treaty, the 1985 Vienna Convention for the Protection of the Ozone Layer (Makhijani & Gurney, 1995, pp. 218–19). Within 18 months, the countries of the world agreed on a strong international protocol to reduce the production and release of CFCs into the atmosphere, the Montreal Protocol. Companies like Union Carbide had already begun research on aerosol propellants that might replace CFCs (Makhijani & Gurney, 1995). To date, 189 countries follow its provisions under international law. The Montreal Protocol has been supplemented with a series of agreements to regulate and phase out replacement chemicals that are themselves major greenhouse gases, and so it has had a positive effect on the effort to reduce climate emissions. The reduction in CFC use led to a gradual shrinking of the Antarctic ozone hole, and most scientists agree that it will likely disappear by the end of the present century, if not before (Solomon et al., 2016).

Many consider the Montreal Protocol to be one of the most successful international agreements ever signed. As host of the agreement, Canada's role was prominent, and Canada continues to host the Multilateral Fund with a contribution of US$6 million annually. The Multilateral Fund is designed to minimize the costs of transitioning away from ozone-depleting chemicals in developing countries (Environment and Climate Change Canada, 2018, p. 64). Canada was among the first four countries (along with Sweden, the United States, and Norway) to institute a total ban on CFCs in the late 1970s (Makhijani & Gurney, 1995, p. 118; Williams, 2012). Actions by governments and corporations were generally swift and urgent and resulted in strong support from some countries that had the most to lose by reducing the market for CFCs. Nevertheless, the urgency of the problem, and the fact that it was limited to one economic sector, did create more favourable conditions for successful cooperation than had been the case for other global issues, such as climate change. As well, the availability of chemical alternatives made it easier for companies to switch, even though there was considerable disruption to the chemical industry in particular.

The problem of stratospheric ozone depletion was also a uniquely global problem, having many of the features of a commons issue. While the ozone hole was first documented over the Antarctic region, it was clear that ozone depletion was happening in both the northern and southern hemispheres, if to a smaller degree in the former (Rees, 2002, p. 255). As well, the discovery of the ozone hole pushed scientists and diplomats alike to accept the idea that "humanity can overwhelm important chemical, physical, and biological processes that modulate the functioning of the Earth System" (Steffen et al., 2011, p. 740). As such, the need for global cooperation and collective action was easily perceived and applied. These features made the problem of ozone depletion ripe for cooperative action. The success of the Montreal Protocol has led experts to use it as a model for solving other global problems, including space junk, marine plastics, and climate change, which display similar properties of global issues.

BIODIVERSITY

Approximately 9 million types of plants, animals, protists, and fungi inhabit the earth, along with some 8 billion humans (Cardinale et al., 2012, p. 1). Biodiversity loss is another important global issue that spans not only countries and regions but the planet as a whole (see Case Study 3.1).

CASE STUDY 3.1. The Sixth Great Extinction

Of all the signposts of the Anthropocene, few evoke a stronger sense of tragedy than the mass extinction of species, a key aspect of the global biodiversity crisis. Globally, it is estimated that species are lost at a rate of 20,000 per year, or over 50 species every day. This is believed to be between 100 and 1,000 times the natural background rate, though enumerating the tragedy – as well as determining the "normal" rate of extinction – is a wildly uncertain task (Pearce, 2015).[1]

In many industries, production has shifted overseas to areas in which the regulations are less strict, meaning the global impact continues to grow. The International Union for Conservation of Nature's annual Red List of Threatened Species evaluates the conservation status of over 142,000 species and indicates that in 2022 over 40,000 of them – about 28 per cent of all assessed species – were threatened with extinction (IUCN, 2022).

By extrapolation, the Intergovernmental Science-Policy Platform on Biodiversity and Ecosystem Services has settled on the figure of a million species that are at risk of extinction (IPBES, 2019). Some extinctions are well known, such as the passenger pigeon, Tasmanian tiger, great auk, and golden toad; others are known only to specialists; and many occur before we are even aware of the species' existence. Many more are extirpated from particular areas with an associated loss of genetic diversity and local lineages and cultures.

The causes of species loss are effectively the same as those that threaten biodiversity as a whole. A distinction can be made between direct and indirect drivers of biodiversity loss. IPBES identifies the direct drivers as changes in land and sea use, direct exploitation, climate change, pollution, and invasive alien species. Indirect drivers include an array of social phenomena that lead to or increase the direct drivers, including values, demographics, technologies, institutional forms, and inequality (IPBES, 2019).

These factors often impact species in combination, and the relationships are not simple or fully worked out (Cahill et al., 2013). Wagner and colleagues (2021) refer to the decline of insect species, for instance, as a "death by a thousand cuts." Most of these "cuts" have to do with habitat loss or degradation – especially deforestation, agriculture, and urbanization – but also occur through impacts like oil spills and air pollution. Moreover, extinction is not a linear function of habitat area: Small islands of biodiversity can help ensure that species survive. El Salvador, for example, has lost 90 per cent of its forests, yet only 3 of its 508 forest bird species have disappeared. Puerto Rico has lost a full 99 per cent of its forests yet only 7 (12 per cent) of its native bird species (Pearce, 2015). On the other hand studies show that rare species are, not surprisingly, often the first to go extinct in disturbed areas – but despite their rarity, these species are often essential components of ecosystem functioning, and their loss tends to have an impact disproportionate to the numerical or biomass loss (Leitão et al., 2016; Dee et al., 2019).

While the irreversible loss of a species is profound, we should remember that this has been the fate of the vast majority of species that have ever existed on the planet. Scientists recognize five "great extinctions" that each knocked out 70 per cent or more of all species then existing on the planet. The last, marking the end of the Cretaceous period, was driven by volcanic activity and the impact of a massive asteroid in the Yucatan Peninsula, which famously wiped out the dinosaurs about 65 million years ago. The Permian extinction, sometimes called the Great Dying, is believed to have wiped out around 95 per cent of all species as a result of warming and chemical changes, including ocean acidification, around 250 million years ago. Many scientists see the current decline of species, driven by human activity and exacerbated by a rapidly warming climate, as the first stages of a sixth great extinction (Leakey & Lewin, 1996; Kolbert, 2014).

Yet halting the loss of those species we are familiar with is certainly not enough to halt species loss, since there are so many species we don't even know about. New research suggests that there may be over 9,000 species of trees on earth that we have not yet identified – a full 14 per cent more than we now know of. The implications for biodiversity are humbling: "If we don't know, in 2022, 9,000 tree species, imagine how many other species we don't know" (Ferreira, 2022). As deforestation, land conversion, and climate change continue, many of these species will be lost before we even have a chance to learn what is disappearing.

It is difficult to consider what kind of thinking can encompass this level of destruction. Even if industrial humanity can make a last-ditch effort in "preventive archaeology … to collect and document as many species as possible before they disappear" (Cowie et al., 2022), what kind of a legacy is this, and what kind of human community is it that can bear responsibility for the sixth extinction? The reality of the sixth extinction shatters the claims of sustainable development discourse and begs for an ethic that recognizes the interrelationships among the species of the earth.

Critical Thinking Questions

1. What responsibilities do Canadians and the Canadian government have to the non-human world?
2. What do you think accounts for the failure of governments to prevent the sixth great extinction?

The implications for human societies of losses in genetic, species, and ecosystem diversity are potentially grave (see Chapter Ten). Biodiversity is an overarching concept that, as described in the 1992 Convention on Biological Diversity, comprises the diversity of species, diversity within species, and diversity among ecosystems. The recognition of species loss as a global issue emerged in conjunction with the growing knowledge among scientists that deforestation, increases in agricultural land, increases in ocean pollution, and the spread of invasive species were undermining the ability of nature to provide what are called **ecosystem services**. Ecosystem services are those functions of nature that benefit people (Pörtner et al., 2021, p. 6). These services are unrecognized and undervalued and may include purification of air and water, mitigation of drought and floods, waste recycling, regeneration of soils, pollination, and many others (Meadows et al., 2005, pp. 83–84). Loss of biodiversity has been identified by the Planetary Boundaries Project (see Chapters One and Two) as one of the gravest problems facing the world.

In 1992, as part of the plans for the Earth Summit, a regime to reduce biodiversity loss was proposed and touted in Rio de Janeiro, Brazil. Plans to implement a Convention on Biological Diversity (CBD) had to overcome a series of challenges characteristic of global issues. The system for measuring and reporting on progress was ill defined, concerns about respect for national sovereignty were strong, and the logic of collective action meant that countries were reluctant to cooperate if their own costly actions were not reciprocated (McKenzie, 2002, p. 246). As well, there were many questions about the efficacy of international agreements for advancing domestic policy changes, rather than just being "good public relations."

Negotiations over the CBD ran into many hurdles before it was finally adopted. Arguments over forests, funding, and pressure from industry hampered agreement. Ultimately, the CBD has three objectives: the conservation of biological diversity, the sustainable use of its components, and the fair and equitable sharing of benefits arising from the use of genetic resources. Global governance over biodiversity was formalized in the CBD, which Canada signed to great acclaim at Rio de Janeiro in 1992, as well as the 1973 Convention on International Trade in Endangered Species of Wild Fauna and Flora (CITES). CITES represents agreed-upon principles and rules to govern the international trade and movement of animal and plant species and parts that are or may be at risk.

In May 2023, following the Kunming-Montreal Global Biodiversity Framework adopted in December 2022, the Government of Canada began a process of new policy development on biodiversity protection to be implemented by 2024 (Canada Energy Regulator, 2023). In 2024, Canada introduced the Nature Accountability Bill in Parliament. It includes "requirements to develop national biodiversity strategies and action plans – like the 2030 Nature Strategy – and to report on their implementation" (Environment and Climate Change Canada, 2024). While promising, the Nature Strategy at time of writing remains largely a roadmap for policy to come rather than a substantive piece of legislation. Canada has an obligation to develop a National Biodiversity Strategy and

Action Plan (known as an NBSAP) under the Kunming-Montreal Agreement (CCME, 2024). To date, the plan has undergone a series of iterations and evolutions but remains incomplete. Together with many other countries, Canada has ratified the CBD and CITES, along with the many other international regimes aimed at protecting flora and fauna as well as habitats like wetlands and the oceans. A wide array of national and subnational laws aimed at protecting wildlife support these regimes, but despite the widely adopted treaties, the recent decades through which they have been in place have been marked by a continued acceleration of habitat and species loss.

The CBD has influenced policies around biosafety, invasive species, genetic research, and international trade in genetically modified organisms (GMOs). Among its most controversial aspects are interactions with global intellectual property rules, ensconced in a large number of international trade agreements, which secure monopoly rights to a given party to benefit from commercial use of the genetic information of living organisms. In effect, intellectual property rights apply Lockean notions to nature's creations, with ownership rights conferred through claims to use and even to "improve" on these creations. The 2014 Nagoya Protocol mentioned earlier and the Convention's Access and Benefit-Sharing (ABS) Clearing-House seek to enhance legal certainty and transparency in procedures for access and benefit sharing, and in monitoring the use of genetic resources along the value chain, including through the use of internationally recognized certificates of compliance.

We often hear reference to the global biodiversity crisis, and in some senses biodiversity must be seen as a global commons: It is often described as the common heritage of humanity (or indeed, of life on Earth). Decades of research, including experimental studies, have concluded that biodiversity loss is sufficiently large to rival many other global drivers of environmental change (like climate change) and that biodiversity losses may have been underestimated because of wider scales on ecosystem services (Cardinale et al., 2012, p. 5). In 2015, the Planetary Boundaries Project identified loss of biodiversity as one of the core planetary boundaries whose transgression on its own could result in such widespread changes as to move the planet into a new, less stable, and less sustainable state (Steffen et al., 2015). The effects of biodiversity loss on ecosystem services are particularly worrying since the overall degree of humans' vulnerability and dependence on those services remains mysterious. As well, as with other global and commons issues, much of this diversity is contained within the borders of nation-states; historically, the self-reproducing resources have been jealously guarded, and their capture and exploitation read something like a spy novel (Crosby, 1986). Where populations are overexploited, the national or global heritage may be undermined and in some cases wiped out entirely.

In Canada, managing compliance with these international conventions is a task coordinated among several government departments, including Natural Resources Canada, Environment and Climate Change Canada, the Canadian Wildlife Service, and the Department of Fisheries and Oceans. It also requires coordination with provincial authorities. A key piece of legislation to recognize and respond to threats to species at the domestic level is Canada's *Species at Risk Act* (SARA). In 1978, Canada established COSEWIC (Committee on the Status of Endangered Wildlife in Canada) to monitor and report on species loss annually (McKenzie, 2002, p. 121). However, it would only be several years afterward that the first species at risk legislation would be established to prevent species loss.

SARA's Schedule 1 lists species most at risk, classifying them as being extirpated (extinct in the wild), endangered, threatened, or of special concern. Schedule 1 is informed by the work of COSEWIC, an independent advisory panel to the minister of Environment and Climate Change Canada. COSEWIC meets twice a year to assess the status of wildlife species at risk of extinction and is made up of wildlife biology experts from academia, government, non-governmental organizations, and the private sector. While COSEWIC informs the ministry about wildlife species in danger of disappearing from Canada, listing these species on Schedule 1 of SARA is a legislative process. At present, COSEWIC indicates that of mammals alone, 32 species are "endangered" (with 16 threatened and 30 of special concern), while only 45 mammals are considered "not at risk."

SARA is also informed and implemented through cooperation with provincial and territorial authorities, notably under the guidance of a National Accord for the Protection of Species at Risk, which aims "to prevent species in Canada from becoming extinct as a consequence of human activities." All the provinces and territories are represented on the Canadian Endangered Species Conservation Council, which publishes a "Wild Species" report every five years (Canadian Endangered Species Conservation Council, 2022). The last report indicated that 80 per cent of species in Canada could be considered "secure," though this left over 1,600 species recognized as "potentially at risk" (Environment and Climate Change Canada, 2019, p. 13).

Most of Canada's provinces also have their own endangered species legislation, and some have committees that perform analogous functions to

COSEWIC. Most of the direct drivers of biodiversity loss fall within the jurisdiction of provincial and territorial governments, which may be less attuned to Canada's international commitments but also tend to be more familiar with local biodiversity and the drivers themselves. Yet even where provincial laws align with SARA, implementation is not always sufficient to protect species and habitats, and tensions between wildlife and development imperatives are ever present. Protests in British Columbia, for example, have sought to draw upon both SARA and the NDP government's abandoned promise to develop legislation to protect some 1,800 species in danger, including mountain caribou and orcas, but the federal government has not sought to enforce SARA over the province's hesitations.

SARA notably has limited reach regarding private land, which limits its ability to protect, ironically, the most vulnerable habitats, such as lands in the southern Great Lakes region. Most of the land in the region is privately owned, and more than 90 per cent of wetlands and 97 per cent of prairie and savannah habitat have already been destroyed (Bocking, 2009, p. 17). While SARA restrictions do apply on private land for aquatic species, as well as a range of birds regulated under the *Migratory Birds Convention Act*, development interests continue to threaten forests, waters, and wetlands, and the federal government continues to be wary of intervening (McDiarmid, 2022).

CONCLUSION: FROM A COMMONS TO A COMMUNITY

Despite its substantial role as a middle power in multilateral agreements and its considerable natural resources and biodiversity, Canada faces challenges in aligning its domestic policies with its international environmental commitments around the commons and global issues. Partly these problems arise from the constitutional makeup of the country (federal relations between levels of government), but inconsistencies also arise from Canada's historical context as a white settler society and its embrace of extractivist approaches to resource management. The complexity of ethical and legal challenges in managing global commons such as the atmosphere, oceans, and polar regions is considerable, since these are beyond the jurisdiction of any single nation. Whether optimism or pessimism will prevail in the global management of the commons remains an open question. The success of the Montreal Protocol on the control of substances that deplete the ozone layer has proven difficult to repeat, as demonstrated by the ongoing efforts to establish a national biodiversity act that might represent a more substantive and effective replacement for SARA.

The increasing importance of non-state actors, including for-profit businesses and multilateral organizations, as well as the need for a whole-of-society approach to global issues is crucial. To that end, a new ecological awareness and global citizenship will prove invaluable to improving effective stewardship of the planet, including the singular diversity and range of life to be found here. These insights underscore the complexity of global environmental governance and the critical role that countries like Canada play in fostering international cooperation to address pressing ecological challenges.

Solving the problems of the global commons requires a corresponding integration among global institutions and legal frameworks. Coordinating policies across diverse geographies, polities, and complex themes is the primary challenge of global issues (Sterner et al., 2019, p. 17). Articulating a new planetary ecological imaginary that will enable societies to overcome the pull of free riding, exploitation, individual self-interest, and rampant growth is challenging but not impossible. A new awareness of the need for human stewardship and global citizenship is needed in the era of the Anthropocene. In 2000, the adoption of the Earth Charter by non-state actors, championed for many years by Canadians such as Maurice Strong, under the heading of "Respect and Care for the Community of Life" enunciated some of the ways in which progress can be made toward a planetary community:

1. *Respect earth and life in all its diversity* – Recognize that all beings are interdependent, and every form of life has value regardless of its worth to human beings. Affirm faith in the inherent dignity of all human beings and in the intellectual, artistic, ethical, and spiritual potential of humanity.
2. *Care for the community of life with understanding, compassion, and love* – Accept that with the right to own, manage, and use natural resources comes the duty to prevent environmental harm and to protect the rights of people. Affirm that with increased freedom, knowledge, and power comes increased responsibility to promote the common good.
3. *Build democratic societies that are just, participatory, sustainable, and peaceful* – Ensure that communities at all levels guarantee human rights and fundamental freedoms and provide everyone an opportunity to realize their full potential. Promote social and economic justice, enabling

all to achieve a secure and meaningful livelihood that is ecologically responsible.

4. *Secure earth's bounty and beauty for present and future generations –* Recognize that the freedom of action of each generation is qualified by the needs of future generations. Transmit to future generations values, traditions, and institutions that support the long-term flourishing of earth's human and ecological communities (Rees, 2002, pp. 265–66).

These steps can be taken as a call for future Canadian action and contribute to the construction of a worldview (see Chapter Two) that demands we see beyond extractivism as the only way forward.

NOTE

1 A notable exception is freshwater river habitats in G7 nations; pollution regulations have helped in recovering habitats, and many species have returned.

CHAPTER FOUR

Canadian Ecopolitical History

LEARNING OBJECTIVES

1. Analyze the impact of staples theory on Canadian economic development and its implications for environmental management and resource extraction.
2. Examine the evolution of Canada's national parks system and protected areas, including the tensions between preservation, conservation, and economic development.
3. Assess the role of Indigenous ecological knowledge and governance systems in shaping Canada's early environmental history and their ongoing influence on contemporary ecopolitics.
4. Examine Canadian ecopolitical history from pre-Confederation times to the current era, including key institutions of Canadian governance.

INTRODUCTION: THE STORY OF ECOPOLITICAL HISTORY

The area today known as Canada would not have been recognizable some 245–65 million years ago, when dinosaurs roamed what we now call the North American continent. This environment was shaped by climate changes, geological shifts, mass extinction events, and even changes in earth's orbit.

Humans have only occupied the area for a fraction of geological history (MacDowell, 2012, p. 14).

In this chapter, we introduce readers to the **ecopolitical history** of what is now known as the Canadian state. The purpose of this chapter is not to simply recount the factual events and stories that happened in the past, but rather to improve our understanding of the origins of the Canadian ecopolitics of today. Continuing the book's focus on political issues and conflicts among the variety of groups that share the ecology of the country, the idea here is to assess the origins of current struggles to develop, protect, manage, and distribute the land, waters, oceans, and mountains of a vast territory in North America. In this, the aim is to provide a comprehensive overview of the evolution of ecopolitical issues in Canada from prehistoric times to the present. The chapter includes six key themes that we have identified as "touchpoints" for Canadian ecopolitical history:

1. Indigenous influence and early ecopolitical structures
2. The establishment and impact of Canadian constitutional agreements and treaties
3. The effect of changing Canadian worldviews on ecopolitical history, particularly the establishment of parks and protected areas
4. The history of resource development, particularly staples like agriculture and forestry
5. The role of environmental movements in fostering policy changes
6. The contemporary ecopolitical challenges of the Indigenous rights movement and the impact of globalization

As will be seen, history shapes the way environmental problems become identified, which worldviews are acknowledged and integrated into decision making, and which material industries and projects are approved or sanctioned. These issues are intertwined with broader ecopolitical challenges, including climate change and environmental justice. It is difficult, for example, to appreciate the full scope of the decline in biodiversity without also understanding how the drive for prosperity, security, and state consolidation have impacted the land and waters. Similarly, for example, a full understanding of the debates around the constitutional division of powers is needed to appreciate the current battles over federal carbon pricing legislation.

PRE-CONFEDERATION HISTORY: EARLY ECOPOLITICAL STRUCTURES

By the time Europeans first arrived in Newfoundland around 1,000 years ago, the land supported a population of roughly 500,000 (although estimates vary widely). Indigenous Peoples had developed sophisticated systems of governance, including legal systems, agreements on elaborate trade routes, treaty relations, rules for warfare and peace, patterns of conflict and cooperation among settlements, and forms of communication and economic development across vast territories. For example, the Hopewell Interaction Sphere encompassed a vast region from as far north as Hudson Bay to the Gulf of Mexico. Although some Indigenous societies in the western hemisphere developed systems of written records centuries before Europeans arrived, others created complex systems of oral history. These histories established attachment to the land and animals and legitimated the society's claim to "be where it is"; the veracity of these claims has been upheld by major court decisions, such as the 1997 case of *Delgamuukw v. British Columbia* (Belshaw et al., 2020, pp. 4, 13, 33).

Indigenous Peoples also substantially altered the environment, shaping it for their economic, social, cultural, and even military needs (Cook, 2006, p. 92). Survival was generally a harsh and unforgiving challenge, especially in the northern reaches of the continent. Oral histories created a bedrock of traditional ecological knowledge based on observation, conclusions of cause and effect, empirical checks for accuracy, and a continuance of intergenerational skills necessary for thriving, creative, and unique cultural governance systems. For example, a Huu-ay-aht story of a major flood on the west coast of Vancouver Island around 1700 was treated by settler scholars as a kind of allegory until it was correlated to a significant seismic event and consequent tsunami that occurred on January 26, 1700 (Belshaw et al., 2020, p. 9).

The variety and distinctiveness of Indigenous Peoples across the continent became extensive, with numerous languages, political systems, and beliefs shaped by a wide-ranging set of bioregions, from the ocean coasts to the plains to the polar north and the mountains. Adaptation to these bioregions accelerated after the end of the last glacial period, approximately 13,000 years BCE. As the continent deglaciated and warming encouraged new plant growth, lichens, mosses, and small shrubs began to sprout on moraines (masses of rocks and sediment carried down by glaciers), followed eventually by the boreal forest. As people migrated north and west into the polar and coastal regions, three distinct groupings emerged: Amerinds, the Na-Dené, and the Aleut-Inuit peoples (Mann, 2009). Settlements were established based on fishing; the hunting of large mammals such as whales, bison, and bear; and agriculture, specifically beans, squash, and corn. Over time, whether through hunting of the large mammals such as mammoth and mastodon that had first migrated to the centre of the continent around 14 million years after the end of the dinosaurs, or through fishing on the Pacific west coast, all of these groups modified the environment in some measure to improve the availability of game, increase agricultural yields, and create sustainable food stores (Belshaw et al., 2020, p. 32; MacDowell, 2012, p. 14).

The arrival of early European settlers would have been first noted by Indigenous Peoples with anomalous environmental changes brought about by the settlers. As honeybees brought by settlers spread westward, it is said that they were seen as unwelcome harbingers of the white man's approach (Cook, 2006, p. 147). Close to follow were domesticated animals, pests, weeds, and pathogens in what Alfred Crosby (1986) has termed a "demographic take-over" of North America (p. 263). The lack of large, domesticated animals in the Americas proved to be disastrous for Indigenous Peoples who, as a result, did not acquire immunity from animal-borne diseases brought by Europeans (Belshaw et al., 2020, pp. 17–18). Indeed, in some parts of the Americas pathogens arrived even before large-scale military engagements and therefore weakened the ability of even large city complexes to fight against the conquerors (Mann, 2009, p. 72). **Bioimperialism** generally refers to the purposeful or incidental spread of biota from core to peripheral states or regions (Crosby, 1994). The impacts of the spread of disease during colonialism should not be underestimated; not only did it result in waves of disease-related deaths, but it limited the ability of communities to carry out daily survival tasks (Hill, 2017, pp. 86–88). This was particularly the case for northern communities. As Liza Piper writes, epidemics made it

> much more difficult for people to harvest food in Subarctic and Arctic environments. The illness itself, whether it was influenza, typhoid, or another disease, weakened those who were afflicted, and healing demanded considerable energy resources that otherwise would be put to hunting, fishing, trapping, or harvesting activities … By the late nineteenth century, hunting and trapping relied upon dog teams that also

needed to be fed (typically with fish) during an outbreak. By the turn of the century, quarantines were an increasingly commonplace response to northern epidemics.

… Yet, quarantines also acted to prevent healthy persons from harvesting as effectively as they might otherwise, because they restricted the travel necessary for extensive harvesting practises across the North. (Piper, 2011, p. 69)

We return to the links between biosecurity and health in Chapter Ten, but it is particularly important to stress the massive change that resulted from European colonization. This is the case across every biome in North America, including the Arctic: "In the last 200 years, the process of survival has been complicated by the clash of cultural traditions, the introduction of asymmetrical power relations, and the impact of Western technologies in the Arctic … The problems are complex, and their resolution will depend on whether other cultures can respect the need of arctic peoples to have the power to manage the environment and ecosystems in which they operate" (Dick, 2001, p. 488). Box 4.1 addresses the impact of a concept that impacted the events described here: the Doctrine of Discovery.

BOX 4.1. The Doctrine of "Discovery"

The Doctrine of Discovery was codified by the US Supreme Court in three cases known as the "Marshall trilogy." In decisions that are now widely contested, the courts found that "American Indians were not the full sovereigns of the lands that they possessed but were rather the users of the lands that they roamed and wandered over for purposes of shelter and sustenance" (Barker, 2005, pp. 6–8). While there is some debate over the degree to which the Marshall decision was integrated into British (and later Canadian) law, Miller (2019, p. 38) has noted that the doctrine was cited numerous times by the Privy Council and applied in cases in Canada. Despite the conflicts with the Royal Proclamation (which is discussed in Case Study 4.1) and with the series of political treaties that had been signed with Indigenous Peoples over the previous centuries, the finding of the US court in the Marshall rulings gave legal cover to the project to subjugate Indigenous Peoples to the rule of the European powers. In the Canadian context, the doctrine was taken as an extension of the principles set forth in the Royal Proclamation, especially regarding the notion that the Crown alone enjoyed the right to treat with and purchase lands from Indigenous Peoples. As in US case history, this logic provided an "efficient justification for Canadian nullification of 'Aboriginal title' by treaty, by purchase, or by the default of colonization" (Barker, 2005, p. 16).

The Doctrine of Discovery came under scrutiny in much later court decisions that tended to validate Indigenous customary title to land, such as 1997's *Delgamuukw v. British Columbia* and 2014's *Tsilhqot'in Nation v. British Columbia* (Beaulieu, 2021, pp. 4–5). Even earlier, the Supreme Court of Canada's decision in the 1973 case *Calder v. British Columbia* found that the Crown's underlying title was subject to Nisga'a title to occupy and manage their lands. In *Calder*, the court found that Aboriginal title is a legal right derived from Indigenous Peoples' historic possession of their lands. However, the court was split on whether that title still existed or whether it had been extinguished by colonial legislation prior to Confederation.

Through the establishment of legal obligations such as the duty to consult and recognition of self-determination, Indigenous Peoples continue, right up to today, to work through the courts to establish legal recognition of their rights to land upon which they have existed for millennia. Through land claims and constitutional negotiations, royal commissions and civil proceedings, Indigenous Peoples have seen only limited progress toward recovering what the Doctrine of Discovery took away from them. In its effect, the Doctrine of Discovery made the inhabited and settled lands of Turtle Island available for European settlement and enclosure into swaths of private and publicly managed property ruled by the British Crown. It was not until 2021, with the incorporation of the United Nations Declaration of the Rights of Indigenous Peoples into Canadian law, that the Doctrine of Discovery was officially and finally rejected, with the legislation calling it "racist, scientifically false, legally invalid, morally condemnable and socially unjust." Activists were disappointed when Pope Francis did not formally reject the doctrine on his trip to Canada in the summer of 2022, but the doctrine was officially denounced by the Catholic Church in 2023.

Figure 4.1. Canada and Newfoundland: Natural and Industrial Resources

Source: Wikimedia Commons/David Rumsey Map Collection.

While colonization occurred rapidly in some places, in others, like Acadia (which includes present-day Nova Scotia, New Brunswick, Prince Edward Island, part of Quebec, and Gaspesia, a portion of Maine), the process was slower. In Acadia, populations of Mi'kmaq and colonists lived side by side for a long period (Duke, 2006, p. 158), at least partly due to the separate agricultural practices and territories of each community (MacDowell, 2012, p. 41). Nevertheless, relations between the two communities were one-sided, as colonists adopted an explicit plan for domination of both the people and the territory even from an early era. As settlers moved westward along the St. Lawrence into Ontario, especially following the US War of Independence and the influx of Loyalists, the country began to feel the effects of industrialization in Europe (Cook, 2006, p. 263). While Indigenous Peoples retained Treaty rights to hunt and fish, the influx of settlers pushed them to the margins. Settlement in the northern reaches of Ontario was hindered by the geography of poor soils and the difficult terrain of the Canadian Shield, and the establishment of permanent settlements was also hampered by the fact that "France and Britain first focused on fish and fur resources and were slow to realize the new continent's agricultural potential" (MacDowell, 2012, pp. 40–43). The transportation and communication networks of the pre-Confederation era eventually became established to move goods, specifically primary or semi-finished resources, for the European markets.

CASE STUDY 4.1. The *Royal Proclamation of 1763*

The conflict between French and British forces in expanding their control over colonies in North America and gaining power in the upper Great Lakes ignited the first global war in 1756 until France ceded Canada in 1763. The Indigenous Peoples supported the French troops in the Seven Years' War, but they did not immediately surrender their sovereignty to the English. Ojibwa Chief Minavavana from west of Manitoulin at Michilimackinac described in a speech how the king of France established a good relationship with the Indigenous Peoples.

The first agreement made by the Indigenous Peoples and the British Crown was the development of articles of capitulation, wherein the rights of the Indigenous Peoples to their lands were stated. It was followed by the issuance of the *Royal Proclamation of 1763* by King George III. The Royal Proclamation was only recognized as a legitimate treaty following a meeting between Indigenous

Peoples and the British in Niagara in 1764. The Proclamation addressed the distribution of the French and Spanish territories, incorporated Quebec as part of the four new British colonies, and empowered governors to rule the territories over which they were appointed. The Proclamation became the most significant document in the history of Canada, part of the legal foundation of the country. It is referenced in section 25 of the *Constitution Act, 1982*. It also outlines the treaty-making process between Indigenous Peoples and the Crown. The Royal Proclamation has been referenced in the 11 numbered treaties between Canada and Indigenous Peoples signed in the nineteenth and twentieth centuries, as well as in the 1973 *Calder* case, which affirmed that it was applicable even in British Columbia, where the majority of land remains unceded by treaty (Hall et al., 2019).

Despite the significance of the Royal Proclamation for Indigenous Peoples, they were not involved in its drafting, although Anishinaabe legal scholar John Borrows argues they were not passive but active participants in the process and that the Proclamation was a "positive guarantee of self-government" (Borrows, 1997, p. 169). Nevertheless, the Proclamation set down the recognition of mutual respect, including mutual obligations and duties, that affirmed the government-to-government nature of the relationship between Indigenous Peoples and the Crown. Today, despite its colonial origins, the Royal Proclamation is both lauded for its treaty-like provisions that ultimately recognized Indigenous Peoples' right to their land and condemned for the way in which it was subsequently ignored or abused by provincial, colonial, and national governments in their dealings with Indigenous Peoples.

Critical Thinking Questions

1. Why do you think the Royal Proclamation was essentially ignored after it was made?
2. Why do you think the Proclamation has had such a large impact on Canadian laws?

POST-CONFEDERATION PERIOD AND STAPLES

From 1867 to today, Canadian ecopolitical history has demonstrated a pattern of development that rested squarely on resource extraction, territorial consolidation of the state, and regional economic growth. Canada moved from being a colonial society and offshoot of the French and British Empires to a continental industrializing nation centred on metropoles along the St. Lawrence and hinterlands to the west. As agriculture became mechanized, farmland became consolidated and shifted from subsistence to commercial production and export.

Depletion of farmland was common, and as the economy shifted westward farmers pivoted to growing fodder for animals, grain for beer and whiskey, and kitchen gardens for fruit and vegetables (MacDowell, 2012, pp. 50–53). Moving on from early staples such as beaver pelts and furs, the country became an agricultural powerhouse as immigration and permanent settlement fuelled the establishment of a wheat economy. The completion of the national railway facilitated the transportation of agricultural products to international markets as well as the importation of needed production goods and tourists. Smelting and lumber milling permitted the production of semi-processed goods that were more easily transported abroad. The railway also fostered the growth of settlements as the waterways had for earlier waves of immigration. The growth of industry followed on the heels of forestry, mining, and later fossil fuel development. The shift from agriculture to industrial production had political impacts through urbanization, technological development, and the establishment of national transportation and communication corridors. Pressures to establish continental integration with the United States prompted the union of the British colonies in 1867, and the drive to complete a continent-wide system of economic production, transportation, and communication continues up to today (Stoett & Temby, 2015). The connection with Britain acted as a counterweight to the push to the United States and eventually drew Canada into World War I in 1914. Throughout this time, an evolving system of colonial relationships with First Nations, the challenge of growing US power, and the pull to greater degrees of provincial autonomy were the most important features of Canadian ecopolitical history. The push and pull of these international and domestic forces shaped the evolution of Canadian ecopolitics from the nineteenth to the twenty-first centuries.

Harold Innis, a prominent economist and historian at the University of Toronto, developed a theory to explain the pattern and pace of Canadian economic development (Innis, 1930, 1940, 1949; Innis & Innis, 1986). He argued that **staples** (in other words, specific export-based commodities) have tended to become leading sectors because of their material abundance and the relative weakness of the domestic capital and labour markets in a settler economy.

A staple refers to a raw, unfinished commodity rather than one that is manufactured, processed, or has additional "value-added" (Hessing et al., 2007, p. 28). Innis argued that staples, rather than settlement patterns or the growth of industry and urbanization, were more important to set the pace and direction of economic development. The "comparative advantage" in resource-intensive exports leads to that staple commodity affecting the degree and form of economic, political, and even social and cultural development of the country. For Innis, the *type* of staple was key, since its properties (whether inputs are domestically available, whether outputs encourage investment in other sectors, the availability of land, etc.) determined the effects on other sectors (Watkins, 1963, p. 145). Also key were the technologies of transportation and communication used to develop the staple (Buckley, 1958). For example, in the case of wheat, the development of this staple necessitated waves of immigration and the establishment of homesteading settlers from abroad on the Prairies. In turn, this spurred the construction of the railway and the extension of political control over the west. The extension of control led to a series of rebellions and protests against the central government in the east. The most prominent of these was the North-West Rebellion of Métis and Indigenous groups led by Louis Riel in 1885, but struggles over the staple of wheat continued into the 1920s with the rise of farmers' movements and protests against policies that favoured industrialization in central Canada over the development of agriculture in the west (see more below in the discussion of the expansion westward).

Ultimately, for Innis, staples development determined the form of political and cultural institutions of governance; there was a direct causal relationship between the ecological endowments of a country and its political systems of governance. The theory seemed to closely fit the Canadian experience; indeed, it might even be argued that staples theory constitutes a distinctly and specifically Canadian theory of ecopolitical development. Staples theory has been used to examine the role of the fur trade, the cod fishery, the timber industry, the production of wheat and flour, and even phosphorus mining and other industries and sectors. In sum, "around the staple trades there grew up characteristic patterns of commercial and financial organization, and these in turn did much to mould the culture of colonial society and the boundaries of political jurisdiction on the North American continent" (Aitken, 1958, p. 451; see also Drache, 1982).

From the viewpoint of ecopolitical thinking, therefore, the formation of Canada in 1867 and its historical progression as a global, continental, and regional entity was as much a function of its geography as of its social, legal, or political makeup. Confederation marked the emergence of a new country that, while not yet completely sovereign, was much more empowered to govern its affairs than it had been previously. The *British North America Act, 1867* (BNA Act) included important provisions that concerned the governance of Canadian territory, resources, and products. Drafting an agreement that was similar in principle to the laws of the United Kingdom, the new Canadian Constitution would consolidate the power of Parliament to be the supreme source of legislative authority, ensure accountability of the Crown under a system of responsible government, maintain a new federal division of powers between the provinces and the federal government, and lay the groundwork for the extension of Canadian sovereignty continent wide. The BNA Act, while bringing together the four British colonies of Upper and Lower Canada, New Brunswick, and Nova Scotia into a single dominion, also put in place the mechanisms of democratic accountability that had been developing since the mid-1800s through a system of **responsible government**. Under this system, the original colonial governors gradually gave up their monopoly on power to share it with Parliament, which would hold final say over the government of the day through elections. Elected members of Parliament would then be able to check the government through a confidence system, which required the executive branch (the prime minister and cabinet) to answer to Parliament or be removed through a majority vote of confidence.

Federalism was a unique feature of Canada, not originally included in the Westminster model, which was the basis of Confederation, but one that suited the needs of a religiously and linguistically divided territory. Federalism, or the co-equal sharing of sovereign powers between provinces and the federal government, was also well suited to a large country with a small, dispersed population and a wide variety of regional geographies and natural resources. Sections 91 and 92 of the BNA Act spelled out the respective powers of the provinces and the federal government. Notably, natural resources lay within the powers of the provinces (eventually for the western provinces as well), along with the as yet minor "civil matters" of hospitals, social welfare, and education. Canada's first prime minister, John A. Macdonald, preferred a strong federal government, which could use its powers of disallowance to set aside provincial laws and legislate on matters of national significance such as trade. In the years following Confederation, these federal powers were resisted by leaders in Ontario and the Maritimes. History since that time has seen a gradual erosion of federal powers in favour of the provinces, with the logic of growing provincial powers accompanying the rise of the welfare state following World War II. While taking a different form in different parts of the country, province building has been a theme in Canadian ecopolitical history with important implications for the management of natural resources and the patterns of development of industry and agriculture.

NEW NATIONAL PARKS AND PROTECTED AREAS

While it was not yet contemplated that the environment would become a significant area of legislative authority, there was some recognition of the need for coordination and shared jurisdiction of federal and provincial authorities over waterways, travel, agriculture, immigration, forestry, and land management. In particular, the story of the establishment of Banff National Park is indicative of the ways in which the "environment" was approached through legislative change.

Interestingly, Canadian national parks were not at first viewed as vehicles for the protection of natural wilderness so much as they were sources of government revenue from tourism. The Canadian Pacific Railway's (CPR) William Cornelius Van Horne worked closely with the government to advance the cause of national parks creation. Van Horne viewed the railway mountain section as a source of tourist revenue to recoup some of the losses incurred in constructing the railway line through the mountains. Paraphrasing Pierre Berton, Page and colleagues have said that the "CPR became the symbolic linchpin of the nation, and the mountain parks, led by Banff, became part of this national dream" (Page et al., 1996, p. 16). Canadian society began to view natural areas as inviting scenes for recreation, leisure, and health, and the Canadian parks as symbols of Canadian identity and a national imaginary.

In 1885 the Banff Hot Springs Reserve was established and then renamed as (or incorporated into) the Rocky Mountain National Park that same year, while Ontario followed suit by establishing Algonquin Provincial Park in 1893 (Conrad, 2011, p. 180). The drive for the park's establishment included an element of preservationist worldviews, drawn from the imaginary of romantic wilderness protection (see Chapter Two's discussion of ecocentrism and deep ecology worldviews). This **preservationist view** was paradoxically coupled with a contrasting parks management philosophy informed by scientific management principles of natural resource conservation. Environmental ideas informed by **conservationist thinking** (leaning toward an anthropocentric ethic) led to the formation of the Canadian Commission of

Conservation in 1909 under the leadership of Clifford Sifton, who examined "everything from fur farming and migratory birds to power development and urban planning" (Conrad, 2011, p. 180). In general, the push for parks was spurred more by commercial considerations than for ecocentric or protectionist principles, especially, but not only, in the case of Banff National Park (Mason, 2008, p. 222).

These same commercial considerations led to a system of parks and protected areas modelled on Banff, many of which displaced Indigenous Peoples from their territories (McNamee, 1909) even while inviting some bands back in to the parks to entertain visitors in festivals and to act as guides for hunters and sightseers (Mason, 2015, p. 77; Mason et al., 2022). The establishment of Banff National Park was accompanied by the exclusion of the Nakoda people from their traditional hunting grounds to allow for sport hunting by white and settler tourists. The Canadian tourism market was global, with promotion reaching across the Empire, the United States, and domestically to Canadian middle-class urbanites looking for a "natural" vacation.[1] The public's view of wilderness and nature had changed drastically as Canadians began to see the benefits of a connection with nature. If not yet a wholly ecocentric view, the idea that some parts of nature should be protected in perpetuity and for the benefit of future generations began to take root in the public imaginary. This newfound appreciation for nature should be distinguished from Indigenous Peoples' reverence and respect for the natural world, which arose from a very different and specific viewpoint of nature as co-evolving with humans in a common community of kinship. For the Nakoda people who were separated from their ancestral lands, the removal from the site that would become Banff National Park was a cultural and spiritual loss with lasting and profound generational impacts. The encounter of most white settlers with natural experiences, however, was comparatively brief and ephemeral.

It is with these early encounters that the beginnings of Canadian political environmentalism began. Early environmentalism was quite different from what we are familiar with today. Conservationists largely focused on the efficient stewardship of natural resources so as not to exceed the land's capacity to provide sustained yields. Early conservationists in Canada favoured reform and regulation to protect natural resources in the public interest but did not go so far as to argue for wilderness protection, nor did they understand the ecological importance of forests as homes to plants, insects, and wildlife in an ecological system (MacDowell, 2012, p. 100). It was during this time that fire suppression in the forests became the norm, with little understanding of the natural role of fire in the forest ecosystem as practised by First Nations for centuries. The approach was a narrow vision of "the environment," which was essentially a problem of managing and engineering projects that would effectively provide resources for human use (and perhaps avoid the worst destruction of the more attractive natural areas). The industrial revolution in Canada, the rise of a socially and economically mobile middle class, and the consolidation of European empires created a demand for leisure experiences and travel to remote locations. In competition with the United States for access to these spaces, Canada moved quickly to consolidate national control over prime areas for the use of hunters and fishers, which would create appealing travel experiences for the growing and mobile middle classes of Britain and the rest of Europe. Business interests, rather than environmental concerns, dominated the government's approach to economic development and environmental and resource management.

THE WESTWARD EXPANSION

Despite the calls for protection, deforestation ran virtually unchecked from Confederation up until the early twentieth century because of the close relationship between governments and forestry companies. Corruption allowed these companies to treat forests as unlimited stores of wealth, and the forestry industry had significant negative impacts on waterways, fishing, local recreation, and the production of waste. Pollution from sawdust and wood burning was rampant. Government policies also encouraged settlement beyond agricultural towns by requiring logs to be milled locally before export, leading to the growth of small, isolated sawmill towns in rural Ontario and British Columbia. The signing of the Reciprocity Treaty in 1854 rapidly opened up the US markets for lumber from British North America, resulting in a rapid expansion of the lumber milling industry (Gillis, 2006, p. 265). Mills began dumping larger and larger deposits of sawdust and mill waste directly into rivers and lakes, resulting in destruction of fish habitats, unsafe drinking water, and other hazards. The resulting "sawdust question" led to the first contestation of the extractive model by early conservationists, starting with sport fishers concerned about the decline of fish populations, particularly salmon, leading to the passage of *Fishing Acts* in 1857 and 1858. Concerns came from urban dwellers, public health advocates, naturalists, scientists, and water navigators who expressed the need for government regulation to protect fish and the natural beauty of waterways. Similarly, one of the earliest environmental groups of the century, Ducks Unlimited, was formed in 1938 to protect game habitat (Doern et al., 2015, p. 298). These early critics became the first harbingers of the *preservationist* wing of the environmental movement, whose full expression would not be realized until several years later with the expansion of national parks (Gillis, 2006, pp. 267, 280).

As the country grew, social, economic, and technological factors were creating a society of increased mobility and urbanization. Until 1920 Canada had been primarily a rural and agricultural country, but a turning point came with the industrial revolution. An iron and steel industry grew up around coal mines in Cape Breton Island, Nova Scotia, and Hamilton, Ontario. Mining, chemicals, and pulp and paper development was dominated by Ontario and Quebec, based on their proximity to natural resources (Conrad, 2011, p. 175). As industrial development spread from Britain around the world, it led to the need for more concentrated sources of energy to power steam engines and other machinery, and hence a transition from human labour to wood to coal and from there to oil and hydroelectric power. Eventually Canada became the largest producer of hydroelectric power in the world, with hydro dams producing some 60 per cent of Canada's electricity (see Chapter Six). At the same time, while relatively clean compared to fossil fuels, hydroelectric projects did extensive damage to landscapes and natural habitats (MacDowell, 2012, p. 163). Urbanization crowded Canadians into dirty, polluted urban environments, leading to the rise of environmentalism and an awareness of the regenerative purposes of wilderness.

As it turned out, the inclusion of natural resources in the provincial realm of jurisdiction under the BNA Act had lasting effects and shaped decades of conflicts. Battles over energy governance and revenues, trade policy, investment, and regional economic development consistently accompanied the growth and consolidation of Canada over a wider geographic area. The government's annexation of the west sparked the Red River Rebellion of 1869–70, which resulted in the creation of Manitoba and the granting of some land for the Métis community. The loss of the fur trade and incentivized buffalo hunting resulted in mass starvation and poverty for Indigenous and Métis communities (MacDowell, 2012, p. 56), whose population had already been decimated by diseases for which they lacked immunity. The Red River Métis Rebellions accompanied the incorporation of the Prairie provinces of Manitoba and Saskatchewan into Confederation. Although the terms of the BNA Act indicated that provinces should control natural resources, these powers were denied to the western provinces until years after they joined the country, with the western provinces essentially occupying a subordinate position relative to other regions. This different treatment was a result of the dominance of an extractivist worldview, which demanded centralized control of the terms by which new provinces entered Confederation to ensure access to the resources of the west to fuel the growth of central Canada.

Immigration and settlement of the west was accompanied by violent displacement and deliberate policies designed to undermine the control of territories by Indigenous Peoples. The *Dominion Lands Act* (1872) offered free land to new settlers to establish farming in the west, and vast tracts were granted to the Canadian Pacific Railway and the Hudson's Bay Company (Conrad, 2011, p. 160; MacDowell, 2012, p. 56; see Case Study 4.2), and 3 million immigrants arrived in the space of one generation. Sport hunting of buffalo, the primary source of food and supplies for Prairie Indigenous Peoples, was unregulated and even encouraged by a national government whose goal was ultimately to eliminate the ability of Indigenous Peoples to be self-supporting. The population of bison went from roughly 60 million to as few as 1,000 individuals by mid-century. Along with the enabling legislation of the *Indian Act*, which allowed for the extensive exercise of governmental authority over Indigenous Peoples, the program of forcible removal of children into residential schools, and the abrogation in some provinces of Treaty rights, successive Canadian governments made maximal use of legal and constitutional authority to suppress and control dissent and resistance among Indigenous Peoples to colonial rule. For example, section 91(24) of the BNA Act granted the federal government jurisdiction over Indigenous Peoples and Crown lands reserved for them and included the requirement that bands elect band councils in keeping with Canadian models of governance rather than traditional models. Furthermore, the *Indian Act* subjected Indigenous Peoples to differential treatment under Canadian law, as they were considered "wards" of the state living on government reserves rather than automatically enjoying full citizenship.

CASE STUDY 4.2. The Hudson's Bay Company

On May 2, 2020, The Hudson's Bay Company (HBC) marked 350 years since its founding. It is the oldest North American corporation still in operation, having been incorporated in 1670 by virtue of a Royal Charter granted to Prince Rupert by King Charles II. Uniquely, as historian Stephen Bown (2020) writes, the "Company always had a legal responsibility to the Crown that was not imposed on any other purely commercial entity operating out of London" (p. 43). The company started its beaver pelt operations in the Hudson Bay region and soon boomed as Europeans began to demand luxurious furs. The company built hundreds of trading posts across James Bay and northern Manitoba. Over time, Hudson's Bay Company expanded its business into oil and gas, real estate, and retail goods under the brand HBC, with 89 department stores across Canada. Having once claimed, traded on, and governed some 8 million square kilometres of the earth's surface, including large parts of Canada and the northwestern United States, today it is a global company (Gismondi, 2020).

The Royal Charter issued to Prince Rupert granted him and a group of English businessmen sole control of the fur market in the huge Hudson Bay area as well as exclusive land rights to the Hudson Bay watershed. King Charles II renamed Hudson Bay to Rupert's Land and named the English merchants as the "true and absolute Lords and Proprietors of the land which encompassed 3,861,400 square kilometers" (Centre for Rupert's Land Studies, 2022). The Royal Charter gave the company full authority in the territory, disregarding the existing sovereignty of the First Nations who lived there. The company also performed much of the early prospecting of lands and wildlife for their commercial applications, sometimes even before species could be scientifically categorized and analyzed (Hammond, 2006).

In the early 1780s, HBC established itself as a large operation covering areas of what is now Alberta, Saskatchewan, Manitoba, Nunavut, Ontario, and Quebec. Behind the company's success was the knowledge and labour of Indigenous People, especially women, who as wives of the traders advised their husbands in the ways of fur trapping and trading (Gismondi, 2020). Forts along Hudson and James Bays were provisioned by the Cree even as they were decimated by smallpox in 1779–83 (Duke, 2006, p. 174; Bown, 2020, p. 150). After the fall and winter trapping seasons, Indigenous People would travel to trading posts during spring to barter their furs for the HBC's stock of manufactured goods. This business operation created considerable wealth for the company: Its capital stock averaged a 10 per cent increase per year during its first half century of trading (Saldanha et al., 2020, p. 3). After 1870, the remaining territory of the HBC became part of the new nation of the Dominion of Canada, and the company "would now have to float or sink as a regular business, albeit one powerfully entrenched, with sprawling landholdings in western Canada, a web of efficient supply lines and depts and forts spanning half a continent" (Bown, 2020, p. 427).

The Hudson Bay Company exploited Indigenous hunters, whose use of age-old trapping methods and knowledge of nature were invaluable to the business. However, the company's activities also cleared the way for the industrial transformation of the Canadian economy from a relatively sustainable system based on hunting and trapping to a more intensive political economy of settlement, railway development, mining, and banking. In 1870, Indigenous territory was sold to the Canadian Crown through a Deed of Surrender that excluded them.

Eventually, the company would earn much of its profit through land sales. According to Frank Tough (1992), "although Native peoples [*sic*] were kept at a subsistence level … between 1905 and 1922, the company's dividend rate ranged from 20 to 50 percent and between 1891 and 1930, HBC's land earnings netted profits of $96,366,021" (p. 233).

The Hudson's Bay Company was established to assure English colonial control over the lands, resources, and people of the vast uncharted North American interior. The establishment of both formal and informal networks of trade created opportunities for settlers to establish new businesses and commerce reliant on natural resources and the knowledge, skills, and goods of Indigenous People. Hudson's Bay trading posts, as in the case of Victoria, British Columbia, became capital cities, centres of commerce, and sites of public administration for the new colonies.

Arguably, the HBC did more to spread the worldview of extractivism discussed in Chapter Two than any other commercial enterprise.

Critical Thinking Questions

1. What was the nature of the relationship between the Hudson's Bay Company and the state in the past, and what is that relationship like today?
2. Identify and explain three positive and negative implications of the fur trade for Indigenous communities and their wellbeing.

The gaps in provincial powers eventually became even more acute as the country industrialized, more people moved away from rural to urban areas, and service industries grew. John A. Macdonald's National Policy, which sought to encourage market investment in industrial manufacturing in the St. Lawrence corridor, imposed high tariffs on machinery imports to encourage industrialization in eastern Canada. These tariffs, however, had to be paid by western farmers, which disadvantaged them by raising the price of needed equipment like tractors and machinery. Coupled with the high rates charged to wheat farmers to ship their grain to major ports for export (the Crow rate), discontent among western farmers reached a high point in the 1930s and 1940s, when the Prairies gave rise to farmers' and workers' protest movements and the formation of new parties to challenge the domination of the industrial east. In 1914, Canada was the world's second-largest wheat producer by volume, and by 1969 western wheat was Canada's second-largest export and provided 6 per cent of the world's supply (Conrad, 2011, p. 175; MacDowell, 2012, p. 224). The importance of wheat in the larger economy buttressed farmers' movements in the 1930s, which articulated alternative economic and political models based on cooperative agriculture and populist critiques of big banks and industrialism. Concerned by the depopulation of the countryside through urbanization and the growing power of the financial system centred in urban areas, the United Farmers of Ontario political party was established in 1914 with direct political action as its goal (Conrad, 2011, p. 182). However, despite these movements and protests, the relative subordination of Canadian hinterlands continued to deepen, fuelling discontent over everything from agriculture to natural resources like oil.

To the east, **province building** in Quebec began in earnest in the 1970s, as the rise of the Parti Québécois brought more attention to the possibility of Quebec sovereignty into the national discussion. As the Quiet Revolution gained steam through the 1960s, the Quebec Liberals under Jean Lesage began to take control over key economic engines such as hydroelectric power development, which offered a means for the province to increase its independence and autonomy from the federal government. In 1971 Quebec Premier Robert Bourassa announced a major new hydroelectric project in northern Quebec, to which the 5,000 Cree and 3,500 Inuit of James Bay objected. The resulting negotiations led to Canada's first major land claim agreement in 1975 (see Case Study 6.1). A 1969 Canadian government discussion paper, the White Paper, proposed an end to the different legal status of Indians under the *Indian Act*, as well as an end to any further land claims and the removal of reserves. The White Paper proposed nothing less than the complete assimilation of Indigenous Peoples into wider Canadian society, along with the loss of what little land was made available under the reserve system. While some bands supported the idea of removing the *Indian Act*, most recognized that the provisions would leave First Nations much more vulnerable and were resistant to the proposal. Most favoured a movement toward recognition of the autonomy and self-governance of Indigenous Peoples within the Canadian Constitution, one that treated First Nations on an equal footing with other levels of government (more on this later in the chapter).

THE EFFECTS OF GLOBALIZATION IN CANADA

Along with the extraction of natural resources and the manufacturing industries, a service-based economy had grown in Canada in the 1960s and beyond, including the banking, clerical, retail, and legal sectors. Government programs for pension, health care, welfare, and education expanded, along with bureaucracies at the federal and provincial levels of government. The contemporary narrative of the evolution of the Canadian polity suggests that, increasingly, Canadian public opinion moved from a "material" to a "post-material" cultural attitude. Priorities shifted away from material needs like jobs, public order, and defence and moved toward equity, freedom, health, and identity needs. Growing environmentalist social movements would emerge as well, as national and provincial governments began to introduce anti-pollution policies and legislation. International conferences such as the UN Conference on the Human Environment (held in Stockholm in 1972) brought concerns about industrial and chemical pollution, acid rain, and whaling to the forefront of political agendas. Chaired by Canadian business leader Maurice Strong, the Stockholm Conference marked the emergence of the environment as an issue of global concern. The prospect of sparking new environmental protection legislation led to the formation of groups bringing legal arguments to the fore, including the Canadian Environmental Law Association, the Canadian Institute for Environmental Law and Policy, and West Coast Environmental Law (Doern et al., 2015, p. 302). In 1970, over 20 million people in the United States and Canada gathered to celebrate the first Earth Day.

Greenpeace, formed in 1971, began as a group conducting direct-action demonstrations against nuclear testing in Amchitka, Alaska, and the Pacific; they soon moved on to the fight against whaling and other issues (see Case Study 2.1 on the history of Greenpeace). The 1960s and 1970s saw environmental activism spread to pollution concerns, air quality, wilderness protection, and acid rain. Inspired by the 1962 publication of *Silent Spring* by Rachel Carson (1962), new concerns emerged regarding the use of chemicals such as DDT and their accumulating environmental impacts. Major environmental organizations still active today were founded at this time: the Canadian Wildlife Federation (established 1962), the Sierra Club of Canada (as a chapter of the US organization, established 1963), Canadian Parks and Wilderness Society (established 1963), World Wildlife Fund (WWF; Canadian office established 1967), and Pollution Probe (established 1969) (Doern et al., 2015, p. 299). Many of these groups had international ties and were engaged with global issues such as anti-whaling campaigns, opposition to the seal hunt, and UN agencies and bodies. The 1972 publication by the Club of Rome, *Limits to Growth* (Meadows et al., 1972), fuelled concerns once again about resource shortages and environmental destruction, as its computer models projected severe social, environmental, and economic disruption to human civilizations in the twenty-first century. Environmentalists, operating in a **post-material political culture**, attacked consumerism, modernization, and the precepts of classical economics, which touted the need for unlimited growth.

The patriation of the Constitution in 1982 marked a transition point in Canadian ecopolitical history. Although the *Charter of Rights and Freedoms* would not contain any explicit recognition of Canadian environmental rights, some of its provisions would have implications for natural resource development, the development of a system of national environmental review of major projects, and an evolution on the question of Indigenous Peoples' role in control over resources on their unceded lands. The logic of growing Quebec powers over education, social welfare, and natural resources would continue, while other provinces increasingly pressed their demands for greater control over natural resource projects like mining and energy extraction. While much of the constitutional negotiations centred on language protections and demands for greater provincial control over constitutional provisions, some issues had direct relevance to ecopolitical concerns. For example, the question of whether to include a *Charter of Rights and Freedoms* to entrench rights like mobility, expression, and association was perceived by some as potentially threatening provincial control over natural resource development, as Indigenous Peoples' protests and environmental protection movements grew in their opposition to hydroelectric power projects, oil sands pipelines, and clear-cutting practices in forestry.

In particular, the 1980s would prove challenging for governments seeking to create a national mission on key environmental issues. The Brundtland Commission of the United Nations toured several countries, including Canada, seeking input on the meaning of and challenges to sustainable development and published its final report in 1987. The Conservative government under Brian Mulroney, elected in 1984, sought to advance environmentalism internationally while promoting a free trade agenda with the United States. There were key early successes in negotiations on air pollution, control of chemicals like CFCs (a refrigerant whose properties eroded the ozone layer in the atmosphere), and on biodiversity (see Chapter Three).

While there was more success on the international stage, relations with the provinces on natural resource policy were rocky. High inflation and unemployment during the 1970s, coupled with global increases in oil prices, had led the government of Alberta to strongly protest the federal government's effort to introduce a National Energy Program (NEP) to limit the price of oil. The NEP meant the creation of a national energy company and price controls; the economic effect of these measures was designed to shift resources from oil exporters in Alberta to oil consumers in the rest of Canada. These plans provoked outrage in the oil-producing provinces, who viewed them as an attack on their revenues.

In 1992, the UN Conference on Environment and Development (UNCED) in Rio de Janeiro, Brazil, brought together countries from the Global North and South to negotiate an agreement that would reconcile economic development needs with the need for environmental protection for future generations. From the Earth Summit (as it became known) emerged several new international agreements: the Convention on Biological Diversity (CBD), the UN Framework Convention on Climate Change (UNFCCC), and Agenda 21, a statement of principles for the twenty-first century. Canada was a key player in the finalization of the CBD, being the first "developed" country to sign the convention and offering to host its secretariat in Montreal, although progress on this file at home was slow. The UNCED also produced a Statement on Forest Principles to guide the world toward more sustainable forestry practices. By 1997 the UNFCCC, which was non-binding, produced the Kyoto Protocol, which mandated countries to set and keep carbon emissions targets up until 2012. Canada's target, 6 per cent below the level of greenhouse gas emissions in 1990, was not met and was replaced with less ambitious targets by 2012, which were negotiated at the UN World Summit on Sustainable Development in Johannesburg in 2002.

THE ROAD TO INDIGENOUS SELF-GOVERNANCE

Through the 1990s, pressure rose to negotiate self-governance arrangements with Indigenous Peoples. The Canadian courts had passed down decisions that affirmed First Nations' pre-existing title to lands that they had never legally ceded, and the neglect of calls for constitutionally protected self-government rights during the constitutional negotiations that led to patriation in 1982 had led to an uptick in First Nations political activism. The Oka Crisis erupted in 1990, prompted by municipal approval of a golf course that would be built on land considered sacred by the Kanien'kehá:ka (Mohawk) of Kanesatake (Belshaw et al., 2020, p. 169). The dispute erupted into a nationally televised confrontation when a firefight led to the death of a police officer and the Canadian military became involved. In other cases, Indigenous Peoples allied with environmentalists to resist old-growth logging. A 1980 land claim by the Nuu-chah-nulth Tribal Council to stop logging on Vancouver Island led directly to the formation of the Friends of Clayoquot Sound (Doern et al., 2015, p. 307; see also Case Study 5.2). The legal and political battles over old-growth logging became international concerns when Greenpeace and other groups called for international boycotts and used naming-and-shaming campaigns to influence Canadian trade partners and multilateral organizations.

In 1991 the Royal Commission on Aboriginal Peoples made several recommendations to affirm self-government rights. In the Meech Lake Accord of 1987, Prime Minister Mulroney and 10 premiers agreed on a new formula for constitutional ratification, language rights for Quebec, and provincial ability to "opt out" of federal programs, all while deferring the question of Indigenous constitutional status. The failure of the Meech Lake Accord occurred in 1990 when the ratification vote in Manitoba was held up by Indigenous legislator Elijah Harper, holding an eagle feather to symbolize the lack of action and Indigenous inclusion on the issues. This action was enough to ensure that Indigenous self-government would not be neglected again. The Charlottetown Accord, agreed to in 1994, included a Canada clause and a clause respecting the rights of Indigenous governance; however, it failed in a national referendum.

Despite these efforts, Indigenous Peoples still had few clearly defined rights in the *Constitution Act, 1982*, which did not go much beyond recognizing Treaty rights and made no guarantees for self-government, nor did it address the colonial relationships entrenched in the *Indian Act*. First Nations in the 1990s moved from direct action toward the pursuit of justice through the courts and negotiated agreements on compensation for residential schools. In 2008 victims of the residential schools' abuses received an apology from Prime Minister Stephen Harper. However, the inequalities between mainstream Canadian society and Indigenous People living on and off reserves persist, prompting leaders to seek redress. In some parts of Canada, Indigenous Peoples have poverty rates three times those of other Canadians. Less money is spent on reserve schools, and Indigenous children are 10 times more likely to end up in foster care (Kelm, 2016, p. 187).

Frustration with the government's inaction boiled over again when the small community of Attawapiskat in northern Ontario declared an emergency due to lack of housing in winter 2012, initiating a national conversation on poverty, housing, and lack of fresh drinking water on reserves. A hunger strike by Chief Theresa Spence in response to the federal government's continued neglect of poverty conditions sparked a national movement of resistance. Bill C-45, a 457-page omnibus bill that loosened legal restrictions inhibiting investment in Canadian resources, was also contested since the changes to the *Indian Act* would have made it easier to lease or surrender reserve land by removing the democratic requirement for a community-wide vote. Indigenous Nations were not consulted on any of these changes (Kelm, 2016, p. 189), so they staged a national campaign, driven by the social media hashtag #IdleNoMore, to bring these issues to malls and highways across the country and to the attention of the Canadian public. The Idle No More movement and the protests over federal legislation governing land and water further revealed the close association between Indigenous Peoples' rights and environmental causes.

In 2008, the federal government struck a Truth and Reconciliation Commission to come to terms with the Canadian history of residential schools. Its final report was released in 2015, shortly after the election of the Trudeau Liberal government. For some 100+ years, the Government of Canada had forced First Nations children to attend residential or day schools, often run by Christian churches, to integrate them into Canadian society and to eliminate traditional languages and cultural practices. By the time the last school closed in 1996, over 130 had operated and over 150,000 Indigenous children had been forced to attend what would ultimately be deemed tools of cultural genocide (Belshaw et al., 2020). Residential schools were highly abusive: Children were poorly fed, subjected to medical experiments, forced to work, and subjected to physical, psychological, and sexual abuse. These conditions were documented as early as 1909 in a report by Dr. Peter Bryce, who noted that 42 per cent of children who attended the schools over the course of 10 years died (First Nations Education Steering Committee, 2024).

The Truth and Reconciliation Commission's recommendations included 94 Calls to Action, of which to date only a fraction have been implemented. Spurred as well by the Government of Canada's recognition of the UN

Declaration on the Rights of Indigenous Peoples (see Box 4.2), there has been a rise in activity in response to the mobilization of Indigenous Peoples across the country. The recommendations of the report are designed to serve two purposes: first to redress the legacy of residential schools and the intergenerational trauma these schools inflicted, and second to chart a pathway forward toward a joint vision of mutual respect and recognition. A National Inquiry into Missing and Murdered Indigenous Women and Girls (MMIWG), which looked into the disappearance and probable murder of anywhere from 1,000 to 4,000 Indigenous women, girls, and 2SLGBTQ+ individuals, delivered its final report in June 2019. The report noted the neglect of Indigenous women and girls in the Canadian legal system and common experiences of racism at the hands of police, including the disproportionate number of Indigenous women who are incarcerated or are victims of homicide, which as one author notes are consequences dating back to the federal government's annexation of the Prairies (Belshaw et al., 2020, p. 156). The report also noted the harms imposed on Indigenous communities by resource extraction projects on their territories, including both environmental damage and risks of physical violence associated with large numbers of mostly male workers located in remote locations. Ultimately, it framed the systematic violations of the human rights of Indigenous women and girls as undermining their human security. Many of these harms stem from the sexist and racist discrimination enshrined in the *Indian Act*, which treated Indigenous women differently under the law than men for many decades prior to changes instituted in the late twentieth century.

BOX 4.2. The UN Declaration on the Rights of Indigenous Peoples

Around the world, Indigenous Peoples have raised their voices to push countries to affirm their rights to exist, to practise their languages and cultures, and to enjoy self-determination. The calls for Indigenous rights have emerged as an important global issue in recent years. As a global ecopolitics issue, Indigenous rights and recognition are closely linked with other global efforts to protect biodiversity, eliminate environmental racism, and address climate change. Canada was considered an early leader in the recognition of the rights of Indigenous Peoples when it "recognized and affirmed" Indigenous Treaty rights in 1985, as it was one of the first Commonwealth countries to do so (Gunn & Fitzgerald, 2021, p. 69). Canada was also an active participant in the negotiations around the UNDRIP (United Nations Declaration on the Rights of Indigenous Peoples) in the years prior to its UN approval (Gunn & Fitzgerald, 2021, p. 72). The need for international cooperation and leadership on the issue, and the questions of sovereignty and self-governance that it implied for the international community, meant that the issue of Indigenous Peoples' rights was one that could not be addressed by states acting alone. In addition, the United Nations took a leadership role to achieve multilateral agreement on a declaration that would respond to the voices of Indigenous Peoples for a greater global political role in recognition of their distinct and unique position as rights holders arising from their centuries of self-governance on their lands and territories.

However, the road to recognition of Indigenous rights has been rocky, both in Canada and abroad. The 2007 UN Declaration is the most comprehensive international agreement on the rights of Indigenous Peoples; it "clearly recognizes Indigenous peoples not merely as stakeholders but as rights-holders" (United Nations, 2019, p. 1). The declaration itself was the result of a 20-year process of negotiation and revision by Indigenous Peoples, members of civil society, and UN member states. The declaration was signed by 144 countries. Canada initially voted against acceptance of the declaration and only recently signed it and began implementation. In May 2016, the Government of Canada, under the leadership of the Liberal Party and Justin Trudeau, announced its unqualified support for the declaration and legislated its adoption in the 2021 *UNDRIP Act*. This legislation had widespread public support and was received warmly by most Canadian Indigenous leaders and civil society members (Gunn & Fitzgerald, 2021, p. 73). Canada's Truth and Reconciliation Commission (TRC) included a request for all levels of government to fully adopt and implement the declaration as the framework for reconciliation in Canada, supported by a national action plan for implementation (United Nations, 2019, p. 33). To date, only one province, British Columbia, has integrated UNDRIP into legislation with the *Declaration on the Rights of Indigenous Peoples Act* (Dusyk et al., 2021, p. 16).

The declaration outlines a core minimum standard that states should respect to ensure the rights of Indigenous Peoples to existence, self-determination, and protection of their cultures and heritage (United Nations, 2019, p. ix). The declaration itself does not define "Indigenous" but developed a standard for self-definition and self-identification of Indigenous communities. However, the use of the term "peoples" was at times contentious, as by using "peoples" in this way Indigenous leaders were claiming a difference from minorities and a status akin to the status of nations (Barker, 2005, p. 19). At the same time, self-determination in the declaration has been taken to mean a degree of self-government that stops short of legal sovereignty (as it might be applied to full members of UN member states). For example, UNDRIP requires governments to obtain "free and informed consent" prior to developing any project affecting (not merely on) lands and territories of Indigenous Peoples (Hoekstra & Isaac, 2018), a provision that has been criticized by some experts as "unworkable" and potentially disruptive to existing Canadian Treaty rights. The Canadian government also initially expressed skepticism over the potential for this principle to veto development projects on Indigenous lands (Gunn & Fitzgerald, 2021, p. 1). This ambiguity about self-determination means fully incorporating UNDRIP into national legal systems, as in Canada, presents challenges. For example, the question of self-determination and self-government is at the core of recent disputes regarding control of traditional Indigenous territories under natural gas pipeline development in British Columbia.

The strong support for Bill C-262 (*An Act to ensure that the laws of Canada are in harmony with the United Nations Declaration on the Rights of Indigenous Peoples*) among legislators, Indigenous groups, and the general public in Canada demonstrates that there is political will for addressing the rights of Indigenous Peoples and for incorporating international human rights instruments into Canadian policies and laws. This is heartening for other global initiatives, including Agenda 2030, the effort to achieve the 17 Sustainable Development Goals by the year 2030. It also bodes well for Canadians' will to address global issues at home and for Canada to be a strong contributor to the resolution of issues like the management of the commons and the solving of problems that affect the globe as a whole, not just Canadians.

CONCLUSION: A MIXED HISTORY

Canadian ecopolitical history is rife with colonialism, resource extraction, conflict, and violence visited upon a continent that was home to Indigenous civilizations that have managed to survive all of these changes, but at great cost. The Canadian pattern of natural resource development involves the growth of regional economies governed by a federal system with divided jurisdictions, and an ongoing conflict between French and English Canadians, central Canadians and westerners, and Indigenous Peoples and the Crown. This pattern of conflict is reflected in debates regarding the Canadian Constitution, the distribution of rights and responsibilities among political institutions, and an ongoing tussle over Canadian national unity and its relationship with the rest of the world. The shift from integration with and reliance on the British to the US economy continues, even as American interests have often been distracted by global security concerns. The promise of Canadian leadership on environmental issues that arose in the 1980s under the Mulroney government has given way to decades of lag, and as a result Canada has yet to fully realize its potential as a global environmental citizen.

Despite its history, the prospects for change and even transformation in Canada are present. Canadians are concerned about the growing effects of climate change. Unprecedented forest fires in 2023, a heat dome and flooding in British Columbia in 2021, along with the advent of the zoonotic coronavirus pandemic starting in 2020 have made the environment one of the top political issues for Canadians. Grassroots activism was mobilized by the Black Lives Matter movement in 2020, and continuing attention is being paid to Indigenous concerns in battles over pipelines, resource development, and old-growth forests. Many of the solutions to climate change mitigation and adaptation are less an issue of technology and more an issue of political will (see Chapter Nine for a detailed history of climate governance). Canadians are increasingly recognizing that a consumer society is resulting in an **ecological debt** that will have to be paid by future generations. There is a growing appreciation for the need to protect and preserve natural spaces and to work with, rather than against, nature to obtain human needs for infrastructure and adaptation. Socioeconomic equity and a concern for the need to address marginalization of Indigenous Peoples, racialized people, and women in the environmental movement is growing. The chapters that follow will explore in greater detail how this history has enabled or constrained ecopolitical progress.

NOTE

1 Mason (2008) states: "When environments or objects are constructed as 'natural' by individuals or groups, these constructions reflect as much about the orientations of those people as they do about what they attempt to identify" (p. 222).

CHAPTER FIVE

People, Products, and Planning

LEARNING OBJECTIVES

1. Analyze how human movement, demographic changes, and urbanization impact environmental sustainability in Canada.
2. Evaluate the environmental ramifications of production and consumption patterns, including the life cycle impacts of products.
3. Examine the complexities and controversies surrounding urban planning, land management, and development projects in Canadian communities.

INTRODUCTION: CANADA'S PRODUCTION PROFILE

As described in Chapter One, the ecopolitics of life in the Anthropocene consists of interdependence and complexity. Complex systems are "more than the sum of their parts" in that each component reflects not only the initial conditions of the system but the patterns of interaction between these various sectors. As such, students of Canadian ecopolitics need to be sensitive to the changes happening at different levels and across long timeframes.

The COVID-19 pandemic caused a series of "break points" in human, natural, and governance systems. Today, the effects are still being felt in inflation, labour shortages, and disrupted supply chains for goods. Canadian ecopolitics involves looking at how these interconnections work as a system, shedding light on them and analyzing how they play an integral role in shaping the state of our environment and with it the wellbeing of Canadian communities.

The United Nations' Department of Economic and Social Affairs has identified five global megatrends that are poised to affect the prospects for sustainable development: demographic change, international migration, urbanization, climate change, and technological change. These changes are critical to societal functioning (Trask, 2020). According to UN population predictions, the world's population is projected to increase to 8.5 billion in 2030 and to 9.7 billion in 2050. This represents a 121 per cent increase since 1970 (Global Footprint Network, 2024a). However, as in other regions, declining fertility rates are also changing Canadian demographics (Trask, 2020), with populations of older people increasing faster than other age groups. Similarly, urbanization is continuing. Globally, 55 per cent of the world's population in 2018 lived in cities, with that number expected to increase to 68 per cent by 2050. In contrast, in 1950 only 30 per cent of the world's population was urban. The greatest increases in population and urbanization are anticipated in lower-income countries, and by 2030 the world is projected to have 43 megacities, most of them in developing regions. More than 80 per cent of Canadians live in cities, ironically making it one of the most urbanized countries in the world, despite the abundance of forests, lakes, mountains, grasslands, and rivers. Montreal, Ottawa, Toronto, Vancouver, Calgary, and Edmonton account for more than 50 per cent of the population and more than 50 per cent of Canada's GDP (Roussopoulos, 2017, p. 9).

Following the spirit of this book, which is to focus on multiple levels of governance and interdisciplinary approaches that incorporate the concerns of ethics both within and among humans and nature, this chapter will consider three dimensions of Canadian ecopolitics that are inextricably intertwined: people, products, and planning. While to some degree Canadians have been more tolerant of state involvement in specific sectors, Canada remains largely situated in a capitalist economy. The government does not generally decide what goods are produced, where they are produced, or how they are produced. The government does not restrict movements of Canadian citizens as a general rule and leaves most of the key decisions about investment, labour, manufacturing, and resource use to private, for-profit industrial and technology firms. This means that Canadian ecopolitics are largely reflective of the structural power of capital to determine how resources are allocated and toward what ends. More often than not, as has been recounted in previous chapters of this book, the driving force of development for the accumulation of capital has been paramount over other concerns.

The ecopolitics of people, products, and planning arise when decisions about community futures intersect with challenges like scarcity, overconsumption, waste, and distributive inequality. The Canadian state is expected, through democratic institutions of accountability, to provide equitable opportunities for economic development. At the same time, the pace and uneven nature of changes is often outside the state's direct control or even influence. The migration to cities has led to unprecedented innovation, wealth, and opportunity. It has also brought increased inequality, marginalization, overconsumption, and environmental degradation. The growth in population creates new employment opportunities, an increased tax base, and an increased capacity to innovate with new technologies. It also brings housing shortages, pressures on land use, higher demand for energy, and increases in pollution. Some of the constraints are within the bounds of actionability, while others are only subject to political influence or "nudging."

Nevertheless, the state looms large in managing and affecting decisions in a capitalist economy and so must use a wide range of economic, political, and educational levers to enable Canadian society to achieve prosperity and sustainability and to maintain social stability. The pressures will continue to be significant, and whether this means changes in budgeting, natural resources management, or recovery from disaster, the need for states to be *anticipatory* rather than *reactive* is clear.

The subjects of this chapter are all united by the tension between reactive decision making on the one hand and deliberative forms of planning and management on the other. A second tension emerges between democratic accountability and the need to ensure social equitability on the one hand and the necessity of acknowledging ecological boundaries that limit the range of action that can be taken on the other. As McAllister (2016) points out, "a great number of environmental issues ... exceed temporal, spatial and political boundaries" (p. 156). This chapter examines in greater detail the ecopolitics of human movements and demographic changes (people); the environmental ramifications of production and consumption of materials, energy, waste, and "forever chemicals" (products); and finally the multifaceted aspects of local communities and the controversies over infrastructure, urban planning, land management, and development projects (planning).

PEOPLE

The ecopolitics of migration, movement, and population have a profound impact on both local and global environmental sustainability. At the time of writing in the summer of 2024, the Calgary Stampede has just wrapped up its most successful year, with nearly 1.5 million attendees over the 10-day event. Large numbers of other local festivals, concerts, and celebrations across the country are drawing visitors from around the globe. Most visitors come only for a short time and focus on specific experiences suitable for their families, friends, and workmates. On the other side, Canadians are also among the world's biggest travellers. Whether it's young people backpacking through Thailand or seniors travelling to Florida to avoid the challenging Canadian winter, travel is a huge industry with a large and growing ecological footprint. As discussed in Chapter Four, Canada's history has been strongly influenced by the economic impact of tourism. The establishment of national parks and protection of natural assets such as hot springs and hunting grounds, and even the construction of the national railway, was motivated by the potential to attract visitors and dollars. After a drop in travel due to the COVID-19 pandemic, the Canadian travel and tourism industry grew by 33.6 per cent in 2022, and forecasts to 2027 anticipate an increase in market value of travel and tourism to $217 billion (Marketline, 2023). Tourism accounts for 5 per cent of the Canadian economy, and the sector is anticipated to contribute 7 per cent of Canada's GDP and grow to employ 1 in 11 workers by 2027 (World Tourism and Travel Council, 2023).

As well, immigration to Canada has been ramping up. The country recently reached the population milestone of 40 million, and the federal government has taken active steps to encourage skilled immigrants in professional fields of high demand to permanently settle here. Canada has an explicit target to welcome 1.5 million new residents in 2023–25. After a post-pandemic slowdown, in 2022 net migration to Canada was more than double the previous record (*The Economist*, 2023b). Add to this the growth of migrant seasonal workers' travel to participate in agriculture, domestic work, and customer service work and the movement of people constitutes a significant factor in Canadian ecopolitics. The number of international students coming to study in Canada is also at an all-time high, as the country hosted just over 1 million young people with study permits in 2023 (although recent changes have reduced admissions) (International Consultants for Education and Fairs, 2024).

As climate change affects populations in some of the world's poorest countries, Canadians should anticipate an increase in environmental migrants seeking to settle in Canada. Already, for example, some analysts have noted that deforestation, land degradation, soil erosion, and pollution have prompted "environmentally induced migration" from Haiti to Canada (Mezdour et al., 2016). Most of the current and anticipated international migration is directed toward North America and Europe. The "push" factors that lead to increased immigration are also accompanied by "pull" factors from the domestic scene. One of these "pull" factors is the aging of the population, identified as one of the "megatrends" of the coming decades. The largest increasing age group globally is those aged 65+, a trend likely to persist until the end of the century (Swiaczny, 2019). The proportion of working-age Canadians able to support dependent populations, including the elderly, is likely to continue to decrease, prompting calls for greater immigration of younger working people. Demographics, too, play a role as population shifts affect resource consumption, land use, and energy demands. For example, a rise in single-person households increases consumption of land, materials, resources, and services. In 2016 one-person households became the predominant household type (28 per cent) for the first time in Canada's 150-year history (Statistics Canada, 2022b).

Against the backdrop of movement and development, the complex interactions between humans and nature are also at the forefront of the public mind. Much of the travel and tourism industry in Canada rests on a particular approach to nature that prioritizes utilitarian values. As Canadians became historically concentrated in cities and separated from rural areas, there emerged a clash of imaginaries, often centred on ideological differences between city and country dwellers. The romantic vision of rural life inspired by the English countryside or the Swiss mountains heavily influenced peoples' views of nature as they arrived in Canada as settlers, and Indigenous Peoples were also affected by these changes. Urban dwellers flocked to the mountains and lakes, inspired by the accounts of John Muir, a Scottish naturalist whose exploits in the wilderness of the American West shaped the entire continent's vision of "nature's Cathedral." Wilderness adventures like whale watching appeared to construct a metaphor of nature as a "performer," while efforts to protect endangered species and to preserve habitats like wetlands and corridors suggest that nature is more of a complex system in which humans are a part, not just passive "observers" (Milstein, 2016). The romantic visions of nature motivate visitors to come to places like Banff National Park, and even (for the more adventurous) to visit polar bears in Churchill, Manitoba, or to camp in mosquito-ridden northern Ontario.

While the rural–urban divide can sometimes be overstated, there are also distinct political and ideological differences between urban, suburban, and rural areas in Canada. Alan Walks (2005) identified a growing political cleavage between left-leaning inner-city dwellers and right-leaning suburbanites that started in the 1980s and has deepened up to the present day. This cleavage also seems to persist at both the federal and provincial levels and is pan-Canadian in scope (Armstrong et al., 2022; Walks, 2005). With respect to environmental policies, the picture is more mixed.

Introduction of the carbon emissions pricing system in 2018 (see Case Study 12.1) may have had stronger effects on suburban and rural households required to commute longer distances, and so resistance to environmental measures might logically be associated with more rural geographic locations. Indeed, in British Columbia, following the introduction of a provincial carbon tax in 2008, there was a noted rise in complaints about the unfairness of the tax on rural communities. At the same time, as noted by Beck and colleagues (2015), the revenue recycling scheme that accompanied the tax blunted the effects on rural consumers, although these and subsequent measures did little to satisfy critics. At the same time, some studies show few significant attitudinal differences between rural residents and city dwellers on other environmental issues (Huddart-Kennedy et al., 2009). The picture is complex, with much depending on the economic profile and availability of services in a community. The pattern of economic and geographic development in Canada has created extractive rural–urban relationships – while much of the wealth of the country is driven by rural activities, most services and opportunities are concentrated in urban areas. The high level of dependence of rural communities on staples commodities and industries means that the patterns of development are highly uneven (see Chapter Four).

Human movements and settlement patterns also create human–nature conflicts. Human movement often aids the migration of invasive species, and human migrations affect the fates of species in interface areas, greenbelts, and grasslands. Today, the paradoxes of human–wildlife interactions are good examples of how movements and changes in land use have set up clashes. Human–bear and human–cougar interactions in urban areas are on the increase in British Columbia, raising issues of how to balance wildlife protection with the need for housing and development. Campaigns such as community Bear Smart efforts designed to reduce these tragic interactions are fighting a losing battle because of human folly and lack of knowledge about wildlife. Despite huge fines, people continue to remove moose calves, disturb whales, and feed bears. Partly this arises from a sense of **biophilia**, an attraction to the wilderness and a heartfelt desire to interact with nature (Lunney et al., 2008). While the impulses for nature protection are often well intentioned, as Camacho (2009) argues, most policies have historically been focused on protecting areas of "beauty" and recreation in as pristine a state as possible and have been averse to more proactive controlled policies based on adaptive management or the preservation of ecological integrity.

Humans often light the spark of devastating forest fires, trample delicate undergrowth under all-terrain vehicles, and divert waterways needed for salmon spawning, requiring active human management and intervention to protect remaining land and resources for nature. Additionally, the growth of the travel and tourism industry has resulted in heightened pressure on fragile ecosystems, accelerated carbon emissions, and degradation of natural landmarks. Therefore, promoting sustainable migration policies, responsible tourism practices, and community-based demographic planning is essential to mitigate the adverse environmental consequences of human movement. For its part, under the Harper Conservatives Canada withdrew from the World Tourism Organization and has yet to rejoin.

PRODUCTS

In 2024 Earth Overshoot Day fell on August 1, but for Canadians it was much earlier, on March 15. This date is calculated by dividing the planet's biocapacity (the amount of ecological resources earth is able to generate that year) by humanity's ecological footprint (humanity's demand for that year) and multiplying by 365,[1] the number of days in a year (see Chapter Two for a discussion of the **ecological footprint**). By this calculation, we would need 1.75 earths to match the total amount of consumption on the globe (Global Footprint Network, 2024a). Canada's **ecological deficit** is much higher. The amount by which Canadians are exceeding the biocapacity of the country was roughly 5.1 earths in 2024 (Global Footprint Network, 2024b). Despite the ecological wealth of the country and our relatively small population, Canadians are unusually high consumers of energy, products, and services. You can calculate your own ecological footprint at FootprintCalculator.org.

As discussed in Chapter One, the **life cycles of products** have become a significant environmental concern in recent times. From the extraction of raw materials to manufacturing, distribution, consumption, and eventual disposal, each stage in a product's life has the potential to leave a lasting impact on the environment and affects people differently at different stages. As well, one must account for the transportation and finishing of products through a global supply chain as part of the ecological impact of production. Resource-intensive industries, such as mining, agriculture, and forestry, are crucial for ensuring food security and sustaining livelihoods, but they can also lead to habitat destruction, flooding, and chemical pollution. The transport of products around the world through the expansion of container shipping, which is facilitated by free trade arrangements, has historically enabled control of price inflation; it has also spread production around the world through supply chains and vertical integration. Production and consumption are increasingly distanced from each other, as is the distribution of environmental goods and harms. As products reach the end of their life cycles, improper waste management exacerbates the problem, with landfills and incineration emitting greenhouse gases and toxins, and plastics contaminating waterways and the oceans.

For example, virtually all Canadians have some sort of telephone in their household: 91.3 per cent report having at least one cell phone, and the number of households with more than one has been increasing. Canadians retain their phones for an average of 33 months before they decide to repair or replace them. Repairing damaged cell phones and computers has become increasingly challenging in recent years as devices have become smaller and more complex in nature. Often the costs of repair or purchase of a replacement are similar, and the options to dispose of them are limited since they are considered hazardous waste (Dewis, 2022). Another example is the widespread use of plastics. The discovery of the Great Pacific Garbage Patch, the largest concentration of marine debris in the world, raised awareness of the impact of this plastic waste on the ecosystem. The ingestion of plastics by seabirds, entanglements by whales and turtles, and the persistence of microplastics in the environment have raised public consciousness of the permanency of such materials. Every year, plastic pollution costs up to $2.5 trillion in ecological, economic, and social impacts (Environment and Climate Change Canada, 2021b; see also Stoett & Vince, 2021).

Plastics have been found virtually everywhere on earth, from the highest mountaintops to the deepest seas, and microplastics have recently been found in human blood and in the clouds (Carrington, 2022). As a result, plastics are also implicated in global climate change (as a source of emissions), health (as possible causes of disease like cancer), and air pollution (as incineration releases toxic chemical compounds). Globally, around 6.3 billion tonnes of plastic waste were generated up until mid-2017 (Wang, Zhang, & Li, 2023). Canadians throw away over 3 million tonnes of plastic waste every year. Only 9 per cent is recycled, while the rest ends up in landfills, waste-to-energy facilities, or the environment (Environment and Climate Change Canada, 2021b). While highly useful, plastics are extremely persistent in the environment, with some varieties taking 450 years to degrade completely (Krogh, 2020, p. 2).

The COVID-19 pandemic further aggravated the problem of plastics in the environment. Countries adopted measures such as social distancing and isolation, which increased consumption through ecommerce platforms, online service delivery, and food delivery. This preference has led to a sharp increase in the production of multilayer plastic film and foam. The use of masks and the demand for PPE (personal protective equipment) increased exponentially, to the point that it is now estimated that approximately 1.56 billion masks (approximately 5.66 million tonnes of plastic) will eventually enter the ocean (Wang, Zhang, & Li, 2023, p. 40406). As a global commons problem (see Chapter Three), reducing plastic waste requires international cooperation. At the 2018 G7 meeting, Canada joined with other countries to adopt the Ocean Plastics Charter (Environment and Climate Change Canada, 2018; Murray & Gecelovsky, 2021, p. 238). Following that, the Canadian Council of Ministers of the Environment (CCME) published the Strategy on Zero Plastic Waste, which introduced regulatory, research-based, and public education measures. The strategy focuses on support for innovative product design, recycling, and extended producer responsibility (Environment and Climate Change Canada, 2021b). The strategy also includes the first legislation in Canada to ban particular forms of single-use plastics, including shopping bags and plastic utensils and straws. A global treaty on plastics is also currently being negotiated (see Chapter Eight for details).

As part of its 2018 G7 presidency, Canada spearheaded the Ocean Plastics Charter, which contains commitments and targets aimed at stopping plastic waste and the flow of plastics into the environment. Work on this front is continuing throughout the G7, and Canada continues to play an active role in advancing international collaborative efforts on plastics. Domestically, the government worked with provinces and territories through the CCME to develop the Canada-Wide Strategy on Zero Plastic Waste, which ministers approved in November 2018.

In sum, the current way to "manage" plastics is a "take-make-waste" model, in which products are made from resources and then discarded. In a circular economy, products follow a "make-use-return" model, in which products are reused, repaired, remanufactured, or recycled (Environment and Climate Change Canada, 2021c). The Government of Canada's Strategy on Zero Plastic Waste defines a circular economy as one in which "the flow of materials and energy aims to keep products and materials in use as long as possible and to maximize their value" (Environment and Climate Change Canada, 2021b, p. 4). These are termed **VRPs (value retention processes)**. VRPs are activities that keep products in use for longer, either through direct reuse, repair, refurbishment, or remanufacturing (Service Canada, 2021). While these represent positive steps forward, it should also be remembered that no attempt to improve recycling rates or to reduce waste in the long run can succeed as long as plastics continue to be produced at the current high rate and volume. It should also be noted that recycling in a circular economy is no panacea, since recycling brings with it new forms of pollution, including the release of carbon emissions and other new pollutants during the recycling process (Hird, 2021).

DEALING WITH POLLUTANTS

The pathway toward regulation of pollutants, whether in the air, water, or on land, began with the environmental movement in the 1950s. The growth of environmental regulation was prompted by several high-profile crisis events, including the 1952 Killer Smog of London, the Love Canal chemical contamination in the 1970s, the proliferation of oil spills, litter on sidewalks and highways, and the eutrophication of the Great Lakes. In response, action began at the provincial level to protect clean water and air and was carried forward by new Departments of Environment in Ontario, Quebec, and Alberta (Macdonald, 2013, p. 70). At the UN Stockholm Conference on the Human Environment in 1972, Canadians were strong proponents of international agreements to reduce pollution, especially acid rain. Consequently, much national legislation has been in response to these international agreements arising from this conference. Over time, new chemical toxins, materials, and pollutants have made their presence felt. In recent years, there has been an increasing focus on **persistent organic pollutants (POPs)**, which are compounds with serious health consequences, especially for people with diets rich in fish and marine mammals, as in Canada's north. Due to this, Canada was the first industrialized country to ratify an international agreement on POPs. Nevertheless, Canada has been both a leader and a laggard, since many of these chemicals remain in widespread commercial use. Regulators have often responded to industry calls for voluntary rather than regulatory measures, as in the **National Pollutant Release Inventory (NPRI)**, which relies on "naming and shaming" to incentivize industry to reduce its pollution. Predictably, corporate support for these mechanisms waned when industry realized the negative impacts on reputations as a result of public disclosure of their polluting activities.

Another example is the case of Canadian mining and mineral development. As noted in Chapter Four, mining is one of the most lucrative Canadian industries, and Canada is a "mining superpower." Mineral extraction has a large and permanent ecological footprint, but the pattern of mining development in Canada has also had significant socioeconomic and social justice implications, since rural and isolated regions "pay a relatively high price, in their economies, environments, and health, and receive relatively few benefits of lucrative oil, gas, uranium, and hydroelectric sales" (Sandwell, 2016, p. 20). There are also extreme regional variations between extractive industry concentrations and their effects that continue to define Canada – east and west, north and south, urban and rural. Mine cleanup and remediation in Canada, and in Canadian mining enterprises abroad, have been persistent sources of complaint from environmentalists and development critics. (For more, see Case Study 5.1.)

CASE STUDY 5.1. The Mount Polley Mine Disaster

The Mount Polley mine in British Columbia started operation in 1997 to process copper and gold. According to a report published by UN Environment in 2017, Imperial Mining (parent of the Mount Polley Mining Corporation) processed 22,000 tonnes of ore per day, and in 2010 it was the largest mineral exporter from British Columbia. On August 4, 2014, the mine's tailings dam collapsed and released 25 million cubic metres of wastewater and tailings (Marshall, 2019), which resulted in flooding in Polley Lake and flows into Hazeltine Creek and Quesnel Lake. The Cariboo Regional District declared a local state of emergency because of the poor quality of water for humans and aquatic health. In August 2014 the BC Ministry of Environment issued a pollution abatement order to the company with the goal of cleaning up the area to an acceptable standard for drinking water, archaeological site preservation, and reducing threats to human and environmental health (Government of British Columbia, 2014).

The collapse of the Mount Polley dam is the largest environmental disaster in the mining industry in Canada. The global scale of the spill was noted in 2019's Global Assessment Report by the UN Program on Disaster Risk Reduction, which stated that although there are no data available publicly about the total volume of tailings ponds that exist around the world, the Mount Polley spill released more than 25 million metres cubed of hazardous substances. The spill into Polley Lake, Hazeltine Creek, and Quesnel Lake had a significant impact. The incident impacted the communities, activities, and health of several First Nations communities, such as the Xatśull, T'exelc (Williams Lake Band), and Lhtako Dené, which were directly impacted. The BC government's approach to the spill came under fire from the First Nations communities affected, in part because the measures to handle the spill were insufficient to address the full range of social and health effects experienced. In addition to the income and health effects, the threat to the salmon habitat on the Fraser River posed a sociocultural threat to First Nations for whom the fishery was a source of community cohesion. For Indigenous Peoples, the spill was part of a pattern of environmental dispossession, affecting their "access to sacred land and territory, traditional food sources, and medicine" (Shandro et al., 2017). Richmond and Ross (2009) define **environmental dispossession** as the "processes by which aboriginal people's access to the resources in their traditional environments are reduced" (p. 403).

In addition, the approach of the government was to rely on environmental regulation and mitigation rather than to redress the concerns of Indigenous communities. For example, to date there have not been any federal charges laid against the Mount Polley Mining Corporation after the incident. Critics argue that this is an example of the continued political power imbalance between natural resource companies and Indigenous communities, indicative of a failure to account for the larger impacts of extractive industries on human and ecosystem sustainability.

Critical Thinking Questions

1. What are some reasons that any level of government has not laid charges against the Mount Polley Mining Corporation?
2. Describe some of the things the Mount Polley Mining Corporation might have done before, during, and after the incident to avoid the significant impact of the spill on the Indigenous Peoples affected.

FOOD AND AGRICULTURAL PRODUCTION

In general, Canadians enjoy opportunities to access a wide variety of foods from all around the world, whether grapes from Mexico, lettuce from California, or lamb from Australia. Globally, container shipping has revolutionized the distribution of goods such that prices have, until recently, defied inflationary expectations, increasing the types and volume of foods available to the Canadian consumer. But the transport of food across longer distances has also increased its carbon footprint and contributed to deforestation and land degradation around the world. Like many other countries, the Government of Canada deploys a series of favourable policies to support agriculture, from wheat marketing boards to stockpiles of maple syrup. Canada is the world's sixth-largest producer of wheat in the world. Domestically, dairy producers enjoy considerable protection from international competition, despite the recent (2020) removal of some protections in the new North American free trade agreement (United States-Mexico-Canada Agreement, or USMCA). In general, these protections raise prices to the Canadian consumer but offer stability to farmers who would otherwise be outcompeted by larger multinational firms capable of flooding the Canadian market. The country also produces large amounts of grains, oilseeds, and beef cattle. Ontario and Quebec lead in dairy production, as well as fruits and vegetables. British Columbia is known for horticulture and greenhouse production. Potatoes from Prince Edward Island and fruits from British Columbia's Fraser Valley and Okanagan regions are sold around the world (Statistics Canada, 2022a). Canada's agricultural production has contributed to the health and food security of the country, a fact that many observers noted when COVID-19 shutdowns affected food supply chains that fed people across the country.

However, agriculture has also increased forms of environmental degradation. As mechanization has grown, agriculture has grown its significant carbon footprint and has radically altered the landscape in ways that have reduced the amount of carbon sinks and increased overall emissions. The use of pesticides, herbicides, and fertilizers have leached poisons into water supplies, resulting in substantial problems with nitrogen runoff and algae blooms. Food waste is a significant contributor to carbon emissions from landfills (Environment and Climate Change Canada, 2023, p. 134). Since the fading of the COVID-19 pandemic, Canadians have seen food prices rise exponentially. Troubles with the supply chain from floods, fires, heat, war, and labour unrest have plagued the food supply in the last three years (Global Affairs Canada, 2022). This has left many people relying on food banks to stock their shelves with items they are not able to afford. (For more about the health and biosecurity implications of food production, see Chapter Ten.)

A concern with food security and the health and nutrition dimensions of the food supply has led to greater action by the federal government. In September 2012, *E. coli* tainted meat was discovered coming from the XL food processing plant in Edmonton, Alberta. This and other incidents have heightened the awareness of the Canadian public of the environmental and ethical implications of food production on human and ecosystem health. The industrial model of food production, which gives rise to concentrated feedlots for cattle, inhumane caging of chickens in overcrowded and dirty warehouses, and abuses of workers with poor working conditions and low pay are all factors to be considered in the evolution of food production.

THE FOREST INDUSTRY

Forestry in Canada is concentrated in the west, Ontario, Quebec, and the province of New Brunswick. However, British Columbia holds by far the lion's share of production and employment in the industry (Statista, 2022). While in the recent past Canada was dotted with "forestry towns" built up around pulp and paper production, lumber mills, and other forestry activities, a recent Bloomberg report claims that there are now only four large communities that are "forestry towns," three of which are in the province of British Columbia: Quesnel, Merritt, and the Cariboo region (Quinn, 2018).[2] Forests cover roughly two-thirds of the province of British Columbia, or around 60 million hectares. During the 1950s–1970s, British Columbia experienced a "timber frontier," and forestry accounted for more than half of provincial exports, which continued to grow throughout the remainder of the twentieth century (Barman, 2007, p. 350). By the early 1990s, the industry was worth around $13.8 billion and directly employed 101,000 people (BC Ministry of Forests, 2024). The BC government granted private logging companies long-term rights to harvest trees in particular areas on the condition that they pay royalties, called "stumpage fees." One of these companies, MacMillan Bloedel, dominated BC wood sales. Foresters maintained that clear-cutting and aggressive harvesting could continue at a high, sustainable rate, and that "natural restocking" would be sufficient to replenish the harvested areas (Kamieniecki, 2000, p. 182; Barman, 2007, p. 357).

In the 1960s–1970s, organizations such as the Western Canada Wilderness Committee, Greenpeace, and the Sierra Club were born, and tensions escalated between the forest industry and environmentalists as the latter decried an economic culture that depended on the continued liquidation of forests and called for a halt to clear-cutting, arguing that it was important to conserve ecological diversity, preserve nature for future generations, and sustain the tourism sector (Wilson, 1998). By the early 1990s, public opinion polls showed that 85 per cent of British Columbians were alarmed about the number of trees being harvested and were against continued clear-cutting (Kamieniecki, 2000, p. 182).

In 1991, the BC New Democratic Party (NDP) under Michael Harcourt was elected to government. The NDP's election platform promised "peace in the woods" through stronger environmental measures and protection of forest industry jobs (Wilson, 1998, p. 264). Harcourt pledged that the size of protected areas in British Columbia would be doubled along with an abstract commitment to "improved ecosystem representation" while simultaneously promising to protect forestry jobs threatened by "conservation activity" (Cashore, 2001, p. 38). As a report presented to the provincial cabinet stated:

> Opinions were sharply polarized, emotions were high and many community members were already frustrated and burned out. As the largest block of old-growth on Vancouver Island, Clayoquot Sound is both a key resource for the timber industry and a place of totemic importance for environmental groups and the wilderness movement. Options for deferrals or log-around "without pain" proved to be non-existent. All of this made for an extremely narrow window for compromise and mutual accommodation. (Wilson, 1998, p. 271)

The Clayoquot Sound protests quickly emerged as a "poster child" of the international environmental movement (Barman, 2007; see Case Study 5.2). The visibility of the peace camp was increased through visits by activists and celebrities, and Premier Harcourt travelled to Europe to counteract this negative impression (Stoddart & Tindall, 2010). However, campaigners saw this as an opportunity to drum up more support for their blockade and followed Harcourt on his trip to draw attention to the logging practices occurring in British Columbia. Their persistence made a strong impression and led to protests outside Canadian embassies in the United Kingdom, Germany, Japan, and the United States, countries where BC wood pulp was used to make toilet paper, newsprint, and disposable chopsticks (Moore, 2015, p. 56). The forest industry, already highly globalized, encountered global opposition to its activities.

CASE STUDY 5.2. Clayoquot Sound: The War in the Woods

Located in the homeland of the Nuu-chah-nulth people, the Clayoquot watershed crosses the traditional territories of the Ahousaht, Hesquiaht, and Tla-o-qui-aht First Nations. The first anti-logging blockade in the area began in 1984 after MacMillan Bloedel announced plans to log more than 4,500 hectares of Meares Island, close to Tofino (Kuehls, 2003, p. 179). The Tla-o-qui-aht protested logging on their unceded territory and gained support from local residents and environmentalists, including a newly formed group, the Friends of Clayoquot Sound. The Tla-o-qui-aht declared Meares Island a "tribal park" and subsequently received a court injunction to prevent logging until their outstanding land claims were resolved (Shaw, 2003, p. 30).

In 1993, Premier Harcourt announced a "compromise solution" that would increase the amount of protected area in Clayoquot Sound from 39,100 to 87,600 hectares, protecting a total of 33 per cent of its land area. However, much of this area was shoreline or bog forest, leaving many pristine watersheds, mountainsides, and rare ecosystems unprotected (Wilson, 1998, p. 271). MacMillan Bloedel retained permission to clear-cut up to 49 per cent of the Clayoquot Sound land area (Walter, 2007). The Nuu-chah-nulth First Nation opposed the government's decision as the area in question was subject to unresolved land claims and they had not been consulted during the decision-making processes. Other organizations, such as Friends of Clayoquot Sound, the Western Canada Wilderness Committee, Greenpeace, and Forest Action Network, also resisted the NDP's proposed compromise solution.

In July 1993 activists arrived to "put their bodies on the line to save the trees" (MacGregor, 2001, p. 49). The camp was modelled after Greenham Common in England, which was the longest-running women's peace camp from 1981 to 2000 and successfully pressured the Royal Air Force to stop operating and testing nuclear cruise missiles (Gaard, 2011). The Clayoquot Sound camp received far more protestors than expected; by the end of that summer, 12,000 had passed through the camp, with the blockades averaging 300–400 people per day. Over 800 people were arrested, two-thirds of them women (Stoddart & Tindall, 2010, p. 77).

In October, an independent advisory panel was set up, composed of scientists and Nuu-chah-nulth Elders with a mandate to "develop world-class standards for sustainable forest management by combining traditional and scientific knowledge" (Scientific Panel for Sustainable Forest Practices in Clayoquot Sound, 1995). In April 1995, the panel concluded its final set of recommendations for logging in Clayoquot Sound, advocating an "ecosystem-based" approach (Mabee & Hoberg, 2006, p. 879). The recommendations also promoted the importance of First Nations values within forest management, such as protecting cultural sites and allowing the Nuu-chah-nulth to identify culturally significant areas before forestry planning occurred (Mabee & Hoberg, 2004, p. 231). Although the general public saw these changes as a resolution to the "War in the Woods," environmental critics argued the recommendations were insufficient as they did not provide permanent protections for the area (Stoddart & Tindall, 2010).

Since Clayoquot Sound, environmentalists have continued to campaign for better protection against clear-cutting and other damaging logging methods on the mainland and on Vancouver Island, often working with local First Nations. A few Nuu-chah-nulth people participated in the Clayoquot Sound protests, but environmentalists still advanced a narrative wherein they were supporting the Nuu-chah-nulth's efforts to preserve the wilderness and save the old-growth forest. Arguably, then, the Friends of Clayoquot Sound practised a form of "green colonialism" that asserted their own views of how people should interact with the environment regardless of the views of the Indigenous inhabitants (Clapperton, 2019, p. 193).

Critical Thinking Questions

1. Why was the NDP government's effort to achieve a compromise on clear-cutting old-growth forest an immediate failure?
2. What is the "ecosystem approach" advocated by the panel, and how can it be effective in conserving nature?

Climate change in British Columbia and across the western provinces, including the boreal forests of the north, has made winters warmer and accelerated infestations of the mountain pine beetle (*Dendroctonus ponderosae*), a highly destructive invasive insect that kills mature pine trees, such as lodgepole pine, by boring through the bark and mining the phloem (BC Ministry of Forests, 2024). The beetle has affected over 18 million hectares, or 58 per cent of the merchantable pine volume between 1990 and 2017 (Natural Resources Canada, 2013). The outbreak has resulted in a large increase in the volume of fuel for wildfires, as beetle-killed wood becomes highly flammable. As well, the infestation has led to a large reduction in the supply of trees for harvesting. In recent years, the BC government has introduced legislative measures to both reduce losses to wildfires and maintain the struggling forestry industry. The government introduced changes to the *Forest and Range Practices Act* (FRPA) to increase the participation of Indigenous Peoples in forest management, including through cultural burns and community forest management that incorporates principles of selective harvesting as opposed to clear-cutting (BC Ministry of Forests, 2024). The province has also taken steps to protect "old-growth" forests (definitions vary, but generally referring to more than 140-year-old trees) following a 2020 review (Old Growth Review Panel, 2020). However, progress has been slow, and demonstrations continue as clear-cut logging practices also continue, leading to recent protests at Fairy Creek and continuing efforts by Indigenous bands to increase their control of forestry activities on their lands (Pawson, 2023).

INTERNATIONAL TRADE

Since the end of World War II, the world's trade in products has been loosely governed by a liberal regime that encouraged the expansion of trade in goods with scant attention given to the environmental consequences of this growth. Toxic waste transport and disposal is governed by the Basel Convention, which forbids the export of waste to countries lacking the ability to safely treat it (Hird, 2021, p. 3). Other agreements provide for the protection of biosafety agricultural protocols (see Chapter Ten). However, Canada's position as an export-dependent resource producer has made the country highly exposed to foreign markets, and as Harold Innis argued in the 1930s, this has shaped the country's political, economic, and social development (see Chapter Four).

Nevertheless, Canada's trade relationships have often been highly politically contentious, with crisis points in 1911, when the Reciprocity Agreement was being considered, and in 1988 with the free trade agreement proposal under the Conservative government of Brian Mulroney. Known as the "Free Trade Election," the debate in 1988 pitted pro–free trade Conservatives against the Liberals under John Turner. The erosion of environmental protections, especially concern over bulk water exports (see Chapter Seven), animated much of the opposition to the free trade agreement. Energy, food, and health concerns also informed much of the opposition from civil society groups, including environmentalists. Mulroney won the election with a resounding majority, despite the fact that many Canadians had voted for parties opposing free trade.

Canada is a member of the World Trade Organization and has signed 15 bilateral and multilateral trade agreements in the last 25 years, mostly with the United States, Mexico, Europe, and countries of the Pacific (Global Affairs Canada, 2022). As well, Canada is a participant in some 115 international environmental agreements and instruments, 23 of which are with the United States (Paquin, 2021, p. 142). The United States looms particularly large in the history of Canadian trade, with continental trade having grown significantly in recent years. Canada sends approximately 75 per cent of all goods exports to the United States, and Canada and the United States are the world's largest trading partners. Since 1993 (just before the North American Free Trade Agreement [NAFTA] came into effect), Canadian goods exports to the United States are up 187 per cent (US Trade Representative, 2023).

In 1994, during the negotiations for a new agreement to replace the Canada–US Free Trade Agreement of 1988, the United States issued a ban on imported tuna on the grounds that Mexican fleets did not meet US standards for minimizing dolphin kills in tuna fishing (Lester & Leitner, 1991). Due to the "purse-seine" net fishing technique for yellowfin tuna, dolphins are often unintentionally caught in nets and killed. Despite the fact that a Global Agreement on Tariffs and Trade (GATT) Dispute Resolution Panel found against the dolphins and allowed the continued importation of tuna that exceeded US standards for dolphin "bycatch," the recognition that trade rules could conflict with environmental standards led to the inclusion of the North American Agreement on Environmental Cooperation (NAAEC, which established the Commission on Environmental Cooperation) in NAFTA. The tuna–dolphin case also led to widespread use of "Dolphin-friendly" labelling on cans of tuna to inform the public in both the United States and Canada.

NAFTA, which was enacted in 1994, included side agreement provisions to address the environmental and labour effects of trade in the region. Despite this, critics of the NAAEC have argued that it has few enforcement provisions (Kukucha, 2021, p. 408). In 2018, rising "America First" rhetoric from the Trump Administration, much of it directed at Canada, prompted a renegotiation of NAFTA and the signing of the new United States-Mexico-Canada

Agreement (USMCA; Global Affairs Canada, 2024a). The new agreement moved the "side deals" on labour and the environment into the main agreement, dropped the energy provisions, and opened up the dairy industry's system of marketing boards to international competition (Kukucha, 2021, p. 408). The impact of the latest agreement has been minimal, but the experience of renegotiating NAFTA led the Liberal government under Trudeau to more strongly affirm support for the inclusion of environmental, gender, and labour protections in future agreements.

In general, the overall deepening of the trade relationship with the United States has had negative implications for environmental protections and policies in Canada. Arguably, Canadians now have less control over natural resource development, must allow greater freedom for international investors, and have had to harmonize many environmental regulations with their largest trading partner. A key example here is the ongoing softwood lumber dispute, in which provincial policies on stumpage fees have been adjusted to more closely match the prevailing practices in the United States, which are market based rather than set by the government. Despite these efforts, the United States continues to battle Canadian softwood lumber regulations in international trade courts. In August 2024, the United States significantly increased its duties on Canadian softwood lumber, with the Canadian Minister of Export Promotion expressing "extreme disappointment" in the decision (Global Affairs Canada, 2024b).

PLANNING

Municipal governments are on the "front lines" of ecopolitics in Canada. As urbanization and population growth expanded, people became disconnected from the natural resources that sustain them, and the relationship between urban centres and rural hinterlands became more distant and separated. Even today, the pattern of staples-and-resource commodity exports (explored in earlier chapters of this book) has continued to shape patterns of settlement and at least partially explains the wide variation of economic regions across the country. Rural communities remain dependent on resource extraction, with little development of secondary or service-based industries. Hinterlands are also largely controlled and governed by the urban centre(s), as well as being subject to economic fluctuations because of their reliance on global markets and trade (Hessing et al., 2007, p. 38). Canada has a large proportion of **resource towns**, communities that grow up specifically to serve a particular industry or economic activity. They can include mining towns (Murdochville, Quebec, for copper), fishing villages (Black's Harbour, New Brunswick), or forestry-dependent towns (Grand Falls-Windsor, Newfoundland and Labrador). Typically, such towns have limited control over their own economic base since the extractive or processing activity is managed by outside agents. Because the natural resource products are most often exported with little processing or value added, resource towns tend to see few benefits from the economic activity and tend to suffer more from "boom and bust" cycles (Stelter & Artibise, 2021).

Rapid industrialization and urbanization early in Canadian history brought new strains on urban planning, including pollution, poverty, crime, and disease. These issues in turn led local businesses to call for beautification efforts to make cities more attractive places to live and work (McAllister, 2016, p. 148). The profession of urban planning grew to advise cities on systems of zoning that separated industrial, commercial, and residential areas. The drive for revenues to fund city services and infrastructure like sewers and roads led to a focus on property development and a bias toward business in local governments (Roussopoulos, 2017, p. 12). The result in most Canadian cities is that rapid growth has consumed rural lands and hinterlands around cities, and the public relies inordinately on cars to go to work, shop, and school.

In 1987, the Brundtland Commission report, which originated the term "sustainable development," identified local–global linkages as integral to the pursuit of practical efforts and actions to respond to environmental crises. Perhaps a bit ironically, the United Nations has often been a lead agency in moving local issues forward through programs such as UN-HABITAT, the World Urban Forum, and the campaign to localize the Sustainable Development Goals' 2030 agenda through voluntary local reviews (Robinson, 2009, pp. 160, 164). The federal government adopted a new sustainable development strategy in 2023, which boosted federal spending on local initiatives such as the Green Municipal Fund, the Federal Gas Tax Fund, and Indigenous local clean energy and food security projects (Canada Energy Regulator, 2023). Despite the strong involvement of the federal government in municipal affairs, provinces and territories have sole constitutional jurisdiction over municipal institutions. Local governments therefore have little control over many of the decisions that most strongly affect them, since they are "creatures of the provinces" under Canada's constitutional division of powers (McAllister, 2016, p. 148).

Accordingly, local governments typically have direct or indirect control over things like land use planning, waste management, water and wastewater supply and treatment, parks and recreation, building code implementation, public transit, policing, and public health (Robinson, 2009, p. 168). Despite this wide range of responsibilities, the tax base for local government is limited to property taxes and commercial licences, which can lead to budgetary pressures on social spending needs such as policing, infrastructure, and housing. Indeed, the effort to fund sustainability activities through the allocation of fossil fuel revenue and arm's-length agencies demonstrates some of the "dysfunctions" of Canada's sustainable development governance institutions. The country lacks any long-term federal transit strategy or transit investment policy, for example (Robinson, 2009, pp. 169–70).

At the same time, cities have been the sites of some remarkably far-reaching experiments in ecologically minded political management and planning. There is growth in the adoption of innovative asset management that includes ecosystem services and benefits in city planning. The Natural Assets Initiative has documented over 100 communities across the country who have started the process of accounting for their stocks of natural resources and ecosystems that contribute to the provision of services required for the health, wellbeing, and long-term sustainability of their communities (Natural Assets Initiative, 2023). Additionally, approaches that focus on watersheds and bioregions are looking for ways to "transcend the limitations created by jurisdictional boundaries" (McAllister, 2016, p. 146). Cities are using bylaws and zoning to develop greener neighbourhoods through local food charters, tree protection, pesticide bans, community gardens, green roofs, anti-idling laws, active transportation initiatives, and more. Eco or "green" infrastructure approaches try to consider ways to reduce flooding by restoring river flows to their natural courses, regenerating wetlands, and managing urban forests. Other plans focus on densification of urban cores to reduce suburban sprawl and "smart growth" to improve energy efficiency. Confronted with the growing prospects of increased heat, flooding, fires, and invasive species, many cities are now working to develop adaptation plans to improve their resilience in the face of climate change.

Municipal governments are confronted by instabilities caused by environmental changes, indeterminate and unreliable sources of revenue, and difficulties in managing the conflicting demands of local populations. Effective governance and sound urban planning are instrumental in determining the sustainability of cities and towns. By implementing green infrastructure and promoting public transport, cities can reduce carbon emissions, alleviate traffic congestion, and improve air quality. Furthermore, community activists advocate for environmentally conscious policies and hold institutions accountable for their ecological impact. Parks and green spaces play a pivotal role in fostering biodiversity, providing recreational opportunities, and mitigating urban heat islands.

The race to keep environmental regulation ahead of ecosystem changes, including climate change, has been a challenge for governments, whose timeframes are often shorter than even the typical infrastructure planning cycle of mid-sized cities in Canada. Technological changes often leap ahead of the government's ability to anticipate, and so legislation needs to be updated and reviewed on a regular basis. The *Canadian Environmental Protection Act* (CEPA), which brought together a suite of environmental protection regulations begun in the 1960s, was enacted in 1988 (Macdonald, 2013, p. 158) and has gone through a series of amendments. The most recent amendment, in July 2023, enacted a new *Strengthening Environmental Protection for a Healthier Canada Act*, which was the first significant change to CEPA in over 20 years. The new Act, when combined with pre-existing provisions, requires the government to consider the right of Canadians to a healthy environment; the provisions of the UNDRIP to respect the right of Indigenous Peoples to free, prior, and informed consent of development projects on their lands; as well as "the importance of considering vulnerable populations and the risks posed by the cumulative effects of toxic substances in substance toxicity assessments" (Gordner, 2023, p. 1). These amendments have been challenged in the courts, so future legal rulings may restrict the range of motion for the federal government to act on plastics and other pollutants.[3] In addition to these considerations, legislation must also be responsive and transparent to the needs, desires, and interests of the Canadian public and the need to respect constitutional provisions for federalism as well as rights and freedoms.

Aside from the recognition of UNDRIP of the role for Indigenous Peoples in development project consultations, there has also been an effort to incorporate **traditional ecological knowledge (TEK)** in environmental planning and project assessment. Along with a series of court victories recognizing the right of Indigenous Peoples to manage their ancestral lands, Indigenous Peoples have been active in the establishment of co-management boards in northern Canada. **Environmental co-management** refers to "the sharing of power and responsibility between government and local resource users, [this being achieved through] various levels of integration of local and state level management systems" (Notzke in Houde, 2007, p. 3). In this approach, the priority is to integrate TEK in different forms at all stages of the planning process, especially when "multiple futures are still possible" (Houde, 2007, p. 12). This system of co-management is based on a participatory model in which decisions are adaptive and responsive to communities on the ground.

Box 5.1 describes how a biodiversity strategy in the Okanagan region of British Columbia has been integrated into land use planning.

BOX 5.1. Planning and Land Use with Nature in Mind: Okanagan Biodiversity Strategy

Biodiversity is a key characteristic of sustainable ecosystems, and regions that support higher levels of biodiversity and protection for intact natural areas enjoy the full benefits of ecosystem services like flood control, wildfire mitigation, cleaner water and air, recreation, and climate change adaptation. An **ecosystem** "is a community of organisms and their physical environment that can be defined at a range of scales, for example, from the very small (a pond) to the very large (all the grasslands in the southern interior)" (Bezener et al., 2012, p. 2). In 2014, a report prepared by Okanagan civil society groups, governments, and Indigenous groups used a sensitive ecosystem-level approach to assess threats to biodiversity in the region and to make recommendations for policies and processes to protect the most ecologically important areas, or **biodiversity hotspots** (OCCP & SOSCP, 2014).

The Okanagan region of British Columbia is one of the most biodiverse areas in Canada while being uniquely endangered. It is a region "full of freshwater lakes, rolling hills, grasslands, mountains, forests, and Canada's only desert" (Iverson et al., 2007). As described in the report *Keeping Nature in Our Future*, a regional approach to ecosystems is preferred because of the need to keep ecosystems connected. The Okanagan is part of a larger basin that stretches north to the city of Armstrong and is an important corridor between the arid Columbia Basin to the south and the grasslands of the central interior of British Columbia. The Okanagan also has important northern and southern connections to other biodiversity hotspots in the Thompson–Nicola region and is part of a north–south corridor that overlaps national, regional, and municipal boundaries (Bezener et al., 2012, p. 13; OCCP & SOSCP, 2014).

The interior dry plateau region has a hot and dry summer, mild and short winters, lower levels of precipitation, and has some of the greatest concentrations of species and ecosystems in Canada. In particular, grasslands, which cover only 1 per cent of the area of British Columbia, are home to a fragile, easily disturbed crust of lichens, mosses, and algae that enables moisture retention, provides nitrogen, and reduces erosion (known as a microbiotic crust) (Iverson et al., 2007). Plants such as balsamroot, ponderosa pine, pinegrass, and prairie lupine are found in the region. There are 15 species of bats in the South Okanagan, 2 of which are found only in this region. The region is also a home for immigrant species of birds.

Off-roading, farming, and property development activities in the Okanagan have endangered and disturbed the habitats and species of plants and animals. "About one-third of the grassland areas has been lost to development; the North Okanagan has lost nearly half of its native grasslands" (Iverson, 2004). The population of other species of animals has declined as well. It was estimated 50 years ago that 1 million Okanagan Lake kokanee spawn every year. However, the population has decreased to 10 per cent of what it was in the 1990s. Numerous species of birds and mammals that can only be found in the region have been classified as threatened or endangered.

A process to establish a national park reserve to protect the grasslands of the South Okanagan Grasslands Protected Area was proposed in 2012 after a feasibility study and was brought forward with public consultations in 2018 and 2019. In July 2019, the governments of Canada and British Columbia and the Syilx/Okanagan Nation signed a memorandum of understanding to formally work toward establishing a national park reserve in the South Okanagan–Similkameen (Parks Canada, 2019). In its summary document reporting on consultations, Parks Canada reported that, unprompted, over half (53 per cent) of participants in the consultation survey, especially non-local residents, felt that the South Okanagan–Similkameen area is special because of conservation and protection-related factors (NRG Research Group, 2019, p. 8). At the same time, the proposed park had significant opposition from local residents (41 per cent of respondents), whose concerns focused on

> increased visitor activity, potential fees, encroachments on private land, and potential restrictions on recreational uses of the area (especially hunting, fishing, and trapping). Overall, the consultations did show that there was a high degree of interest (73 per cent of respondents) in the ecological value of the region (NRG Research Group, 2019, p. 9).

CONCLUSION: CONNECTING ECOPOLITICS WITH EVERYDAY LIFE

This chapter explored the interconnected aspects of people, products, and planning in Canadian ecopolitics. It highlighted how human movement, demographic changes, urban development, and production and consumption patterns impact the environment and sustainability efforts. One of the things that stands out is that Canadian ecopolitics is not only about governments, but is also about people and their everyday lives and activities. Much of the environmental awareness that people have today comes from the popular environmental movements that emerged in the 1970s. These early movements urged everyone to "reduce, reuse, and recycle" to change the way they used products. Anti-consumerism urged "buy nothing days" or high-profile boycotts of polluters to encourage companies to change their ways. Today, purely individual efforts to change consumer preferences are recognized as highly limited. Without collective action, markets are resistant to changes that impose costs on production. This is particularly true in an open economy like Canada's, where many economic drivers and important decisions on investment, planning, and strategy come from outside the country. While it is important to have an awareness of how your individual decisions impact the environment, it is also vitally important to recognize that everyone is both a consumer and an "ecological citizen." We will return to this theme in Chapter Twelve.

The intricate linkages between people, products, and planning underscore the undeniable role of human activities in shaping the environmental future of our planet. By understanding the ecopolitical implications of flows of people and products through the economy and the environment, we gain a comprehensive perspective on the challenges and opportunities in achieving sustainability. Embracing ecoconscious policies, responsible consumption, and community-driven initiatives are vital steps in safeguarding the health and prosperity of both present and future generations.

NOTES

1 Because 2024 is a leap year, the calculation used 366 days instead of 365.
2 The fourth "forestry town" is La Tuque in Quebec.
3 In November 2023, the Federal Court struck down an order that had designated "plastic manufactured items" (PMIs) as toxic substances under CEPA. The court found this designation was too broad and posed a threat to the balance of federalism, as it did not restrict regulation to only those plastic items that truly have potential to cause environmental harm. The court ruled this order was both unreasonable and unconstitutional (*Responsible Plastic Use Coalition v. Canada*, 2023).

CHAPTER SIX

Energy

LEARNING OBJECTIVES

1. Explain the historical development and current state of Canada's energy sector, with a focus on fossil fuels and renewable energy sources.
2. Assess the environmental and political implications of Canada's oil sands development and related pipeline projects.
3. Analyze the challenges and opportunities associated with Canada's transition to electric vehicles and other low-carbon technologies.

INTRODUCTION: THE VITAL NEED FOR ENERGY

Energy is a fundamental part of modern ecopolitics in what is today known as Canada. Defined as *the ability to do work*, energy is a deceptively simple concept for articulating the resources that allow people to accomplish daily tasks. Energy is derived from many sources, all of which are ultimately "natural," whether ecological processes such as solar radiation, blowing wind, or flowing water, or the burning of stored carbon energy from wood and other fibres, or minerals such as coal, oil, gas, and bitumen. These sources of energy are produced across different geographies and timescales and reflect the inherent diversity and complexity of discussing "energy" in an overly general fashion (Daggett, 2019).

At the time of European arrival, energy for daily life across the Americas was derived from various basic and renewable sources, notably wood, plant fibres, peat, and running water. By the mid-nineteenth century, industrial technologies had led to the widespread adoption of fossil fuel energy in much of the world, particularly burning coal for heat, steam, and later electricity. In the twentieth century, the global energy landscape transformed once again as liquid fossil fuels, called hydrocarbons, gained global prominence. Closely related to the shift in fuels used by modern naval vessels during World War I, petroleum oil became the single most important global commodity, leading to shifts in global politics and great power competition as European and other powerful state actors sought secure supplies of oil and gas. With its relatively isolated position in North America located next door to the emerging US superpower, Canadian fossil fuel reserves became a key strategic resource for the United States, and exports of oil and gas became one of the backbones of the national economy. In the late twentieth and early twenty-first centuries, framed by a growing awareness of global climate change and the emergence of a multilateral governance regime devoted to reducing greenhouse gas emissions (see Chapter Nine), fossil fuel development became the source of some of the most divisive disputes in Canadian ecopolitics. In the context of the Anthropocene, the ecopolitics of energy and the environment are among the key points of interaction and contestation between citizens, civil society, global actors, and federal, provincial, territorial, and Indigenous governments in Canada.

This chapter explores energy as a central theme for the development of Canada and the source of some of its greatest ecopolitical disputes. The UN's SDG 7 calls for affordable and clean energy, drawing attention to the need for fair energy access for all, as well as the need to develop renewables to reduce emissions from fossil fuels (United Nations, 2017). However, oil and gas extraction today is responsible for the largest and growing share of greenhouse gas (GHG) emissions in Canada. Emissions from oil and gas have grown by 88 per cent since 1990 and accounted for 28 per cent of Canada's total GHGs in 2021 (Environment and Climate Change Canada, 2023b). Through the lens of ecopolitics, energy appears as a fundamental long-term process of ecosystem functioning, with patterns of entropy and exchange, transformation and consumption that have ethical implications for the future that span from generations to millennia. Examining timescales from prehistoric to modern eras brings the ecological risks of continued fossil fuel energy consumption into sharp relief. Exploring energy in historical and contemporary settings, this chapter analyzes how economic processes of production, consumption, and trade are governed by energy needs and uses, and how energy contributes to the goals of economic prosperity. It outlines some of the ways that energy is central to ecopolitics in Canada, while contributing to conditions of local and global ecological and human insecurity.

EARLY ENERGY

During the early period of European arrival and permanent settlement in North America, energy on both sides of the Atlantic was derived from various basic and renewable sources. Solar energy fuelled agricultural crops; heat from fire provided heating and cooking; rivers and streams powered water wheels and propelled boats and canoes across distances near and far; and wind-propelled ships sailed across the oceans, transporting both willing and unwilling passengers as well as goods, invasive species, and diseases. Most other energy used for everyday activities was supplied by the brute labour of humans and animals, including large numbers of enslaved people from the early seventeenth century onward. These forms of energy were drawn from ecological systems using technologies that reflected, on the one hand, Indigenous systems of knowledge and relationships with the land, and on the other the limits of sixteenth-, seventeenth-, and eighteenth-century technology prior to the innovations of the early modern era. The development of the steam engine in Europe, particularly James Watt's more efficient model invented in the 1760s, catalyzed the Industrial Revolution and led to the rapid transformation of global energy systems. Industrialization fundamentally altered the nature of the global political economy, and the key to industrialization was the ability to access increasingly concentrated, efficient forms of energy using ever-more complex technologies.

Sandwell (2016) divides the history of energy in Canada over the last 400 years into two energy eras: the organic and the mineral. The organic energy regime era derived from pre-industrial renewable sources such as wood fibre, biomass, animal labour, and kinetic energy extracted from wind and flowing water. Organic forms of energy were characterized by the renewable and decentralized nature of their energy flows. The mineral energy regime is characterized instead by concentrated sources of energy, necessitating access through high-tech interventions and industrialized extraction, thus requiring unprecedented levels of centralized control. These technologies include fossil fuels, electricity, and nuclear power, which Canada transitioned to significantly later than comparable countries. The persistent use of wood fuels, in particular, is attributable to the abundance of forests across the Canadian landscape. Approximately 39 per cent of Canada's land area is covered by forests, representing one of the three most globally significant forested areas, along with the Russian boreal and Amazon rainforest. This abundance also informed the emergence of the lumber and forestry industries as significant economic sectors in much of the country, particularly in heavily forested provinces such as British Columbia, Ontario, Quebec, and New Brunswick (see Chapter Five for more). Even prior to colonization, Indigenous Peoples in what would become Canada likely had among the highest rates of per capita energy usage in the world due to the combination of high energy demand for heating and light during the long winter months at relatively high latitudes, and the abundant availability of organic energy sources such as wood and running water.

Prior to transitioning to the mineral energy regime in the mid-twentieth century, Canada's energy system was closely entwined with its largely rural and agrarian economy. In that context, energy principally came from two sources: solar energy to produce animal muscle (i.e., the growth of crops to feed farm animals) and burning wood for heat. Horses in particular provided a key source of energy until well into the 1900s, including labour for agricultural, industrial, and transportation activities, including in cities and urban areas. The unusual confluence of a modern, industrializing economy that nonetheless retained a substantial component of its energy mix from organic sources complicates the historical division between the organic and mineral regimes in Canada. The use of horses and other animals co-existed at large scale for decades alongside wood fuels, coal, early fossil fuels, and hydroelectricity, making Canada unique among comparable societies of the time. Whereas western European countries were overwhelmingly reliant on fossil fuels by the mid-nineteenth century, and the United States by the early twentieth century, Sandwell (2016) notes that "it was only in 1955 that Canada reached the 90 per cent mark [for fossil energy], and it was only in 1980 that Canada joined other industrialized countries in obtaining 98 per cent of its energy from modern [sources]" (p. 21). Thus, although late to the fossil energy transition, by mid-last century Canada was fully committed, with fossil fuels set to play a critical role in the development of its ecopolitics.

OIL AND GAS

In many ways, energy is a broad meta-concept, but it has often been associated narrowly with fossil fuels. By the mid-nineteenth century, technological change had led to the widespread adoption of fossil fuel energy across much of Europe, Asia, and the Americas. The global expansion of fossil fuel energy consumption would lead the twentieth century to be called the "fossil century," with all of humanity integrated into a single "hydrocarbon society" premised on a global system of high-carbon political and economic organization (Yergin, 2003). The ubiquity of fossil fuels within the global energy mix made twentieth-century energy virtually synonymous with fossil fuels and fundamentally connected the political economy of coal, oil, and gas with issues of political power, organized labour, democracy, and human rights in many parts of the world (Mitchell, 2011).

The conflation of energy with fossil fuels has been a key, though contested, feature of Canadian ecopolitics. Oil was first drilled commercially in Canada in the mid-1800s, leading to the establishment of the first North American oil boom towns of Petrolia and Oil Springs in southern Ontario. These communities experienced only temporary prosperity as their accessible oil reserves were soon depleted, but they provided something of a model for boom-and-bust resource communities that would be replicated many times over across the country in the following years. In 1920, federal government prospectors struck an oil geyser at Norman Wells in the Northwest Territories, marking the beginning of sustained fossil fuel production in Canada. Northern Canada was far away from the infrastructure and markets necessary to support large-scale extraction, and production at Norman Wells ceased in 1924 before being restarted in 1935 to provide oil to the fast-growing mining sector in the territory. Production levels boomed when Norman Wells was expanded during World War II to provide fuel for the construction of the Alaska Highway and Canol pipeline projects and to support the Allied military effort in the Pacific. Shortly after the war, however, reduced demand led to the termination of the pipeline and reduction to modest pre-war levels of oil production. Oil came relatively early to northern Canada but would not endure as a significant feature of the region's political economy (see Chapter Eleven).

At the same time that oil production was declining in the north it was emerging as a major feature of western Canada's political economy, when the first major discovery was made in 1947 at Leduc, Alberta. The Alberta "oil patch" developed rapidly in the following years, with national implications. By 1957, Alberta possessed 85 per cent of all known crude oil reserves in Canada and had already achieved annual production of 137 million barrels (as well as 89 per cent of all Canadian natural gas production). "The significance of the oil discovery in Leduc in 1947 was not merely in terms of the size (an estimated

100 million barrels in reserve) or the quality of the oil (light crude suitable for gasoline production), but that the find literally transformed the economy of the province" (Fairbairn, 1980, p. 91). Alberta rapidly transformed from an agrarian economy to the heart of Canada's petro economy and a player in the global energy market. Alberta's fossil fuel transformation reconfigured political relations in Canada, with the rise of the western provinces' economic strength accompanied by increasing political power and political grievances toward the federal government in Ottawa. Throughout the 1970s and 1980s, disagreements between conservative provincial governments and the Liberal government of Pierre Trudeau were major issues in Canadian federalism, notably the animosity in western provinces caused by the National Energy Program implemented between 1980 and 1985 (discussed in Chapter Four). This federal policy was blamed for the rise of "western alienation" and the re-emergence of populist conservative politics, particularly in Alberta. It foreshadowed a similar dynamic in the first decades of the twenty-first century over federal regulation of Alberta's bitumen sands, environmental impact legislation, and restrictions on oil tankers on Canada's Pacific coast.

ALBERTA'S BITUMEN SANDS

Conventional oil production in Alberta peaked in 1973 amid high global energy prices caused by the first Organization of Petroleum Exporting Countries oil crisis. Although conventional production continued, the oil industry increasingly turned its attention to developing unconventional bitumen deposits in the Athabasca, Peace River, and Cold Lake regions of northern Alberta. The bitumen sands – a viscous mixture of clay and sand saturated by water and a particularly heavy type of oil – were first surveyed by federal agents in 1875, and the first bitumen mine opened in 1967. However, large-scale development remained uneconomical throughout the post–World War II period because of the high costs of extraction, discovery of large conventional oil deposits, and limited infrastructure and other practical obstacles to development. Various extraction schemes were put forth – including a proposed underground nuclear detonation to super-heat the bitumen and force it closer to the surface (Marsden, 2007) – but development remained modest until the late 1990s and early 2000s, when multiple factors, including rising global oil prices; rapidly growing oil demand in emerging economies, particularly China; declining production in many conventional oil fields; and geopolitical tensions with several key oil-producing states, renewed interest among American policymakers for a more reliable supplier to meet US energy demand (Chastko, 2004; Humphries, 2008; Levy, 2009).

By the turn of the millennium, Alberta's crude oil reserves had been depleted by around half, and bitumen had overtaken conventional oil as the majority of Alberta's fossil fuel energy production. A high-level panel chaired by then–US vice-president Dick Cheney concluded in 2001 that development of Alberta's bitumen sands "can be a pillar of sustained North American energy and economic security" (National Energy Policy Group, 2001, p. 8). The US Energy Information Administration (USEIA) stimulated further interest when it estimated in 2003 that at least 175 billion barrels of Alberta's bituminous oil – 11 per cent of the estimated 1.7 trillion barrels located in the province – were "economically recoverable," giving Canada, by way of Alberta, the second-largest oil reserves in the world after Saudi Arabia (Government of Alberta, 2023), later revised to third largest in the world after Venezuela. By 2007, bitumen accounted for 64 per cent of Alberta's oil production, and by 2017 it was nearly 90 per cent. Excluding bitumen, Alberta has around 39 per cent of Canada's oil reserves, only somewhat greater than Saskatchewan or Newfoundland. Including bitumen, however, Alberta has approximately 98 per cent of all proven oil reserves in Canada, making the growth of the bitumen sands the province's primary economic priority for the last three decades and the future of the fossil fuel energy sector in Alberta and the entire country.

Bitumen development has had a powerful impact on Canada's economy. The "bitumen boom" that followed the USEIA's 2003 estimates generated more than $10 billion of capital investment by 2009, with continued investments of approximately $10 billion per year between 2009 and 2022 (Government of Alberta, 2023; Alberta Energy Regulator, 2023). Bitumen has driven the Alberta economy, which in the mid-2000s underwent "the strongest period of economic growth ever recorded by any Canadian province" (Statistics Canada, 2006). In the wake of the 2008–9 global financial crisis, the bitumen sands were often described as an engine of the broader Canadian economy and were the centrepiece of the Harper Conservative government's vision of Canada as an emergent "energy superpower" (see Chapter Nine). Between 1995 and 2004, bitumen production had doubled to more than 1 million barrels of oil per day, and though the pace of growth slowed after the 2008–9 Great Recession amid slumping global oil prices, the 1.7 million barrels of crude bitumen Alberta produced per day in 2011 had doubled to 3.3 million

Figure 6.1. Primary Energy Production in Canada

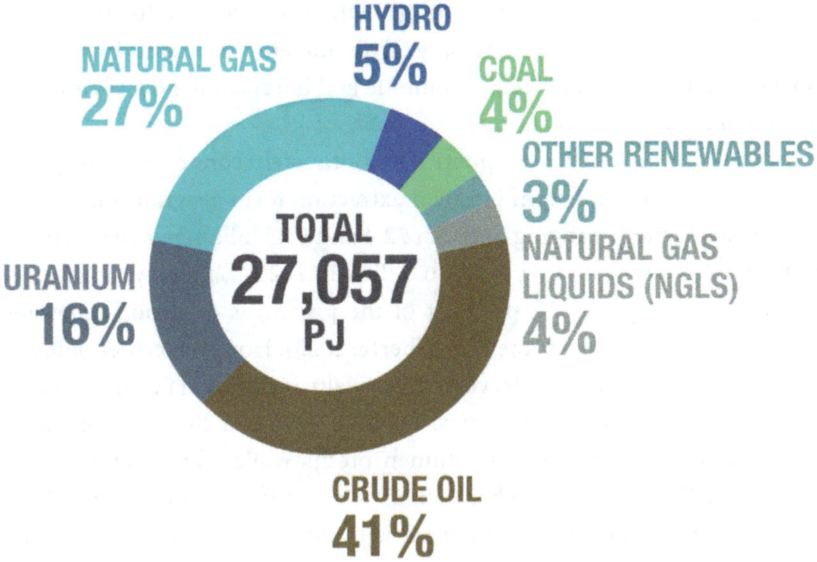

Source: "Energy Fact Book, 2023–2024." Energy Systems Sector, Natural Resources Canada, 2024. Reproduced with the permission of the Department of Natural Resources, 2024.

barrels per day by 2022 (Alberta Energy Regulator, 2023; Energy Resources Conservation Board, 2012). To put this in perspective, that is enough oil to fill roughly 210 Olympic-sized swimming pools per day every day of the year.

The flip side to the bitumen sands' contribution to the Canadian and Albertan economies is their contribution to Canada's and Alberta's GHG emissions. Between 1990 and 2021, Canada's national GHG emissions increased by 13.9 per cent despite significant decreases in emissions in its two largest provinces: Ontario (16 per cent) and Quebec (8 per cent) (Environment and Climate Change Canada, 2023b). By contrast, Alberta's emissions increased by nearly 55 per cent over the same period, with emissions from bitumen specifically surging from 15.1 megatonnes in 1990 to 85.3 megatonnes in 2021. Put differently, Alberta's emissions increase from bitumen alone during the roughly three decades of the global multilateral regime to reduce GHG emissions and address climate change has driven Canada's overall emissions increase despite steep reductions in the central and Atlantic provinces (see Chapter Nine). British Columbia's, Saskatchewan's, Manitoba's, and Yukon's emissions also increased during this time, but their collective increase of 36.1 megatonnes over 30 years is only a fraction of Alberta's total increase of 89.6 megatonnes during the same period. In short, the growth of bitumen production cannot be separated from Canada's increasing GHG emissions relative to 1990, nor its corresponding failure to meet its domestic and international GHG emissions reduction targets since that time.

In the case of Alberta, ecopolitics are intimately connected with political economy. Royalties from bitumen extraction form a significant share of provincial revenues, ranging between $2.4 and $5.2 billion per year between 2006 and 2021, and surging to $11.6 billion in 2021–22. That year, bitumen royalties accounted for 72 per cent of the province's total non-renewable resource revenues (Government of Alberta, 2023). However, critics note that Alberta has significantly undervalued its royalty regime and failed to account for the full costs of the oil industry. Between 1986 and 2012, oil companies reaped $260 billion in pre-tax bitumen profits while governments earned less than $25 billion (Campbell, 2012). One analysis found that Alberta received around 4.5 per cent of the market value of the fossil fuels extracted from the province in royalties, increasing to 6 per cent when other taxes and fees are considered. The remainder is privatized as corporate profit, leading some to decry the "misplaced generosity" shown by Alberta toward the fossil fuel sector (Campanella, 2012, p. 9). This reflects what a former provincial energy minister described as a "give-it-away" formula, whereby investment in the oil patch was stimulated with a royalty regime that transferred the bulk of Alberta's oil wealth to corporate stakeholders from outside the province (Nikiforuk, 2010, p. 159). Moreover, it fails to account for the unfunded liabilities left behind by the oil industry to be borne by federal and provincial taxpayers. A recent journalistic investigation found more than $30 billion in liabilities related to cleaning up so-called orphan oil wells alone, with Alberta's energy regulator in possession of less than 1 per cent of that sum in security from the industry (Anderson, 2023; Wilt, 2018). The emerging prospect that the actual costs of the oil industry *to* Alberta vastly outstrip the benefits *for* Albertans threatens to upend the social contract in that province, where for nearly 80 years the oil sector has been legitimized as the engine of shared prosperity. Should it turn out that private corporations have exploited Alberta's resources then abandoned it without properly funding the clean-up of those activities, the political, economic, and social consequences could be significant.

Box 6.1 discusses the ecopolitics of transnational energy projects using the Keystone XL Pipeline as an example.

BOX 6.1. The Keystone XL Pipeline

The bitumen sands have been intimately linked to national debates over expanding pipeline infrastructure to transport bitumen from Alberta to the global market. Multiple pipeline projects have attracted public and political attention and disagreement, serving as proxies for broader debates over climate and energy policy. The Keystone XL pipeline project is a notable example that featured prominently in contrasting visions of North American energy security, the Canada–US trade relationship, and the future of the bitumen sands. First proposed in 2005 to transport additional bitumen from Alberta to the United States, thus relieving the problem of insufficient pipeline capacity that has depressed prices for Alberta crude oil and limited opportunities for bitumen sands growth, Keystone XL was approved by Canadian regulators in 2007. The proposal encountered fierce opposition from environmental organizations and Indigenous Peoples along the route, leading to widespread protests and intense political pressure on the Obama Administration. Prior to the 2012 US election, Obama announced a decision to delay a final decision, which was denounced by some political commentators. To them, "the construction of the Keystone XL pipeline should have been an easy diplomatic and economic decision … [and] Obama's choice marked a triumph of campaign posturing over pragmatism and diplomacy" (Burney & Hampson, 2012). Then–Prime Minister Stephen Harper similarly opined that approving Keystone XL should be a "no-brainer" for the United States and lobbied hard for its approval, but President Obama rejected the project in the final 14 months of his presidency.

Keystone XL represented a significant challenge for the Obama Administration, challenging its environmental bona fides while posing a significant electoral issue during the 2012 presidential campaign and a bilateral irritant with Canada. During the review period, Obama invoked climate change to justify his administration's evident reluctance to approve the pipeline. He situated Keystone XL and America's continued reliance on "dirty" sources of foreign energy (including Alberta's bitumen sands) in the context of the global climate crisis, specifically listing hazards including extreme weather, sea-level rise, and access to freshwater (Greaves, 2017). Ultimately, in his November 2015 statement rejecting the pipeline, Obama deemed that approval "would not serve the national interest of the United States" because "approving this project would have undercut [America's] global leadership [on climate change]." Although he acknowledged that Keystone XL was not "the express lane to climate disaster proclaimed by others," Obama argued that rejecting the pipeline would not significantly affect the US economy, while accepting it would worsen America's energy security by maintaining its reliance on "dirty fossil fuels" (see also Chapter Nine).

President Obama also presented an argument never before made by a US president or leader of a major industrialized economy: Noting the success of US shale gas production and significant reduction in demand for foreign oil, he reiterated that transitioning to a clean energy economy would require continued, though diminishing, consumption of fossil fuels. Then, anticipating the COP21 climate summit in Paris occurring in the following weeks, he said: "Ultimately, if we're going to prevent large parts of this Earth from becoming not only inhospitable but uninhabitable in our lifetimes, we're going to have to keep some fossil fuels in the ground rather than burn them and release more dangerous pollution into the sky" (quoted in Greaves, 2017, p. 113). Obama's acknowledgement of the need to "keep it in the ground" – a popular rallying cry of climate change activists – was a milestone brought about by the Keystone XL pipeline.

Although Obama's successor tried to revive the project, it became mired in the courts, and ultimately the construction permit that Donald Trump had attempted to issue was revoked by Joe Biden on his first day in office in early 2021. After nearly 16 years of political tug-of-war spanning four presidencies and three Canadian governments, the Keystone XL project appeared to be dead, though it was among the first issues Trump raised after being re-elected in November 2024. But it serves as a warning of the deeply contested nature of building new fossil fuel infrastructure in the era of the climate crisis and the difficulty of getting transnational projects approved given the number of regulatory and political chokepoints where opponents can apply leverage to stop them. It also demonstrates the adage that to stop new extractive projects activists need to win again and again, whereas to get them built industry and governments that support such projects only need to win once.

LIQUEFIED NATURAL GAS

The complex ecopolitics of liquified natural gas (LNG) extraction is illustrated by the $40 billion LNG Canada project in British Columbia. Approved by its investors in 2018, it consists of a coastal LNG export terminal at Kitimat, fed by the 670-kilometre Coastal GasLink (CGL) pipeline from the northeast interior region of the province. The joint venture is supported by some of the largest fossil fuel corporations in the world, including Shell, Petronas, PetroChina, Mitsubishi, and the Korean Gas Corporation. It is the largest private sector and natural resource investment in Canadian history and the cornerstone of the NDP provincial government's "CleanBC" economic policy (Government of British Columbia, 2019). The project promises to provide 10,000 jobs during construction and up to 950 permanent jobs once fully operational, as well as CAD$5 billion in additional provincial GDP per year and CAD$23 billion in new revenues over the life of the project (LNG Canada, 2023). With predicted benefits in the rest of Canada estimated at CAD$2 billion per year, including approximately CAD$500 million in new federal revenues and increased value for all Canadian LNG exports of between CAD$519 million–$5.8 billion per year depending on market prices (Coad et al., 2016; Cross, 2018), the governments of Canada and British Columbia have strongly supported the project.

Yet LNG sits at the intersection of three critical policy areas for ecopolitics in Canada: clean economic growth, GHG emissions reductions to combat climate change, and the inherent and constitutional rights of Indigenous Peoples. The BC and federal governments insist a new LNG industry can be established without compromising emissions reduction targets, but environmentalists have criticized the project based on Canada's poor historical performance in reducing its GHG emissions and the inconsistency between developing a whole new fossil fuel sector and the province's desire to position itself as "CleanBC" (Hughes, 2015). Some see British Columbia as hypocritically championing its own LNG pipelines while opposing new bitumen pipelines from Alberta to the Pacific coast. The province's opposition to the Trans Mountain Pipeline Expansion project even led to a brief trade war with Alberta in 2018, though both provinces had social democratic governments at the time.

Government support for LNG Canada exposes challenging issues related to the political relationship between Canada and Indigenous Peoples in the country. In 1998, the Supreme Court of Canada ruled in favour of a group of Wet'suwet'en and neighbouring Gitxsan hereditary chiefs in a legal case attempting to resolve land title over 58,000 square kilometres of unceded territory in central British Columbia. In the *Delgamuukw* case, the chiefs argued that they have maintained a traditional system of governance over their territories through the practice of feasting, and thus never ceded jurisdiction over their land. The Supreme Court affirmed that Wet'suwet'en hereditary chiefs remain the titleholders of their traditional lands, called Yintah, and that British Columbia and Canada have a constitutional duty to consult with them about developments on their territories.

However, approval for the Coastal GasLink pipeline through Wet'suwet'en territory was negotiated with each First Nation along the pipeline route, including the Wet'suwet'en, through the elected chiefs and band councils created through the federal *Indian Act, 1876*, an infamous piece of colonial legislation used to control and oppress Indigenous Peoples in Canada (see Chapter Four). Following the announcement of the project, hereditary chiefs from all five Wet'suwet'en clans asserted that the elected chiefs and councils lacked authority under Wet'suwet'en law to make such a decision. Claiming their own jurisdiction over Wet'suwet'en territory, the hereditary chiefs rejected the pipeline's passage through their lands and expressed their intention to resist it (Bellrichard, 2019).

Shortly after LNG Canada was launched in October 2018, a campaign of civil disobedience and territorial occupation was reinvigorated by members of the Wet'suwet'en people. Checkpoints were established by members of the Unist'ot'en and Gidim'ten clans to prevent construction workers from accessing the intended route of the Coastal GasLink pipeline. The Royal Canadian Mounted Police subsequently enforced a court injunction supporting Coastal GasLink's right to enter the territory, launching the first of repeated police raids on the Uni'stot'en and Gidim'ten encampments between 2019 and 2021, resulting in dozens of arrests. In early 2020, the conflict escalated further when Wet'suwet'en land defenders and allies blockaded highways and rail lines across Canada in solidarity and symbolically obstructed the main doors of the British Columbia legislature for weeks. Although the movement was disrupted by the onset of the COVID-19 pandemic, the checkpoints have experienced continued police raids, which have in turn been criticized for excessive force, lack of transparency, and unlawful arrests of journalists and Wet'suwet'en members (De Souza & Simmons, 2022).

The situation is further complicated by disagreement within the Wet'suwet'en hereditary leadership. Three female leaders who support the Coastal GasLink project alleged their hereditary titles and traditional roles were removed by other hereditary chiefs in punishment (Jang, 2019a). The women claimed their authority was usurped, violating traditional protocols and compromising the governance process. Critics contend the three matriarchs are funded by the BC government and Coastal GasLink to sow dissent among the Wet'suwet'en, even though the women leaders claim a majority of Wet'suwet'en people support the pipeline (Jang, 2019b). The dispute highlights the legal ambiguities around the respective roles of legislated and hereditary Indigenous governance structures. As former chief of the Wet'suwet'en First Nation and CEO of the First Nations LNG Alliance Karen Ogden Toews stated: "There is no doubt that the hereditary leadership has some responsibility for land and natural resources within our territory. At the same time, the elected leadership has responsibility for our people and the external affairs of their First Nation" (McBride, 2019). This struggle over legitimacy exposes deep divisions between elected First Nations leadership recognized by federal and provincial governments and hereditary chiefs who assert their rightful leadership of their communities. In this case, the disputes complicate both the representation of the Wet'suwet'en externally and the abilities of the BC and Canadian governments to fulfill their consultative responsibilities under section 35 of the *Constitution Act, 1982*.

The Wet'suwet'en conflict captures the complexity of Canadian ecopolitics as it relates to reconciliation, governance, and the legitimacy of decision making over land use and natural resource extraction on Indigenous territories. It should come as no surprise that members of Indigenous communities express different views about the role that natural resource extraction should play on their lands. But with the Coastal GasLink pipeline approved by elected chiefs and councils, and land defenders claiming legitimacy from the authority of the hereditary Wet'suwet'en leadership, the dispute highlights the conflict between legislated and traditional First Nations governance structures in British Columbia and elsewhere in Canada over "who decides?" The natural resource sector's reliance on transporting commodities to market using infrastructure that crosses both First Nations reserve lands and traditional territories poses a series of challenges for ecopolitics in Canada. In addition to the local and global environmental consequences of fossil fuel–intensive or producing activities, new infrastructure projects highlight the tensions that exist within Canadian society and its constitutional system. LNG Canada and the Coastal GasLink pipeline are only a recent example of a resource project receiving strong support from state, private actors, and elected Indigenous leaders only to encounter uncertainty because of grassroots opposition on the basis of underlying questions of Indigenous rights, title, and the appropriate source of Indigenous political authority.

Recently, the Government of British Columbia has doubled down on controversial projects to expand the production of LNG through new fracking, pipeline infrastructure, and port transportation facilities in the north of the province. The Prince Rupert Gas Transmission pipeline project is facing protests similar to those that led to confrontations on the Coastal GasLink pipeline route. This time, however, the pipeline's proposed route is supported by Western LNG and the Nisga'a Lisims government, who have purchased the pipeline from the original ownership of TC Energy (Gottlieb, 2024). Despite the intervening passage of enabling legislation for UNDRIP in British Columbia and changes to the environmental assessment process, the project appears to be proceeding quickly. Environmentalists have raised concerns that the Indigenous ownership of the project is on "paper only" and that it is providing a front for accessing government loan guarantees with little substantial involvement of the people living in the region. At the time of writing the project is undergoing a process of consultation and environmental review, even as construction is already slated to begin. Echoing the divisive conflicts over the Coastal GasLink project, the Prince Rupert project raises many of the same questions and issues regarding Indigenous legal rights and the government's obligation to include cumulative impacts in environmental assessment.

The question of cumulative impacts of LNG development raises further issues regarding the strategy of energy development that continues to follow the established Canadian model of building infrastructure for carbon-intensive production facilities for export markets. The two projects discussed above are joined by others in various stages of development: Woodfibre LNG and Cedar LNG. It is argued that such development "locks in" continued emissions-producing projects in the future, raising the financial and environmental costs indefinitely. Hydraulic fracturing (known as fracking) is the most widespread technology for extracting gas in Canada and releases chemical pollutants that have many known health impacts in the remote communities where the facilities are located, including increased risks of cancer (Elliott et al., 2017). Other emissions from LNG, particularly methane, are often unaccounted for in emissions reduction targets (see Case Study 9.2 on methane for details on this). In addition, there are doubts around the economic viability of further LNG exports bound for the Asian markets since demand is declining in Japan and Korea while China's market is fluctuating (Cunningham, 2024). Much of the argument in favour of LNG exports has been based on the premise that switching to LNG from coal and oil would reduce overall emissions in Asia, however there is little evidence to date to support the idea that natural gas is a "bridge fuel" in this way. Similarly, expansion of LNG has sometimes been justified on geopolitical grounds, as a more secure replacement for the removal of Russian gas exports to Europe following the war with Ukraine. Despite these concerns, and despite the government's continued commitment to emissions reductions (see more in Chapter Nine), provincial and federal governments continue to be committed to LNG expansion.

ELECTRICITY

Electricity production in Canada is diverse, complex, and deeply entangled with ecopolitics related to climate policy, regional interests, and Indigenous Peoples' treaty and constitutional rights. The electrification of Canadian society accompanied the transition from an organic to a mineral energy regime in the mid-twentieth century and reflected the energy sources available in different parts of the country. Recently, concerns about climate change have shifted the energy discussion, as the world looks toward low-emission sources of energy and more innovative ways to mitigate carbon emissions while still meeting large-scale energy needs. Many Canadian energy sources – such as hydroelectricity, nuclear, and renewables – have low GHG emissions, while others, including coal and natural gas, are carbon intensive. Nonetheless, electricity production in Canada has seen a remarkable 45 per cent decline in emissions between 1990 and 2021, largely due to the elimination of coal-fired electricity in Ontario in the mid-2000s (Canada Energy Regulator, 2023). Here, again, regionalism is a key factor; coal-fired electricity remains dominant in Alberta and Saskatchewan, which together account for three-quarters of all electricity-related GHG emissions in Canada (see Figure 6.2). Oil, gas, and coal still account for around 18 per cent of all Canadian electricity generation, though the federal government's Clean Electricity Regulations set a target for Canada's electrical grid to produce net-zero emissions by 2035 that will put significant pressure on provinces to further reduce their use of fossil fuels (Government of Canada, 2024). With highly polluting provinces such as

Figure 6.2. Electricity Production in Canada, 2021

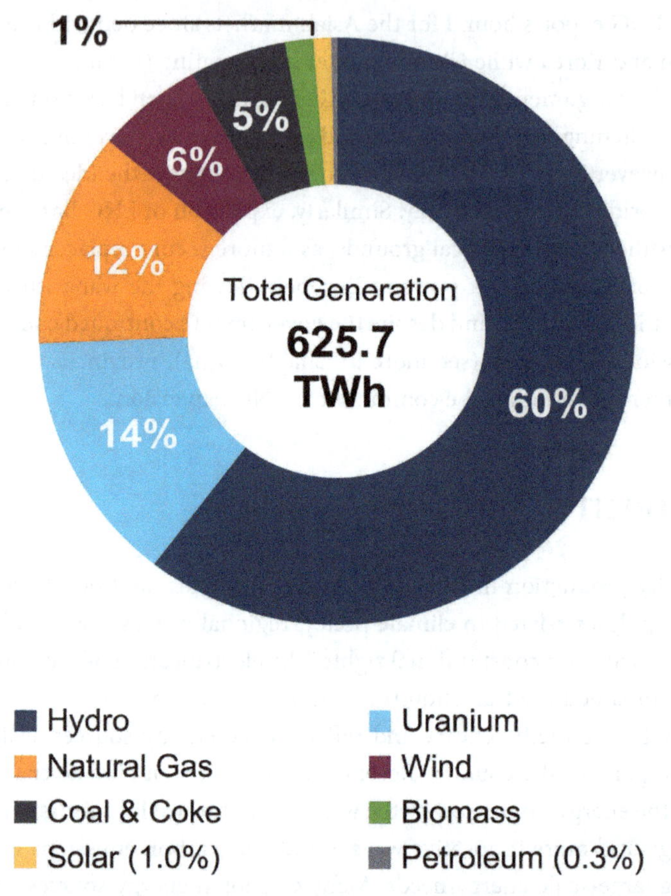

Source: Adapted from "Figure 2: Electricity Generation by Fuel Type (2021)." Canada Energy Regulator. Accessed September 25, 2024. www.cer-rec.gc.ca/en/data-analysis/energy-markets/provincial-territorial-energy-profiles/provincial-territorial-energy-profiles-canada.html. Reproduced with permission.

Alberta and Saskatchewan indicating their intention to resist this new policy, it is likely the Clean Electricity Regulations will eventually be decided by the courts. In the meantime, growth in Canadian electricity production will come mostly from low-carbon sources.

Hydroelectricity

The dominant source of energy in Canada's electricity system is hydroelectricity produced from dams on rivers and lakes. By the early 1880s, some of the first hydroelectric-generating stations in North America had been built on the American side of Niagara Falls to power new factories, and the potential for hydroelectricity to fuel southern Ontario's industrial growth became apparent. Today, Canada is the world's fourth-largest producer of hydroelectricity after China, Brazil, and the United States. Hydro makes up more than 60 per cent of all electricity produced in the country, by far the largest share of any single source, and provides more than 80 per cent of electricity generated in British Columbia, Manitoba, Newfoundland and Labrador, Quebec, and Yukon, and more than a quarter of electricity in Ontario.

By the mid-twentieth century, the goal of new dams shifted from provincial demands for local industrial development to exporting power to feed the massive American manufacturing sector. Under Canada's Constitution, energy is primarily a provincial matter, with the federal government playing a role in energy exports and reviewing major projects through the National Energy Board. With the ability to transport power over longer and longer distances, there often emerged struggles between the provincial and federal orders of government, as well as between rural and urban communities. Over time, energy shifted to reflect more centralized systems capable of powering factories and fuelling the export market. Some came to believe that, similar to the railway, interprovincial hydroelectricity grids could unite the country, while others saw more scope for province building through publicly owned hydroelectric utility companies (Froschauer, 1999).

Early hydroelectric development in Canada occurred in conjunction with the growth of energy needs for mining and minerals, and eventually large-scale hydro projects began to appear across the country. Multinational copper and aluminium investments were lured to Canada at least in part due to the promise of cheap hydroelectricity (Sandwell, 2016, p. 17). Soon, the mighty northern rivers of British Columbia, Labrador, Manitoba, and Quebec were walled, diverted, and dammed to create large reservoirs. These came with many environmental problems: New lakes sometimes covered Indigenous burial grounds, pulp mill effluent floated downriver to the ocean, and salmon were blocked from their traditional spawning grounds (Froschauer, 1999). The environmental and social costs of new dams also include flooded lands, exposure to mercury concentrations, loss of fisheries, and sedimentation of water supplies. These affect those in rural, remote areas the most, and Indigenous Peoples most strongly. Due to this, battles over both the construction of new dams and the distribution of revenues have characterized hydroelectric development in Canada (see Case Study 6.1).

CASE STUDY 6.1. James Bay and the Cree

On April 30, 1971, Quebec premier Robert Bourassa announced plans for a massive hydroelectric-power development in northern Quebec, the largest in North America. Hydro-Québec would build a series of dams, dikes, reservoirs, and power stations and divert major rivers to harness massive amounts of power in the James Bay territory, known as Eeyou Istchee by the Cree people (Royer, 2016, p. 35). The government believed the James Bay Project was the key to its economic future, as well as a means to build independence for the province, because cheap power would encourage new industry and create jobs. The Eeyou/Eenou of Eeyou Istchee (Cree) were not consulted by Quebec on this proposed mega project, though the flooding would affect the Eeyou/Eenou traditional way of life. On November 11, 1975, the Cree and Inuit signed an agreement with Canada to renounce their claim to certain land in northern Quebec in return for $225 million. The far-reaching James Bay and Northern Quebec Agreement (JBNQA) also gave the band special hunting and fishing rights and more opportunity for self-government. It was the first modern comprehensive land claims settlement in the country.

The Cree and Inuit reaped certain benefits from the JBNQA. In their communities, new homes with satellite dishes replaced unmaintained shacks, while new schools and modern health care clinics were built. But the Cree traditional way of life declined as the gigantic hydroelectric project flooded vast areas of the land. The Eeyou/Eenou also became concerned about polluted drinking water, flooded trap lines, and mercury contamination in fish stocks. Chronic social problems such as alcohol abuse and domestic violence increased in the communities.

The James Bay Project helped Quebec become an economic powerhouse, as cheap electricity attracted foreign investment and the sale of surplus power brought in cash. By 1988 Quebec sold electricity worth $700 million a year to Canadian provinces and American states. In 1986, Premier Bourassa – back in power – announced plans to launch the second phase of the project, called the Great Whale Project. This development would generate power entirely for export and was once again proposed with no input from Indigenous Peoples, despite a self-government agreement that had been in place with the Quebec government since 1984.

Fearing further environmental damage, the James Bay Cree launched a massive campaign in the late 1980s to stop the Great Whale Project. They attracted powerful allies among environmental groups and Indigenous rights supporters. As part of the opposition to the Great Whale Project, the groups organized a voyage of the *Odeyak*, a Cree–Inuit canoe that had travelled some 1,500 kilometres to arrive in New York City on Earth Day. The Great Whale Project suffered a crippling blow when New York State cancelled its billion-dollar hydroelectric contract with Quebec in 1992. Two years later, the federal government ordered Hydro-Québec to rework the environmental study it had prepared for the second phase of the project. On November 18, 1994, Quebec premier Jacques Parizeau announced the Great Whale Project was no longer a priority for his government and put construction indefinitely on hold (Froschauer, 1999, p. 77).

Critical Thinking Questions

1. Why do you think the Cree in northern Quebec have been more successful in achieving their independence than other Indigenous Peoples?
2. To what degree did the James Bay and Northern Quebec Agreement act as a precedent for other treaties across the country?

Although hydroelectric power is now a mainstay in Canada, new projects are often controversial and can involve deep disputes between provinces, local communities, and Indigenous communities. The controversial Site C Dam in British Columbia has been the subject of intense debate because of its potential impacts on the environment and Indigenous land rights. While it is a renewable energy project, critics argue that the dam's reservoir will flood large areas of agricultural and culturally significant land along northern British Columbia's Peace River, leading to biodiversity loss, disruption of ecosystems, and harmful impacts on local First Nations. There is also concern that the electricity that Site C will produce is intended to support the province's growing LNG industry in the central and northern parts of the province, which means that "green" hydroelectricity will be used to support the extraction of fossil fuels that make it impossible for British Columbia to meet its emissions reduction targets (Hughes, 2015; Lee, 2021). Site C is thus implicated in the debates over the province's commitment to LNG and the disputed Coastal GasLink pipeline, discussed above.

Elsewhere, hydroelectricity has been a source of major dispute between the neighbouring provinces of Quebec and Newfoundland and Labrador. Beginning in the late 1960s, Newfoundland and Labrador approved damming the Churchill River in Labrador, leading to what was then the largest engineering project in North America. Once completed in 1974, the Churchill Falls

Generating Station comprised 88 dykes along a 64-kilometre stretch of river with a drainage area larger than Ireland, becoming the second-largest hydro project in Canada. However, geography limited the opportunities to get this electricity to customers, and in 1969 the company building the dam signed a long-term agreement to sell most of the power it produced to Quebec at rates that would turn out to be considerably cheaper in the long run than other market rates for electricity. Faced with the prospect of Quebec paying below-market rates until the year 2041, Newfoundland challenged the agreement in court, arguing that Hydro-Québec's high profits while paying such low rates for power from Churchill Falls warranted renegotiation. In 2018, the Supreme Court of Canada ruled in favour of Hydro-Québec, affirming the status quo of cheap hydroelectricity from Labrador to Quebec for decades to come.

In the interim, Newfoundland and Labrador proceeded with a second hydro project on the Lower Churchill River. Instead of being sent west to Quebec, this electricity is sent east and south to the island of Newfoundland and on to Nova Scotia via underwater cables. After being announced in 2010, the Muskrat Falls dam and transmission lines were finally completed in 2023 at nearly double their original budget of $6 billion, and not without further controversy related to the rights and title of Indigenous Peoples affected by the environmental impacts of large-scale development. After protests by Indigenous groups, the government of Newfoundland announced a commission to study ways of mitigating these impacts, particularly the production of methylmercury from decomposing plant matter beneath the flooded hydro reservoir. But the province never implemented the recommendations, instead offering lump sum payments of $10 million each to the three Inuit and Innu groups affected, two of whom accepted. The final report of a public inquiry released in 2020 found the province had failed in its responsibilities by determining that Muskrat Falls should proceed despite a questionable business case, failure to consider all options, and insufficient consultation with Indigenous Peoples. Nonetheless, in 2021 the Government of Canada announced more than $5 billion in funding to support the completion of the project, amounting to a huge federal subsidy so that Newfoundland and Labrador can sell unexpectedly expensive hydroelectricity at a profit to the other Atlantic provinces.

Nuclear Power

Although hydroelectricity is by far the largest source of electricity in Canada, there are many other sources of electric power across the country. After hydro, the largest single source of electricity in Canada is nuclear power produced from uranium, which accounts for 15 per cent of Canadian electricity. Canada was an early leader in nuclear technology research, having contributed to the Manhattan Project to develop nuclear weapons during World War II and developing a civilian nuclear energy program after the war through the Crown corporation Atomic Energy of Canada Limited. The first nuclear generator in Canada was an early model of the CANDU reactor in the early 1960s built at the pioneering nuclear research facility at Chalk River, Ontario. In the 1970s and 1980s, more advanced CANDU reactors were designed and built, becoming a mainstay of Canadian electricity production and a major export product to other countries. Of the 25 nuclear reactors ever built in Canada, only three were built outside of Ontario, with the two generators at Gentilly, Quebec, permanently closed in 2012. As a result, only Ontario and New Brunswick currently have nuclear reactors, though Saskatchewan is one of the world's leading jurisdictions for uranium mining, accounting for 13 per cent of global production in 2019.

While it is a low-carbon energy source, concerns over nuclear waste disposal, risk of accidents, and high upfront construction costs have influenced nuclear power's role in Canada's renewable energy transition. Environmental organizations such as Greenpeace and Sierra Club Canada have long opposed the development of nuclear power, and public opinion across Canada has generally been more opposed to it than favourable. British Columbia explicitly banned all uranium mining and nuclear power generation across the province in 2010. While other provinces and industry have expressed interest in the prospect of small modular nuclear reactors, such as to power remote mines or oil and gas projects, the current reality is that nuclear power generation in Canada is overwhelmingly concentrated in southern Ontario, where it accounts for nearly 60 per cent of that province's electricity and is thus vital to the national economy (Canada Energy Regulator, 2023). The nuclear generators at Darlington and Bruce, among the largest reactors in the world, are undergoing a multiyear $25 billion retrofit to extend their lifespan, continuing Ontario's reliance on nuclear power for decades to come. In 2023, Ontario approved construction of the first new full-scale nuclear generator in three decades at its Bruce nuclear facility at an undisclosed cost.

The context of global climate change has significantly increased the appeal of nuclear power as a reliable, low-carbon alternative with additional environmental and health benefits due to reduced air pollution. Groups like Doctors for Nuclear Energy (2021) contend that the climate and health benefits of nuclear power outweigh concerns related to waste disposal or risk of accident, and instead "see nuclear energy as an irreplaceable part of the just transition to a low-carbon future." The Government of Canada has expressed renewed interest in supporting new nuclear power generation, but given public and political opposition from environmental organizers and local communities afraid of the potential consequences, and the fact that most electrical utilities in Canada are either provincially or privately owned, the path toward expanded nuclear power generation in Canada remains uncertain.

Renewables

Most recently, Canada has begun to develop its significant potential for renewable electricity production from solar, wind, tidal, and geothermal sources. From negligible amounts of renewable electricity before 2005, solar and wind production made up 5 per cent of Canada's electric grid in 2019, mostly from wind power installed in Ontario, Quebec, and Alberta. Solar photovoltaic installations, both residential and commercial, continue to grow, especially in sunnier regions like British Columbia, Alberta, and Saskatchewan, and additional large-scale projects are under development in multiple provinces. The deployment of wind and solar farms has been increasing steadily as both technologies become more cost effective, but new developments in certain jurisdictions have come under political pressure. Shortly after taking power in Ontario in 2018, Doug Ford's Progressive Conservative government spent more than $230 million to cancel renewable energy contracts signed by the previous government before reversing this decision in 2023 and announcing the intent to develop new wind and solar projects. Also in 2023, the United Conservative government in Alberta announced a temporary moratorium on new renewable projects pending assessment of environmental impact guidelines. The decision was widely seen as intervening in the existing energy market in favour of fossil fuel electricity, which Alberta relies on heavily, and was criticized by both environmentalists and the business community.

Other potential sources of renewable energy in Canada include substantial tidal and geothermal resources, but both are limited by the specific geographies where they can be tapped. Tidal energy is concentrated along the coastlines, and wave energy technology is still in the early stages of development, with challenges related to high costs and operating in harsh marine environments remaining (also discussed in Chapter Eight). Geothermal energy in Canada is relatively untapped but has potential in specific regions with favourable geological conditions, mostly in the west, where it could provide a stable and continuous source of renewable energy. Geothermal energy has low GHG emissions and requires minimal land and freshwater, but exploration is risky and development is expensive. Though there are several experimental sites in operation, the only commercial geothermal power plant in Canada was commissioned in January 2023 in northern Alberta. However, with government investment in geothermal energy in Saskatchewan, Alberta, Yukon, and British Columbia, there are considerable opportunities for future development. Debates about these and other new renewable projects and regulations remain active across Canada and demonstrate the complex interactions between economic, political, social, and ecological factors that make up Canadian ecopolitics.

ELECTRIC VEHICLES: THE FUTURE OF TRANSPORTATION?

The transportation sector is responsible for around 23 per cent of global GHG emissions, over 70 per cent of which come from road transport (Intergovernmental Panel on Climate Change, 2014). Electric vehicles (EVs) have long been used in mass transit on land (trains, trolleys, buses), and while there is plenty of room to expand this sector, the personal vehicle market is the big prize: There are hundreds of millions of vehicles on the road worldwide, most of which will become scrap within a couple of decades. When global auto sales declined in 2020 in the shadow of the COVID-19 pandemic, EV sales actually increased by some 43 per cent to more than 3 million, which was over 4 per cent of global vehicle sales (Carrington, 2021). In 2021 this doubled again, with some 6.6 million EVs sold worldwide, representing 10 per cent of all auto sales; this marks a 50-fold increase over the previous decade (IEA, 2022).

Some major car manufacturers have committed to entirely phasing out internal-combustion engine vehicles in the next decade. Government policies and subsidies have helped spur sales, along with installation of infrastructure. The greatest push has been in China, which accounted for around half of global EV sales and almost 90 per cent of the market for electric two- and three-wheelers. The largest markets are the United Kingdom, Europe, and the United States; Canada might be seen as something of a laggard, as only about 4 per cent of new car sales in 2021 were EVs. Challenges in Canada include range limits and distances, cold weather, and limited charging infrastructure, but these are not insurmountable. Technology and infrastructure is improving steadily, and along with many other governments Canada has committed to phasing out fossil-fuelled personal vehicles (IEA, 2022, p. 47); its first target is to achieve 10 per cent of all vehicle sales being EVs by 2025 and to reach 100 per cent non-emitting cars and light-duty trucks by 2035. This is seen as essential to achieving net-zero emissions in the transport sector by 2050 (Canadian Press, 2021).

Canada is actively collaborating in coordination and technology promotion through groups like the **Electric Vehicles Initiative (EVI)**, which Canada co-leads with China under the International Energy Agency's Clean Energy Ministerial. The EVI oversees the EV30@30 Campaign, which has a collective "aspirational goal" to achieve a 30 per cent EV share of new light vehicle sales by 2030, along with the "Global Commercial Vehicle Drive to Zero" campaign that targets transformation of commercial EVs. Canada's automotive sector is closely tied to that of the US industry, too, and is impacted by the comings and goings of EV policies in that country.

Looking inward, federal policies and aspirations can be helped (or hindered) by relevant provincial policies. Quebec and British Columbia have tended to take the lead on EVs among the provinces, while the biggest market, Ontario, has been less consistent in its support as government priorities change. For instance, soon after his election in 2018, Ontario premier Doug Ford cancelled virtually all EV incentives and even oversaw the removal of 24 chargers at GO Transit stations as a way of appealing to his conservative base (Xing, 2019). Resistance stems from legacy industries faced with the prospect of declining demand for their products; calls for decarbonization pathways need to heed the corresponding demand for a "just transition," which among other things would entail an equitable distribution of costs and benefits, especially with regard to employment (Office of the Auditor General of Canada, 2022). In Canada this is particularly acute in relation to the oil and gas sectors, which indirectly employ some 600,000 Canadians (Caranci et al., 2021), but proponents argue that the jobs will follow if governments guide the transition through strong policies to address climate change (IRENA, 2021).

Many forms of transportation are less amenable to electrification: Air and sea travel, long-distance trucking, mining and construction vehicles, and farm equipment are much further from mass electrification than automobiles. Moreover, replacing gas-powered cars with EVs will do nothing to address issues of urban traffic congestion, allocation of public space, the high cost of road and highway construction and maintenance, safety from automobile collisions, and other aspects of "car culture" that have been subjected to increasing criticism in cities and communities across North America and Europe (Nikiforuk, 2022).

If the energy growth driving the EV transition is to avoid worsening the climate crisis, it will need to come entirely from renewable sources. EVs could be used to bring online massive battery storage capacity that could be used to build efficiencies into the system through load balancing (using power that might otherwise be spilled or curtailed) and a range of valuable grid services (see MacDougall, 2018). Still, the scale of changes envisioned evokes the notion of a new industrial revolution – and as such it carries considerable environmental implications. The growing demand for metals is a particular concern, one that could even accelerate the push to mine deep seabeds; as Sir David Attenborough notes, this "risks creating terrible impacts that cannot be reversed" (Fauna & Flora International, 2020, p. 5).

Lithium supplies will need to increase sixfold by 2030 to meet the current aspirations, and prices have risen immensely in recent years – around 700 per cent in 2021–22. Meanwhile geopolitical issues weigh heavily on this sector, as manufacturing is not evenly distributed; China manufactures about 70 per cent of all batteries globally, and 75–85 per cent of major battery components (IEA, 2022). Supply chains were heavily impacted by COVID-19 restrictions, while markets for metals, especially copper, nickel, and cobalt, have been hit hard by recent conflicts and sanctions. Mining's historical association with human rights and environmental abuses continues with the mining of battery materials, especially lithium, which threatens lands, water, and biodiversity, seriously impacting the lives of Indigenous Peoples, particularly in arid areas of the Global South (Jerez et al., 2021; Campbell, 2022). The rush for the mineral supply for a post-carbon economy can accentuate existing exploitive labour conditions and even induce environmental crimes in Africa and elsewhere (see Stoett & Omrow, 2022). Some argue that growth ambitions will need to be curtailed considerably if resource constraints are not overcome through new discoveries and innovations in both mining and battery technologies (Turcheniuk et al., 2018).

Indeed, Canada's path to "net zero" is packaged alongside a vision of continued growth: "Many of the resources and products already produced across the country will still be in demand in a net zero world – and in many cases, demand may increase ... [R]esource sectors such as agriculture, forestry, and mining see continued growth, as do manufacturing sectors like vehicles, chemicals, steel, cement, metals, and paper" (Canadian Institute for Climate Choices, 2021, p. 16). The future of EVs often seems to be in conflict with ideas around walkable communities, work-from-home arrangements, improved public and active transportation, localized or circular economies, and even degrowth scenarios such as those intimated in the most recent Intergovernmental Panel on Climate Change (IPCC) report (Parrique, 2022). Replacing the internal-combustion economy with an EV economy may address a portion of carbon emissions, but more far-reaching and radical efforts will be needed to achieve climate goals.

CONCLUSION: FINDING THE RIGHT ENERGY MIX

Energy remains one of the most complex and challenging issues in Canadian ecopolitics. At the same time the hero and villain of multiple overlapping and interwoven stories and narratives, energy is a multifaceted complex of different natural resources, regional and local needs, geographies and built environments, ideologies, and social identities. Energy in Canada is political, economic, and social, and public policy decisions that guide, regulate, or restrict the development and distribution of different energy systems are among the most contested in contemporary Canadian politics. Canada is distinct among its peer countries for the historical patterns and current variety of energy resources, which range from drawing more than half of all electricity produced in the country from two high-efficiency, low-carbon sources – hydroelectricity and nuclear – to continuing to invest in fossil fuel energy extraction, notably bituminous oil and hydraulically fractured natural gas, as major export commodities still considered essential to regional economies in western Canada, particularly on the Prairies. In turn, the ongoing expansion of Canada's fossil fuel energy sector is one of the most hotly contested fault lines in Canadian ecopolitics and our political economy. It pits against each other diverse regional economic interests, competing industries and corporations, and conflictual political and legal claims to land use authority and rights and title between the federal and provincial governments, elected and hereditary Indigenous leaders, and social movements both supportive of and entirely opposed to the continued extraction and consumption of fossil fuel energy. The competition and negotiation between these sometimes-incompatible actors and interests will continue to unfold in Canadian ecopolitics over the decades to come.

CHAPTER SEVEN

Freshwater and Canadian Ecopolitics

LEARNING OBJECTIVES

1. Describe the key issues surrounding freshwater management in Canada, including water rights, quality, and pollution.
2. Evaluate the multilevel governance challenges in Canadian water policy, including federal–provincial relations and international agreements.
3. Discuss the concept of inherent rights of watercourses, as well as rights to water and its potential implications for Canadian water management.

INTRODUCTION: WATER AND LIFE

Life in the earth's biosphere is simply unimaginable without water. Water makes up over 70 per cent of the human body by weight and is an essential component or ingredient in every biotic (and many non-living) process. Access to freshwater has been recognized by the United Nations as "a basic human need and a fundamental human right" (UNDP, 2006, p. v). Resolutions of the UN Human Rights Council established the right to drinking water and sanitation as binding under international law in 2010 and 2015, respectively. The UN's SDG 6 is to "Ensure access to water and sanitation for all." Still, a quarter of humanity currently lives without clean water in their homes, while 40 per cent lack proper sanitation (UN Water, 2021). Canada is widely recognized as particularly fortunate in this regard, yet as of July 2024 there were 31 Indigenous communities still living under a long-term water boil advisory, and short-term advisories are quite common.[1]

Indeed, everywhere we look access to freshwater is unequal, risky, contested, and often leveraged for political or financial gains. Losing access to water can pose an existential risk to individuals, communities, and even entire countries. Meanwhile, as this book comes to press, climate change has brought unprecedented drought to many areas, including western North America from California to British Columbia, along with Europe, China, and the Horn of Africa; water flow in important rivers like the Yangtze, Loire, Rhine, Po, and Colorado has become exceptionally low, threatening agriculture, transportation, and hydroelectric, nuclear, and thermal power generation as well as drinking water for many millions of people (Seidel, 2022).

The availability or *quantity* of water is partly a function of natural cycles, which are subject to change, especially with climate change, the decline of glaciers, and the impacts of wetland and forest loss on hydrogeological cycles. But existing flows are also impacted by water extraction from rivers and groundwater (for industry, agricultural use, aggregate washing, and urban demand) and through intentional diversions (irrigation, dams). Availability is, for many, further limited by financial constraints driven by the costs of water purification and delivery – costs that must be borne by the users themselves (often at wildly varying rates) or subsidized by governments. Trends toward increased privatization in water infrastructure and services can exacerbate these inequities.

Quantity is one thing, but quality is also important when discussing usable (potable) water, which is most affected by pollution from agriculture and industry, various natural sources, and municipal sewage and other wastes, like road runoff. (One of the major sources of microplastic pollution – now ubiquitous, found even in the Arctic – is the residue from car tires.) Despite such abundant water resources, many rivers and lakes in Canada are unfit for swimming and fishing because of a huge range of pollutants that contribute to eutrophication, algal blooms, disease, chemical accumulations, and fish kills. The continued destruction of wetlands and forests means there are fewer resources to provide essential "ecosystem services," such as groundwater cleaning and recharging. One recent study suggests that levels of so-called forever chemicals (PFAS, or per- and polyfluoroalkyl substances) already exceed safe drinking water standards in rainwater samples taken around the globe (Cousins et al., 2022).

Canada's freshwater endowment is legendary: Some 25 per cent of the surface freshwater on the planet can be found within its borders, including the Great Lakes, though the annual renewable supply (i.e., the flow) is only around 6.5 per cent of the world's supply. Yet while many would envy this endowment, a **myth of abundance** has propagated a widespread misunderstanding of the state of water in Canada and contributed to considerable neglect in water management efforts. Water abundance is limited by a number of factors. For example, some 60 per cent of Canada's freshwater flows northward, to the Arctic Ocean, and is generally not accessible for the vast majority of the population that lives close to the southern border. Also, since a large amount of water falls as snow, flows are seasonally determined everywhere in the country, with spring flooding as common and disruptive as summer dry spells. Water is generally scarce in the Great Plains, where large irrigation schemes have been built to divert major sources like the Bow and Red Rivers. Summer often limits availability in other places too; every year a quarter of Canada's municipalities experience water shortages of some sort (Biro, 2007, p. 331) and prolonged droughts have become quite common (see Map 7.1). An outdated study by the Canadian government found the incidence of waterborne diseases in First Nations communities is 26 times higher than in the general Canadian population (Basdeo & Bharadwaj, 2013), often because of inadequate sanitation facilities; more recent studies are difficult to find (Karunananthan & Willows, 2012; Bradford et al., 2016; De Coste et al., 2024). So, while there is a great deal of freshwater in Canada, there is also a widely shared and mistaken perception that water is available for everyone who wants it.

The ecopolitics of freshwater occur across several dimensions. The most commonly cited is the upstream–downstream relationship, which relates to the impact of drawings, diversions, and pollution on the rights of downstream users within a watershed. There is also the shoreline dimension, especially around drawings and transfers *between* watersheds. In addition, the temporal dimension is vital when thinking in terms of sustainability and intergenerational ethics. Through all these, a number of key considerations guide our relationship with water: Is it appropriate to treat water as a commodity? How far do ownership rights extend (e.g., to rainwater)? Should there be a human right to clean water? Who pays for pollution and cleanup when the source of pollution is diffuse (agriculture), foreign (Great Lakes), or even untraceable (PFAS)? This chapter will explore some of the key discussions emerging from this ecopolitical framework.

Map 7.1. Drought Conditions in Canada

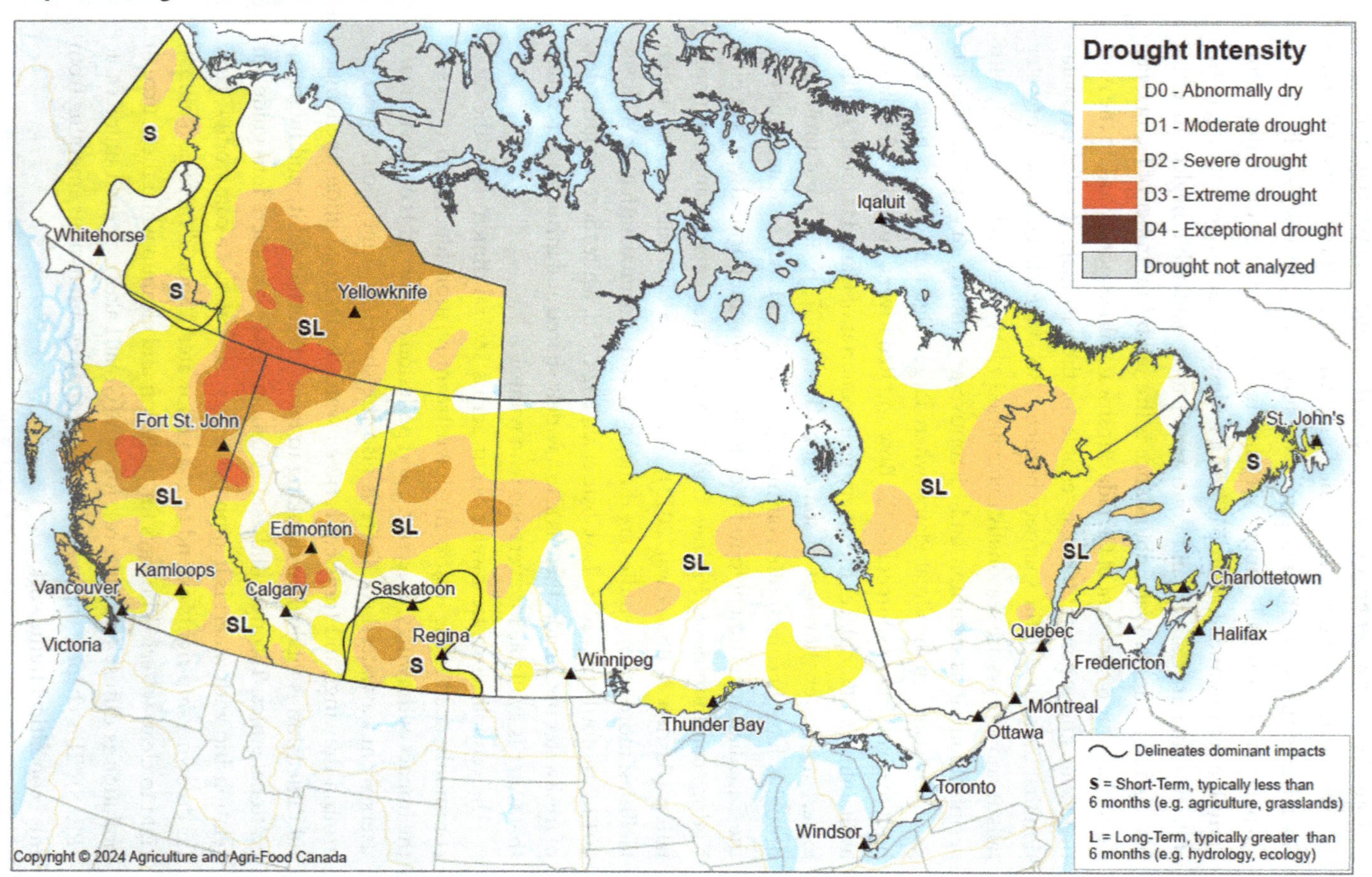

Source: © Agriculture and Agri-Food Canada, 2024. Contains information licensed under the Open Government Licence – Canada.

THE WATER CYCLE AND HUMAN CONTROL

Water, along with air, is perhaps the proverbial common property – or common pool – resource (see Chapter Three). Water travels freely across property lines and borders, potentially travelling through every part of the planet; when it doesn't evaporate "into thin air," it makes its way into food and beverage products or into the animals that provide them; it collects in shared spaces including rivers, lakes, and underground aquifers that are accessible to many users. Water flows are defined by climate and geology, but the natural boundaries that define watersheds rarely coincide with the political boundaries that dictate their management.

It is important to remember that a significant portion of water is effectively locked away in underground aquifers and in glaciers, much of it since the last ice age. Groundwater makes up over 30 per cent of freshwater globally (glaciers and permanent snow hold nearly 69 per cent, and lakes and rivers a mere 0.4 per cent), and underground aquifers can take anywhere from two weeks to 10,000 years to recharge (Environment and Climate Change Canada, 2013). Only around 6 per cent of aquifer waters are replenished within a 50-year period, and these waters are all being depleted much faster than they can be recharged (Barlow, 2016, p. 20). Deeper wells and more powerful pumps create access issues as large industrial users draw down groundwater, requiring other users, including homes and small farmers, to invest in new equipment or supplies or go without. Meanwhile glacial melting rates are increasing (see Chapter Eight), but will not do so indefinitely, and future flows of fresh mountain streams, the birthplace of many of our great rivers, are likely to decline considerably as ice loss proceeds.

To some extent, water can also be controlled, and a visual mark of human civilization are the engineered interventions, such as dams and canals, that move or hold water for various uses. These interventions often impact availability for downstream users – not only other humans and property owners, but also fish and wildlife and ecological communities, thus adding an *interspecies* dimension to the ethical and legal concerns around water use. The damming of rivers has impacted the health, migration, and reproduction of fish and often adds to the pollution load, which further affects the health of wildlife and local and Indigenous communities. Further impacts arise when water is diverted from one watershed to another; Canada diverts four times the volume of water diverted within the United States, the majority (some 97 per cent) for hydroelectric generation. In the United States, by contrast, most diversion is for irrigation, urban use, or navigation. While little water is actually "used up" in these diversion schemes, "the sheer magnitude of some diversions leaves no room for doubt about harm to the environment" (Lasserre, 2007, p. 143). Fortunately, at least in political terms, these diversions only rarely move water across the borders of states or provinces, as this would raise a host of complex jurisdictional issues. We can note an irony, however, in that much of the electricity generated with the help of diversions is itself exported to the United States.

WATER USERS AND RIGHTS

Prior to the arrival of Europeans, the waters of Turtle Island were subject to natural forces and Indigenous customs; Indigenous Peoples generally "sought to ensure that all forms of water usage recognized and respected one's spiritual connection with water" and often included restrictions on use that reflected a deep sense of responsibility toward future generations (Christensen & Lintner, 2007, p. 221). Europeans, however, drew upon a range of legal arguments that allowed the granting of "rights" over water while substantially neglecting responsibilities toward other users. Land was divided and allocated, often along compass lines and imaginary measurements with little regard to the realities of watershed boundaries. Violence was applied generously to the land and its inhabitants as water sources and flows were manipulated to serve the interests of the newcomers. Rights were generally granted on a first-come basis, neglecting the obvious Indigenous presence. Walkem (2007) relays the story of the Twaal Valley (located in central British Columbia), ancestral home of the Nlaka'pamux people, which was fed from a mountaintop water source directed by beaver dams. Settlers came to the neighbouring (dry) valley and sought to divert the water by destroying the beaver dams, but the beavers simply rebuilt them. "The newcomers then went in and systematically killed the entire beaver population on the mountaintop and rerouted the water to their dry valley" (pp. 303–4), leaving little to support life in the Twaal, including its human inhabitants.

As Walkem (2007) notes, "the experience of the Nlaka'pamux people of Twaal is far from unique ... Historically ... land use and development has proceeded with little regard for the indigenous peoples who draw their lives from the land and the waters" (p. 304). Settlers appropriated water for a wide range of industrial projects and built their settlements where water was available, pushing Indigenous Peoples to reserves. Reserves were often assumed to have rights to the waters that flowed on them, but as federal creations they are not in control of surface water flows, as this is a provincial jurisdiction; thus, water rights are often still contested among provincial, federal, and Indigenous governments (Walkem, 2007). Where water supplies have been badly polluted, as in Grassy Narrows (see Case Study 10.1) and Fort Chipewyan (two of the most notorious instances), the deferral of responsibility can go on for decades (Porter, 2017; Willms, 2011).

Access to water was key to the early development of industry and agriculture, from the early Europeans, voyageurs, missionaries, and settlers to the industrialists with their log booms, fisheries, tanneries, pulp and paper mills, water wheels, and hydroelectric dams. Much of this development has left a legacy of interrupted, diverted, dammed, and often polluted waterways and impinges on the ability of Indigenous Peoples and settlers alike to enjoy the many other uses of water, including those guaranteed through Treaty rights. The historical allotment of rights over water has both reflected and served to secure economic powers, while the various historical interventions and institutions have limited subsequent decisions. Thus, while water management institutions may be designed to reduce conflict, "it is also a historical truth that they create conflict by privileging certain uses and users over others" (Johns, 2008, p. 9). The guiding common law principle of **riparian rights** has held a central place in these developments. According to this principle, "every riparian is entitled to the water of his or her stream in its natural flow without sensible alteration to its character or quality" (Johns et al., 2008, p. 60). In addition, according to this principle any user who limits or damages the use of water for downstream users is liable to be sued, a convention from which much private litigation has sprung. But management and governance also have to take this basic principle into account as they seek to avoid and address disputes among users; it has thus been foundational in statutory law and in constructing the "complex layering of legislation, authorities, and agreements [that] exists to manage water resources in Canada" (Johns et al., 2008, p. 61).

To be clear, naturally flowing water is generally not considered "property" (and where it is, it is typically the property of the state), but a range of property-like rights exist around the *use* of water. For instance, the riparian landowner's right to draw from the flow to meet their own reasonable needs can be extended through negotiation with other riparian owners. Riparian norms also entail a right to exclude others; owners of property that does not reach the river have no rights to the water. They may be able to negotiate such rights with the riparian landowner, but their use can be challenged by other riparians. In many cases the broader diversion of waters, such as with irrigation in Alberta, is by necessity led by state or provincial decree. Once such rights are allotted, however, they can be difficult to take back to meet other needs, such as growing urban populations and new industrial demands (Brownsey, 2008).

We should note that groundwater in Canada is even less regulated than the flows of rivers and lakes. Groundwater is not mentioned in the *Constitution Act, 1867* – which is hardly surprising, given that its movements and quantities were largely unknown until the mid-twentieth century. The **rule of capture**, a common law tenet sometimes referred to as "the law of the biggest pump," allows landowners to extract as much water as they can from underground sources without regard to others who may also have access to the same deposit. This can lead to escalating competition among aggregate facilities, bottled water companies, agricultural operations, municipalities, and even golf courses. Much of this extraction is guided by permits issued by provincial and municipal authorities, but across Canada permitting regulations are far from standardized; reporting, public participation, and rights of appeal vary greatly among the provinces. The first licensed extractions of groundwater were issued in Ontario in 1961 and in the Prairie provinces in the 1970s (Nowlan, 2007). In British Columbia, permits were not required to extract water until the *Water Sustainability Act* came into force in 2016 (Nowlan, 2007, Table 4.2, pp. 72–75; Government of British Columbia, 2022). A survey by the Canadian Council of Ministers of the Environment (CCME) found major concerns around the quality and accessibility of groundwater data that could help guide decisions related to the ecological and water impact of withdrawals. It also found that, across the country, "consideration of the cumulative effects of groundwater withdrawals on an aquifer-wide basis is rare" (CCME, 2010, p. 4).

Today, around 30 per cent of the water used for drinking in Canada comes from groundwater sources, yet many unknowns remain around the health and sustainability of these resources. Pollution is a major concern, as it is exceedingly expensive, if not impossible, to clean up contaminated groundwater sources. Common contaminant sources include road runoff (salt, oils), leakage from underground fuel and septic tanks, and landfills and industrial dump sites (including specific **areas of concern**, or AOCs, which will be discussed later in this chapter). Many natural sources of pollution occur as well, including arsenic, mercury, and hydrocarbons (such as the natural seepage from the oil sands). Groundwater contamination is a growing concern in

Canada "primarily because of the large and growing number of toxic compounds used in industry and agriculture" (Environment and Climate Change Canada, 2017). Contamination is often well advanced before it is discovered; a single litre of gasoline from a leaking fuel tank can contaminate a million litres of groundwater but is unlikely to be discovered before somebody smells it in their tap water. And once the water is contaminated it can take decades – or longer – to flush the toxins, but this often only succeeds in moving them to another water body. The issue of contamination turns us now to the second major set of issues around water: water quality and pollution.

WATER QUALITY AND POLLUTION

The rules and institutions that guided water usage in earlier Canadian history are not always well suited to the challenges of a more ecologically informed era. The early emphasis on the economic uses of water has made it challenging to ensure that other uses, such as cultural, recreational, and ecological concerns, can be addressed. The relative absence of pollution regulations and biosecurity provisions for many decades only began to be challenged as health concerns sparked a growing demand for water quality standards, particularly for drinking water. Poor water quality also impinges on recreational users, including bathers, boaters, and fishers, and heavily polluted or damaged ecosystems may not support healthy wildlife or even agriculture. Still, "for most of Canada's history, the institutional arrangements have been designed to manage the quantity of water available for economic development, rather than the quality of water available for Canadian citizens and ecosystem health" (Johns et al., 2008, p. 54).

Water pollution is generally designated as either **point source** or **non-point source pollution**. Point sources, which could include industrial waste dumps, municipal waste discharges, and chemical effluent pipes, were widely recognized as a source of chemical and organic pollutants such as heavy metals, fertilizers, toxic chemicals, and contaminated sediments. Non-point sources, or NPS, were not given much consideration until the 1980s. NPS pollution arises from widely dispersed inputs that can include urban and agricultural areas, roadways, and sewage overflow. These sources collectively add large amounts of pollutants to waterways and even groundwater aquifers, but they are difficult to assess, trace, and control. A major problem is overflow from sewage pipes that carry rainwater and sewage. Heavy rainfalls, which are increasing under climate change, can overwhelm these systems, which then discharge polluted water that mixes with other sources. Agricultural runoff can also overwhelm systems; in the Ontario town of Walkerton in 2000, heavy rain led to agricultural runoff, contaminating the local water supply with *E. coli* bacteria. Seven people died from the poisoning, and thousands were made sick. The Walkerton tragedy led to many changes in agricultural practices and reporting (guided by the *Nutrient Management Act, 2002*), along with municipal water quality testing regimes (under the *Safe Drinking Water Act, 2002*); thankfully the tragedy has not been repeated in Canada, though a similar event in South Battleford, Saskatchewan, in 2001 further boosted the case for improving water safety. However, heavy rainfalls still frequently lead to uncontrolled discharges of sewage, chemicals, and plastic that pollute waterways and beaches, leading to shutdowns and restrictions.

Reducing pollution and ensuring clean water supplies demands continuous investment in water treatment infrastructure, and this demand is a key element in debates around privatization in the water sector. Historically, much of Canada's water services have been managed by communities, and municipal governments own and operate the vast majority of facilities. In recent decades, however, several large municipalities have begun to explore, and in some cases to implement, a variety of public–private partnerships (PPPs) to help finance expanding or upgrading existing systems. Such partnerships can allow access to expertise and financial resources that can enable needs to be addressed quickly. Some argue that involving private actors helps ensure an efficient allocation of resources, allows these market actors to find a price point that reflects the actual value to users, offers financial incentives for conservation, and encourages additional investment to support demand under shrinking municipal budgets. Ideally, more market-based water allotment can also help overcome historical maldistributions and enable the redistribution of water rights to align with new social and economic priorities (Horbulyk, 2006, pp. 210–11).

At the same time, privatization can also lead to conditions in which only those who can pay are able to access water, which is difficult to align with the recognition that water is a universal human right. In addition, it is clear that the many applications of water in agriculture and industry will also tend toward the concentration of access rights, providing economic advantages that those without access cannot hope to enjoy. In municipal settings, for example, it is difficult or impossible to avoid a monopolistic situation in water purification and delivery; this is a primary argument in favour of public ownership, as it helps ensure some democratic accountability around rate increases and user protections, along with concerns about transparency and regulatory oversight. Public opposition has prevented several PPP initiatives from proceeding and has even reversed some that were already contracted – a process known as remunicipalization – as happened in the City of Hamilton in 2004. Much of this opposition extends to the international trade agreements that threaten to lock in privatization trends through investor protection mechanisms and rules on procurement; such agreements can make efforts to reverse privatization extremely difficult and costly. This is just one way in which water policy links many levels of government, a framework to which we now turn.

MULTILEVEL GOVERNANCE OF WATER

The division of powers between federal and provincial governments in Canada emerged from the shadows of fur, lumber, and farming interests, negotiated among the nascent polities of a new country. The federal government's ability to regulate water is guided by its juridical responsibilities under the *Constitution Act, 1867* over fisheries, navigation, shipping, and agriculture; meanwhile the provinces retain the authority to manage natural resources, including water, as well as the wetlands, forests, roads, and infrastructure that impact it. Arguments can be made for greater federal involvement on a number of constitutional justifications, where water concerns can be framed as a matter of interprovincial coordination, international waters, trade and commerce, or the more general duty to uphold peace, order, and good government, especially in terms of understanding water as a "national concern" (Saunders & Wenig, 2007, pp. 122–23). Yet Ottawa has long been reluctant to impinge on provincial powers over water resources, even where intervention could reduce environmental harm. For example, longstanding water drawing rights in Alberta have seriously impacted river flows; the federal government could have leveraged the *Fisheries Act* provision that "no person shall carry on any work or undertaking that results in the harmful alteration, disruption or destruction of fish habitat" to prohibit further expansion. It has not done so, however, which "bodes poorly for the survival of fish and other aquatic species" in some heavily used areas (Saunders & Wenig, 2007, pp. 128–29).[2] Recent pipeline construction in northern British Columbia (see Chapter Six), supported by federal investment and intensive police protection by the RCMP, has generated considerable tension between Ottawa and Indigenous Nations – a fraught relationship that nonetheless generally has little impact on provincial imperatives.

As Council of Canadians head Maude Barlow puts it, "Canada's water management … is a patchwork of uneven and often inadequate regulations and standards in need of firm federal oversight and governance" (Barlow, 2016, p. 26). Indeed, critics claim that the federal government has largely abdicated its role in water management, even while the need for it – in terms of fisheries, biodiversity, and interprovincial and international affairs – is more apparent than ever. In recent decades the federal government's role in infrastructure (including water infrastructure) has shown a steady decline; from the 1950s to the 1990s, the federal share of public capital stock declined from 44 per cent to 13 per cent (Barlow, 2016). Toward the end of this period environmental concerns were also receiving less attention and less funding; many aspects of water quality regulation were taken up by departments whose mandate was economically driven, while water quality concerns of Environment Canada and Fisheries and Oceans Canada were diminished. Though some efforts were made to define a more active role, such as in the 1987 Federal Water Policy put forward by the Mulroney government, implementation has been abysmal: According to Barlow (2016), "it seems to be that the policy is not to have a comprehensive policy" (p. 29). Waves of provincial offloading subsequently thrust many water quality issues onto municipalities, so that today the federal government has only limited influence and "is largely ignored by the provinces when they make their decisions about water" (Schindler, 2007, p. xii). However, interprovincial agreements have emerged over the years, particularly on the eastward and northward flowing rivers of the Prairies and for the Mackenzie River Basin. The Prairie Provinces Water Board helped advise on allocations in a Master Agreement on Apportionment (1969), which it now supervises, while the Mackenzie River Basin Board oversees implementation of a considerably less robust Mackenzie Master Agreement (1997) that continues to seek detailed commitments from the upstream provinces. The general lack of commitment is particularly disconcerting because of the impact on the Mackenzie Basin of the Alberta oil sands, the world's largest industrial project (see Case Study 7.1).

CASE STUDY 7.1. The Mighty Athabasca

Mining and processing of Canada's oil sands takes place across a wide swath of northern Alberta and Saskatchewan, but the largest deposits are found in the Athabasca River watershed, which forms a major tributary of the

Mackenzie River. The massive tailings ponds of these operations, which cover some 250 square kilometres in total, are separated from the "Mighty Athabasca" by sometimes only a single berm with a secondary collection trench. These ponds hold over a trillion litres of oil sands process water (OSPW), "an acutely toxic substance containing, among other things, naphthenic acids and heavy metals … [These] bitumen-derived organics are complex mixtures containing millions of substances that remain impossible to fully characterize, even with the most sophisticated instrumentation presently available" (CEC, 2020, p. 3). The oil sands facilities as a whole take about 15 per cent of the water they use for processing from the Athabasca River, while 85 per cent is recycled from the tailings ponds themselves. Processing each barrel of bitumen requires "from 2–6 barrels of hot water, sometimes mixed with chemical additives to separate out constituent inorganics, silts and clays" (CEC, 2020, p. 26).

The federal government's authority to oversee the oil sands and their tailings could derive from either (or both) the *Fisheries Act* or the *Navigable Rivers Act*. However, the federal government has no effective relationship with the province pertaining to the tailings ponds, and the provincial regulatory system and the federal system have almost no context for coordination. While a joint federal–provincial Oil Sands Monitoring Program is in place, successive Alberta governments have been reluctant to support demands that might reduce production in the popular oil sands projects, and the federal government has been unwilling to act beyond the joint environmental review process, which is invoked only for new facilities approvals (CEC, 2020, p. 5).

Impacts on health have become more serious since the 1960s, when oil sands production began in earnest. As in the forestry and mining sectors, the vastness of Canada's boreal forest has disguised the environmental impacts of resource extraction. Clearly, an extractivist worldview and frontier mentality has dominated in oil sands mining, but even in its beginnings it was clear the processing and tailings were not compatible with other uses of the river, especially the provision of drinking water for and fishing by downstream First Nations as well as settler communities and industrial operations.

In June 2017, a joint submission from Environmental Defence Canada, the US-based Natural Resources Defense Council, and Canadian resident Daniel T'seleie asserted that the Government of Canada was failing to enforce the pollution prevention provisions of the federal *Fisheries Act* in the context of OSPW seepage from the tailings ponds. The submission pointed out that "Syncrude monitoring reports [show] consistent evidence of seepage of OSPW from tailings ponds into groundwater at certain monitoring wells that are close in proximity to surface water, including tributaries to the Athabasca River" (CEC, 2020, p. 3). Groundwater, as a provincial issue, is outside the mandate of the submission, and the evidence to show that OSPW was reaching the river in quantity was found to be conflicting overall. Thus, scientific uncertainty, built from a combination of infrastructure age, inadequate sampling, and limited federal authority to access the site and conduct analysis, left the commission unable to conclude with certainty that OSPW was reaching the fish habitat.

The quality of the conflicting evidence is, perhaps, debatable, but it has the potential to impose change on the status quo. More problematic, though, is that the tailings ponds, similar to abandoned oil wells, decommissioned nuclear facilities, and so many other industrial leftovers, may prove virtually impossible to clean up. At the very least, the costs will be extraordinary.

Critical Thinking Questions

1. Should the federal government play a more pronounced role in environmental regulation?
2. What are the long-term impacts of pollution in the Athabasca River for riparian peoples?

If national Liberal governments have struggled with federal–provincial relations and environmental regulation on water quality and water security, Conservative leaders have tended to side with western energy interests. In 2012, Stephen Harper's government introduced major changes to the environmental assessment process in Canada through a so-called omnibus bill, the *Budget Implementation Act*, which simultaneously amended seven environmental laws, including "a complete re-write of the *Canadian Environmental Assessment Act* and a major shift in direction in the *Fisheries Act*" (Paris, 2012). The new *Fisheries Act* removed reference to protective measures on fish habitat, limited remaining protections to economically relevant (commercial, recreational, and Aboriginal) fisheries, and arguably seriously compromised Canada's obligations under the Convention on Biological Diversity (Taylor, 2014). A second omnibus bill in the same year (Bill C-45, the *Jobs and Growth Act*) amended the *Navigable Waters Act*, removing protections and oversight from thousands of waterways across the country; the final list of protected "navigable waters" comprised just 3 oceans, 97 lakes, and 62 rivers. Thanks also to decimated budgets, the number of projects reviewed annually declined from an average of 4,000 or 5,000 to only 25 (Gilchrist, 2018).[3] A subsequent statistical analysis of a decade of changes to environmental laws and procedures suggested that the federal government had "all but abandoned" its role in protecting Canada's lakes and rivers (Olszynski, 2015).

Bill C-45 drew considerable ire from some members of the Canadian public, especially scientists, environmentalists, and Indigenous representatives. Among the more powerful elements of the backlash was the birth of Idle No More, an Indigenous-led protest campaign that sought to draw attention to environmental issues and Indigenous sovereignty, including issues such as drinking water quality on reserves as well as contested energy sector developments like the Northern Gateway pipeline project. Idle No More grew rapidly in the Harper era and no doubt influenced Justin Trudeau's 2015 election promises on restoring protections to water (see Chapter Four). The change in government did not subdue the movement, and Bill C-69 was introduced in 2018 in a move to respond to its continued pressure (*CBC News*, 2016). Bill C-69 enacted the *Impact Assessment Act* (IAA) along with the *Canadian Energy Regulator Act*, amended the *Navigation Protection Act* into the *Canadian Navigable Waters Act*, and was itself a focus of controversy for many months. Opponents decried the "appalling" rush to pass the legislation with little opportunity for debate, and on its passage the Council of Canadians denounced the Bill "for further cementing market-based, corporate-friendly policies that exploit water and the environment" (Lui, 2018). Others suggested the Bill, which replaced the Canadian Environmental Assessment Agency with the new Impact Assessment Agency of Canada, held some promise of ensuring that new projects would be examined with at least some degree of transparency and greater participation from Indigenous stakeholders. Review decisions would now be required to evaluate projects with explicit regard to sustainability, impacts on the rights of Indigenous Peoples, and the extent to which the ultimate effects of the project would contribute to Canada's ability to meet its climate change commitments. The new regulations still have to contend with the provinces, however; the Alberta Court of Appeal, responding to the Alberta government's concerns over new and expanding energy projects, referred to the IAA as "a classic example of 'legislative creep'" based on concerns it would give the federal government "an effective veto" over every intraprovincial project in the country (Awad & Wiltse, 2022), and the Canadian Supreme Court agreed in a decision made in October 2023 (see Bakx, 2023).

CROSSING THE BORDER

Where water flows across national borders, the ecopolitics, not surprisingly, become even more complicated. North America's geography is characterized by strong north–south contours, with the Rocky Mountains, Great Plains, and the coastal boundaries all spanning from the Far North to the Mexican border and beyond. But if we look at water flows, they suggest a different picture: The Mississippi River drains much of the United States into the Gulf of Mexico, while the Mackenzie and many other rivers, including those in Ontario and Quebec, drain most of Canada's land surface water toward the Arctic. The Great Lakes region is a notable exception, and these shared waters hold a special place in the relationship, subject to the 1909 Boundary Waters Treaty (BWT) and the 1972 and subsequent Great Lakes Water Quality Agreements, among others (MacFarlene, 2017).

The 1909 BWT established a core set of legal principles to govern management of waters shared between the two countries and established the International Joint Commission to oversee implementation and mediate disputes. It is worth noting that the BWT emphasizes the special nature of boundary waters like the Great Lakes (which form part of the international boundary) along with transboundary waters (generally rivers that flow across the border). The former are subject to the principle of "equal and similar rights," while the latter are subject to the "sovereign right to use or divert the waters as [each government] sees fit"; the BWT is silent on the status of groundwater (Saunders & Wenig, 2007, p. 131). While not perfect, the BWT has proven useful and flexible enough to deal with new issues, a key one being the question of bulk water transfers (exports) to the United States from the Great Lakes.

The prospect of exporting Canada's water is not a new idea. Population growth in the dry US southwest has long led dreamers – including politicians and engineers – to look northward for freshwater that could slake the thirst of growing croplands and cities. Recent years have seen the west dry even further in what some call a climate-change-related "mega-drought," with impacts felt even into what remains of the great forests of Oregon and Washington.[4] Schemes for diverting Canadian water have recurred periodically since the 1950s, but upon examination the vast scale and enormous costs involved in realizing such visions has been enough to deter the planners, at least so far. Alternatives, including desalination and conservation measures, have been shown to be more economically and environmentally sensible (Biro, 2007).

Nonetheless, the fears of eventual bulk water exports remain a major platform for groups such as the Council of Canadians, which continues to watch for holes in the containment around this issue. For instance, the controversial Site C Dam, the third major dam on the Peace River in British Columbia, has been flagged as a possible contributing infrastructure, subject to the will of the province (Patterson, 2016). To many, the prospect of exporting Canada's water contravenes a widespread sense of water as a national treasure, part of the national narrative, a key to Canadian identity as a natural, untamed land. Simply put, water is an important part of what Canada means to many Canadians. Ironically, while in many parts of the world the engineered control of water is held as a symbol of national strength (especially big dams and irrigation projects, such as the mammoth Three Gorges Dam on the Yangtze River in China), for Canada the opposite seems to be true: Its identity is strengthened by maintaining the wild rivers and lakes, preserving them from the hands of engineers and water barons who would almost certainly represent foreign capital and foreign interests (Biro, 2007, p. 330). In 2013 the Harper government introduced further legislation to prohibit such bulk exports, but critics point out its weaknesses are substantial, especially in not including non-boundary waters in its protections (Patterson, 2016).

The Great Lakes Basin is the largest freshwater basin on earth, holding roughly 18 per cent of the world's liquid freshwater. Four of the five lakes are shared between the United States and Canada, with the international border readily crossed by boats, wildlife, invasive alien species, and pollutants. The shared waters are of enormous importance for shipping, fishing, and tourism and supply drinking water to the roughly 38 million residents of the basin, which also hosts large amounts of intensive agriculture – nearly a quarter of Canada's – and major industry in urban centres such as Chicago, Cleveland, Detroit, Windsor, Hamilton, and Toronto. The density of activities and population in the relatively small basin has sorely compromised the quality of the water in the lower lakes (Erie and Ontario) especially. Fertilizers, detergents, and other organics have for many decades accelerated the process of eutrophication, leading to greatly increased plant and algae growth that starved insects and fish of oxygen. In the 1960s Lake Erie was often referred to as a "dead" lake, or as one author described it, an "odorous, slime-covered graveyard" (Edmonds, 1965).

The 1972 Great Lakes Water Quality Agreement (GLWQA) between the United States and Canada marked the beginning of a major effort to improve the condition of the lakes' waters. The "non-binding, good faith agreement" led to strengthened regulations, particularly targeting point source pollution such as sewage discharges and industrial effluent. However, sewage spills remained a problem on occasion, and agricultural runoff continued to feed algal blooms, on Lake Erie especially. Meanwhile decades of poorly regulated industrial activity had left contaminated sites that were often suspected of leaching toxins into the lakes. The 1972 agreement was superseded by a revised 1978 GLWQA, amended in 1983 and again in 1987. This third iteration identified 43 specific areas of concern that were prioritized for remedial action; however, after some 25 years, only 3 had been delisted with another 2 designated as "in recovery" (Johns, 2009, p. 100). The agreement was amended again with the 2012 Great Lakes Water Quality Protocol, adding annexes targeting action to slow the spread of invasive aquatic species, prevent further loss of habitats and native species, and consider the effect from longer-term impacts of climate change, such as increased lake temperatures and reduced ice cover. The 2012 amendments included a number of target dates for action and increased public input and accountability with the establishment of the Canada–United States Great Lakes Executive Committee, which includes participants from federal, state, tribal, provincial and municipal governments, First Nations and Métis communities, watershed management agencies, and other public agencies; its mandate focuses on coordinating action and advising the parties on implementation of the GLWQA (Environment and Climate Change Canada, 2022b).

The International Joint Commission (IJC) is tasked with independently assessing progress on the GLWQA through, since 2012, a triennial assessment report, replacing the previous biennial reports from 1978. These reports note improvements and failures across a number of chemical, biological, and physical indicators, such as toxins, nutrient loading, invasive species, and ice cover. Its first triennial report (IJC, 2017) was critical of the governments' efforts, calling them "disappointingly slow" in dealing with toxins and noting that water quality and nutrient pollution in Lake Erie was not improving through voluntary measures. The 2017 report also recommended a binational approach to adaptation to the impacts of climate change. The second report (IJC, 2020) noted that little had been done on these fronts and reiterated its suggestion regarding a binational approach to climate adaptation and resilience, noting recent impacts like cyanobacterial blooms and intense storms on Lake Superior. The IJC offered to take a role in convening stakeholders around this issue, which some commentators suggested is "exactly the kind of role the Commission was meant to play" with regard to the agreements (FLOW, 2020).

Another transnational agency, the Commission on Environmental Cooperation (CEC), was created in 1994 under the North American Agreement on Environmental Cooperation, the environmental agreement signed alongside NAFTA, with a mandate to conduct analysis and make recommendations to the parties on environmental matters. Soon after the CEC was created the governments of Canada and the United States signed the Great Lakes Binational Toxics Strategy, which aimed to "virtually eliminate" a designated set of substances found in the basin in the period 1997–2006. The strategy built on the aims of the 1987 GLWQA while also aligning with emerging global concerns as expressed in Agenda 21 (adopted at the UN's Conference on Environment and Development in 1992) and elsewhere, concerns that eventually led to the Stockholm Convention on Persistent Organic Pollutants (2001).[5]

Subnational governance has also been important in the Great Lakes Basin, particularly via the Council of Great Lakes Governors (CGLG), comprising representatives of the eight states that border the lakes, along with Ontario and Quebec (see Temby and Stoett, 2017). Established in 1955 under the Great Lakes Charter, the CGLG works independently of national governments in committing its 10 members to measures to uphold water quality in the basin. The CGLG also holds that Great Lakes waters should not be exported in bulk outside the basin, a decision confirmed in the 2001 annex to the charter regarding bulk water removals; the annex emerged in response to Ontario's decision in 1999 to grant a private conglomerate a permit to extract 160 million gallons per year for Asian markets (Schulte, 2012). The 2005 Great Lakes–St. Lawrence River Basin Sustainable Water Resources Agreement outlined the framework for management agreed to in the 2001 annex. The eight US member-states signed an agreement in 2008 that lays out common policies and procedures to ensure their own compliance. While a moderate flow leaves Lake Michigan to enable navigation to the Mississippi River, municipalities naturally lying outside the Great Lakes Basin have been refused access by their own states under the CGLG – though some counties continue to press for consideration. The concern is that once transfers are initiated it may be difficult to hold them back; "opening the tap" to bulk water exports may effectively be an irreversible decision. Indeed, despite a voluntary 1999 agreement between the Canadian federal government and the provinces banning bulk water exports, "any province that chose to lift that voluntary ban and approve bulk water exports would put pressure on every other province" through NAFTA's Chapter 11 investor protection provisions (Patterson, 2016).[6]

The recovery of the Great Lakes has been driven by a number of bodies tasked with maintaining and improving the health of these ecosystems, including municipalities and non-governmental organizations, as well as national and provincial/state authorities, but it continues to be challenged by industrial, agricultural, and population trends. The few remaining wetlands in populated areas are often highly sought after by agriculturalists and developers; roadways are still being built across sensitive lands and streams, encouraging vehicle pollution such as exhaust, solvents, particulates, and microplastics from tires; shorelines continue to be hardened through housing and land reclamation; pharmaceuticals and new "forever chemicals" continue to find their way into waters that are increasingly overwhelmed by invasive species. Indeed, the most recent State of the Great Lakes Report declared the overall condition on a number of indicators (drinkability, agricultural chemicals, groundwater) as "fair" (with the overall trend "unchanging") – but every one of the five lakes scored poorly with regard to the ecological impact of aquatic invasive species (SOGL, 2022; see also Chapter Ten).

Overall, Canadian water quality is better than that in most countries, but as we have seen there are still many challenges to be met. Many activists and observers believe that the best way to protect Canadian water is to instil it with its own set of inherent rights, and we turn to that proposition now.

INHERENT RIGHTS FOR WATER?

Many Indigenous cultures recognize natural entities such as animals and rivers as persons, and even as kin, and good relations with the living earth form a foundation of their worldview. The introduction or recovery of Indigenous voices in jurisprudence has contributed to a growing body of legal decisions that reflect this view. The concept of rights revolves around the recognition of capacities and granting of protections to legal persons, enabling them to do things like buy and sell property, trade access to water, and sue others while protecting them from impositions like theft and assault. In recent years a global movement around the rights of nature has sought to extend the recognition of **legal personhood** to other natural entities such as lakes, forests, and mountains. The movement has gained a solid footing in groundbreaking legal protections for the Whanganui River in Aotearoa/New Zealand, the Vilcabamba River in Ecuador, the *Atrato River* decision of Colombia's Constitutional Court, and the Uttarakhand (India) High Court ruling on the Ganges and Yamuna Rivers (see Rights of Rivers, 2020, for an extensive listing; and Lamalle & Stoett, 2023).

The argument gained prominence in western jurisprudence with Christopher Stone's (1972) provocative article "Should Trees Have Standing?," which pointed out there is no inherent reason why rights, in parallel with human rights, should not be extended to natural entities. His argument is not simply about supporting the already recognized *human right* to a liveable environment (clean water, etc.) or even animal protection laws; both of these are cases in which law is a response to human sentiments and needs.[7] Rights of nature, by contrast, "are not rights *conferred* by human beings, but [are] instead a recognition of rights that have always existed" (Rights of Rivers, 2020, p. 12); they are parallel to human rights, which recognize inherent value in the subject of rights simply by the fact they are humans (see Warner, 2021).

These efforts have been assisted in many cases by environmental and legal groups, including members of the Global Alliance for the Rights of Nature (GARN.org), which initiated the International Rights of Nature Tribunal in 2014. While lacking legal standing, the tribunal's decisions illustrate the robust legal logic behind the movement and the enthusiasm of civil society groups and governments (Rights of Rivers, 2020, pp. 14–15). The movement is not without its setbacks, though, as the weight of legal interpretation moves slowly (for a Canadian example, see Case Study 7.2). For instance, when the citizens of Toledo, Ohio, secured a "Lake Erie Bill of Rights" from the city in response to ongoing agricultural pollution and resulting algal blooms, it was immediately challenged in a federal court and struck down on the grounds it was "too vague" and could "invite arbitrary enforcement" (Gersony, 2022).

CASE STUDY 7.2. The Magpie River Case

In Canada, the first formal assertion of the rights of nature came in February 2021, when the Minganie Regional County Municipality (RCM) and the Innu Council of Ekuanitshit adopted resolutions recognizing legal personhood for Muteshekau-shipu, also known as the Magpie River, in Quebec. The Magpie is globally renowned among whitewater rafting enthusiasts, despite already hosting one Hydro-Québec dam. In an effort to contain further development, an "Alliance" of protectors, led by the Innu Council, Minganie RCM, and the Quebec chapter of the Canadian Parks and Wilderness Society (CPAWS), sought legal help to codify the river's rights. Jean-Charles Piétacho, chief of the Innu Council, said he was inspired in part by a visit to the Whanganui River, sacred to New Zealand's Indigenous Maori, and by their long and ultimately successful fight to have the river legally recognized (Stuart-Ulin, 2021).

The resolutions adopted by the Innu Council and Minganie RCM grant the Magpie River nine discrete rights that are "held in conformity with the beliefs, customs and practices of the Innu of Ekuanitshit" (Jang, 2021):

- The right to flow
- The right to respect for its cycles
- The right for its natural evolution to be protected and preserved
- The right to maintain its natural biodiversity
- The right to fulfill its essential functions within its ecosystem
- The right to maintain its integrity
- The right to be safe from pollution
- The right to regenerate and be restored
- The right to sue

The Muteshekau-shipu resolutions also assign the Innu as legal guardians to ensure these rights are enforced, but (for now) these lack the power of parliamentary sanction (Jang, 2021; Remedios & Ardanaz, 2021). The Magpie River's legal rights have yet to be tested in court, and it remains to be seen how the arguments of its guardians will fare against the demands of developers or the province, should it come to that. Nonetheless the declaration itself establishes the Muteshekau-shipu as another support for global recognition of these principles of Indigenous legal thought. As Piétacho said, "We are not the owners of the river. The Innu of Ekuanitshit have always been the protectors of the Nitassinan (ancestral territory) and will continue to be so through the recognition of the rights of the Muteshekau-shipu River" (quoted in Stuart-Ulin, 2021).

Stone's (1972) early argument echoes the Indigenous viewpoint: "The fact is, that each time there is a movement to confer rights onto some new 'entity', the proposal is bound to sound odd or frightening or laughable. This is partly because until the rightless thing receives its rights, we cannot see it as anything but a *thing* for the use of 'us' – those who are holding rights at the time" (p. 455). It can be argued that natural entities, from mice to mountains, have as much inherent right to exist and flourish as do humans. As our law evolves to recognize this as legal fact, it both reflects and impacts our behaviour regarding the natural world.

Critical Thinking Questions

1. What are the arguments for granting rights to nature versus rights for living animals and sentient beings?
2. What would a tribunal that included representation for nature look like?

CONCLUSION: FUTURE FLOWS

A key principle of hydrology is that water, driven by gravity, tends to follow the path of least resistance as it flows to lower elevations. Considerable inputs of energy are required to lift the water up again. As a metaphor for federal water policy, the path of least resistance suggests a weak policy approach that seeks to avoid upsetting strong, entrenched interests and generally avoids committing to strengthening and enforcing policy to accord with new realities and scientific knowledge. The metaphor also embodies the realization that, as with Idle No More and water supply privatization, when the public makes vocal demands with sufficient energy this can impact policy. If provincial governments abandon their own water protection rules in the interests of developers in the energy, agriculture, housing, and transport sectors, they must navigate the resistance from rural communities, rate payers, environmental groups, fishing interests, Indigenous Peoples, and municipalities. Meanwhile a virtual whirlpool around transboundary water exports threatens to draw in all ships if governments are not united and careful. The political will needed to lift water policy to a higher standard is not easy to generate, and from an environmental perspective it is a struggle simply to keep water and habitat protection standards from falling further. Collective pressure from scientists, but also from the many diverse users of water, will need to raise this energy, and so raise the bar on freshwater protection. Similarly, efforts to protect the largest collections of water on the planet – the oceans – need to be amplified moving forward, and we turn to them in the next chapter.

NOTES

1   Long-term drinking water advisories mean the local water supply is unsafe to drink and should be boiled before use or replaced with bottled water brought in from elsewhere. Some of these water advisories have been in place since the 1990s. Since 2015, the federal government has reduced their numbers, but many remain (see Indigenous Services Canada, 2024).

2 This provision of the Act was subject to substantial revision in 2012, as discussed below.
3 Historically, the review process almost never handed down a denial; only two projects were rejected between 1975 and 2012 (Gilchrist, 2018). While this fact was used to justify removing "red tape," the changes removed any incentive for developers to consider their potential ecological impact on most of Canada's rivers and lakes.
4 A recent study (Williams et al., 2022) determined the period between 2000 and 2020 was the driest in over 1,000 years.
5 The Stockholm Convention has 185 parties as of 2022.
6 Note that under the new, post-NAFTA, United States-Mexico-Canada Agreement (USMCA), investor–state dispute settlement mechanisms will change, effectively eliminating the Chapter 11 provisions of NAFTA between Canada and the United States and significantly scaling it back between the United States and Mexico. However, this does little to assuage the fear that once the freshwater taps are open to export, it will indeed be difficult to turn them off or keep others from opening.
7 While wild animals have "protected" status in a number of national constitutions, in no instance is the term "rights" used (Stilt, 2021). Animals thus are not subjects of law; in legal terms they are a form of property, the treatment of which is regulated.

CHAPTER EIGHT

Oceans

LEARNING OBJECTIVES

1. Explain the importance of oceans to Canada's economy, culture, and environment, including marine biodiversity and ecosystem services.
2. Analyze the major threats to ocean health, including climate change, pollution, overfishing, and invasive species.
3. Evaluate Canada's ocean governance framework, including the *Oceans Act* and international agreements, and identify areas for improvement.

INTRODUCTION: THE CHANGING OCEANS

Freshwater resources – lakes, rivers, and wetlands – are a signature trait of Canada's physical characteristics and identity. But oceans, which stretch long into the horizons on three Canadian fronts, are equally significant. The Pacific, Arctic, and Atlantic Oceans have been instrumental in the geophysical, cultural, economic, and political development of North America/Turtle Island. The total distance of Canada's coastlines, including all its intricate bays, inlets, islands, and fjords, is estimated to be approximately 243,042 kilometres, longer than any other country, and Canada has the second-longest continental shelf. Canada is one of the biggest commercial exporters of ocean fish, and Canadian oceanic shipping lines carry products across the globe. As importantly, Canada imports vast quantities of products that have been carried over the oceans and has imported various aquatic invasive species in the process. Coastal Indigenous communities have special cultural and spiritual bonds with the oceans as well (Bennett et al., 2018); the oceans are intertwined with many Indigenous identities and provide a foundation for cultural heritage, traditional fishing practices, and spiritual beliefs.

Too often underrecognized, ocean ecopolitics is as contentious as any other area where natural resources, biodiversity, community needs, global interconnections, and other dynamic factors are involved. This should not be a surprise, given the geopolitical history of colonialism. Since its contemporary inception, Canada has relied heavily on marine transportation for trade, connecting its remote communities and facilitating international commerce. Ports along the coasts enable the import and export of goods, enhancing economic growth and competitiveness while at the same time bringing pollution and new threats to biosecurity. As we will see in Chapter Eleven, the Arctic region's increasing accessibility because of climate change has opened new possibilities for shipping, resource extraction, and tourism, requiring responsible management to mitigate potential environmental impacts. But not just the Arctic Ocean is changing: The Atlantic and Pacific are also undergoing transformations resulting from climate change, pollution, and other anthropogenic threats to sustainability.

Thinking about the health of the oceans means going beyond traditional extractivist and geopolitical perspectives. There is no doubt that oceans are a vital aspect of the Canadian economy; indeed, the communities that now line the Atlantic coast were to a considerable extent developed on the strength of the fishing industry there, offshore oil drilling has dominated much of eastern coastal economic development, and almost all of Canada's exports bound for non-US or Mexican destinations must be shipped across oceans (the same goes for imports, obviously). Oceans are also at the heart of naval policy, a major aspect of Canadian defence policy. But even these ongoing factors are small in comparison to the role oceans play in sustaining life on the planet, providing key ecosystem services that enable us to breathe, eat, and avoid even greater impacts of climate change due to anthropogenic emissions.

Canadian marine ecosystems are home to a vast array of species, including commercially important fish stocks, marine mammals, and migratory birds. These ecosystems contribute to the overall ecological balance and provide critical habitats for species at risk. Protecting and preserving the oceans' biodiversity is not only crucial for sustaining marine life but also for supporting the broader ecosystem services that benefit human populations, such as climate regulation, carbon sequestration, and water filtration (see Archambault et al., 2010). But the theme of oceans biodiversity goes far beyond the territorial and exclusive economic zone of Canada – as a recently (2023) negotiated international treaty on biodiversity on the high seas indicates. And while much of the public discourse on oceans centres on the construction of additional ports for oil and natural gas distribution abroad and the further pursuit of deepwater drilling, we should not forget that oceans also offer viable alternatives to fossil fuel energy. Indeed, Canada's oceans offer immense potential for renewable energy production, mainly through tidal and wave energy, which can help diversify the country's energy sources and reduce greenhouse gas emissions (see Chapter Six).

So there is little doubt that the oceans are a major factor for Canadian ecopolitics, yet they are not often the subject of sustained political discussion – at least not away from the coasts. As the impacts of overfishing, pollution, climate change, offshore oil and gas drilling, invasive alien species, and other substantive threats to ocean health register on the Canadian public consciousness, oceans will probably play a larger role in the cross-country discussions of Canadian ecopolitics.[1] However, this may be too little, too late. If it is reasonable to assume that most Canadians do not understand the foundational role oceans play in the carbon cycle and other ecosystem services that are absolutely essential for human survival, it is imperative that ocean sustainability is a major part of the ecopolitical agenda.

It is important to note that Canada has exercised jurisdiction over the territorial sea on its east and west coasts (out to 12 nautical miles) since 1970, first under the *Territorial Sea and Fishing Zones Act* and now under the *Oceans Act*. The baselines for measuring the territorial sea were originally set in 1967. The UN Convention on the Law of the Sea (UNCLOS) governs many aspects of ocean affairs, from navigation and fisheries to scientific research and the rights of coastal states to explore, exploit, conserve, and manage resources within 200 nautical miles of their shores and on their continental shelves beyond 200 nautical miles (where applicable). This gives Canada a tremendous amount of marine area to govern and, as naval and coast guard personnel will remind us, protect. The *Oceans Act* is Canada's flagship marine protection law, and it celebrated its twenty-fifth anniversary in 2022. The Act was lauded as the world's first holistic and ecosystem-based law when it came into force in 1997 (see Jessen, 2011). In 2016 it was joined by a new Oceans Protection Plan added by the Trudeau government, which came with $1.5 billion in spending commitments. Nonetheless, there is considerable fragmentation in ocean policy governance in Canada, as responsibilities are often split between federal, provincial, territorial, municipal, and First Nations governments (Kenny et al., 2020; Ricketts & Harrison, 2007; McDorman & Chircop, 2012; Berkes et al., 2001; Jessen, 2011). There are many actors who want different things from the oceans, including large companies invested in shipping, fishing, oil drilling, deep sea mining, and other resource pursuits; coastal communities concerned about local pollution and fishing rights; activists and scientists concerned about climate change and biodiversity; and many others. And when oceans are involved, related issues are immediately international in scope.

CANADA'S OCEANIC BIODIVERSITY

From iconic orcas (killer whales) to once-bountiful cod to far-flying coastal seabirds, Canada's marine biodiversity is well known throughout the world. One study estimated that Canada's ocean biodiversity, including microbes, phytoplankton, macroalgae, zooplankton, benthic fauna, fishes, and marine mammals, easily includes 16,000 different species (Archambault et al., 2010). But as we have seen throughout this book, one cannot discuss biodiversity today without reference to the threats it faces. The same study emphasizes the exploitation pressure that has been put on marine mammals in particular: 42 per cent of marine mammals are at risk of extinction (compared with roughly 36 per cent at risk globally). Fisheries operations kill untold numbers of marine mammals – especially cetaceans (whales, dolphins, and porpoises), otters, and seals – each year. Yet the largest threat remains habitat alteration due to climate change and pollution; bioaccumulation is clearly a factor in populations of St. Lawrence beluga whales and polar bears, for example.

The direct exploitation of species has always been a cause of concern for biodiversity conservation, and Canada is no stranger to these threats. We've already discussed overfishing, but the history of whaling, in which several species of large cetaceans have been driven to or are near extinction, and the contemporary saga of the bluefin tuna, which Canada insists can be harvested sustainably despite many claims to the contrary (see Pinchin, 2023, for a fascinating delve into the bluefin tuna fishing industry), permeate our understanding of the human exploitation of ocean biodiversity. Even the most casual observer of Canadian coastal ecopolitics will be aware of the intense controversy that has swirled around the east coast seal hunt. Indeed, the Inuit and others have relied on sealing for centuries, and sealing on the west coast was so prodigious it threatened to drive seals extinct and propelled the establishment of one of the first international wildlife conservation conventions, the 1911 North Pacific Fur Seal Treaty. The Atlantic sealing industry dates back to the 1500s, driven primarily by a combination of local consumption and the export market of fur seal (and other body parts). Footage of baby harp seals (whitecoats) and hooded seals (bluebacks) being skinned alive in the 1950s and 1960s established a negative connotation of the seal hunt (this practice has been banned for decades, but the hunt remains a bloody spectacle). The International Federation for Animal Welfare was particularly prolific on the seal front; it began an anti-sealing campaign in the 1960s that continues to this day. A legendary animosity persists between the seasonal sealing industry in Newfoundland, represented by groups such as the Fur Institute of Canada and the Canadian Sealers Association, and star-studded groups opposing it on animal welfare grounds (even though harp seals are not endangered), suggesting the hunt is only allowed to continue to compensate for the mishandling of cod stocks (see Case Study 8.1 later in this chapter).[2] In many cases, without solid European or American export markets[3] seals are killed for body parts, including the male penis, to be exported to Asia. While the humaneness of the hunt has been found largely satisfactory by the Canadian Veterinary Medical Association (see Daoust et al., 2002), sealing has become a hard line for many animal rights activists, though many of them accept Inuit sealing (mainly for subsistence purposes). The Government of Canada continues to struggle between the pull of these two strong currents.

Direct exploitation of species is not the only threat to oceanic biodiversity, however. For example, many biologists consider aquatic invasive species one of the gravest threats to marine life. Familiar culprits include the zebra and quagga mussels, the round goby, the sea lamprey, the dreaded Asian carp, the alewife, the lionfish, and many others: The majority of these arrived in Canadian freshwater lakes and rivers after having been transported across oceans. Pathways include ship ballast water, aquaculture, recreational activities (including stocking for sport fishing), aquarium releases, live food and bait, biological controls, ecological restoration efforts gone awry, and even melting sea ice (which could release pathogens against which there is no contemporary immunity). An international convention on ballast water is helping to reduce the numbers of introduced species in the shipping industry, but the threat remains acute, especially as climate change and water temperatures reconfigure the natural ranges of species.

Indeed, all the threats to global biodiversity identified by a landmark assessment compiled by the Intergovernmental Science-Policy Platform on Biodiversity and Ecosystem Services (IPBES) apply to Canadian marine biodiversity: habitat destruction, direct overexploitation, invasive alien species, climate change, and pollution (including, in this case, marine noise pollution,

Figure 8.1. World's Largest Bluefin Tuna, Nova Scotia, 1979

Note: In 1979, Ken Fraser landed this 1,496-pound bluefin tuna, the world's largest, near Auld's Cove, Nova Scotia.
Source: Photo courtesy of the International Game Fish Association (IGFA). Reproduced with permission.

a theme we discuss later in this chapter; IPBES, 2019). While certain marine species have emerged as iconic in the Canadian public imagination, such as the polar bear, orca, snowy owl, or northern fulmar, and they all face these threats to greater or lesser degrees, what is really at risk is the very fabric of life itself – the biodiversity that makes ecosystems possible. This applies to oceans in particular: Phytoplankton are the bottom of the oceanic food chain, and if it is significantly reduced from pollution or temperature fluctuations or ocean acidification, the entire chain could collapse. A United Nations Regional Global Outlook Assessment outlines the seriousness of this issue of acidification, which

> is expected to harm a wide range of ocean life, particularly those that use calcium and carbonate ions from seawater to produce calcium carbonate for their shells. Larval molluscs and some other calcifying organisms are already showing impaired shell formation at some locations, and calcareous plankton ... corals, and shellfish are also threatened. Water off the North American Pacific coast already has a low carbonate saturation state. When surface winds blow the top layer of water out from coastal regions, deeper water with higher acidity can well up, and harm shellfish ... There has been a reduced natural set of juvenile oysters in some Pacific coast estuaries where the commercial shellfish industry relies on natural reproduction of oysters ... Behaviour is also altered in many animals, especially that related to the olfactory system. Fish in acidic water in the lab or living next to natural seeps, where carbon dioxide is released by volcanic activity, lose their natural fear of the odour of predators and become attracted to them. But predatory behaviour can also be impaired. (UNEP 2016, pp. 97–98)

In 2023, working under the legal umbrella of the UNCLOS, the international community arrived at a legally binding agreement to protect biodiversity in areas beyond national jurisdiction – the high seas, basically, which cover two-thirds of the ocean. This landmark agreement took over a decade to construct and calls for governments to set up large-scale protected regions and to share genetic information about biodiversity (though fishing and military activities are largely beyond the Biodiversity Beyond National Jurisdiction Agreement). As a signatory, Canada (which has yet to ratify the agreement as of the summer of 2024) has made a commitment to respect this aspect of conserving marine biodiversity (see Box 8.1 and Map 8.1), but the extraordinary variety of life within the country's coasts and the vast Arctic Sea also require urgent and steadfast protection in the midst of multiple threats and economic development. As we see now, the stakes could not be higher. But it would be chimerical to suggest that the Canadian state and provincial governments, despite pressure from conservation groups, are prepared to put ocean biodiversity high on the list of national concerns moving forward (see Map 8.1).

BOX 8.1. Marine Protected Areas under Canadian Jurisdiction

One often-celebrated response to threats to marine life is the establishment of marine protected areas (MPAs). This can involve complete bans on human activity within designated coastal zones or severe limitations on it. The general idea is to allow nature to take its course without human interference, though in the context of global climate change this is, in the pure sense, not possible. But by banning commercial or recreational fishing, boating, camping, industrial activity, and other human pursuits, the marine area at least has a chance to recover from prior human activities. MPAs can provide much-needed sanctuary for vulnerable and threatened species, and they can also provide natural laboratories for scientists such as biologists to do their important work. Canada has made significant progress in establishing MPAs. Notable examples include the Gwaii Haanas National Marine Conservation Area Reserve and Haida Heritage Site in British Columbia, the Saguenay-St. Lawrence Marine Park in Quebec, and the St. Anns Bank Marine Protected Area in Nova Scotia. However, there is room for improvement in expanding the MPA network, ensuring adequate representation of different marine habitats, and strengthening collaboration with Indigenous communities and stakeholders.

At the 2022 Conference of the Parties of the Convention on Biological Diversity co-hosted by Canada and China, the international community agreed to the Kunming-Montreal Global Biodiversity Framework, which includes a commitment to protect 30 per cent of the world's oceans by 2030. As of January 2023, Canada has protected 14.66 per cent of its oceans, totalling 842,822 square kilometres; jurisdiction is shared among the following federal government departments:

- the *Oceans Act* Marine Protected Areas led by Fisheries and Oceans Canada
- National Wildlife Areas led by Environment and Climate Change Canada
- National Marine Conservation Areas led by Parks Canada

But there are also ample criticisms of MPAs, which we should keep in mind. First of all, they can be seen as exclusionary, keeping people such as Indigenous communities, who had little to do with establishing the problem, away as a solution. They can also present the public with the false notion that the problem of protecting marine biodiversity has been solved, whereas in reality MPAs are temporary and limited solutions that cannot overcome climate change and other threats. And they cost resources to maintain, demanding long-term commitment from both provincial and federal governments.

CLIMATE CHANGE AND THE OCEANS

No oceans, no people: It is really that simple. But the interactions between the oceans and human society are quite complex. For example, the oceans serve to regulate global climate by transferring hot and cold water that rises and sinks, thus affecting local temperatures everywhere.

We've taken this for granted, until recently, but major shifts in ocean temperatures could have potentially disastrous impacts in terms of climate regulation on a global scale, affecting food security and habitat for humans and non-humans alike. In the summer and autumn of 2023 scientists noticed a major temperature anomaly in the Northwest Atlantic, for example, raising concerns that this will result in increased sea ice melting, more hurricanes affecting the Canadian east coast, and in the long run could even disrupt the ocean currents that prevent Arctic-like conditions in the United Kingdom and elsewhere. Most scientists believe that 90 per cent of the extra heat associated with global warming has been absorbed by the oceans, leading to decreasing oxygen concentrations and hypoxic zones. "Climate-related changes to physicochemical properties have repercussions for the vertical transport of carbon and nutrients as well as the biogeochemical properties of marine waters,

Map 8.1. Federal Marine Bioregions for Canada's National Network of Marine Protected Areas

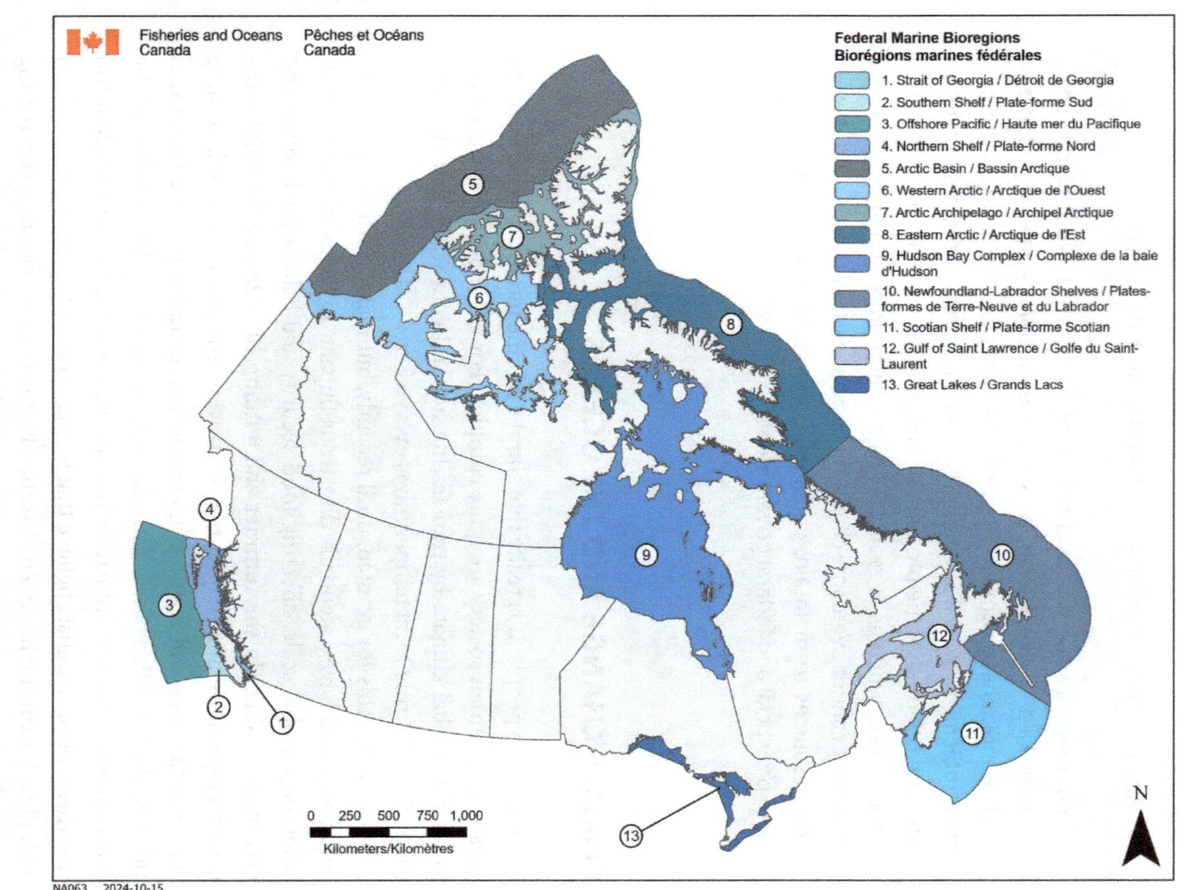

Source: Fisheries and Oceans Canada. Reprinted with permission.

marine microflora, primary productivity, trophic dynamics, and species distributions" (Kenny et al., 2020).

Rising sea levels will certainly impact Canadian coasts, and the increased frequency of extreme weather events (including hurricanes) has already taken an expensive toll over the past two decades. Perhaps the biggest future concern is the Arctic. We discuss this in more detail in Chapter Eleven, but it should be stressed that the impacts of climate change are no longer a future concern but a present reality with significant geopolitical implications and daily impacts for northern peoples, including the Inuit. Alaskan and Canadian glacier ice loss continues at a predictable pace, part of a global trend that is contributing to accelerating patterns of sea level rise:

> Long-term observations show that glaciers around the world are in retreat and losing mass. The World Glacier Monitoring Service, which has a series of datasets collected since the 17th century, coordinates worldwide glacier monitoring activities that provide an unprecedented dataset of glacier observations from ground, air, and space … Glaciological and geodetic observations show that since 2000 the rates of glacier-mass loss are unprecedented on a global scale, at least compared to the centuries of observation and probably also for recorded history, as indicated in reconstructions from written and illustrated documents. (UNEP, 2016, p. 98)

Global ocean temperatures recorded in 2024 have, by all accounts, been extraordinarily high, even when compared to the steady rise in temperatures illustrated in Figure 8.2; indeed, between April 2023 and June 2024 we saw a streak of 15 consecutive monthly record highs (National Ocean and Atmospheric Administration, 2024). The implications of climate change for Canadian security are explored elsewhere (see in particular Greaves, 2021), but it is painfully evident that the impact of rising ocean temperatures, which is linked directly to the continued emissions of greenhouse gases, poses an existential threat to the human and environmental security of everyone on earth. In some coastal communities and small island states the threat is immediate, but no one can escape it entirely. And yet the national ecopolitical discourse on climate (see Chapter Nine) is virtually silent on the grave issue of climate and oceans. We might come to regret this absence greatly in the coming decades.

One source of hope on the climate change front pertains to "blue carbon," which is presently being discussed within the broader context of an emerging

Figure 8.2. Average Sea Surface Temperature, 1880–2023

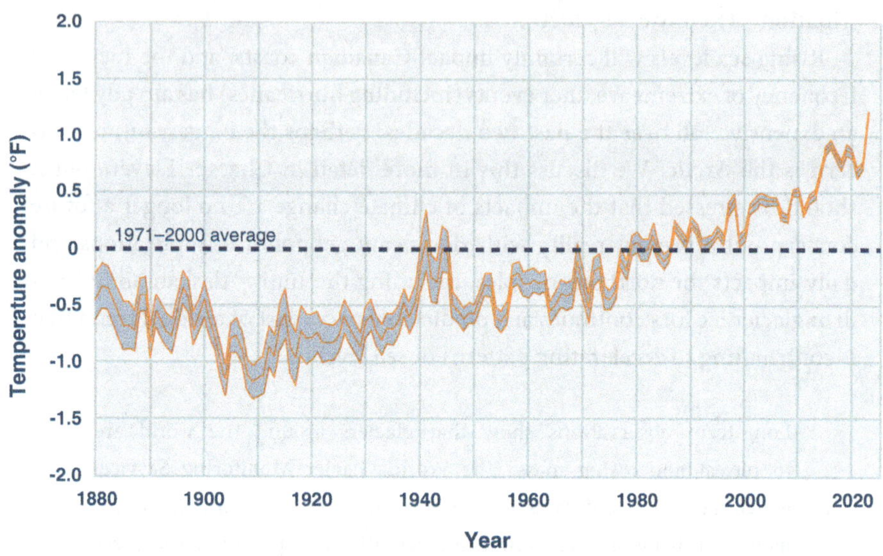

Note: This graph shows how the average surface temperature of the world's oceans has changed since 1880. The graph uses the 1971 to 2000 average as a baseline for depicting change. Choosing a different baseline period would not change the shape of the data over time. The shaded band shows the range of uncertainty in the data, based on the number of measurements collected and the precision of the methods used.
Source: Adapted from US Environmental Protection Agency, "Climate Change Indicators: Sea Surface Temperature," www.epa.gov/climate-indicators/climate-change-indicators -sea-surface-temperature. Data retrieved from Huang, B., Thorne, P.W., Banzon, V.F., Boyer, T., Chepurin, G., Lawrimore, J.H., Menne, M.J., Smith, T.M., Vose, R.S., & Zhang, H.-M. (2024). "NOAA Extended Reconstructed Sea Surface Temperature (ERSST), version 5 (dataset)." https://doi.org/10.7289/V5T72FNM.

"**blue economy**." Terrestrial carbon stored in plant biomass and soils in forested land, plantations, agricultural land, and pastureland is often called "green carbon." Blue carbon is the carbon captured by the world's oceans and represents more than 55 per cent of total biological carbon (Nellemann et al., 2009). It is stored or sequestered in marine and coastal ecosystems including mangrove forests, tidal salt marshes, and seagrass meadows, as well as coral reefs and oceanic carbon sinks in the form of marine algae. These habitats provide important ecosystem services as spawning habitat and defence against storms as well as for nutrient cycling and pollination, and they provide economic resources including livelihoods and food, materials, and medicine. The growing kelp forest industry is an example of how commercial success and climate change mitigation can work together. The need to conserve estuaries, mangrove forests, seagrass ecosystems, and other wetlands is well recognized as we adapt to rising sea levels and extreme weather events, but viewing these areas as carbon sinks can give extra incentive to pursue related policies and to build on experience.

THE FISHING NATIONS

As discussed in Chapter Four, it is impossible to conceive of contemporary Canada without the historical record of several varieties of natural resource extraction, but the most formative variety might well have been fisheries. Indeed, Indigenous communities on the Atlantic coast (such as the Mi'kmaq), on the Pacific coast (such as the Haida), and in the Arctic (such as the Inuit) relied heavily on the oceans for thousands of years before European arrival. This was for survival and trade, but oceans and the wildlife contained within them are central aspects of many Indigenous cultures and worldviews (Berkes, 1990; McMillan & Prosper, 2016):

> Possessing place-based knowledge systems and equipped with fishing technologies passed down for generations …, Indigenous fishing practices were governed by laws and customs embedded into their worldviews and languages, often centering on sustainable uses and conservation for generations to come. For example, the Mi'kmaw concept of netukulimk describes achieving nutritional and economic standards of wellbeing for the community without jeopardizing ecological integrity, diversity, or productivity in the future. (Castañeda et al., 2020, p. 304)

Similarly, it is impossible to think of the development of the Pacific Coast First Nations without reference to the anadromous salmon that provided the basic food for so many communities. Nor is it possible to think of the advent of colonialism without fisheries to both draw and sustain the settler European presence. As the group of prominent historians quoted above describe it:

> The European experience in Canada began with fish. The Portuguese and Spanish Basques in the late 15th century (followed by the English and French in the early 16th century) undertook migratory fisheries, travelling from Europe in March/April to fish Atlantic Cod in the coastal and offshore waters of Newfoundland, returning to Europe to sell their catch

> in early autumn … By the early 17th century, Atlantic Salmon became
> another strategically and economically important species, albeit minis-
> cule relative to the value and catch of cod … Although prominent today,
> the earliest commercial fishery for an invertebrate was for lobster Homa-
> rus americanus in the mid-19th century. (Castañeda, et al. 2020, p. 306)

Some believe the Norse reached what is now eastern Canada as early as the year 1000 and were fishing for cod even then (Ledger et al., 2019). Long before the *British North America Act, 1867,* fishing was one of the main economic activities of European settlers; contestation and diplomacy over North Atlantic fishing rights between the United States and Great Britain began soon after the American Revolution, and American investment in shipping operations off the coast of Nova Scotia was an early indication of the coming strength of American capital (see Payne, 2005; Earle, 2023). Whaling was also an important economic factor in the development of many small coastal communities in the north (see Francis, 1984) and further linked colonial Canada to the world economy (commercial whaling has not occurred off Canadian shores since the late 1960s, though small "aboriginal subsistence whaling"[4] operations continue in the Arctic). Fisheries are so central to the Canadian state that, at the federal level, Canada has never had a department solely devoted to "oceans" (such as the US National Oceanic and Atmospheric Administration) but has, since 1867, operated some version of the Department of Fisheries and Oceans. At one point even the work of the future Canadian Navy was included within the fisheries administrative context; today, at the federal level, the relevant official in the cabinet is the Minister of Fisheries, Oceans and the Canadian Coast Guard.

Despite the challenges of conservation, fishing remains central to the Canadian economy today. Even during the COVID-19 pandemic fishing provided thousands of jobs. Canada's fish and seafood exports were worth $8.79 billion in 2021, a 36 per cent increase over 2020 and an 18 per cent increase over the previous high in 2019. Unsurprisingly, the United States is the primary destination of most (70 per cent or higher) of Canada's fish and seafood exports, followed by China and then the European Union. The top species exported included lobster, crab, and salmon. The main exporting provinces are all on the east coast, relying principally on the Atlantic: Nova Scotia, New Brunswick, and Newfoundland and Labrador account for 70 per cent of Canada's fish and export value, though British Columbia is a close fourth.[5]

In 1992, the Canadian government imposed a moratorium on extraction of cod and other groundfish stocks from the North Atlantic fishery (see Case Study 8.1). This drastic policy resulted from the collapse of reported populations of fish in the region and ensuing fears about the short- and long-term viability of the fishing industry, which directly and indirectly employed more than 50,000 people, primarily in Newfoundland and Labrador. The causes of the collapse and its ecological, economic, and social implications have been widely studied, and there is general agreement that it resulted from the interaction of a variety of phenomena (Myers et al., 1997; Myers & Worm, 2003; National Research Council of Canada, 1999). Most observers agree that "the practice of [fisheries] management, which has led to depletion and dependence, points to the inability of resource management frameworks to control destructive fishing practices, the realities of which are connected to economic and technological realities that are present in modern society generally" (Rogers, 1997, p. 81). There is general agreement that the primary cause was commercial overfishing that was ineffectively managed by government regulation. The profit incentive to develop extractive technology greatly exceeded efforts to manage the level of resource extraction, namely the development of methods to ameliorate the social, economic, and ecological damage caused by the fishery's collapse. Following the collapse, the regional economy, particularly that of Newfoundland and Labrador, was only saved from greater loss "to the extent that public funds substitute for cash inputs from the fishing industry" (Ommer & Sinclair, 1999, p. 64), illustrating the claim that under neoliberal capitalist economics profits from production accrue to private actors while costs and risk are borne by the state (Saurin, 2001).

CASE STUDY 8.1. The North Atlantic Cod Fishery Collapse

The overexploitation and ultimate depletion of the North Atlantic cod fishery was intimately connected with technological developments in the fishing industry. Of particular note was the changing nature of fishing vessels in the postwar period, with traditional side trawlers giving way first to stern trawlers, whose extractive potential remained limited by their necessary proximity to port, and later to factory-equipped freezer trawlers capable of spending months at sea and catching and processing hundreds of tonnes of fish before returning to shore (Blake, 1997, p. 208). As a result of such massive extraction, by 1995 the total biomass of groundfish stocks in the Atlantic Canadian fishery had declined to 11 per cent of 1982 levels (National Research Council, 1999; Davies & Rangeley, 2010). Foreign fishers, primarily from Europe, also reduced cod stocks in the 1970s before the modernization of the Canadian fleet, but the assertion of sole Canadian fishing rights to a 200-mile coastal economic exclusion zone (EEZ) enabled domestic extraction to push the fishery beyond a sustainable threshold in the early 1990s (Blake, 1997; National Research Council, 1999; Ommer & Sinclair, 1999). Within the context of a global neoliberal economic system, the distinction between foreign and Canadian fishers is largely irrelevant; both signify market actors pursuing private profit according to the accumulative logic of a common pool resource. But it is of immense political importance to Canadian politicians.

In the wake of the technologically induced collapse and the federal fishing moratorium, bureaucratic actors at all levels engaged in denial and finger-pointing to avoid responsibility for the devastating social, economic, and ecological impacts. To avoid accepting responsibility for insufficiently protecting the public interest, bureaucrats and politicians engaged in three sets of tactics: (1) They claimed that decision-making power, and thus responsibility, actually rested with some other authority – delegation; (2) they initially refused to accept the scale of the problem, denying the need to alter existing regulatory mechanisms or management schemes – institutional paralysis; and (3) they claimed that causes other than overfishing were responsible, despite the scientific agreement that overfishing by private actors was the definitive cause – regulatory capture. Fishers blamed government, seals, and foreign vessels; government denied its responsibility and vacillated about the cause, so "rather than analyze the relationships and procedures which have caused the collapse of the fishery, most relevant fishery discussions have demonized the foreigner, the seal, and changing climatic conditions which allegedly caused the cod to freeze to death off the coast of Labrador" (Rogers, 1997, p. 83).

The delegation of responsibility by government and industry was largely based on denial that overfishing was the fundamental cause of the collapse. This involved two distinct phases: Preceding the collapse, policymakers at the Department of Fisheries and Oceans (DFO) ignored the advice of their own scientists and set limits for the total allowable catch that exceeded what the data suggested was the sustainable yield of cod. By the mid-1980s, it was apparent that DFO's projections of fish stocks had been wildly optimistic, but in 1989 the minister declined to follow his scientists' advice and reduce the total allowable catch by half, reducing it by one-tenth instead. As a result, in 1991 more than half of the total volume of all remaining fish in the waters off Newfoundland was extracted, and just seven months before the imposition of the moratorium, the DFO set the same quota for the following year (Kunzig, 1995). The capacity of the government to take action had been compromised by the political and economic imperative of keeping the fishery open. This phase of denial was followed by a second round after the collapse, in which officials ignored, challenged, or lied about the scientific findings that overfishing had caused the collapse (Brubaker, 2000).

The story of the North Atlantic fishery shows signs of regulatory capture, insofar as the decisions and actions of the government were taken primarily with industry's interests in mind. The data collected by DFO scientists to determine estimates of fish populations were gathered partly from the logs of commercial fishing trawlers (Ommer & Sinclair, 1999, p. 64). Providing industry with the ability to influence scientific estimates of fish stocks that are then used to determine the total allowable catch clearly gave private actors the opportunity to affect the stringency of their own regulation. Even the post-collapse financial assistance provided to the fishing industry served the interests of private capital more than it helped manage the structural problems of the industry and region. The Atlantic Groundfish Strategy (TAGS) was intended to help the fishing industry transition following the collapse and moratorium by reducing fishing capacity. In a report on federal spending to help Atlantic Canada "adjust" to the moratorium, the auditor general concluded that despite the intention that TAGS and other federal subsidies would help reduce the chronic overcapacity and overcapitalization of the east coast fishery, five years later effective fishing capacity was 160 per cent of what it had been in the early 1990s. That the collapse of groundfish stocks as a result of commercial overfishing should result in government programs whose end result is the further subsidization and modernization of those private commercial interests such that the physical capacity to exploit the now-exhausted resource actually increases is simply stunning. In retrospect, the DFO "was cheerleading rather than regulating" (Kunzig, 1995), but the overall decision making and response of the government to management of the fisheries strongly suggests the satisfaction of commercial over public needs.

Critical Thinking Questions

1. Who is ultimately responsible for the cod fishery collapse: fishers, the government, technology, or seals?
2. What is meant by "regulatory capture" in this case, and what effect did it have on the cod fishery leading up to the collapse?

Unsurprisingly, Canada is no stranger to serious fisheries disputes. Much of the contention over fishing has been between Indigenous communities and recreational fisheries, such as the ongoing **Mi'kmaq lobster dispute** between Sipekne'katik First Nation members and non-Indigenous lobster fishers in Nova Scotia. The dispute relates to differing interpretations of *R. v. Marshall*, a 1999 Supreme Court of Canada ruling upholding the Peace and Friendship Treaties and empowering Indigenous People with the right to fish. Meanwhile, much of the resource conflict on the oceans has involved other countries, such as the so-called **Pacific Salmon War** with the United States, which began in 1992 after the expiration of the first Pacific Salmon Treaty. The treaty had been ratified in 1985, expired, and lasted until a new agreement was signed in 1999. In 1997 Canadian fishers decided to pursue unlimited salmon catches, leading Alaskan fishers to follow suit, which in turn resulted in a flotilla consisting of over 100 Canadian fishing boats surrounding an Alaskan ferry in the port of Prince Rupert, British Columbia, for three days. At the time, BC premier Glen Clark even threatened to further disrupt Canadian–American cooperation, though a new agreement was signed in June 2001.

Even more famous was the so-called Turbot War (*Guerre du flétan*) of 1995, which evolved on the east coast on the Grand Banks of Newfoundland when a Canadian fisheries patrol vessel fired over the bow of a Spanish trawler, forcing it to port and arresting its crew. Overfishing by the Spanish and other countries was long viewed as a cause of the decline of the cod and turbot fisheries, so it was not a surprise that confrontations would ensue, though many observers were startled by how quickly this led to an international diplomatic scuffle. In the end, the conflict helped usher in a new international fisheries treaty on "straddling" and "highly migratory" fish stocks and reinforced the importance of the Northwest Atlantic Fisheries Organization (NAFO). But these disputes leave social scars, often pitting people against each other because of competing interests and associations, and they illustrate the fragility of both fish stocks and geopolitical relations (see Stoett, 2001).

However disturbing or transformative these disputes have been, they should not overshadow the more alarming fact that a global fisheries crisis is upon us. The United Nations Food and Agriculture Organization (FAO) indicates that overfishing threatens nearly every species, which in turn has severe implications for global food security (FAO, 2022, 2023), and illegal, unregulated, and unreported fishing remains a serious global issue, often accompanied by severe exploitation of workers (see Stoett & Omrow, 2022; Urbina, 2019).

The hard fact is that Canadian marine fisheries have been in a state of "acute crisis" since the early 1990s, and political disputes over fishing jurisdiction and international allocation persist to this day (Schrank, 1995). Several layers of international collaboration have failed to overcome these crises, which have been fed by chronic overfishing by Canadians and others, heavy subsidies given to the fishing industry (though the World Trade Organization now has a much-welcome Agreement on Fisheries Subsidies), illegal fishing operations, and other issues; despite the success of the NAFO (founded in 1979 and headquartered in Halifax), the often-amended Pacific Salmon Treaty between Canada and the United States, and the UN Fish Stock Agreement on high seas fishing in operation since 2001, fisheries remain challenged and stocks are slowly dwindling. The advent of climate change is adding to the challenge as fish try to adapt or migrate to cooler water temperatures. Even recreational fishing, which is much less resource intensive but an important source of revenue and employment across Canada, contributes to the global fisheries crisis; it is difficult to monitor all recreational catches, and many invasive alien species were introduced to enhance local recreational fishing, with deleterious impacts (see Cooke & Gowx, 2004). We will turn our attention to aquaculture next, but it remains politically contentious even as it takes over the global fishing industry as the main mode of fishery operation. In short, and despite continuous and well-informed management of fisheries across Canada, over-reliance on this sector of the economy for food security and economic development has become a perilous exercise at best.

No matter how it is done – whether through concentrated management programs, the drastic reduction of fisheries subsidies, or the fall of profits due to increased scarcity of fish stocks – Canada will be less reliant on open seas fishing in the future.

AQUACULTURE

As suggested previously in this chapter, if overfishing is such a systemic problem, it is often asserted that the solution – assuming people still want to consume vast quantities of fish products – is in moving away from pelagic and coastal commercial fishing and toward farmed fishing on a large scale, commonly known as **aquaculture**. This transition (in addition to shrimp farming and other food sources that have always been related to harvesting non-wild species) has been taking shape across the globe for several decades (see FAO,

2022). Small-scale aquaculture has been practised in Canada for thousands of years, but the involvement of industrial capital changed the complexion of the politics of aquaculture forever.

In Canada, the DFO manages aquaculture collaboratively with the 10 provincial governments and the territories. While Canada has approximately 80,000 kilometres of marine coastline capable of supporting aquaculture and fisheries, it ranks only twenty-fifth in terms of world aquaculture production (FAO-IPPC, 2018). Though there has been progress on the management front, including important collaborative work with Indigenous Peoples, aquaculture remains controversial and is certainly a site of ongoing ecopolitical conflict. Back in 2010 the authors of a detailed analysis of the industry suggested that the debate over the ecological and economic costs and benefits of aquaculture is a "knowledge battlefield," a "political and cultural struggle that reaches across courtrooms, laboratories, governments, newsrooms, scholarly journals, and virtual and street-level activism" (Young & Matthews, 2010, p. 3). Promoting large-scale aquaculture on both coasts are private firms and governments who see great potential for growth, especially as wild stocks continue to decline, touting the health benefits of eating fish over livestock meats such as beef and pork. Those opposed, including many First Nations, non-governmental organizations, and scientists, see it as an especially dirty and dangerous industry that harms wild fish, pollutes local waters, and puts fishers out of business. The spread of sea lice; the release of farmed populations that can interbreed with local populations; the use of antibiotics, pesticides, and artificial colourants; the contamination of seabeds by excess feed: These are all serious issues that large-scale aquaculture struggles to overcome, especially when increasingly violent weather patterns make securing netting difficult. As we mentioned in Chapter Three, the "commons" are always political hotspots, and large-scale aquaculture basically involves capturing the oceanic and lake commons for private purposes.[6] Indeed, many of the industry leaders are not even Canadian-owned businesses.

While the ecopolitics of aquaculture is experienced in many countries (see Osmundesen & Olsen, 2017, who refer to the controversy in Norway as "imperishable"), it is particularly acute in Canada for several reasons. As Young and Matthews (2010) suggest, aquaculture is a very late entry in the extractive industry game: It did not have the benefit of building entire communities and support from politicians – in other words, it had no prior opportunity to establish the narrative of its virtues. The First Nations element should not be underestimated either, especially on the west coast, where wild salmon are of immense cultural significance to Indigenous communities. The First Nations Wild Salmon Alliance has been particularly vocal in its criticism of the dual role – to both regulate and promote the industry – it believes the DFO plays. This was juxtaposed by the BC Salmon Farmers Association's claim that the industry provides nearly 5,000 jobs and $1 billion of economic activity. In mid-June 2024, Diane Lebouthillier, minister of Fisheries, Oceans and the Canadian Coast Guard, announced that the Government of Canada will ban open net-pen salmon aquaculture in British Columbia coastal waters by June 30, 2029 (Fisheries and Oceans Canada, 2024c). But the pressure to delay this ban will no doubt be intense, and inland aquaculture – regulated largely by the provinces – will continue its controversial growth.

POLLUTION

Pollution is an obvious concern regarding Canadian ocean space. Oil spills are perhaps the most dramatic example of disasters that capture public attention while also destroying wildlife and harming fisheries and other activities. While most oil spills in Canada have been onshore, often related to pipeline leaks (see Kheraj, 2020), there have been large spills from both coastal storage units and shipping. And though major oil tanker catastrophes, such as the *Exxon Valdez* spill in Prince William Sound (off the south coast of the US state of Alaska) in 1989, get more media attention, smaller spills from other ships also occur. For example, in February 2022 a Dutch-owned cargo ship accidentally discharged roughly 30,000 litres of an "oil-water mixture over 12 hours and 175 nautical miles after the ship's fuel tank was punctured during heavy sea conditions" (*CBC News*, 2022). On the west coast, a cargo ship spilled 2,700 litres of fuel into English Bay near Vancouver in 2015. An American-owned tugboat sank and leaked 110,000 litres of fuel into the ocean in Heiltsuk First Nation territory the next year, devastating the local marine food industry, which included clam harvesting, and throwing the Indigenous community's relationship with its coastal area into a period of prolonged mourning. The Heiltsuk filed a lawsuit against the BC and federal governments and the ship's owner, which has yet to be resolved; since Canada's *Marine Liability Act* does not recognize cultural losses, a group of elected and hereditary leaders appealed to the International Maritime Organization to recognize such non-economic losses in conventions in the future (see Wood, 2024). This is quite significant since the opening of the Arctic to more shipping could lead to similar situations for the Inuit and others.

Oil and fuel spills are traumatic events for the wildlife and coastal communities that are affected, but most pollution is much more pernicious and takes place on a slow but steady level with equally deleterious results. For example, nutrient leakage into waterways such as freshwater rivers and lakes is largely the result of agricultural practices, but many Canadian waterways lead eventually to the open seas. Harmful algal blooms (HABs) and hypoxia are not only deadly, they are also occurring at alarming levels in most coastal zones in North America, caused by a combination of warmer waters (linked to anthropogenic climate change) and excess nutrient runoff (mainly nitrogen and phosphorous) from agriculture and wastewater. Non-point pollution sources (roadways, farms, suburban sewers) are largely unregulated across the North American continent, and a large amount of this pollution ends up on coastal beaches and in oceans (see Chapter Seven). Though we have known about the global spread of HAB events and coastal eutrophication for decades (see Hallegraeff, 1993), it has reached crisis proportions in Florida and elsewhere, and scientific models predict that HABs will increase on Canada's east coast, too. For example, "*Dinophysis* blooms are most likely to increase in the St. Lawrence Estuary. *Pseudo-nitzschia* blooms will move to the northeastern part of the Gulf of St. Lawrence and will increase in the Bay of Fundy/Gulf of Maine regions" (Bolvin-Rioux et al., 2022). This presents catastrophic dangers to coastal aquaculture, such as the east coast mussel industry. The ecopolitical problem here is that the inputs used in the agricultural system end up affecting water bodies that are quite distant from the farms involved. Accustomed to a level of agricultural production dependent on the heavy use of fertilizers and pesticides, politicians can have a hard time regulating farming practices. Similarly, despite improvements in regulatory capacity, other sources of pollution stem from industrialized society. According to Kenny and colleagues (2020): "Contamination of marine-source foods by metals and new persistent organic pollutants (e.g., per- and polyfluorinated compounds) remains a significant and complex public health concern, particularly for Indigenous Peoples in the Arctic."

Another major source of pollution in the oceans is plastic waste. We've already covered this phenomenon in Chapter Five: Plastic waste is a major problem everywhere today and is often conceived of as part of the product life cycle of plastic products, which are largely derived from fossil fuels and contain thousands of chemical additives. But the issue is particularly acute in oceans, since they experience not only plastic discarded at sea but so much onshore waste also ends up in them. Marine plastic pollution can be subdivided into three basic categories: (1) macroplastics, including debris such as fishing nets, large pieces of Styrofoam, and parcels that have been lost or discarded from cargo ships; (2) microplastics, which comprise particles under 5 millimetres in diameter that remain when plastic objects, including plastic nurdles (which are used in various production processes), enter the sea and phytodegrade; and (3) nanoplastics, the end state of microplastic degradation, which, because they are so small (1,000 times smaller than an algal cell), are more likely than microplastics to pass through biological membranes. The sources of microplastics are a reflection of their ubiquitous presence in modern society, including microbeads used in cosmetic cleansers (at one point, even toothpaste commonly contained them), pellets used to produce plastic products, discarded water bottles (and, during the COVID-19 pandemic, a large spike in personal protective equipment including gloves and masks), microfibres in clothing released during washing processes, plastic discarded from wear on automobile tires, plastic bags, bottle caps, six-pack rings, straws, cigarette butts, and many other sources. Though lost fishing gear is an obvious source of plastic pollution, it is estimated that three-quarters or more of plastic waste is derived from land-based sources (see Stoett & Vince, 2019).

A number of international frameworks or approaches exist that address plastics governance, such as the Basel, Rotterdam and Stockholm Conventions; the World Trade Organization Informal Dialogue on Plastic Pollution and Environmentally Sustainable Plastics Trade (IDP); the EU Waste Directive; and voluntary environmental approaches for corporate responses (e.g., the Ellen Macarthur Foundation Global Commitments). In February 2022, to facilitate an accelerated and concerted effort to tackle the plastic pollution problem, a resolution for the development of a legally binding instrument to end plastic pollution was passed during the fifth session of the United Nations Environment Assembly. As this book comes to press, the Canadian federal government is engaged in multilateral talks to establish an international plastics treaty – one that, hopefully, will limit plastic production and not just promote recycling, which has proven to be a less-than-adequate response to what many refer to as the global plastics crisis.[7] An international conference to further negotiate the treaty was held in Ottawa in April 2024, but by the end of a week of negotiations it was clear that there is a large divide between a coalition of countries interested in firmly limiting plastic production and others (who are reliant on fossil fuel production) who want only to promote recycling as the answer to this tremendous problem. Canada hosted the conference and was quick to proclaim its support for a strong treaty but held back on being a vocal proponent in the actual negotiations. At the federal level, Canada has passed nationwide legislation banning the sale of single-use plastic products (though this has been contested in Alberta and elsewhere). Many municipalities have gone further (see Chapter Five for more on the plastic product life cycle).

The concern with plastic pollution in the oceans is particularly visible because it is extremely difficult to remove it, and once it degrades into microplastic and nanoplastic, removal is nearly impossible. Plastic pollution has killed millions of seabirds, turtles, and other forms of ocean biodiversity and has been found in a wide range of fin fish and crustaceans (including the species humans consume). It even threatens the entire food chain, if indeed early reports that plastic pollution is ingested by zooplankton are accurate (this, in turn, could limit the oceans' ability to cycle carbon, which is vital for human survival). So the problem is large, and concerted efforts by activists and scientists were needed to push governments into seeking a coordinated legal response. The federal government faces legal and political pressure to limit plastic production and consumption regulations and has passed relevant legislation, as discussed in Chapter Five. Another important factor is the international plastic waste trade, to which Canada has contributed. A vast plastic waste trade, both legal and illegal, exists; recycling in countries like Canada has a low effectiveness, and much of the plastic put out for recycling ends up in landfills or is shipped elsewhere. Until recently, the majority of recycling has taken place in China. However, a January 2018 decision by the Chinese government to cease imports of plastic destined for recycling processors has disrupted the entire industry, and other countries such as Vietnam, Indonesia, and Turkey are not receiving more waste. The plastic waste trade can be quite lucrative for traders, but the plastic is often not recycled properly in destination countries, where it is dumped, or worse burned, posing health risks for those involved and communities living nearby (relatedly, the electronic waste trade faces similar challenges). This is relevant for ocean sustainability as the waste is shipped over oceans and can be lost at sea in the process but, as importantly, it challenges Canadian society to recycle properly and reduce plastic consumption considerably to avoid further contributing to this affront to environmental justice.

MARINE NOISE POLLUTION

The "soundscape" of the oceans has changed enormously since pre-industrial times (Duarte et al., 2021). Human sources of ocean noise include "commercial shipping and recreational vessel traffic, detonation of explosives, seismic exploration, navy and scientific sonars, pingers and acoustic deterrent devices used in directed fisheries and aquaculture, pile-driving and other construction work, and operational noise from marine industries," in addition to air traffic noise and the pending growth of industrial deep sea mining (Nienke et al., 2022, p. 1). Increased runoff and calving from glaciers and icecaps are special concerns in Arctic waters (Halliday et al., 2021; Stafford, 2021). Anthropogenic noise pollution can disrupt the feeding and social behaviour of a variety of ocean wildlife, from whales and dolphins to crabs, turtles, squid, fish, and even zooplankton. Sometimes animals react to human-made noises as they do to predators' sounds; dolphins and others flee from the construction noise of offshore wind turbine installations for up to 25 kilometres (Merchant, 2019), and naval sonar (especially mid-frequency active sonar) has long been associated with induced mortality in deep-diving beaked whales (Bernaldo de Quieros et al., 2019). Noise from blasting, military sonar, and seismic testing can cause temporary or long-term hearing loss and can cause bodily harm and even death through stress, trauma, and behavioural impacts (i.e., whale beaching); at the very least, it poses serious questions around animal welfare and unnecessary cruelty (IFAW, 2021).

The problem is especially acute with regard to large ships and marine mammals: "The predominately low-frequency sounds associated with large commercial vessels directly overlap typical low-frequency communication sounds and hearing of many marine mammals, particularly large whales and some seals and sea lions" (Southall et al., 2017, p. 3). The roar from large tankers and freight ships can reach over 200 decibels, while sonar can generate low frequency noise of up to 230 decibels (Scott, 2004, pp. 288–89).[8] Another area that remains difficult to manage is military activity. Mid-frequency active sonar and the testing and use of explosive ordinance, as national security matters, consistently trump the environment. Canada's military, while self-regulating in this regard, has been working with allies since the early 2000s to find ways to mitigate the impact of these activities (Thomson & Binder, 2021).

As the short- and long-term costs of marine noise pollution came to be understood, a precautionary approach to the "dumping" of noise has been embraced by conservation interests. It is often contested, however, by the commercial, research, and state interests whose activities entail – and sometimes rely on – adding noise to the marine environment. Governments often seek a cost–benefit analysis, but given the poor state of understanding of the impacts of ocean noise pollution and disagreements over animal welfare concerns, assessing the value of mitigation measures is a profound challenge (Merchant, 2019). And since sound can travel very far through the ocean, noise pollution will frequently cross national boundaries, which makes management a necessarily intergovernmental issue.

Transport Canada regulates shipping and related activities under the *Canada Shipping Act*; in 2019 this legislation was amended "to provide additional authorities to enact regulations to protect the marine environment from the impacts of navigation and shipping activities, which includes underwater vessel noise." In 2019 Transport Canada also launched its Quiet Vessel Initiative, which "aims to advance research and promote the adoption of safe and environmentally-responsible quiet vessel technologies, including retrofits, new vessel designs, and operational practices to mitigate noise" from shipping (Breeze et al., 2022). Canada has also directed considerable funding under the Oceans Protection Plan (OPP), which specifically aims to protect the endangered populations of whales from key threats, including noise. The OPP's Whales Initiative focuses on the southern resident killer whale (*Orcinus orca*), or SRKW, the North Atlantic right whale (*Eubalaena glacialis*), and the St. Lawrence estuary beluga (*Delphinapterus leucas*), species that are also protected under SARA, Canada's *Species at Risk Act*. Transport Canada administers the OPP, while both SARA and the Whales Initiative fall under the purview of the DFO, which also draws on the *Fisheries Act* in managing noise pollution to protect the whale populations. SARA in particular prohibits "killing, harming, or harassing" species listed as threatened or endangered, and for aquatic species, it makes it illegal to damage or destroy any part of their critical habitat, including the acoustic environment. In 2020 work began on an ocean noise strategy for Canada, which would inform "a whole-of-government approach" to addressing marine noise; the strategy was finalized in 2023 (Fisheries and Oceans Canada, 2024a).

Clearly, managing the impacts of marine noise on just ocean mammals involves many regulations and policies being split across several departments (Breeze et al., 2022, p. 2). The ecopolitics become even more complex when we consider other sources of noise pollution, such as seismic activity. Seismic surveys are widely used by the oil and gas industry and by mining interests as well as for navigation and mapping. Oil and gas–related activity is generally managed by Natural Resources Canada, Indigenous and Northern Affairs Canada, the National Energy Board, and a number of intergovernmental agencies. Non-oil and gas–related seismic activity falls under the *Oceans Act*. The Government of Canada and the provinces of British Columbia, Quebec, Newfoundland and Labrador, and Nova Scotia developed a "Statement of Canadian Practice with Respect to the Mitigation of Seismic Sound in the Marine Environment" in 2008. "The Statement of Canadian Practice is intended to formalize and standardize the mitigation measures in Canada with respect to the conduct of seismic surveys in the marine environment. It will consist of minimum standards which will be given effect through existing regulatory authorities" (Government of Canada et al., 2008). The statement sets out mitigation requirements for planning of seismic surveys, establishment and monitoring of a safety zone, prescribed marine mammal observation and detection measures, prescribed start-up, and prescribed shut-down. The challenge is that most remedial measures have either considerable upfront costs or unwelcome impacts on delivery times and the economics of shipping (Merchant, 2019).

Nevertheless, some successes have been seen. For example, the Vancouver Port Authority's ECHO program (Enhancing Cetacean Habitat and Observation) has provisions to reduce port fees for vessels that meet noise certification requirements (Merchant, 2019, s. 4.3.2). The port has also implemented a voluntary speed/noise reduction scheme for the Haro Strait, part of the SRKW feeding grounds, which has enjoyed the compliance of some 80 per cent of vessel operators; yet the port is also gearing up to expand operations by up to 25 per cent, and this could quickly overcome the benefits from the speed reductions (Haskell, 2022).

DEEP SEABED MINING

Mining the seas has been an enticing prospect for many investors and companies for decades. Of course, offshore oil rigs are, in essence, mining the sea for oil or natural gas deposits, and Canada's main offshore oil operations are some 300 kilometres off the coast of Newfoundland and Labrador; the four largest projects, Hibernia, Terra Nova, White Rose, and Hebron, produce up to 4 per cent of total Canadian oil output, most of it destined for export to the United States and Europe. These rigs will stay in operation for many years to come, assuming the global demand for oil is maintained; controversies over their initial costs (including heavy government subsidies) have largely faded, though concerns about ecological and worker safety remain relevant, and new regulations introduced by the federal Liberal government in 2022 were criticized as weak by environmental groups.[9]

Deep seabed mining is another type of extractive activity that has stirred the media and environmental activists. For many decades the promise of mining the ocean floor, including in areas beyond national jurisdiction (i.e., outside the 200 nautical mile exclusive economic zone along the coast), was held out as a possible avenue to share the wealth that lay there. But technical challenges and political uncertainty combined to delay the development of deep seabed mining, which was to be arranged through the UNCLOS and the International Seabed Authority (ISA), which hears applications for establishing operations. At the time of writing, the ISA is actually considering applications.

The demand for metal ores such as lithium, cobalt, and graphite is steadily rising as efforts to replace fossil fuels increase; evidence suggests that the ocean floor, hundreds of metres deep (or deeper), has deposits of polymetallic nodules that could, theoretically, be pumped to the ocean surface for processing. This would entail scraping the ocean floor over large areas and displacing the sediment that is home to thousands of species that inhabit the deep sea (we know now that these are not barren spaces but are quite biodiverse; see Rabone et al., 2023). The operations would also produce intense marine noise pollution (see above), they would discharge wastewater and sediment that could in turn damage fish habitat, and the mining could disrupt the ecosystem services offered by marine environments, especially carbon cycling (see Ashford et al., 2024). Advances in battery technology might decrease the demand for rare earth minerals associated with the swing toward a post-carbon economy.

At the international level, divisions are forming on the issue. Norway and Nauru, for example, want to begin mining soon, and China and Japan also have plans, while the European Union, Brazil, Costa Rica, and Chile are formally opposed to it. (To complicate matters further, the United States has not yet ratified UNCLOS, but there is pressure on the US Senate to do so if only to allow American companies the ability to mine under the ISA arrangements.) Given the centrality of mining as an extractive economic activity both in Canada and by Canadian firms abroad, it is somewhat surprising that the Liberal government under Justin Trudeau has demonstrated firm policy resolve on this issue, announcing in July 2023 that it supports

> a moratorium on commercial seabed mining in areas beyond national jurisdiction and will not support the provisional approval of a plan of work. This position is consistent with our approach to commercial seabed mining in areas under Canada's jurisdiction, which was announced on February 9, 2023. The Government of Canada has been clear: seabed mining should take place only if effective protection of the marine environment is provided through a rigorous regulatory structure, applying precautionary and ecosystem-based approaches, using science-based and transparent management, and ensuring effective compliance with a robust inspection mechanism. (Global Affairs Canada, 2023)

Deep seabed mining is a fascinating case of a potential large-scale extractive industry that was once viewed as a way of offering wealth to many countries, even land-locked ones, with a resource-sharing regime based on the UNCLOS; this grand scheme never materialized, and the debate now is between a handful of countries and companies (including some Canadian firms) who want to engage in the activity on a for-profit basis and a large coalition of environmental and Indigenous groups that see it as a grave threat to environmental security and an affront to environmental justice. It will be interesting to see how market pressure, the post-carbon transition, and environmental concerns all play out in this evolving ecopolitical space.

CONCLUSION: THE OCEANIC IMPERATIVE

From energy provision through waves and wind, to both wild capture and farmed fisheries, to minerals on the seabed floor – all these resources can be used and are often touted as part of an emerging new "blue economy." But as we've seen, they all have both historical and recent ecopolitical contexts characterized by debates and struggles over regulatory control. In June 2024, the federal government announced a "Blue Economy Regulatory Roadmap" focused on "marine renewable energy and environmental protection, marine spatial planning, maritime autonomous surface ships, ocean technology, and sustainable fishing gear and practices" (Fisheries and Oceans Canada, 2024b). The strategy was developed by Fisheries and Oceans Canada in collaboration with Transport Canada, Innovation, Science and Economic Development Canada, and the National Research Council of Canada. While some believe this avenue of economic development finally shines much-needed light on oceans and offers a way to diversify economies and move away from fossil fuel extraction and land use change, others suggest it is just another way to open up the rapid exploitation of the oceans and there is very little that is "blue" about it.

One of the most interesting ecopolitical questions about Canadian oceans, perhaps, pertains to national identity. While oceans policy and politics are clearly of central importance to coastal communities, are the oceans really part of the broader common understanding of Canadian futures? In the landlocked provinces of Alberta, Saskatchewan, and Manitoba (though, of course, they have far more lakes than most countries!), are oceans of any significance? The maritime history of Canada, both pre- and post-colonial, suggests they certainly are. More importantly, Canadians need to know more about the impact industrial civilization is having on the oceans moving forward. While this may be more apparent in the case of receding ice cover in the Arctic Ocean (discussed at length in Chapter Eleven), we cannot afford to take the ecosystem services offered by the Pacific and Atlantic Oceans for granted either.

Simply put, without the oceans there is no Turtle Island. The coastal Indigenous communities not only recognized this but also built it right into their worldview, their ceremony, and their cultural context. This might not be possible on a Canada-wide scale, yet the battle against climate change is to a large degree dependent on the oceans' ability to control the global climate. One thing is certain: If we continue to see oceans as vast resources, and not as sustainers, we will lose that battle.

The *Oceans Act* in Canada recognizes that three oceans – the Arctic, the Pacific, and the Atlantic – are the common heritage of all Canadians. Furthermore, this Act holds that conservation based on an ecosystem approach is of fundamental importance to maintaining biological diversity and productivity in the marine environment. So one could plausibly argue that not only are the oceans vital for our collective health, but that we have an inherent right to enjoy that health and a collective responsibility to conserve the oceans that provide it. All of the climate justice issues outlined elsewhere in this book apply to ocean ecopolitics, especially as coastal communities will be most severely affected by sea-level rise, but the stark reality is that every person on earth is ultimately affected by the state of our oceans.

NOTES

1 Recent polls conducted by the World Wildlife Foundation suggest that Canadians "strongly value ocean protection as a way to reduce human impact on the environment. When asked about four potential ways to reduce our

environmental impact, seven in ten or more say it is very important to protect oceans and their ecosystems (73%), protect wildlife and habitat on land and in oceans (72%) and reduce the use of toxic chemicals (71%). Slightly fewer (61%) place the same degree of importance on reducing greenhouse gas emissions. In all four cases, very few say these actions are unimportant" (Environics, 2019, p. 6).

2 Note that the Inuit have similar animosity toward the European Union (EU), which moved to completely ban seal product imports in 2009 (though there is an exemption for Inuit products). The Inuit Circumpolar Conference and others argue that the EU ban has essentially driven demand for Arctic seal products into oblivion. Some ire is reserved for Canadian politicians as well: The Labrador Inuit do not even have an accreditation body (only the Northwest Territories and Nunavut governments can formally designate seal products as of genuine Inuit origin).

3 In the United States, seal product imports are, with few exceptions, banned by the 1972 *Marine Mammals Protection Act*.

4 This is the term used by the International Whaling Commission (IWC) to describe whaling by Indigenous communities. Canada withdrew from the IWC in 1982, avoiding a painful vote on what amounted to a complete moratorium on whaling at that time.

5 These statistics are from the Government of Canada (2022). Canadians also import significant quantities of fish and seafood: The value of Canada's fish and seafood imports in 2021 was $4.61 billion, a 16 per cent increase over the previous year. Top suppliers of fish and seafood to Canada were the United States ($1.67 billion), China ($520 million), and Vietnam ($314 million), accounting for 54 per cent of Canada's total fish and seafood import value. The top three species imported were salmon, shrimp and prawns, and lobster.

6 Though the argument that farmed fish is a public good is often advanced by proponents (see Canadian Aquaculture Industry Alliance, 2023).

7 One of this book's authors has been attending related meetings and is an active member of the Scientists' Coalition for an Effective Plastics Treaty, which lobbies governments to agree to a strong Convention that will limit plastic production in the future (see https://ikhapp.org/scientistscoalition).

8 These numbers are not directly comparable to noise on the surface, where humans feel pain at 120 decibels and find 150 decibels intolerable. But this is an area of tremendous uncertainty; what we know of marine animals' hearing is based on educated guesswork from studying the vocalizations and other sounds animals produce, modelling from anatomical studies, and measuring behaviour responses through playback experiments and observation where possible (Matthews & Parks, 2021, p. 2).

9 The World Wildlife Fund (2022) is critical of regulations that seem much weaker than those implemented by other countries, including the United States, where the disastrous Deepwater Horizon "blowout" spill occurred in the Gulf of Mexico in 2010.

CHAPTER NINE

Climate Ecopolitics

LEARNING OBJECTIVES

1. Understand the historical development and current state of climate change policy in Canada, including key milestones, challenges, and policy approaches.
2. Analyze the complex interplay between federal and provincial governments in addressing climate change, including tensions around carbon pricing and emissions reduction targets.
3. Evaluate Canada's international role and commitments on climate change, including participation in global agreements and frameworks.

INTRODUCTION: THE CLIMATE CRISIS

Unlike some other global issues, such as the accumulation of plastic pollution, climate change is not a new phenomenon. The physical processes that lead to warming caused by the accumulation of greenhouse gases (GHGs) in the atmosphere were first identified in the mid-1800s by Eunice Foote, who was a physicist, inventor, and women's rights advocate (Suzuki & Hanington, 2020; Ortiz & Jackson, 2022). There were many specialists who suggested that burning fossil fuels would lead to atmospheric changes, but this wasn't really identified as a major problem by scientists until the 1960s. Climate change is now having a profound impact on citizens in all countries, and Canada is far from an exception; on the contrary, we are seeing impacts that are much more substantial than other countries, and these are occurring much more frequently. And yet climate governance involves a considerable mismatch between ecological timescales on the one hand and political timescales on the other: While climate change looks like it is developing "rapidly" when framed against the millennia of geological change, it is a relatively slow process when viewed from the standpoint of a given electoral cycle.

The Intergovernmental Panel on Climate Change (IPCC) identifies five key sectors that are sources of GHG emissions: energy systems, industry, buildings, transport, and AFOLU (agriculture, forestry, and other land uses) (Lamb et al., 2021). Steffen and colleagues (2015) argue that climate change is one of the planetary boundaries that is currently being exceeded due to "anthropogenic perturbation levels" (p. 736). Climate change is also closely intertwined with biodiversity loss, the spread of invasive species (see Roy et al., 2023), the impact of pollutants (including plastics), and the accumulation of toxins. As suggested in Chapter One, climate change represents an existential risk for human civilizations if the worst-case scenarios affecting food security, mass migration, sea-level rise, heat extremes, and freshwater supplies come to pass. It is perhaps the most distinguishing characteristic of the Anthropocene.

Though the main culprit of global warming is carbon dioxide, other gases, such as methane and nitrous oxide, also contribute. These gases are emitted through relatively common industrial activities, including manufacturing, resource extraction, industrial forms of agriculture, the heating and cooling of buildings, combustion of fossil fuels for energy production, transportation of goods and people, and land use changes such as deforestation. The pathways to reducing these emissions are numerous, and the effort required is multilevel, encompassing economic activities at municipal, regional, national, and international levels. Climate change, as mentioned in Chapter Three, is a "commons problem" in that achieving solutions will require collective action on the part of many state and substate actors. However, the distribution of costs and benefits is a key ethical question, since the historical sources of emissions are primarily in industrialized economies, yet the effects of climate change are mostly felt in lower-income countries. In Canada, it is well established that the effects of climate change are also disproportionately borne by Indigenous Peoples (Asfaw et al., 2019; Downing & Cuerrier, 2011; Wang, Kinay, et al., 2023; Theriault, 2013), which has led many groups to organize and agitate for Indigenous-led action and climate governance that respects Treaty rights and self-determination (Kahn et al., 2014). For example, the

Shut Down Canada campaign in 2021 was inspired by the resistance of the Wet'suwet'en hereditary Elders to the expansion of fossil fuel infrastructure (the Coastal GasLink pipeline) through their traditional territories without consent, in contravention of the United Nations Declaration on the Rights of Indigenous Peoples (discussed in Yousif & Smith, 2020).

As climate change accelerates, intergenerational justice and ethics come to the fore – a fact that has led to an increase in climate-related political and legal action by young people. Since young people in the current generation and future generations will bear the greatest costs, while older generations have disproportionately benefited from emissions that led to economic prosperity, the concern by young people is clear. Climate change, unlike changes in weather, historically happens over the course of millennia, and its effects lag decades behind its initial conditions and are highly uncertain. Intergenerational and cross-generational dynamics are increasingly apparent, as are the distributive ethics in terms of who pays the price for loss and damage and who is responsible for the costs of mitigation. Climate change also demonstrates, in a visceral way, humanity's domination of the planetary system and hence the geological passage from the era of the Holocene to the Anthropocene. The Anthropocene, as described in Chapter One, brings forward uncomfortable questions about the human–nature relationship, ones that arise from the "planetary imaginary" rather than from the viewpoint of the individual or nation. Spatially, the atmosphere is a **global commons** (as discussed in Chapter Three), yet its management is largely ungoverned and fragmented (Abbott, 2011). States are drawn together to share the burdens of climate change mitigation and adaptation yet find that populations on all sides of their borders are reluctant to do so.

As a northern country, Canada has much to lose as climate change progresses. Indeed, Canada has already been hugely affected by extreme events like forest fires, floods, invasive species, and drought (see Case Study 9.1 on the Fort McMurray wildfire). As of the most recent data available, Canada has the third-highest emissions on a per capita basis among the 36 Organisation for Economic Co-operation and Development (OECD) countries. Among the G7 nations, Canada had one of the lowest percentage reductions in GHG emissions per capita between 2005 and 2018 (Dusyk et al., 2021, p. 10). However, the economic impacts of increasingly severe extreme weather events reflect Canada's vulnerability to climate-related risks. Nine of the 10 most expensive years for natural disasters have occurred since 2011, with insured losses averaging nearly $3 billion per year over the last decade. The number of catastrophic events is over three times higher than it was in the 1980s, and insured losses represent only a fraction of the total economic costs, as they do not account for uninsured damages, lost productivity, the costs of emergency relief and assistance efforts, or of rebuilding public services and infrastructure (Insurance Board of Canada, 2024).

CASE STUDY 9.1. The Fort McMurray Wildfire

In 2016, Fort McMurray, Alberta, was shocked by one of the largest population displacements in Canadian history (Blunden & Arndt, 2017) when the city of more than 88,000 people was evacuated due to wildfires (McGee, 2019, p. 14). The wildfire, nicknamed "The Beast" because of its size and intensity, extended for more than 5,000 kilometres, permanently altering the environment around Fort McMurray. There were dramatic and frightening scenes of residents fleeing the flames along roadsides, and with losses estimated at $9.9 billion, it was the costliest disaster in Canadian history to date.

Evacuations during wildfires, floods, and other disasters are more frequent and are likely to be larger and more challenging as climate change accelerates. Disaster responses are primarily provincial and local, though there is often strong involvement from the federal government when disasters reach a certain scale. In addition to the personal losses, in Fort McMurray's case it also had an impact on oil sands production. An estimated 1.0 to 1.5 million barrels a day had to be cut, representing around 25–40 per cent of total Canadian oil production (Canada Energy Regulator, 2016). The financial effects were severe, since production was reduced to a third of what it had been (Barclay et al., 2020).

This was not the first time a wildfire affected the area. Climate change has caused Fort McMurray to become a warmer and drier area. In 2016 a study showed that the first months of that year were drier and there had been a temperature increase in comparison to previous years. By April in that same year the soil was dry and contributed to the availability of other fuels easily found in forests, such as dried grass, branches, and logs (Institute for Catastrophic Loss Reduction, 2019). The rapid changes and potential for cascading effects has left governments exposed, and, as argued by Greaves (2021, p. 189), "the shortfall in climate planning and preparedness increases the potential for synchronous or compounding environmental and human security crises in the future."

First responders in Fort McMurray were widely praised for their heroic efforts, but according to the Department of Earth and Atmospheric Sciences at the University of Alberta, many things could have been done to improve the response. As early as January 2016, stakeholders had called for an Alberta climate change adaptation strategy to address these risks (Feltmate, 2016, p. 4), and the province had been warned in 2012 about the need to prepare for catastrophic wildfires. By 2022, a partnership between the Government of Alberta and municipalities provided only $4.5 million for its adaptation programs, and no comprehensive adaptation strategy appeared to be forthcoming. The federal government also released a new climate adaptation strategy in 2023.

Post-incident reports following the fire were strongly critical of the lack of communication, unclear chains of command, and a general lack of organization among respondents. The Government of Alberta has moved to create a more centralized disaster communication system based on the report's recommendations to improve communications with residents, be better prepared, and create an educational program supporting a culture of prevention. Road signalling with predetermined evacuation routes would have improved safety as residents fled the fast-moving fire (McGee, 2019, p. 14). As part of the improvements, real-time warnings are now promoted by the Government of Canada, evacuation procedures are published, and households are encouraged to have a 72-hour plan following an emergency. The 2016 evacuation was difficult and unorganized, but for citizens and authorities who have to act, lack of preparation is no longer an option. Nationally, 2023 was the worst forest fire season on record; the time for a national forest fire response corps has surely arrived.

Critical Thinking Questions

1. Whose responsibility should it be to plan and prepare for disasters: municipal, provincial, or federal governments? How much should individual citizens be expected to prepare?
2. What is meant by a "culture of prevention" and how might this have changed the response in the case of the Fort McMurray fire?

Yet Canada has faced numerous challenges in implementing climate change policies, especially as it occupies a paradoxical position as a fossil fuel extractor and exporter in the global economy. The Government of Canada stated in 1990 that regional variation in temperature changes meant that Canada would likely be impacted more strongly than other countries by climate change (Government of Canada, 1990, p. 97). The uneven nature of these emissions flows from the regional nature of Canada's economy, with high-emitting oil and gas operations concentrated in Alberta and lower-emitting hydroelectric power in Quebec, Manitoba, and Newfoundland. As a result, GHG emissions vary significantly across the provinces, and that disparity is increasing (Harrison, 2010). Such concerns mean that any discussion of climate policy that could affect oil sands production inevitably engages the potential to ignite western alienation and negatively affect national unity and stability (Hayden, 2014, p. 187).

Project Drawdown (https://drawdown.org) keeps an impressive list and ranking of climate solutions that offers much insight into the types of actions that are needed. Indeed, one of the most hopeful dimensions of climate change is that new innovations are not necessarily the fastest or most efficient route to climate mitigation. Project Drawdown reviews and analyzes practices and technologies that can reduce GHG concentrations in earth's atmosphere that are also:

- currently available,
- growing in scale,
- financially viable,
- able to have a net positive impact, and
- quantifiable under different scenarios.

Among the preferred solutions on the Project Drawdown site are reducing food waste and adopting plant-rich diets, advancing renewable energy solutions such as distributed solar power, and changing land use to increase carbon sinks. These options are all within reach for Canadians. In terms of climate governance, there are broad differences between the various worldviews. Resource extractivism, perhaps the dominant view prevailing in conservative circles, focuses on technological solutions such as carbon capture, storage, and utilization. In line with the views of fossil fuel companies, those embracing extractivism tend to speak about "responsible" resource development, energy security, and the need for regulatory change, with a potentially greater role for carbon trading and incentives for innovation. Indeed, the mantra of responsible resource development was at its height under the Harper Conservative government, which emphasized extraction and transportation of resources over emissions reductions (Toner et al., 2016, p. 123; see Chapter Two).

In the political centre, often associated with the federal Liberal Party, solutions have taken the form of carbon pricing (either in terms of direct taxes or cap-and-trade systems), energy conservation measures, electric vehicles, voluntary and incentive-based policies for industry, capital investment in renewable energy, energy retrofits for buildings, and funding for research and development. On the left, those embracing the Green Party or New Democratic Party don't always agree on the most appropriate policy approaches. In general, though, Green parties at both the federal and provincial levels favour more rapid decarbonization with the potential for degrowth and reduction or transition away from fossil fuel extraction and export, which remains one of the most significant sources of Canada's emissions. Parties of the centre and left tend to agree on the need for a **just transition** that supports workers in moving away from fossil fuel development toward renewable energy and other, broader societal changes focused on welfare and educational efforts. On the outer fringes of climate solutions, one also finds proposals for large-scale technological geoengineering, such as seeding the atmosphere to reflect more sunlight. Seeding the atmosphere may mean cloud seeding to increase rainfall (Desert Research Institute, 2024), marine cloud brightening (University of Washington, 2024), or other means of reflecting sunlight back out into space, such as sulphur aerosol injection (which remains highly theoretical and likely very expensive; *Global News*, 2024). These ideas have become more mainstream as climate impacts have proliferated, but governments have been slow to respond.

EARLY CANADIAN ACTIVISM

Canada's climate change policies have undergone significant changes over the years, with periods of early activism and leadership followed by neglect and decline. As discussed in Chapter One, it is important to remember that Canada has oscillated between high-minded promises and "isolationist climate change denialism." Canada has had at least 11 different climate plans and nine emissions targets since 1988 (JWN Energy, 2022). While the problem of climate change weaves throughout this book, the challenges of climate are severe and have implications specific to Canadian ecopolitics, and so this chapter will dive deeper than others into the governance conundrums and issues faced in the arena of climate governance both domestically and internationally. The chapter will focus especially on the historical setting for Canada's climate change policies, the ins and outs of policy changes, and the degree to which these have impacted the country's "green" identity.

As discussed in Chapter Four, Canada was among the first countries to establish a Department of Environment and was active in the lead up to the 1992 Rio Earth Summit. The Montreal Conference in 1987 and the Green Plan of 1990 represented high points of Canadian diplomacy. At the Montreal Conference in 1987, the international community produced a detailed protocol to the 1985 Vienna Convention on ozone layer protection. This early success led Brian Mulroney's Conservative government to sponsor a major international conference on atmospheric change in Toronto in 1988, followed by active participation in the IPCC, formed in 1988 by the World Meteorological Association (Government of Canada, 1990, p. 97). The purpose of the IPCC was to synthesize the recent scientific data on mitigation, adaptation, climate science, and vulnerability to assist decision makers. IPCC reports have undergirded Canada's and the world's climate actions and policies, with successive reports starting in 1990 and continuing to the present day (Doern et al., 2015, p. 100). In that same year (1988), Prime Minister Mulroney recommended that global GHG emissions be reduced by 20 per cent by 2005 (Harrison, 2007, p. 98).

This early activism did much to shape Canadians' self-identity as environmental leaders, but the follow up was lukewarm. The Conservative government's Green Plan, issued in 1990, was touted as "a comprehensive national strategy and $3 billion action plan for sustainable development." The Green Plan also established the National Action Strategy on Global Warming, with the aim of information sharing between municipalities, provinces, and industry to foster GHG reduction. Ultimately the Green Plan was modest in its targets, calling for further study of the "technical feasibility" of the 20 per cent reduction called for at the Toronto Conference (Government of Canada, 1990, p. 101). Despite these early efforts, problems emerged in Canada's climate change policies. The promise to implement a comprehensive review of the environmental implications of Canadian law stalled. The ambitious rhetoric of the Toronto Conference on comprehensive atmospheric law was replaced with a more focused statement on the need for a framework convention on climate change (Smith, 2002, p. 78). The National Action Plan on Climate Change was developed in November 1993, followed by the Voluntary Challenge and Registry Program in 1995. The registry operated from 1994 to 2004 and offered tax incentives and support for technological adjustments for heavy industry. However, this program had a negligible impact on emissions because of weak participation and incentives, relying on altruism to encourage companies to register their plans for reduction. The program had even fewer mechanisms for ensuring companies followed through on their plans. Firms had few reasons to participate, and the tendency for participation in the registry to take the form of "strategic behaviour" or "greenwashing" to simply improve a company's environmental reputation was endemic (Brouhle & Harrington, 2010, p. 522; Campbell, 1998).

THE KYOTO ROLLER COASTER

As discussed above, Mulroney's environmental accomplishments were capped off with an ambitious Green Plan that fully launched in 1993. The plan was a response to the fall of the Berlin Wall, the rise of environmentalism, and awareness about climate change among the Canadian public (Smith, 2002, p. 78). Canada's Green Plan and the signing of the UN Framework Convention on Climate Change (UNFCCC) in 1992 committed the government to stabilize carbon dioxide and other GHGs from 1990 levels by 2000. As the country approached the negotiations for the first protocol agreement for the UNFCCC in 1997 in Kyoto, several factors shaped Canada's position. The first was a desire to appear more activist than the United States, seen as Canada's primary competitor and trade partner. The second was an imperative to control any adjustment costs that might be associated with a GHG emissions reduction plan. And the third was a traditional commitment to multilateral efforts similar to those for peace and disarmament as the Cold War wound down.

Toward the first consideration, Canada at first touted a target of 3 per cent below 1990 GHG emissions, but it later agreed to a 6 per cent reduction target, in response to US commitments that looked like they might exceed Canada's. This motivation did not last long, however, as after 2002 the United States signalled that it no longer cared about appearances and withdrew its support of Kyoto, leaving Canada with little choice but to backtrack toward a more competitive stance with respect to its oil and gas exports (Doern et al., 2015, p. 102). The desire to control costs was more persistent. In the lead up to the **Kyoto Protocol** negotiations to bring specificity to the UNFCCC in Berlin, Canada was part of the JUSCANZ (Japan, US, Australia, and New Zealand) coalition, which resisted calls by European countries for greater progress on climate change. As part of this group, Canada made credit for carbon sinks and flexible market-based mechanisms key to its acceptance of the agreement (Bernstein, 2002, p. 220; Doern et al., 2015, p. 102). These policies would have moderated Canada's commitments by ensuring that the country would gain carbon credits from its vast forests and land areas with carbon absorption potential. The focus was on "flexibility mechanisms" such as the clean development mechanism, emissions trading, and joint implementation, which would allow industrialized countries of the Global North to earn credits by investing in emissions reduction projects in the Global South. These mechanisms shored up the market-based effort to reduce emissions by pricing carbon credits – in other words creating domestic credit for investments abroad – by allowing for emissions trading among signatories (Bernstein, 2002, p. 210).

These efforts to create more efficiencies in climate change policies were also accompanied by a concern with equity, which was "built in" to the Kyoto negotiations. The concern with equity was framed domestically in terms of a principle that the costs of transition be borne relatively equally across the country, designed especially to bring in Alberta, the highest carbon-emitting province and energy producer (Bernstein, 2002, p. 217; Doern et al., 2015, p. 101). Internationally, the Kyoto Protocol included distinctions between Annex I and Annex II countries, the former composed of the industrialized high-emitting countries and the latter the less developed countries that could become higher emitters in the future (notably China). The argument was that the developed western industrialized countries were largely responsible for the problem and remained high emitters, while developing countries would need room to increase their energy use to develop. This prompted an alternative strategy on the part of the United States to bring in China and India to avoid the potential negation of American policies by increased emissions from the Global South (Doern et al., 2015, p. 105). This norm of **"common but differentiated" responsibilities** for climate policies was resisted by countries like the United States, which challenged the idea that less developed countries should be exempted from burdens that would be more strongly borne by American consumers.

The Kyoto Protocol negotiations ended with a final agreement on Canada's part to reduce GHG emissions by 6 per cent below 1990 levels by 2012. These targets would have been difficult for an energy-intensive and trade-dependent economy like Canada to reach, but they were nevertheless touted as progressive and innovative. Finally, the effects of the end of the Cold War and the need to buttress multilateralism was also a consideration, even more so by

2002, when Prime Minister Jean Chrétien brought the ratification vote to Parliament. By that time, Kyoto was viewed as weakening and seemed unlikely to achieve its targets, in large part due to US domestic opposition. Canada's and Chrétien's renewed leadership on climate change leading up to the 2002 anniversary of the UNFCCC was motivated in part by its self-image as a multilateralist "middle power" capable of affecting international negotiations and playing its role as a responsible global citizen (Bernstein, 2002). Environmental issues provided an important international arena for the assertion of Canadian "middlepowermanship" while also avoiding or mitigating some of the most politically divisive issues of domestic burden sharing of the costs of transitioning in the energy sector.

By 1998, the Chrétien government's Action Plan 2000 to bring Kyoto into force committed the federal government to spending a total of $1.1 billion over five years, leading to a targeted reduction of Canada's GHG emissions by about 65 megatonnes per year during the commitment period of 2008–12. This program also included modest subsidies for renewable energy and energy information programs for consumers and businesses. Climate Change Plan 2002 would produce a system of tradable permits based on emission intensity caps for each sector and a combination of information and modest subsidies to encourage voluntary actions by firms and households. The government estimated that through these programs, as well as education, each Canadian would reduce their average annual CO_2 emissions by one tonne (Government of Canada, 2000). Accordingly, the 2002 Climate Change Plan and "One Tonne Challenge" was also launched.

The Chrétien government announced it would ratify Kyoto at the World Summit on Sustainable Development in 2002, over the objections of the province of Alberta. Alberta's Progressive Conservative government, led by Ralph Klein, feared the economic impact of the agreement and put forward its own competing plan the same year (Boyd, 2018, p. 191). As the Official Opposition, Conservative Party leader Stephen Harper had been highly critical of the Kyoto Protocol, and in 2011, when he was prime minister, the Conservative government announced that it would not be able to fulfill its commitment, citing the target as impossible to meet (Nossal et al., 2015, p. 164). Canada now became the only country to have withdrawn from Kyoto. Despite this, the country did not suffer any penalties, aside from shaming and reputational damage (Olive, 2016, p. 231). The government did not pursue international carbon credit purchases as an option to fill the gap between domestic emissions and the target. Instead, in 2007, the government introduced its own goal of a 20 per cent GHG reduction below 2006 levels by 2020, equivalent to only a 3 per cent reduction below 1990 levels, to be achieved long after the Kyoto deadline. In 2007, Canada introduced the *Kyoto Protocol Implementation Act*. Interestingly, this was a private members' bill that garnered support from all opposition parties. The law passed despite opposition from the Conservative government, which subsequently repealed it once they achieved a majority government in 2011 (Boyd, 2018, p. 167). Canada also pushed to use 2006 as the base year in international negotiations, rather than the established norm of 1990, which would effectively wipe the country's large emissions increase in the intervening years off the slate.

Following the 2009 UNFCCC meeting in Copenhagen, which allowed countries to make their own voluntary emissions reduction pledges, Canada weakened its target further. Harper committed at most to a GHG emissions reduction target of 17 per cent (relative to its 2005 emission levels) by 2020. This was equivalent to a 2.5 per cent *increase* above 1990 levels (Olive, 2019, p. 231). Canada has since ratcheted up its reduction targets through the signing of the Paris Agreement in 2015, with the latest increase coming in 2021 (Environment and Climate Change Canada, 2021a). Although under the Paris Agreement countries are obligated to review their nationally determined contributions (NDCs) every five years and to increase their level of ambition each time, Canada has also reserved the right to change its target again if the United States enacted a weaker goal in its domestic climate legislation.

AFTER KYOTO

Up to 30 per cent of Canada's GHG emissions come from fossil fuel production and consumption, and Alberta is responsible for 38 per cent (the largest component) of the country's total emissions (Dusyk et al., 2021, p. 11), a statistic that is not lost on any informed observers of the issue. By the early 2000s, Canada's reputation as a leader on climate issues had been progressively eroded, and the oil sands themselves have become targets of celebrity and popular criticism, such as by Leonardo DiCaprio and James Cameron (Boyd, 2018, p. 184).

Climate consciousness reached a height in the popular imagination in 2006, the year that Al Gore made his famous Oscar-winning documentary *An Inconvenient Truth*. Upon election to a minority government in 2006, the Conservatives under Stephen Harper began to back away from Canada's international commitments and put forward an alternative plan, largely based on Alberta's proposals for a "made in Canada" solution to GHG emissions reduction.

Alberta's provincial plan, put forward in 2002, for the first time touted "intensity-based" reductions, which would mean the government would lower emissions based on gross domestic product. The effect would be that emissions would be allowed to continue to rise. Other measures in Alberta's plan included industrial intensity-based emissions, liberal use of carbon credits and trading, and a technology fund (Boyd, 2018, p. 185). Not surprisingly, this plan was more friendly to the fossil fuel extraction that constituted the source of Alberta's wealth and export-based economy (see Chapter Six).

However, Harper went even further in response to the attacks on the oil sands, beginning to tout Canada as an "energy superpower" capable of flexing its resource wealth in the global and continental economy. As part of this strategy, the Harper government began targeting climate and energy policies in the United States and the European Union that could limit the ability to export oil from the oil sands. In 2007, the election of Barack Obama in the United States led to a slew of climate policies that threatened the competitiveness of Canada's oil sands in the US market. Activity at the subnational level in the United States, especially California's *Global Warming Solutions Act* (2006) and the "anti-tar sands" agitation by US environmental groups, led to pressures on the Obama Administration to put restrictions on imports of Canadian "dirty oil" (Boyd, 2018, p. 193). The potential for disruption of the plan for the development of the Keystone Pipeline and for the introduction of clean fuel standards were viewed as direct threats to Alberta's (and Canada's) economy, which depended on oil exports (Engler, 2014, p. 59). In 2007, California adopted a low-carbon fuel standard, which required fuel producers to reduce the carbon intensity of their products by 10 per cent by 2020 (CERES, 2013). Canada feared the possible precedent, and so it intervened numerous times to try to alter California's policy.

In addition to lobbying vigorously against low-carbon fuel standards, Canada and Alberta worked to exempt the tar sands from section 256 of the US *Energy Independence and Security Act* of 2007, which prohibited US federal agencies, including the military and postal service, from buying alternative fuels with higher life cycle GHG emissions than conventional petroleum (Climate Action Network [CAN], 2011; Hayden, 2014, p. 191). Canada, Alberta, and industry allies became heavily involved in the US debate over approval of the $7 billion Keystone XL pipeline linking Alberta to Gulf of Mexico refineries (see Chapter Six). Many observers saw the issue as decisive in determining whether the United States would become increasingly dependent on the oil sands or prioritize green energy alternatives – a choice that caused divisions within the Obama Administration. Canada lobbied hard behind the scenes to influence that choice. Canada's US ambassador and former NDP premier of Manitoba, Gary Doer, spoke of his "grinding" work in lobbying US politicians at all levels and from coast to coast (Yakabuski, 2011). Meanwhile, Gary Mar, Alberta's former representative in Washington, claimed to have personally contacted every Congressperson and governor from states that the Keystone XL pipeline would cross (Kaufman, 2007). In 2010, the Oil Sands Advocacy Strategy was introduced to promote the oil sands as a sustainable, responsible, and "ethical" source of energy. Environmental groups have documented the similarities between the arguments and figures presented by the federal and Alberta governments and those of the Canadian Association of Petroleum Producers (CAPP), the main industry body (CAN, 2011, p. 17). Despite these efforts, ultimately the Keystone XL project was cancelled by the Biden Administration in 2020, leaving the industry to focus on the development of the Trans Mountain Pipeline to reach "tidewater" and enable Canadian exports abroad.

THE PARIS AGREEMENT

The ousting of Stephen Harper and ushering in of a new Liberal government led by Justin Trudeau in 2015 resulted in a shift away from the defensive and reactionary policies on climate change that had characterized the Harper years. In a marked change from earlier policy, Trudeau attended the negotiations of the Conference of the Parties to the UNFCCC in 2015, loudly pronouncing that "Canada is back" in the agreement (VanNijnatten & del Buey, 2021, p. 415). The Paris Agreement provided that countries should develop their own NDCs to reduce emissions, aligned with the goal of keeping warming to 2 degrees Celsius globally, with most agreeing to aim for the more ambitious goal of 1.5 degrees. Shortly afterward, the Pan-Canadian Framework on Clean Growth and Climate Change was agreed to after consultations with provinces, territories, and Indigenous Peoples. While the strategy had four main "legs," the primary one was the implementation of a price on carbon before 2018 (Environment and Climate Change Canada, 2016; Olive, 2019, p. 232). It seemed as if a new consensus was achieved, released in the form of the Vancouver Declaration on Clean Growth and Climate Change in March 2016 (Flanagan et al., 2016).

The framework plan would develop a common measure of emissions reduction across the country and establish standards for the provinces to follow. Those provinces that already had an emissions tax in line with the federal standard would be relatively unaffected, while those provinces that did not would be expected to establish their own or adopt the federal plan by 2018. Following the Paris Agreement's direction to review Canada's NDC every five years and to ratchet up its ambition each time, Canada's initial target NDC was increased in 2021 to 40–45 per cent below 2005 levels by 2030. In 2022, the Emissions Reduction Plan outlined the federal government's plan for achieving its most recent 2030 target. Measures included innovation incentives, funding for clean technology, and regulations to implement the phase-out of high-polluting industries such as coal (Office of the Commissioner of the Environment and Sustainable Development, 2021). Throughout the following years and up until the present, there has been significant growing opposition to the federal plan in the provinces and from populist movements that are growing in stridency in their attacks on climate policies, hardening the political opposition to the Liberal climate agenda at home. In 2024, Canada had three conservative provincial premiers who were staunch opponents of carbon pricing: Scott Moe in Saskatchewan, Doug Ford in Ontario, and Danielle Smith in Alberta (VanNijnatten & del Buey, 2021, p. 420; see Case Study 12.1). However, faced with political pressure from their conservative opponents to abandon an increasingly unpopular policy, in 2024 New Democratic premiers Wab Kinew in Manitoba and David Eby in British Columbia also indicated their support for eliminating a government price on carbon, leaving the Trudeau Liberal government isolated in their support for the federal carbon price.

In 2020, the Canadian government introduced the Healthy Economy and Healthy Environment Plan, partly in response to the challenges of the COVID-19 pandemic, which had a significant impact on the economy (Environment and Climate Change Canada, 2020). In 2021, the government announced an enhanced contribution goal as well as a new plan to achieve net-zero emissions by 2050 (Environment and Climate Change Canada, 2021d; 2023a, p. 152). In addition, the Government of Canada has recently released a National Climate Adaptation Plan to help Canadians deal with the effects of climate change in local communities and across the country.

While we have discussed GHG emissions in general throughout this chapter, Case Study 9.2 outlines the significant role methane plays in these emissions.

CASE STUDY 9.2. Methane: A Problem Too Long Overlooked

Methane accounts for more than 18 per cent of the heat generated from GHG emissions and is up to 80 times more potent than carbon dioxide in terms of trapping heat in our atmosphere. There is no doubt that rapid and sustained reductions in anthropogenic methane emissions are both cost effective and necessary to limit global warming to 1.5–2 degrees Celsius above pre-industrial levels (Azar et al., 2023). Yet, despite a significant reduction in carbon dioxide emissions during the pandemic-related lockdowns of 2020, atmospheric methane increased. Among other sources, livestock production, gas pipelines, shale fracking, waste dumps, and wet rice agriculture all contribute to methane emissions (Scoones, 2023), and this output is compounded by methane release associated with wetlands and (increasingly) melting permafrost (Strack et al., 2022). Recent computer modelling by the US Geological Survey predicts that natural methane release will continue to increase as the climate warms (Collier & Bansel, 2023). Put bluntly, we have an accelerating crisis on our hands with multiple feedback loops.

The policy dilemma facing all collective action problems at the international and national levels involves the need to deal with emerging crises, persistent governance challenges, and the ethical demands of social and environmental justice (see Stoett, 2019). Given the potency of methane, it is obviously imperative that it is addressed at a global level; the Global Methane Pledge, an action plan launched at COP26 in November 2021, promised a 30 per cent reduction by 2030. The pledge also targets the accuracy, transparency, consistency, comparability, and completeness of national GHG inventory reporting under the UNFCCC: A global methane budget has been established to track emissions, and a thorough global methane assessment has been conducted (UNEP, 2021).

Canada adopted a plan to reduce methane emissions by 35 per cent from 2020 levels by 2030 through a combination of regulation and incentives. Yet it is clear that methane is not considered with the same gravity as carbon by policymakers or the public. For example, even though methane has come "front and center in climate change policy" in North America, with both Canada and the United States playing a leadership role (Rabe, 2022, 2023), "Canadian regulators said they were unaware of a methane cloud spotted by the European Space Agency's Sentinel-5P satellite … near gas pipelines, highlighting a disconnect between the nation's climate ambitions and its emissions, which are the second highest per capita among G-20 countries" (Clark et al., 2022). In a joint global assessment, the United Nations Environment Programme (UNEP; 2021) concluded that reducing farming-related methane emissions is key to mitigating climate change. For example, livestock emissions from manure and gastroenteric releases account for approximately 32 per cent of human-caused methane emissions (Dillon, 2021). Recent studies suggest that phasing out meat production over the next 15 years on a global level could achieve a 68 per cent reduction in GHG emissions by the end of the present century and start global cooling as early as 2030 (Eisen & Brown, 2022).

It is clearly an affront to climate/environmental/social justice that large-scale methane emissions, which harm the general public and future generations, are not subject to greater scrutiny. Public-facing organizations focused on methane emissions reduction in the United States are growing, but with notable exceptions such as the David Suzuki Foundation and Common Earth, growth has been slower in Canada. Reducing coal, oil, and gas usage remains the most effective way to cut emissions from the energy sector, though this has proven challenging in the policy context of countries such as Canada and the United States, where "natural gas" has been sold as a stepping stone to the greater use of renewable energy sources (see the discussion of liquified natural gas exports in Chapter Six).

Multilateral partnerships such as the Global Methane Initiative and the Climate and Clean Air Coalition (CCAC) underscore the importance of mitigation efforts such as (1) sustainable ventilation of methane in coal mines (McKain et al., 2015), (2) the covering of landfills to reduce methane emissions while producing biogas for energy and transport usage, and (3) the creation of farm biodigesters (Lebuhn et al., 2018). Satellite data has been used to monitor methane gas and analyze its changes over time, planning for macroeconomic policies and environmental measures to help GHG mitigation. Since methane sinks are also playing a role in the rapid rise in atmospheric methane over the last decade, nature-based solutions, such as conserving peatlands, are vital and can mitigate not just methane release but enhance carbon storage (Strack et al., 2022).

Critical Thinking Questions

1. Why do you think this issue has been "too long overlooked" in climate change policies and programs?
2. Is "natural gas" a stepping stone to the greater use of renewable energy, given the findings of this case study?

CONCLUSION: FUTURE PROSPECTS FOR PROGRESS

How effectively will the policies set down in these plans lead to emissions reductions? Will they stop climate change? Put simply, we don't know, and much depends on Canadians' efforts and responses to these changes in regulation and policy. The cost of implementation, degree of scope across the economy, as well as issues of equity and unevenness in costs and benefits will affect the kinds of actions the government is able to take going forward. While we have come a long way since the 1990s, when much of the debate focused on the costliness of mitigation, today there is a discursive shift to focus on the opportunities for economic prosperity and employment that emerge from new technologies and industries in the renewable energy sector. There remains considerable resistance to costly and unjust policies that marginalize Indigenous Peoples and poorer Canadians. Even more problematic is the entrenchment and influence of fossil fuel industries in the governance process, as suggested by the continuation of fossil fuel subsidies. As well, the tendency for "carbon lock-in," the trend for investments in high-emitting infrastructure like pipelines to take on their own momentum and permanence, continues to affect governance. For example, while there is little evidence that carbon capture and storage is a scalable solution to carbon emissions, these solutions remain immensely popular among lobbyists and politicians because of the influence of the fossil fuel industries in provincial and federal arenas. A briefing note for federal and Alberta ministers marked "secret" and revealed by the media said of the oil sands: "Only a small percentage of emitted CO_2 is 'capturable' since most emissions aren't pure enough. Only limited near-term opportunities exist in the oil sands and they largely relate to upgraded facilities" (*CBC News*, 2008).

Despite these efforts, total GHG emissions in Canada increased by 13.9 per cent between 1990 and 2021, and emissions from the oil and gas sector have grown overall by 88 per cent from 1990 (Environment and Climate

Change Canada, 2023b). While there are few who continue to tout Canada as an "energy superpower," the prospects for reducing Canada's emissions seem bleak given the poor historical record. More radical "solutions" such as geo-engineering remain nascent and could end up increasing problems because of the many unknowns and risks associated with such climate "tampering," while presenting complex environmental justice issues.

Conflicts over climate governance are likely to continue among Canadian regions, whose economic profiles and varying experiences make cooperation difficult. As well, as discussed in other chapters, the constitutional division of powers continues to bedevil efforts at a pan-Canadian solution. National leadership will likely continue to be haphazard and modest, even as the human and economic costs of climate impacts continue to rise. These costs will likely be borne most acutely by marginalized and poorer Canadians, especially in the north, and future generations. The future remains uncertain, but what does seem clear is that adaptation to climate change will be necessary, and the longer we delay emissions reductions the more costly those adaptations will likely be.

CHAPTER TEN

Biosecurity and Health

LEARNING OBJECTIVES

1. Explain the interconnections between environmental issues, biosecurity threats, and human health in the Canadian context.
2. Assess the impacts of climate change on biosecurity and public health in Canada, including emerging disease risks and food security challenges.
3. Critically examine Canada's policy approaches and governance structures for addressing biosecurity and health issues related to environmental change.

INTRODUCTION: HEALTH IS ECOPOLITICAL?

You may not be accustomed to thinking of health, conventionally defined, as an ecopolitical issue. We argue that it certainly is, since human health is directly and indirectly tied to biosecurity – the protection of nature and ourselves from biological invasion, biodiversity loss, ecosystem failure, the destruction of food crops, and other calamities (see Box 10.1). There are several ways in which the myriad environmental issues already covered in this text intersect with biosecurity and human health. It is important to remember that Canada is a nation-state constructed largely through the exploitation of natural resources and the dispossession of Indigenous Peoples: Related threats to biosecurity and the health of some sections of the population continue today. The spectre of ecosystem collapse is especially frightening if human survival is, indeed, a desired outcome. There are four general types of "human health functions" of ecosystems:

1. Ecosystems provide us with basic human needs, such as food, clean air, clean water, and clean soils (i.e., ecosystem services).
2. Ecosystems prevent the spread of disease through biological control.
3. Ecosystems provide us with medical and genetic resources that are necessary to prevent or cure diseases.
4. Biodiversity contributes to the maintenance of mental health by providing opportunities for recreation, creative outlets, therapeutic retreats, and cognitive development (Sala et al., 2009; see also Chivian & Bernstein, 2010).

BOX 10.1. Defining Biosecurity and Health

Both terms that animate this chapter have been defined in numerous ways over the years. Biosecurity is often viewed as the protection (of human beings) from threats posed by biology, or the manipulation of biology. For example, according to the US Department of Agriculture (USDA), biosecurity is about the protection of "the food supply" and, specifically, responses to food safety emergencies. After 9/11, the USDA formed the Food Biosecurity Action Team to assess potential vulnerabilities along the farm–table continuum (FDA, USDA, & Homeland Security, 2015). The implied threat here is, in essence, terrorism – more specifically, terrorists – yet attacks on the "farm–table continuum" are far less realized threats to human habitat than the agricultural production system itself, which is heavily reliant on oil products, pesticides, antibiotics, and land erosive practices. In this rather militarized definition, the main concerns would be protecting the national imaginary (see Chapter Two) from the use of biological agents, such as anthrax, or the protection of water supplies from purposeful contamination. A slightly broader definition would include protection of crops and domesticated animals from pests and disease (whether the threat is from terrorists, plagues, or others). We use biosecurity in a much wider sense: *the protection of the environment (whether it is human-built or "natural" areas) from threats to biological integrity, including threats to species, to ecosystems, and to climate and other characteristics of earth's natural systems that support biodiversity, including human life.*

Health, meanwhile, can be defined very narrowly as the physical health of human beings – mainly the avoidance of disease, or even pain – but it is more broadly defined by the World Health Organization as "a state of complete physical, mental and social well-being and not merely the absence of disease or infirmity ... The enjoyment of the highest attainable standard of health is one of the fundamental rights of every human being without distinction of race, religion, political belief, economic or social condition" (World Health Organization, 1946). We define health along these terms but insist, as the ongoing discussion on One Health suggests, the health of the environment – of animals and plants (wild and domesticated) and of the ecosystems (on land and in water) on which we all depend – is just as important as human health itself. The interface between biosecurity and health is thus a fundamental aspect of ecopolitics.

As ecopolitics play out, key ethical decisions will be made regarding ecological futures, limiting the range of choice for future generations and affecting human, animal, plant, and ecosystem health. Today, many specialists prefer to adopt a "**One Health**" approach that takes into consideration the interlinkages between these aspects of health, noting that, since they are so tightly interconnected, compromising one will threaten them all (see IPBES, 2020). Beyond this foundational interdependence, another key element of ecopolitics is that the structural inequality that characterizes most countries today, including Canada, is manifested in differentiated access to the benefits of nature as well as protection from the threats posed by pollution, climate change, biodiversity loss, and other contemporary impacts of industrialization and extraction. These discrepancies often reflect and perpetuate inequities along racial, ethnic, and gender lines, and health is a prime indicator of this relationship.

For example, in an area commonly referred to as "Chemical Valley" near Sarnia, Ontario, there are around 60 industrial facilities within a 25-kilometre radius of the homes of the Aamjiwnaang First Nation. They constantly face high exposure rates to pollutants; have an extremely high girl-to-boy birth ratio; report high miscarriage, cancer, and childhood asthma rates; and have faced ongoing resistance to even getting accurate measurements of sulphur dioxide and other chemicals; the pollution could also be affecting medicinal plants upon which the Aamjiwnaang have traditionally relied (Jarvis, 2021; see Bedeau, 2006). This can be seen as an egregious example of environmental injustice, but it is clearly a health issue for the Aamjiwnaang First Nation (see Case Study 10.1 for another example of environmental injustice). The extensive use of antibiotics, both by people and on farms, is another example. Excrement containing antibiotic residue gradually finds its way into the water system, including the Great Lakes, increasing the risk of waterborne infectious diseases. According to a report by the International Joint Commission, "some experts believe that the massive and largely unregulated use of antibiotics in agriculture, coupled with the increasing number of antibiotic-resistant pathogens found in nature, may present the greatest risk," resulting in the evolution of "superbugs" we would be unable to resist (Spears, 2004). Other threats to water supplies have harmed local communities, and there is often a correlation with racial minorities (see Waldron, 2018).

CASE STUDY 10.1. Grassy Narrows[1]

The Grassy Narrows reserve was created in 1882, five years after Treaty 3 was negotiated between the Ojibwe people and the Canadian government. The agreement reserved the Indigenous right to pursue traditional hunting and fishing activities throughout their traditional land use area (Asubpeeschosee-wagong Anishinabek). Several events since that agreement have violated that right. In 1961, residents were coerced into relocating five miles southeast by the Indian Affairs agent, which disrupted their traditional economy and lifestyle and made them highly dependent on fishing with 85 per cent of their population working in the commercial or tourist fishing industry (Vecsey, 1987).

Between 1962 and 1970, Dryden Chemicals dumped an estimated 9,000 kilograms of untreated mercury 130 kilometres upstream from the new Grassy Narrows reserve until the Ontario government found mercury concentrations up to 50 times the upper limit considered safe in the fish. Because of the high concentrations of mercury they banned commercial fishing, and "within the space of a year, Grassy Narrows moved from 95% employment to 95% unemployment" (Vecsey, 1987), which was followed by increased rates of violence, suicide, and alcoholism. A study in 1975 found that 45 of 89 Grassy Narrows residents had symptoms consistent with mercury poisoning and were diagnosed with Minamata disease (Harada et al., 2005). However, there was resistance from the government, and "some Canadian officials blamed the symptoms on alcoholism, venereal disease, laziness, and so forth" and claimed evidence for mercury poisoning was inconclusive (Vecsey, 1987). In 1985, the Indian Affairs agent claimed no "federal legal obligation" but encouraged a settlement to "assist the band" and to "save against future social disruption" (Vecsey, 1987). They reached a settlement, and the Canadian government passed the *Grassy Narrows and Islington Indian Bands Mercury Pollution Claims Settlement Act* in 1986, which established the Mercury Disability Board to manage claims of mercury poisoning. The board acknowledged the symptoms but did not agree with the diagnosis of Minamata disease (Harada et al., 2005).

Grassy Narrows continues to have issues with mercury poisoning and fears that logging risks are exacerbating the contamination. Grassy Narrows residents created a blockade in 2002 to stop all logging trucks from coming into the community. After lengthy litigation, Ontario's Superior Court ruled in 2011 that the province was infringing on their Treaty rights, but that ruling was overturned by the Ontario Court of Appeal and dismissed by the Supreme Court of Canada (Ilyniak, 2014). After subsequent litigation, Ontario has committed to prohibit logging in the area until 2034 (Canadian Environmental Law Association, 2024).

In 2024, a new lawsuit was filed claiming the government violated its duties under Treaty 3 by failing to protect against or remedy the effects of mercury contamination. The suit cited the federal government's commitment to building a mercury treatment centre, the Ontario government's commitment to remediation of the river system, and the lack of progress on both fronts several years later. In July 2024, the Grassy Narrows First Nation took their fight to the Inter-American Commission on Human Rights (IACHR) (Law, 2024b). Judy Da Silva of the Grassy Narrows First Nation called for an end to environmental racism, comparing their situation to the Walkerton water crisis that killed 7 people and made 2,300 sick from *E. coli*-contaminated water and saw liability and compensation determined within a year of the outbreak (Law, 2024a).

Passed into law in 2024, Bill C-226 (*National Strategy to Assess, Prevent and Address Environmental Racism and to Advance Environmental Justice*) was developed in Canadian Senate committee hearings that considered Grassy Narrows and its history. The purpose of the law is to develop the framework to consult with First Nations on how to address environmental racism. It differs from other legislation regarding Indigenous rights and the environment in its specific focus on racism and the goal of consulting with First Nations and affected communities on how they perceive environmental justice to move past the often one-sided and performative consultation process.

Critical Thinking Questions

1. What considerations do you think should be presented to the Inter-American Commission on Human Rights with regard to this case?
2. Does the legislation passed in 2024 properly address the biosecurity and health issues connected with the longstanding grievances of Indigenous and other rights holders in Canada?

It has even been suggested that some 80 per cent of all cancers are likely due to environmental factors that could be reduced or even eradicated, including toxic industrial and agricultural chemicals, excessive sunlight, nuclear radiation from power plants and military operations, and other factors (Burdon, 2003). The United Nations Environmental Programme (UNEP) has indicated for nearly a quarter century that "some 25 per cent of all preventable ill-health, with diarrhoeal diseases and acute respiratory infections heading the list," is directly attributable to poor environmental quality (UNEP, 2002, p. 27). Of course, these linkages are all controversial in the causal sense, but the point is that in pursuing economic and military security, environmental security for the common citizen is compromised. Indeed, health is in many ways at the centre of the ecopolitical debate, and this includes mental health as well as the physical variety. Recent studies linking positive mental health outcomes (and even reduced crime rates) with exposure to green spaces and biodiversity are again leading us toward a One Health vision, even if policymakers have been slow to actively respond (see, e.g., WHO-CBD, 2015; Barton & Rogerson, 2017; Bratman et al., 2019). The longstanding Japanese practice of *shinrin-yoku*, or "forest bathing," which involves deeply inhaling the scents of trees and other forest dwellers, is an example of a human health activity that has become nearly impossible for most low-income urbanites to engage in (see Mathews, 2020, p. 246). It stands to reason, then, that threats to biosecurity are threats to human health and should be easily pegged as policy priorities if governments exist, even nominally, to promote the health and welfare of citizens. Yet we have seen that ecopolitics is not so simple.

As with the other issues covered in this book, Canadian biosecurity is best viewed as a range of sub-issues that, taken together, present significant challenges for policymakers with ethical dilemmas around every corner. For example, one of the most efficient and successful approaches to managing invasive species is to kill them – an action called "eradication" by conservation managers and policymakers. It might be viewed as a necessary evil, but many environmentalists and some Indigenous communities disagree about its ethical validity: What right do humans have to kill off species that have spread largely because of our own negligence or misadventure? With public health and safety, ethical questions abound. The use of mask mandates and vaccine programs to combat the COVID-19 pandemic is, of course, an obvious example. Future pandemics could prove even more intrusive as society struggles to cope, demanding forced quarantines such as those seen in China during the year 2022 (entire sections of major cities were effectively shut down upon the slightest detection of the virus). For a country with such a pronounced immigration experience, shutting down airports to foreign nationals is indeed a significant ethical decision. And if, as we suggest in this chapter, climate change is the ultimate threat to both biosecurity and human health, then hard decisions need to be made about transitioning to a post-carbon economy, both in Canada and across the planet.

This chapter will focus on several threats to biosecurity that, arguably, should concern us all. Disease – an undeniable policy priority if there ever was one, following the COVID-19 pandemic of 2020–22 – is often linked to environmental destruction. Food security, often considered a major aspect of biosecurity, is as frail as ever despite the massive input of chemicals (fertilizers and pesticides) that drive today's industrial agriculture. An "insect apocalypse" may well be upon us, which will reduce food security even further as we lose the erstwhile services of pollinators. Biological invasions are not the stuff of science fiction movies but occur daily, driving native species toward extinction and threatening human health and livelihoods. The illegal wildlife trade, beyond harming biodiversity across Canada, has the potential to bring both pathogen vectors and invasive alien species to Canadian shores. And all of these factors are exacerbated by the advent of escalating climate change. It is probably needless to say at this point that these are all global issues, affecting every citizen in every country on earth, but Canada has its own unique problems and abilities to deal effectively with them. Harsh ethical decisions await the Canadian ecopolitical landscape unless there is a fundamental change in how we approach, value, and use nature.

DISEASE

Few events polarize a citizenry while harming them like the rapid spread of a serious disease. It is widely accepted that, whatever its exact origin may have been, COVID-19 was a zoonotic pathogen that spread from China to the rest of the world, affecting every Canadian and Indigenous Nation in the process. A zoonotic pathogen (viruses, bacteria, parasites, fungi) is one that has spread to humans from non-human animals (meanwhile, zooanthroponosis is the reverse: pathogens transmitted from humans to non-human biota). The species that infects humans may or may not be the origin of the pathogen; it is often the case that another animal, such as a bat, has infected a species that subsequently has contact with humans. (Many diseases are also spread by vector transmission: an arthropod (insects and arachnids) transmits a virus, bacterium, or parasite from one host to another, mainly through feeding on blood.) It is believed that COVID-19 was zoonotic: It probably originated in bats, then lived in an intermediate animal host, then made the jump to humans in a so-called wet market (where live animals are sold) in Wuhan, China.[2]

While COVID-19 may have shocked the medical and public health establishment and added a new politics of dissent to the Canadian political landscape, it should not have come as a major surprise, since infectious disease has played such a visible role throughout human history and we know that increased exposure to nature is increasing the likelihood that we will encounter new dangerous diseases (IPBES, 2020; Machalaba et al., 2017). Any casual student of history is familiar with the Black Death (bubonic and pneumonic plagues originating in the Eurasian steppes that killed roughly a quarter of the European population in the fourteenth century), the impact of viral infections on Indigenous Peoples during colonization (Crosby, 1986; Lovell, 1992), the advent of tuberculosis and other diseases during industrialization, the flu pandemic of 1916–20 (Collier, 1974), the HIV/AIDS epidemic that has resulted in over 40 million deaths worldwide so far (UNAIDS, 2022), and other incidents that demonstrate the ability of infection to spread with alarming and deadly speed. SARS took Canadian health officials by surprise in 2003, and though the death count was low, it did cause billions of dollars in economic damage as tourists avoided Canada.[3]

COVID-19, itself caused by the SARS-CoV-2 virus, was yet another assault on the biosecurity of Canada, killing over 60,000 Canadians (as of August 2024) and straining health systems to the breaking point in many areas. The response to COVID-19 involved shutdowns, lockdowns, transformed educational environments, mask mandates, and vigorous vaccine programs, as well as anti-mask and anti-vaccine protests and many other social factors that Canadians had never really experienced before. That this pathogen probably originated in a bat cave in China and was spread through transmission in the wildlife trade and to a human being before affecting every country on earth is quite astounding. As this chapter is being written, concerns are spreading about the re-emergence of polio and new introductions of the monkeypox virus.

Circling back to our definition of biosecurity, we are not only concerned with diseases that harm humans. On the farm, foot-and-mouth disease, mad cow disease (or bovine spongiform encephalopathy), and the avian flu H7N3 have had immeasurable animal kill totals in many countries, including Canada (see Stoett, 2006). Similar concerns riddle the aquaculture industry, particularly among net-pen-reared Atlantic salmon in British Columbia (St-Hilaire et al., 2002), though there are strict protocols in place to prevent diseases in the National Aquatic Animal Health Program delivered by the Canadian Food Inspection Agency and Fisheries and Oceans Canada (Fisheries and Oceans Canada, 2017). In general, food security is constantly at risk from the spread of invasive alien species and pathogens. It is safe to say that though there remains understandable concern that disease will be used as a weapon or a bioterrorist threat (Chyba & Greninger, 2004), the main threat to human health and industry stems not from deliberately released anthrax spores or smallpox, but the incidental spread of disease in a highly interconnected global economy. And, ultimately, if we accept the argument that the destruction of nature (or, at least, severe land use change) and the spread of disease are linked, we need to consider the impact of development (IPBES, 2020). (We return to the impact of climate change on biosecurity and human health later in this chapter, but it is clear that the threat of disease emergence is a primary concern.)

Canada has an ongoing gap in the provision of biosecurity as it relates to zoonotic disease. While health is subject to provincial jurisdiction, the global nature of pandemics clearly demands a national preventive regime. While the Canadian federal government reacted to COVID-19 by controlling flights and making vaccines available, and biosafety protocols are in place for experimental laboratories and agricultural contexts, a new Canadian biosecurity strategy "must prepare Canada for all biological risks [and] include communicable and non-communicable infectious diseases, and address risks of species crossover, accidental release and deliberate acts by hostile agents"

(Levy, 2021). At present, efforts to legislate the development of a national strategy are being made by parliamentarians, but they face various pressure points, including a strong populist revolt against centralized decision making on health-related issues, provincial governments reluctant to follow Ottawa's lead (especially on the health profile), and limited resources. For example, by June 2020 Canada had the worst record among OECD countries for COVID-19 related deaths in long-term care facilities, a situation that only worsened as the pandemic dragged on. Largely a provincial policy responsibility, the call for a national strategy to protect the elderly during a pandemic has been resonant. And when it comes to prevention in a highly interconnected world economy, border control and surveillance is essential. This is in effect an eco-political battlefield as well: Since we can link modern disease with land use change and climate change, environmental policy clashes between different levels of governance also affect the viability and ultimately the effectiveness of any national strategy.

BIODIVERSITY LOSS AS A THREAT TO BIOSECURITY AND HEALTH

We are learning continuously about the relationship between the health of nature and humans; a landmark WHO-CBD report outlined much of this in great detail nearly a decade ago (WHO-CBD, 2015). For example, we will have a difficult time surviving in the absence of pollinators, and we are probably doomed without insects in general.[4] There's a popular cartoon on X (formerly Twitter) that depicts a driver smiling behind his bug-spattered windshield, captioned "1980." Then the same driver is shown, with an almost perfectly clean window this time, with the caption "2020." In one version a third image shows the clean windshield and car, but with no driver: it is captioned "2050." The generations that remember the windshields of the 1970s and 1980s know well that there are fewer insects now; a recent study of licence plate spatter in the United Kingdom indicates a 60 per cent plunge in insect numbers over only the last 17 years (Wilkins, 2022). In recent years many studies have appeared that show massive declines in insect populations, indicating declines in the range of 1–2 per cent per year among all insects, with up to 40 per cent of species at risk of extinction (Wagner et al., 2021; Sánchez-Bayo & Wyckhuys, 2019). A few significant and well-documented declines, like that of the honeybee (*Apis melliflua*) and the monarch butterfly (*Danaus plexippus*) that have been known for decades (Inamine et al., 2016), have helped bring awareness of the disheartening situation for insects, and headlines about the "insect apocalypse" have begun to seem almost cliché (Jarvis, 2018; Leahy, 2019; Soroye et al., 2020; Goulson, 2021).

Milman (2022, p. 11) cites a study (Hebert et al., 2022) suggesting that Canada alone has close to 100,000 species of insects. While insect declines are evident and in many cases well documented in areas with relatively high human populations, less certain is the severity of declines in the tropics; while the equatorial regions house a large portion of insect diversity and numbers, it is often not well documented, especially with regard to populations over time. With some exceptions (Kimbrough, 2021), data are sparse or non-existent if we want to assess insect declines over decades in areas like the boreal forests of Canada and Russia or the tropical forests of Africa, South America, and Southeast Asia. Still, scientists and conservationists are concerned; if the facts we know are indicative of the facts we don't know, insects around the world are in trouble. And as the cartoon suggests, we may be as well.

Members of the Krefeld Entomological Society in Germany have been keeping records on insects in parts of Europe since 1905 and have noted marked declines, especially in recent decades. In 2017 they made international headlines when data were published showing, in one German nature reserve, a decline in the total mass of flying insects of nearly 80 per cent between 1989 and 2013 (Vogel, 2017). The group also noted local extirpations of relatively common species, including half the nation's known bee varieties. Groups like Monarch Watch in North America (www.monarchwatch.org) and popular apps like iNaturalist (www.inaturalist.org) have generated loads of new data, but much is only recent – there is almost no way to reliably estimate background population levels of 50, 100, or 500 years ago. And even today our ignorance of the insect world is vast: While there are more than a million described species of insects, even the most modest estimates calculate that another 4.5 to 7 million remain unnamed (Wagner et al., 2021, p. 4). The decline of what biologist E.O. Wilson called "the little things that run the world" is a special aspect of the global biodiversity crisis, as insects fill a number of specific ecological roles, including nutrient conversion and pollination, and are an especially important food source for many birds. Vast populations of ants, wasps, beetles, flies, butterflies, moths, and bees, along with a few vertebrates, play a role in pollinating 90 per cent of flowering plants and around one-third of global food crops by volume (IPBES, 2016). (The remainder are pollinated by wind or, increasingly, through human intervention, including by hand.)

Concern over domesticated pollinators, especially the honeybee (*Apis mellifera*), has been an important driver of media and public attention. Colony collapse disorder (CCD) is a growing concern, with widespread reports of 40–60 per cent declines in colony numbers through consecutive spring counts, and declines in the number of colonies themselves measured at 16 per cent in 2017–18 (Gray et al., 2019). The causes are complex and include impacts of parasites and disease, the impacts of pesticides, and severe weather events that can wipe out hives and foraging opportunities. Yet honeybees, while suffering, are far from being endangered. Millions of bees are bred annually, to be trucked around continents to provide pollination services on apricots, apples, peaches, and other crops. Globally, these pollination services are valued at up to US$577 billion (IPBES, 2016), but quoting E.O. Wilson once again puts this in perspective: "If invertebrates were to disappear, I doubt the human species could last more than a few months" (quoted in Kimbrough, 2021).

Far more concerning for ecologists, however, is the loss of native and wild bees, including bumblebees, sweat bees, mason bees, mining bees, masked bees, leafcutters, wool carders, cuckoo bees, and carpenter bees. Not to mention the ants, wasps, beetles, springtails, mayflies, dragonflies, stoneflies, caddis flies, butterflies, moths, mantis, and grasshoppers, to consider only the major groups of insects. Ironically, many members of these groups are also great pollinators, but industrial-scale agriculture has eroded the habitat that makes their survival possible while undermining the biodiversity and ecological integrity that support their co-existence and resilience. The United Nations estimates that almost 40 per cent of the earth's surface is currently used for agriculture (IPBES, 2020, p. 109). Notably, almost 77 per cent of this agricultural land is used to raise and feed livestock, and only 23 per cent of it – less than 10 per cent of the world's land – grows all the grains, fruits, nuts, and vegetables that humans consume directly (Ritchie & Roser, 2019).

Not surprisingly, it is in those areas in which agriculture has intensified in recent decades, especially in Europe and much of the Americas, where the insect decline is most evident. The issue is not just the scale of agriculture but the impact of modernizing practices like the removal of hedgerows to accommodate larger machinery and "wall-to-wall" annual ploughing that destroys the many beetles and bees that nest underground. Pesticide- and herbicide-treated crops, including genetically modified varieties (GMOs), are by now the norm; in 2015 89 per cent of soy and 94 per cent of corn in the United States were GMOs, primarily to enable weed spraying with herbicides, especially Roundup. These methods often include eradicating all the "weeds" in an area, leading to even greater loss of habitat. Monarch Watch director Chip Taylor stated in 2013 that the monarch breeding habitat in the United States was "virtually gone" (Conniff, 2013), though the Obama Administration did try to engineer a resurgence with a special pollinator highway approach. Neonicotinoids, a widely used group of pesticides typically applied to seeds prior to planting, have also been found in nearby foraging plants, which can disrupt navigation and mating behaviours among both domesticated and wild bees (and almost certainly other classes of insects). The use of fertilizers has all but eliminated fallow lands, which regenerated both soil and plant biodiversity. Runoff polluting waterways has also seriously impacted aquatic insect species. All these factors combine to reduce habitat and forage for wild insects.

We will return to this theme below, but it is important to realize that climate change is also having an impact, as changes in temperature, rainfall, and humidity as well as severe weather events disrupt food availability and nesting and may induce insect relocation – often at rates that cannot be matched by the host plants they use for food and shelter. Milman (2022) argues that, if we experience "3.2 degrees Celsius of warming, which the world is on track for by the end of the century in the absence of major emissions reductions, half of all insect species will lose more than half of their current habitable range" (p. 115). In other cases this leads to a shift in habitat, as the abundance of insects from warmer regions move toward the poles. The decisive success factors seem to be related to interactions among species, such as when a population moves away from predator or forage species (Cahill et al., 2013); but the opposite can also happen, as when a warmer climate enables invasive species like the pine beetle (see Chapter Five) and the emerald ash borer to move into areas where food is abundant (at least until their food source is wiped out). The improvement of land-based pollution standards, especially since the 1970s, has also improved prospects for the many species that live some or all of their lives in freshwater (Wagner et al., 2021). The research is difficult to extrapolate, however; degraded or developed sites, for instance, are often excluded from studies, even though these are the very sites where declines would be most evident. As one researcher points out, "It's not an experiment. It's ... observation of this massive decline. The data themselves are strong. Understanding it and knowing what to do about it is difficult" (Vogel, 2017).

Agricultural modernization is driven by many factors, including globalized markets, subsidies, and the sanctity of private property, which for decades has tended toward larger farms and increasingly mechanized farming. High land values and larger machinery have led to the removal of hedgerows, which historically provided habitat for insects and birds. Chemical inputs, including fertilizers and pesticides, are often promoted by agricultural extension agents and marketed as essential for productivity, but their cost can lead to debt traps and put pressure on farmers to maximize land use, even when it is detrimental. Yet pesticides also hold the promise of protecting crops from insect losses, thus keeping yields high and reducing pressure to expand agriculture into new landscapes, including in highly diverse tropical locales. (Palm and coconut oils can readily replace canola or corn in many products.) Widespread concern around bees and other pollinators from environmentalists, beekeepers, and others has led to prohibitions on the use of neonicotinoids (neonics) in several jurisdictions. Ontario began to restrict their use in 2015, despite opposition from grain farmers; seed treated with neonics was actually designated a Class 12 pesticide, and farmers had to complete training in **integrated pest management** (IPM) and verify they actually had losses due to insects before they would be able to plant it (Ontario Ministry of Agriculture, Food and Agribusiness and Ministry of Rural Affairs, 2015). In 2018 neonics were banned from fields in the European Union, and in 2019 Health Canada imposed limited restrictions across the country.

IPM is widely supported by international agencies including the WHO, the Food and Agricultural Organization (FAO), and the Convention on Biological Diversity. The FAO-WHO International Code of Conduct on the Distribution and Use of Pesticides established a set of voluntary actions for government and industry that could reduce impacts on the environment and insects, and a majority of member-states claim to be using the guidelines (IPBES, 2016, p. xxiii, note 6). But the agricultural and agrochemical industries continue to fight restrictions, even claiming that neonics have benefits for pollinators, and in many areas they are still widely used: Research in the United States found that the overall agricultural environment is almost 50 times as toxic to bees as it was only 25 years earlier. As one scientist at Friends of the Earth US put it, "This is the second *Silent Spring*. Neonics are like a new DDT, except they are a thousand times more toxic to bees than DDT was" (Leahy, 2019).

Unlike the first fears over a *Silent Spring*, described in Rachel Carson's groundbreaking book of that name, today's pesticides are more targeted, less acutely toxic to workers, and less bio-accumulative. In the 1960s concerns were raised about poisoned birds and workers, whereas now "only" insects are directly impacted. But the fact remains that insects are a primary source of food for a great many bird species, and so it's no coincidence that bird numbers have been falling drastically alongside the numbers of their prey in many of the same agricultural-intensive regions. Ultimately, the decline of this vital aspect of biodiversity harms the biosecurity of every Canadian and Indigenous community.

The broader link with diseases, as discussed above, should not be lost on us either. Healthy ecosystems are essential for healthy people to thrive, and failing ecosystems will present more direct and indirect health threats to humans. This is why experts have called for ecosystem restoration as an essential component of any viable COVID-19 recovery plan (see Robinson et al., 2022), and biodiversity conservation needs to be a Canadian and provincial priority moving forward.

BIOLOGICAL INVASION

We do not need to worry only about species leaving; many of those coming are highly problematic (see Roy et. al., 2023). The most commonly accepted definition of an "invasive alien species" is probably "widespread nonindigenous species that have adverse effects on the invaded habitat" (McNeely et al., 2001; see also Colautti & MacIsaac, 2004), though some feel that the term "invasive species" has such a negative connotation it "over-emotionalizes," thus betraying the standards of dispassionate science (Theodoropoulas, 2003). (Of course, the ultimate invasive species, and the one with the uncontested title for most "ecological damage done" in the process, is humankind.)

For several centuries, **bioinvasion** has been a global affair. Such species displacement is often referred to as "human-mediated global dispersal." There are, of course, non-human mediated dispersals, such as ice flows in the Arctic, changing wind patterns, tsunamis, and even "kelp rafts" in the Antarctic (Smith, 2001). But these are not known to cause lengthy migrations; this takes human intervention. Some of the introductions have been deliberate, in efforts to affect biopest control, or the introduction of game species for hunting and fishing purposes. The North American Great Lakes (after being ravaged by the invasive sea lamprey) have been populated largely by introduced species, and terrestrial species such as ring-necked pheasant and sika deer have been introduced for hunting purposes (Cox, 1999). The Asian carp was originally introduced to clear vegetation from fish farms; an electric barrier between the Chicago Sanitary and Ship Canal and Lake Michigan is the last line of Great Lakes defence against this ravenous fish. The carp are so plentiful that their acrobatic jumping has injured boaters. As Elizabeth Kolbert (2021) writes, "the sight of silver carp arcing through the air is at once beautiful – like attending a piscine ballet – and terrifying – like facing incoming fire" (p. 22). Tens of millions of dollars have been spent by the US federal government to avert the arrival of the carp into Lake Michigan, and efforts to reduce their abundance in the Mississippi River by exporting the carp as food to Asia and elsewhere have met with limited success. The most damaging invasions, however, have been incidental: In general, human-mediated transport is the most important factor for the range of invasive species, while conducive temperatures, competitive ability, and lack of enemies is more important once generous transportation services have been provided by unwitting economic actors.

According to one estimate, since the completion of the St. Lawrence Seaway in 1959 at least 43 non-indigenous species have been established in the Laurentian Great Lakes, including the dreaded sea lamprey; US-Canadian bilateral efforts to combat the lamprey resulted in the Great Lakes Fishery Commission, which has made some impact on mitigating its harm (Abramovitz, 1996, p. 47). The majority of invasive species have arrived courtesy of ballast water from commercial ships (Grigorovich et al., 2003). In 2008, almost 50 years after the seaway began operation, the United States and Canada agreed on an (unimplemented at this stage) inspection system for incoming ships. Arguably, what is perhaps the most infamous example of transoceanic bioinvasion in Canadian history, the inedible *Dreissena polymorpha*, or zebra mussel, was the main impetus.

The mussel invasion has had a significant economic impact, clogging intake valves in ship engines and power plants. In the words of one analyst, the clogging caused by zebra mussels is akin to "an acute hardening of industrial arteries" (Bright, 1998, p. 181). Some environmentalists might argue this may be good for the environment (the mussels also filter water as they consume), but it is decidedly bad for biodiversity. In areas where they are highly concentrated and the technology permits, colonies can be eradicated. This involves using chemical agents (known as molluscicides), freezing and boiling (through steam injection), acoustical vibration, electrical currents, and the introduction of biological agents (such as predators, parasites, and disease). All of these techniques present obvious problems for the greater aquatic environment and may in fact cause more problems than they solve. As van Driesche and van Driesche (2000) remind us, "no examples of successful biocontrol of aquatic invertebrates exist" (p. 74). Manual removal is possible for small boats but presents an enormous challenge (in terms of safety and humanpower) for large ships and underwater pipelines. Reporting the sighting of mussels in non-contaminated areas is vital, so that protected areas (such as clam grounds along the Mississippi River) can receive immediate attention. But there will be no large-scale eradication program. Like the purple loosestrife, which spread inexorably across Canadian fields after its introduction from Europe in ballast soil used in sailing ships (White, 1993), the zebra mussel is here to stay; it would seem that co-existence, rather than counterinvasive warfare, is the only reasonable response.

Indeed, zebra mussels are but one problematic invasive species that has been specifically linked to ballast water discharges by the International Maritime Organization, Global Environment Fund, and UN Development Programme, which have together instituted an international Global Ballast Water Management Programme. The others include cholera, the cladoceran water flea, various sources of toxic algae, and the self-fertilizing hermaphroditic North American comb jelly. Many of these species have literally criss-crossed the globe because of the expansion of trade, secured in freshwater ballast tanks and emptied in awaiting ports.

Alien species do more than challenge competitors: They can even change the ecosystem itself, fundamentally altering its characteristics (see Beisner et al., 2003). For example, there is ample concern that the large numbers of introduced salmonine fish stock in the Great Lakes – in excess of 745 million fish between 1966–98 – have also fundamentally altered the recipient ecosystems (see especially Crawford, 2001). When invasive species actually transform ecosystems, they can also create hybrid taxa, or "genetic pollution" resulting from introgression, and this can only be studied at the level of gene analysis (Petit, 2004; see also Hengeveld, 1989). This becomes even more important with the agricultural introduction of GMOs, invasive species in their own right, when they pollinate adjoining farmland, leading to vigorous calls for precaution as well related bioterrorism fears.[5] Though biological control efforts have vastly improved over the decades, fixing the problem with natural predators can lead to even greater problems: The deliberate introduction of so-called biological-control agents can release them from the constraints imposed by their natural enemies, further homogenize the world's biotic communities, and affect non-target species; they can also lead to unpredictable evolutionary changes (see Edwards, 1998). Indeed, containment measures are especially counterproductive when biodiversity conservation efforts demand more connectivity between bioregions and transborder conduits for species migration (Sanders & Stoett, 2006).

There is also evidence that warming trends will induce species migration northward (see Hughes, 2000). Such "unassisted migration" will prove difficult for rare species of plants and trees, and adaptation or extinction is likely (see Iverson et al., 2004). Not so for insects: For example, warming patterns have vastly extended the range of the mountain pine beetle, now ravaging Yoho National Park in British Columbia and threatening forests in Washington and Banff. Mathews (2020) refers to the "landscapes of death" left behind by the pine beetle: "By far the biggest patch of pine mortality, an area bigger than Wisconsin, happened [in British Columbia,] killing more than half the pine timber volume in the entire province. Flights of beetles during the B.C. outbreak formed swarming dark clouds" (p. 60; see Chapter Five for a more in-depth discussion of the impact of the mountain pine beetle). We are likely to see further zebra mussel northward migration as appropriate reproduction temperatures become more common, and flooding could expand zebra mussel territory even further. It is believed that "climate change will affect the incidence of episodic recruitment events of invasive species, by altering the frequency, intensity, and duration of flooding … by allowing aggressive species to escape from local, constrained refugia" (Sutherst, 2000; Kolar & Lodge, 2000). The 2021 Arctic Report Card produced by the US National Oceanic and Atmospheric Administration includes a disturbing discussion on the impacts of the North American beaver spreading northwards; since beavers are fantastic ecosystem engineers, they can change entire landscapes and accelerate permafrost melt and methane release (see Tape et al., 2021). Thus, the discourse on bioinvasion must now be seen as nested within the broader global debate on the mitigation of and adaptation to climate change; importantly, this challenges the logic of placing trade in the global marketplace on an unassailable pedestal.

Canada does have a national invasive species strategy, but it is badly in need of updating. It was published in 2004 (!), and in fact the federal government discontinued the Invasive Alien Species Partnership Program in 2012. (Invasive alien species continue to be monitored and regulated to varying degrees by provincial governments.) As a firm contributor to the Convention on Biological Diversity (CBD), Canada implicitly recognizes that invasive species are a primary threat to biodiversity and thus to the biosecurity of every Canadian, but more robust policy action is needed. But again, ethical questions are rife: Is eradicating a species because it has proven inconvenient to humans, even when its spread is because of human negligence, ethically justified? How do we decide which species are in need of this eradication, especially as high-tech genetic methodology is developed that will allow us to be even more specific and effective in terms of targeting? Which rights holders and stakeholders should have a say in this evolution of policy priorities?

THE ILLEGAL WILDLIFE TRADE

Another threat to biosecurity, at both the national and global levels, is the burgeoning trade in wildlife, both alive and dead. This form of ecoviolence (Stoett & Omrow, 2022) continues to grow despite measured efforts by many countries and organizations and the Convention on International Trade in Endangered Species of Fauna and Flora (CITES) to limit it. Phelps and colleagues (2016) define the illegal wildlife trade broadly as the harvest, trade, and exploitation of wild, biological specimens through activities that contravene environmental regulations and government legislation; the violation of rules governing private/community resource-holder rights; and the non-observance of international agreements such as CITES. The trade is typically valued at over US$20 billion per year, though the total costs of environmental crimes including illegal forestry, fishing, mining, and hazardous waste dumping are easily in the hundreds of billions (Stoett & Omrow, 2022, p. 43; Phelps et al., 2016).

The illegal wildlife trade encompasses trade in everything from exotic mammals such as pangolins and tigers (and their body parts) to eels to endangered butterflies and other insects, as well as a plethora of endangered plants that are used for various purposes and highly valued timber made from endangered tree species. Timber poaching is a particularly acute crime in North America. As Lyndsay Bourgon (2022) writes, "it's estimated that $1 billion worth of wood is poached yearly," with $20 million worth taken from British Columbia alone (pp. 6–7; figures in US dollars).

On the demand side, the trade is often animated by collectors who are in it for the money, by those who view endangered species as especially exotic pets or meals, or by consumers convinced that certain medicinal qualities (including aphrodisiacal) can be obtained (this partly explains the lucrative market in rhinoceros horn, tiger bones, and other body parts). On the supply side, the trade is driven largely by the greed of traders mixed with the poverty of poachers and others who supply the species for the market. Illegal hunting has often been a form of protest against unfair rules and property structures in European history, but today it is more a function of desperate hunters trying to provide for their families. In some cases, governments are partially or fully complicit, either through corruption (accepting payoffs for not stopping the trade) or actively promoting it (such as Russia's well-known efforts to sell Siberian timber to China without formal authorization or permits; see Stoett & Omrow, 2022, p. 128).

The illegal wildlife trade creates many problems. First of all, it spreads animals and animal parts that could be invasive alien species or that could distribute diseases, as mentioned above. But it also places precious biodiversity, including highly vulnerable or endangered species, directly in danger of extinction. In this sense it is a threat to global biodiversity, not just to species found in Canada or imported into Canada illegally but to all species. Overfishing is bad enough; illegal fisheries are draining the oceans of invaluable species as well as protein for human consumption. Environmental crime also enriches organized criminals, many of whom are involved in other forms of illicit activity. It has been low on policy priority lists for most of the preceding century, though more international action has been taken in recent decades as western environmentalists, biologists, Indigenous communities, and others have drawn attention to it.

One of the more problematic illegal wildlife trades in the Canadian context involves the expanding illicit market for ginseng, which grows naturally in southern Ontario and southwestern Quebec. Environment Canada suggested that ginseng can fetch from $500–$1,000 per pound in Asia, where it is highly coveted as an aphrodisiacal medicine (Crawford, 2017).

American ginseng is listed in one of the appendices of CITES, so special permits must be obtained to trade it, yet in certain areas in the United States and Canada "ginsenging" – poaching wild ginseng – has become a profitable illicit industry. The Canadian Wildlife Service and border agents do their best to limit the trade, meaning that Canada's reputation is relatively free of the charges of corruption applied to many other countries, and Canada is a longstanding member of CITES. But much of the trade in endangered species does not cross borders and is difficult to discover, despite advances in surveillance technology and DNA testing. Illegal fisheries are a good example: While fishing permits can limit seasonal catches, it would be beyond resource capacities to monitor all of Canada's coasts and freshwater lakes and rivers.

It may seem that there are less ethical dilemmas inherent in the fight against the illegal wildlife trade, but issues remain (see Sollund, 2019).

For example, many people around the world are dependent on harvesting and trading endangered or vulnerable species. Who has the right to tell them what they can and cannot do, especially if there is no effort to compensate them for the opportunity cost of refraining from this harvesting? Another argument concerns cultural relativity: The debates over the European Union's ban on seal products and how this has hurt the Inuit who became partially dependent on this trade raise questions about how consumers in one place can condemn activities they may know very little about and how politicians can jump on the bandwagon. The rise of internet commerce has only complicated things, since much of the trade in endangered species is now conducted online and on the dark web (Sollund, 2019).

CLIMATE CHANGE: THE ULTIMATE BIOSECURITY AND HEALTH THREAT

We've referred elsewhere to climate change as the "ultimate ecopolitical challenge," but we might also consider it the ultimate ongoing threat to Canadian biosecurity and human health. It is important to understand that environmental change is, of course, unavoidable, and it would be as futile as disingenuous to refer to this in itself as a threat to biosecurity. It is the rapid rate of human-induced change that is at issue, and we are making unprecedented alterations at both the macro and micro levels that present incalculable risks to human, animal, and plant life, prompting geologists to speak of entering the Anthropocene age, which is essentially a "no-analogue" condition, incomparable to any before it (Dalby, 2006, p. 21; see also Chapters One and Two). At the macro level, climate change is a severe threat to biodiversity, itself challenged by the centuries-long process of agricultural production, since it moves us toward homogenous ecosystems and is reliant on unnatural inputs, especially fossil fuels, for increased yields. But the links between climate change and threats to human health are growing on a yearly basis, and their impacts are most pronounced among communities that have the least resources to avoid them (Greaves, 2021; Machalaba et al., 2015).

The 2021 "Report of the Lancet Countdown on Health and Climate Change" (Romanello, 2021) makes the link quite apparent: Record temperatures in 2020 resulted in billions of person-days of heatwave exposure among people older than 65 years and children younger than 1 year; record-breaking temperatures of over 40 degrees Celsius in the Pacific Northwest areas of the

United States and Canada in June 2021 resulted in hundreds of premature deaths from the heat and exposure to smoke from forest fires; populations in countries with low and medium levels of the UN-defined human development index (HDI) have had the biggest increase in heat vulnerability during the past 30 years, with risks to their health further exacerbated by the low availability of cooling mechanisms and urban green space; and agricultural workers in countries with low and medium HDI were among the worst affected by exposure to extreme temperatures, bearing almost half of the 295 billion potential work hours lost due to heat in 2020. The massive flooding in Pakistan in 2022, which scientists agree is climate change related, resulted in over 1,000 deaths and untold suffering and compromises the health of some of the most vulnerable people in South Asia.

During any given month in 2020, up to 19 per cent of the global land surface was affected by extreme drought; a value that had not exceeded 13 per cent between 1950 and 1999. We do not yet have reliable numbers for the early 2020s, but a quick scan of severe droughts in Europe, California, the Canadian Prairies, and China give an indication that they will be higher than ever. These warm temperatures are affecting the yield potential of the world's major staple crops: 6.0 per cent reduction for maize; 3.0 per cent reduction for winter wheat; 5.4 per cent reduction for soybeans; and 1.8 per cent for rice in 2020, relative to 1981–2010 (combined with the effects of severe limitation in trade resulting from Russia's invasion of Ukraine in early 2022, this is a disastrous scenario). As discussed above, changing environmental conditions are also increasing the suitability for the transmission of many waterborne, airborne, foodborne, and vector-borne pathogens and invasive species. For example, the number of months with environmentally suitable conditions for the transmission of malaria rose by 39 per cent from 1950–59 to 2010–19 in densely populated highland areas in the low HDI group.

The concurrent and interconnecting risks posed by extreme weather events, infectious disease transmission, and food, water, and financial insecurity are overburdening the most vulnerable populations. We've discussed this above, but it's important to note that this was easily foreseen. As Andrew Price-Smith (2002) suggested over two decades ago, there is a "link between temperature increases and a shortened extrinsic incubation rate coupled with increased biting activity of many arthropod vectors … Since global environmental change is expected to generate significant long-term shifts in abiotic phenomena (temperature, humidity, water resources, etc.), we can reasonably expect attendant shifts in pathogenic virulence" (p. 168; see also Ewald, 1994;

McMichael & Bouma, 2000). COVID-19, malaria, and yellow fever, among other tropical diseases, remain serious health threats in many countries also struggling to deal with the AIDS pandemic, land and forest degradation, and civil or international military conflict.

Indeed, there is an increasing recognition of the right to a healthy environment in international law (Schrijver & Weiss, 2004), and the UN General Assembly recently declared access to a clean and healthy environment a universal human right (see UNGA, 2022). The stark realization that this right cannot be realized without drastic changes in the carbon-based global economy is undeniable.

CONCLUSION: AN OVERLOOKED AGENDA

The pursuit and maintenance of biosecurity provides what is perhaps the ultimate example of the need to apply the precautionary principle (see Whiteside, 2006; Burns, 2006), raising further ethical dilemmas and demands related to the construction, social distribution, and prevention of risk (Beck, 1992; Leiss, 2001). At the most basic level, since Canadian biosecurity cannot be viewed in national isolation, we are forced also to consider not only Canada's relatively privileged place in the world but the discrepancy between the health risks endured by people in peripheral regions, such as the Inuit, and the average suburban Canadian. Even within Canada's cities there are marked differences between the health status of those in upper- and lower-income neighbourhoods, and this is often correlated with race.

Canada has a patchwork of biosecurity measures in place across the country, and the strong link to human health we describe in this chapter seems underrepresented. Much Canadian legislation and regulations seem more related to import and export control to adhere to CITES and the World Trade Organization than to building a biosecure future. Since health is a provincial jurisdiction, there are limits to what the federal government can do, but nationwide policies are as vital as ever. Health is an obvious policy priority for all governments, though we have seen that the ecopolitical arena is a contentious one and there is still much work to do to make biosecurity the priority it deserves to be if we are to take a holistic vision of health seriously.

Prevention and preparedness are obviously necessary; with invasive species and infectious disease, we can predict patterns of prevalence, but we would be foolish to believe we can do so with great accuracy or do so enough to eliminate the element of unpleasant surprise. Environmental change is even less manageable. But what may be needed, more than ever, is a healthy dose of introspection. Many of the invasive species we face today are approaching, leaving, or crossing Canada because of economic processes that need to be tightly regulated if we stand a chance of controlling further spread. Similarly, the processes of mass industrialized agriculture – the feeding of bovine spinal matter to cattle, the close quarters in chicken coops, the water contamination resultant from excessive untreated farm excrement, the "massive application of antibiotics to livestock that would otherwise perish in the lethal miasma created by industrial agriculture" (Glasser, 2004, p. 36) – are responsible for the speed with which biosafety can be compromised. Our eating, driving, and recreational habits, all consumer activities, have a profound effect on human health but also ecosystem maintenance capacity. In short, the pursuit of a sovereign biosecurity begins at the kitchen table. Indeed, we might ask how we can use such security threats to broaden civic participation and reduce structural inequities instead of lowering and reinforcing them, respectively.

NOTES

1 Thanks to Joshua Lee for his assistance in writing this case.
2 There is controversy over the origin of COVID-19, as some are convinced it was the result of an accidental lab leak in China, or even a purposeful one; others feel it may have resulted from multiple spillover events (zoonotic transmissions) and not just a singular one (see Katwala, 2022).
3 Parts of this chapter have been adapted from Stoett (2010).
4 Thanks to Shane Mulligan for providing parts of this section.
5 For a good description of the GMO science, see Leiss and Tyshenko (2002). Risks associated with GMOs include impacts on human health (such as allergens) and environmental risks (crossing of GMOs with wild relatives, acceleration of insect resistance, effects on non-target species). For a good discussion of how industry and the Canadian government mismanaged the optics of GMOs, see Leiss (2001); and for an engaging discussion of the international biosafety regime, see Mulligan (2000). Note, however, that there are measures in place to outlaw the "hostile use of GMOs"; the African Union (AU) has put forth a Model Law on Safety in Biotechnology, related to the Cartagena Protocol on Biosafety, and the possibility of deliberate release of GMOs to cause harm cannot be overlooked. However, in the AU case this may apply more to fears of ecoimperialism, and subsequent demands for legal reproach, than to armed conflict situations, and there would seem to be little relevance to Canada here (see Sunshine Project, 2002).

CHAPTER ELEVEN

The Arctic

LEARNING OBJECTIVES

1. Describe the unique ecological, political, and social dynamics of the Arctic region and Canada's role as an Arctic nation.
2. Analyze the impacts of climate change on Arctic ecosystems, Indigenous communities, and geopolitical relations in the region.
3. Evaluate governance frameworks and policy challenges for sustainable development and environmental protection in the Canadian Arctic.

INTRODUCTION: THE VIEW FROM THE NORTH

The circumpolar Arctic region is experiencing a combined magnitude of interconnected changes that is virtually unprecedented in human history. Climate-related impacts to ecological systems across the northernmost part of the planet are profoundly affecting the human societies that have developed in close relationship with the challenging Arctic environment. As the Arctic's natural environment changes, so do the social, political, economic, and knowledge systems that have developed over decades and centuries by European-descended societies on the one hand and over centuries and millennia by Arctic Indigenous Peoples on the other. These changes both reflect and propel global climate change, meaning the Arctic has never been more relevant to distant events and peoples, nor so intimately connected with global processes occurring far beyond the region itself.

The Arctic region contains roughly 4 million inhabitants spread across 40 million square kilometres surrounding the Arctic Ocean, approximately 8 per cent of the earth's surface. Governance of this area and population rests with the eight Arctic states: Canada, Denmark, Finland, Iceland, Norway, Russia, Sweden, and the United States. These countries represent two distinct groups: the two most powerful states of the late twentieth century and Cold War rivals in the US and Russia (formerly the Soviet Union), alongside six countries closely aligned with the United States as capitalist liberal democracies and NATO allies. Russia is the foremost Arctic state, with approximately half the Arctic's population, land area, and coastline under its sovereignty, resulting in a de facto division of the region into two roughly equal blocs (Greaves, 2023). However, many Arctic jurisdictions experience relatively high levels of autonomy or devolved political authority from their national governments, as well as Indigenous governments and institutions of varying sorts. As a result, the Arctic consists of a surprisingly complex web of relations between states, subnational governments, regional organizations, and Indigenous governments and institutions who are all making decisions over the unique ecological context that links them together (Chater et al., 2020).

More recently, the Arctic has been understood first and foremost as an ecological region. Ecological distinctiveness is so central to the Arctic that the region's warming because of human activities destabilizes our very understanding of what the Arctic is. Most definitions of the Arctic are based on distinct natural features such as high latitude, extreme winter temperatures, specific plant and animal life, and the frozen Arctic Ocean. For instance, the Arctic Climate Impact Assessment and the Arctic Human Development Report both define the Arctic in ecological terms, such as the area above the Arctic Circle at 66°30′ N latitude, the 10 degrees Celsius July isotherm (i.e., places where the average July temperature has not historically exceeded 10 degrees Celsius), and the northern tree line. Other definitions emphasize human factors that constitute the region as a distinct area of global politics. But the Arctic is easier to define as an ecological region than a sociopolitical one. As the Arctic Human Development Report notes:

> There is nothing intuitively obvious about the idea of treating the Arctic as a distinct region … It is possible to resort to the use of biophysical criteria to determine the extent of the Arctic as a region [but because]

this approach has little to recommend it in cultural, economic, or political terms, it also fails to produce a clear cut result. [Many] writers have questioned the appropriateness of treating the Arctic as a region at all. (Steffanson Arctic Institute, 2004, pp. 17–18)

If the Arctic was already difficult to define, climate change complicates its assessment further. Atmospheric and ocean warming are changing the very basis for how we conceptualize a shared, global Arctic region and forcing governments, peoples, and communities to make hard assessments about what their interests are now and what they want the future to look like. The Arctic is one of the most ecopolitical regions of the world, where the natural environment is inseparable from the conditions of daily life, both of which are being fundamentally reshaped by human decisions and activities.

This chapter explores the interactions between environmental and human factors in the global Arctic. It outlines the state of climate change impacts in the region and examines how environmental issues have been central to political organization and regional governance. It examines different levels of governance in the Arctic, including states, subnational governments, regional organizations, international law, and Indigenous peoples, and shows how environmental issues form a thread that links all these actors into a dense web of Arctic ecopolitics. While focused on the Arctic as a global region, the chapter identifies key features of Canada's role in the region and the role Canada plays in Arctic ecopolitics. As human-caused climate change accelerates, it has profound implications for people and political organization at all scales across the region, presenting some opportunities but also many challenges for a region that has been rapidly thrust from the margins of global politics to the ecological and geopolitical centre of a fast-changing world.

CLIMATE CHANGE IMPACTS IN THE ARCTIC

The physical effects of climate change are reshaping diverse forms of human and non-human life. The polar regions are the most environmentally sensitive in the world, but Antarctica has no permanent human population, making the Arctic the oft-cited "canary in the coalmine" of global climate change because it is experiencing the fastest and most dramatic climate change impacts on the planet. Numerous studies have observed that Arctic sea ice is melting rapidly, glaciers are receding, snow cover is reduced, and temperatures are increasing at approximately three to four times the global average (Larsen, 2014; Pörtner et al., 2022). Seasonal changes on land are also dramatic, including warmer temperatures with more extreme winter–summer variation, melting permafrost, changing terrestrial water systems, increased lake temperatures, invasive species, and stress on plant and animal populations.

The Arctic is a cryosphere largely composed of frozen water, and so particularly significant climate effects are occurring in marine systems. Arctic sea ice volume decreased by an estimated 12 per cent per decade between 1979–2022, reaching an historic low in the summer of 2012. In 2023, sea ice extent was nearly 40 per cent less than in 1980, with scientists observing that sea ice is melting faster than predicted by climate change models. The result has been record low summer ice levels years before they were predicted, with the Arctic Ocean expected to be free of summer sea ice by the 2030s. The loss of seasonal ice cover will mark a dramatic and irreversible transformation to the most definitive feature of the northern polar region and promises a bleak milestone of the climate crisis in the coming years.

Other regional climate impacts vary in their effects and are limited to specific areas and communities, but they still pose serious challenges to human and non-human life. Researchers have identified direct and indirect climate-related impacts on Arctic human health, including physical hazards related to the changing landscape (including increased accidents and fatalities due to unpredictable ice and weather patterns); new communicable diseases; changes to food- and waterborne pathogens; increased exposure to environmental contaminants released from thawing soil and permafrost; and ozone depletion increasing exposure to ultraviolet radiation (Hild & Stordahl, 2004; Meakin & Kurvits, 2009; Séguin, 2008).

The quality and availability of traditional food sources, particularly large mammals, fish stocks, and plant life, have also eroded, making individuals and communities reliant on more expensive and less healthful store-bought foods as they are increasingly unable to subsist using traditional methods. This, in turn, makes people more reliant on market-based waged labour and thus more vulnerable to shifts in local and regional economies (Meakin & Kurvits, 2009). The consequences include fewer people being able to maintain healthy relationships with the land or traditional food sources, which particularly affects Arctic Indigenous Peoples who remain closely connected to the natural environment, including to animals whose hunting and consumption is central to cultural and spiritual practices (Hild & Stordahl, 2004).

The warming environment also affects critical infrastructure across the Arctic, particularly in rural, remote, and coastal communities. The combined effects of glacier melt and seawater expansion (due to global warming) have raised average global sea levels by around nine inches since 1990 and are expected to increase them by at least one foot (over 30 centimetres) above the 2000 average by 2100 (Lindsey, 2022). This will threaten communities, infrastructure, military installations, and industrial facilities located on coastlines or in low-lying areas around the world, including in the Arctic where most communities are close to water. Impacts are already apparent in damage to roads, bridges, airstrips, pipelines, homes, and sewage systems as a result of coastal erosion and thawing of the permafrost on which many Arctic communities are built. Some communities have already been relocated as environmental changes render their homes uninhabitable, while others may face similar choices in the near future. We discussed the possible tipping points associated with thawing permafrost and other climate change impacts in Chapter One.

Taken together, these changes amount to nothing less than a radical transformation of the Arctic environment. According to the Arctic Climate Impact Assessment (ACIA, 2004), "The sum of these factors threatens to overwhelm the adaptive capacity of some Arctic populations and ecosystems. The increasingly rapid rate of recent climate change poses new challenges to the resilience of Arctic life" (p. 5). Written more than 20 years ago, this assessment of how seriously climate impacts affect the Arctic was confirmed by the more recent findings of the Intergovernmental Panel on Climate Change (2014), which noted that "the rapid rate at which climate is changing in the Polar Regions will impact natural and social systems and may exceed the rate at which some of their components can successfully adapt" (p. 3). Overall, the Arctic is clearly experiencing profound ecological changes that affect all human and non-human species in the region and requires significant efforts to facilitate adaptation and mitigation of their worst impacts.

ARCTIC NATURAL RESOURCES

The warming of the Arctic has also enabled access to vast stores of resources that were previously either inaccessible or uneconomical to extract. At stake are fisheries, critical minerals, hydrocarbons, and new polar shipping lanes that offer the potential to reduce transit times between Asia and Europe. Each of these ecological and economic resources is connected to climate change.

The Arctic contains vast stores of hydrocarbons, estimated at 90 billion barrels of oil (13 per cent of undiscovered global resources) and 46 trillion cubic metres of natural gas (30 per cent of undiscovered global resources) (Gautier et al., 2009). The extraction and consumption of these reserves would be catastrophic for the global climate, but fossil fuels have been a central pillar of economic development and modernization in Arctic jurisdictions from Alaska to Norway to Russia. Along with mining, fossil fuels have provided many communities the opportunity for economic development that has proven difficult to resist, and this has been widely embraced as a means to finance greater political autonomy and economic self-reliance by subnational governments and Indigenous Peoples in Alaska, Greenland, and the three Canadian territories. Indigenous participation in new resource extraction projects is now the norm across most of the Arctic outside Russia, including a trend toward Indigenous-owned and -led initiatives. However, ownership stakes for Arctic Indigenous Peoples can complicate already-complex assessments of which projects are in the best interests of local people and which primarily benefit distant financial and government actors.

As one example, critical minerals have emerged as an area of great interest in the Arctic. Critical minerals are key components in the global energy transition away from fossil fuels and toward renewable energy, particularly for the manufacture of solar panels and battery storage. However, most global critical mineral reserves are located in China or controlled by Chinese businesses, making development of critical mineral deposits in the Arctic a high priority to reduce China's control over the global supply chain (Watson et al., 2023). Though current levels of extraction are limited, the presence of ores such as lithium, nickel, zinc, and uranium makes the Arctic a key anticipated site for increased mining over the coming decades. While this may help address the climate crisis by supporting decarbonization of the global energy system, it entails massively expanded mining and resource extraction, with associated impacts for pollution and environmental contamination across the Arctic. Mining for critical minerals thus risks becoming another form of "green colonialism" imposed on Arctic communities and Indigenous Peoples for the benefit of southern populations, perpetuating historical patterns of resource colonization and environmental racism that downloads many of the ecological costs of modern society onto low-income and racialized people.

Global warming has increased the navigability of Arctic waters and their attractiveness to a wider range of marine species. As the oceans warm, fish are migrating north in search of cooler waters that approximate more familiar temperatures, increasing the volume of fish in Arctic waters in relation to their decline further south. This results in increased competition between Arctic and non-Arctic species for aquatic nutrients and the increasing intrusion of warm water fish species into the Arctic Ocean. Fears over increased fishing activity in High Arctic waters led the eight Arctic states and others, including China, Japan, South Korea, and the European Union, to regulate fishing in the Arctic by imposing a moratorium for 16 years, beginning in 2021. The intention is to use that time to study climate change impacts in the fast-warming region to better understand the implications for marine ecosystems.

Arctic marine traffic has also increased in recent years because of the increased navigability of northern waters as a result of high temperatures and a longer ice-free season (Lasserre & Faury, 2020). In particular, the growth of Russian liquified natural gas exports to China from the Yamal region of Siberia being shipped via the Northern Sea Route has led to a large increase in marine traffic in the Eurasian Arctic. While it has been anticipated that shipping traffic will also increase in the North American Arctic via the Northwest Passage, this has yet to occur, and some analysts doubt it will ever come to pass (Exner-Pirot, 2021). Regardless, increased Arctic shipping traffic is closely related to global interest in Arctic resources and has driven the development of new practices and governance regimes related to the growing number of maritime vessels, increased risk of damage to vessels and oil rigs from sea ice and unpredictable weather, and potential harm to the Arctic ecosystems. However, concern over the possibility of a major oil spill, shipwreck, or related accident in the region has led some communities and groups to employ legal, advocacy, or direct-action tactics to prevent new resource projects from taking place nearby.

While some new resource projects have been delayed or stopped, the trend in the Arctic is toward increasing levels of resource extraction to finance not only socioeconomic development in the Arctic but also to profit national governments and corporations located far to the south. This, in turn, has led to ongoing debates over who should participate in governing the extraction of natural resources and other contemporary issues in the Arctic region.

GOVERNING THE ARCTIC ENVIRONMENT

These climate-related shifts in the Arctic are occurring alongside major political and social changes that are in turn affecting the governance of the Arctic environment. The post–Cold War period witnessed the transformation of the region from a zone of conflict to one of cooperation. New governance structures were created to manage regional relations, notably the Arctic Council, which was the first pan-regional institution to include all eight Arctic states. However, growing interest from non-Arctic actors and global economic conditions such as high resource demand have focused significant attention on the Arctic's undeveloped hydrocarbons, minerals, and other economic opportunities. Yet these dramatic regional changes are occurring against a familiar backdrop: sparse population density and few urban centres; limited infrastructure; ongoing and unresolved questions of Indigenous Peoples' rights to land and self-determination; the relative underdevelopment of regional institutions; and persistent rivalry between Russia and its Arctic neighbours. These interrelated factors raise fundamental questions about how Arctic governance will develop over the coming years as its environment continues to transform.

Historically, the Arctic has had a weak network of institutions and an underdeveloped framework for regional governance. During the twentieth century, Arctic states disagreed over a variety of issues, including the legal status of Arctic waters, the appropriate legal regime for the Arctic region, and even the validity of international law (Kikkert, 2021). The Cold War generally stifled cooperative governance in the region, even on inherently transnational issues such as environmental protection. In the absence of strong institutions, circumpolar cooperation was pursued on an ad hoc basis. International law and regulations were often byproducts of other legal or political regimes or resulted from unilateral actions of Arctic states. Only since the early 1990s have pan-regional institutions developed and new governance structures emerged to provide opportunities for political agency to state and non-state actors from across and beyond the circumpolar region.

Since then, however, the politics of the Arctic region have largely focused on issues related to the natural environment, including the management of transnational pollutants, conservation and natural resource management, and research on climate change impacts. Multiple regional institutions, agreements, and practices have been established to cooperatively manage both the Arctic's living and non-renewable resources, particularly in light of the changing climate conditions that have placed many species and ecosystems under strain. These include new international agreements on Arctic search and rescue, fisheries management, oil spill response, and the International Maritime Organization's (IMO) new Polar Code for all vessels travelling in polar waters. Many scholars agree that "the Arctic is exceptional in that the environmental sector dominates circumpolar relations" (Exner-Pirot, 2013, pp. 121–22), making it, in effect, an ecopolitical region.

Map 11.1. Political Map of the Circumpolar Arctic

Source: Map by Winfried Dallmann, Norwegian Polar Institute. Reprinted with permission.

INTERNATIONAL LAW AND INSTITUTIONS

The most important governance institution for the Arctic region is the Arctic Council, which grew out of the 1989 Arctic Environmental Protection Strategy (AEPS) tasked with facilitating environmental cooperation between the west and the Soviet Union as the Cold War was coming to an end. Consisting of four environmentally focused working groups, the AEPS reflects the central role of ecopolitics in the region: the Arctic Monitoring and Assessment Programme (AMAP), the Conservation of Arctic Flora and Fauna group (CAFF), the Protection of the Arctic Marine Environment (PAME), and the Emergency Prevention, Preparedness and Response group (EPPR). To these, the Arctic Council later added the Sustainable Development Working Group (SDWG) and the Arctic Contaminants Action Program (ACAP). No treaty formally established the council; instead, the 1996 Ottawa Declaration stipulated that it "provide a means for promoting cooperation, coordination and interaction among the Arctic States, with the involvement of the Arctic indigenous communities and other Arctic inhabitants on common Arctic issues, in particular issues of sustainable development and environmental protection in the Arctic." Although only the eight Arctic states are full members, they sit around the same decision-making table as six organizations representing Arctic Indigenous Peoples, who have a large influence on the council's decisions given that it makes decisions on principle of consensus between member-states and Indigenous permanent participants. The Arctic Council also includes more than 39 non-Arctic states, international organizations, and non-governmental organizations as non-voting observers, which, until the regional crisis that followed the Russian invasion of Ukraine in 2022, allowed it to serve as the major forum for all political actors interested in the Arctic to meet and converse. See Case Study 11.1 for how the war in Ukraine has affected this regional institution.

CASE STUDY 11.1. The Arctic and the War in Ukraine

In 2014, Russia invaded and annexed the Ukrainian region of Crimea following the US-backed popular overthrow of the pro-Russian president of Ukraine. This strained the relationships between Russia and the other Arctic states, who supported a western-leaning Ukraine and rejected Russia's illegal use of armed force against its neighbour. Western states imposed sanctions on Russian individuals and companies to which Russia retaliated, causing regional relations to decline to the lowest level since the Cold War. The five Nordic countries began unprecedented military cooperation with each other, the nearby Baltic states, and NATO, while both Russia and NATO increased their military activities in northern Europe, conducting the largest Arctic military exercises since the Cold War.

Already strained, the rules-governed Arctic system was shaken when Russia expanded its invasion to the rest of Ukraine on February 24, 2022. This led to a rare joint statement by the other seven Arctic states announcing they would no longer participate in Arctic Council activities involving Russia, which effectively suspended the council's activities until Norway assumed the council's chair in 2023. The decision was taken without consulting the Indigenous permanent participants, demonstrating that ultimately states remain the pre-eminent decision makers on issues of Arctic geopolitics and regional security. In the immediate wake of the expanded invasion, Finland and Sweden both abandoned their longstanding diplomatic neutrality and applied for full membership in NATO. Finland was admitted to NATO in 2023 and Sweden in 2024, deepening Russia's regional isolation. The invasion of Ukraine has thus cemented a new Arctic geopolitics of confrontation between the bloc of Arctic allied capitalist liberal democracies (Canada, Denmark, Finland, Iceland, Norway, Sweden, and the United States) and an authoritarian and mercantilist Russia (Greaves, 2023).

The de facto suspension of the Arctic Council and subsequent disruption to high-level regional cooperation directly affected ecopolitics in the Arctic. Scientific research, particularly on the impacts of climate change, had benefited from a peaceful regional order and consequently suffered due to sanctions, restrictions on research funding, and increased scrutiny of relationships with Russian institutions. Increased tensions between Russia and its NATO Arctic neighbours have led to more military activities in the region, which produce both high levels of greenhouse gas (GHG) emissions and other harmful forms of pollution such as black carbon soot, grey water, and plastic waste that contaminates the Arctic environment. Russia's isolation from the west has forced it to deepen its reliance on a partnership with China, including for the development of Arctic resources such as liquified natural gas, which is transported from Siberia via massive tanker vessels that travel thousands of kilometres across Russia's isolated Northern Sea Route. Other impacts of the Russian invasion of Ukraine are less direct, such as the fact that since 2022 the European Union's efforts to wean itself from Russian natural gas have led to a surge in production in Norway, an Arctic state and major EU energy partner. The conflict has spurred concerns about energy security and energy prices that have rippled out to affect other policy areas, including efforts to reduce carbon emissions, control pollution, and protect the Arctic from further natural resource and hydrocarbon exploitation. In effect, the war in Ukraine demonstrates how Arctic geopolitics and Arctic ecopolitics are intimately connected, with issues of war, peace, and security undermining efforts to achieve greater environmental protection and sustainability.

Critical Thinking Questions

1. How might worsening conflict in the Arctic affect the prospects for environmental protection?
2. As the geostrategic importance of the Arctic increases, how will the roles of the Arctic Council and other multilateral actors change?

Another regional organization is the Barents Euro-Arctic Council, formed in 1993 by Denmark, Finland, Iceland, Norway, Russia, and Sweden. It also allows an observer role for other states, including Canada and the United States, and subnational governments within member-states, which collectively form the Barents Regional Council. The Barents Euro-Arctic Council facilitates cooperation on environmental management and sustainable development in the Barents region, playing a similar subregional role as the Arctic Council does by focusing on the environment and, to a lesser extent, economic development. In summary, a dense network of regional institutions spanning across scales and countries contributes to governing the Arctic region, with a common focus on protecting Arctic ecosystems from the effects of economic development and other human impacts on the natural environment.

These regional institutions are rooted in international law, which enshrines the centrality of state sovereignty within Arctic governance. Yet there have been significant advances in international recognition of Indigenous Peoples' rights globally that also affect Indigenous Peoples in the Arctic, most notably the 1989 International Labour Organization's Indigenous and Tribal Peoples Convention (No. 169) and the 2007 United Nations Declaration on the Rights of Indigenous Peoples (UNDRIP). But international law in the Arctic region primarily remains a tool for states to manage international boundary issues, maritime cooperation, and competitive pursuit of their national interests (Greaves & Lackenbauer, 2021). The **United Nations' Convention of the Law of the Sea (UNCLOS)** underpins the global regime for the control and use of the world's oceans, which directly affects the Arctic as a primarily marine space. Although ratification of UNCLOS is voluntary, its principles are so widely accepted that even states that have not signed, like the United States, comply with it in the Arctic, where it is used to resolve maritime boundary disputes and determine state claims to exclusive economic zones, extended continental shelves, and deep sea resources (Riddell-Dixon, 2017).

Akin to the war in Ukraine, Arctic geopolitics often seem to drive ecopolitics. There are not many territorial disputes in the Arctic, and in recent years border issues have been resolved between Norway and Russia and Canada and Denmark. However, Canada still has a disputed maritime boundary with the United States in the Beaufort Sea, and there is geographic overlap between the Canadian, Danish, and Russian submissions for their extended continental shelves under UNCLOS. Arctic states have thus far relied on the UNCLOS-mandated Commission on the Limits of the Continental Shelf (CLCS) to help resolve these overlapping claims, following the law closely and even collaborating with each other to help support their claims with scientific data. However, since the announcement of large volumes of predicted Arctic resources in 2008, particularly hydrocarbons such as oil and gas, there has been significant speculation over the potential for increased conflict over Arctic resources. Although all Arctic states have emphasized their commitments to an orderly and rule-governed Arctic, given the lengthy and non-binding nature of CLCS determinations, the eventual outcome of their boundary recommendations in the Arctic is uncertain.

These maritime boundary disputes are connected to climate change and thus serve as examples of the transformative ecopolitics underway across the region. When the Arctic Ocean was frozen most of the year, states had little incentive to quarrel over such disagreements. Disputed polar boundaries had little effect on core national interests, and the Arctic states were unwilling to risk provoking a wider conflict over minor Arctic issues. Moreover, the inaccessibility of most offshore Arctic resources made them geopolitically insignificant; what did it matter what resources were where if it was neither technically feasible nor economically viable to extract them? But as the sea ice cover has declined, states have paid more attention to the delimitation of their Arctic boundaries. This coincided with the need to submit claims to their extended continental shelves to the CLCS within 10 years of ratifying UNCLOS, leading to a flurry of claims between 2006–13. At the time of writing, none of the Arctic states' claims had yet been determined by the CLCS.

What lies behind state interests in expanding their Arctic marine territory is primarily the desire for future economic benefits from natural resources. Major interstate conflict over these resources is considered unlikely given that doubt remains over the viability of developing them and because most are believed to lie in undisputed sovereign territory (Keil, 2014). But some scholars consider the link between states' maritime claims and natural resources clear, particularly with respect to oil and gas: "Issues of Arctic energy and development and Arctic sovereignty are linked … When no one was talking about actually developing Arctic resources, the many sovereignty issues could be and were ignored" (Beauchamp & Huebert, 2008, p. 342).

Though all Arctic states continue to emphasize the absence of conventional military threats in the region and reaffirm their commitments to peaceful resolution of Arctic disputes, many have also constructed Arctic resources as central to their national economic security interests. There is little evidence the warming environment will directly result in interstate violence, but the opening of the Arctic has led to a renewed emphasis on military activity, and the prospect of resource wealth has raised the stakes for states asserting and defending their Arctic sovereignty claims. Arctic resources provide a potential incentive for conflict at the same time that their development poses severe challenges for Arctic ecosystems through the risk of a major oil spill, marine disaster, industrial pollution, and contributing GHG emissions that accelerate global climate change.

THE URBAN ARCTIC

Contrary to popular depictions of the Arctic as a frozen tundra where everyone lives in very small or isolated communities, it is actually a relatively urbanized region. Though definitions of "urban" in the Arctic vary by jurisdiction (Greaves, 2020a), most people in the northern parts of Arctic states reside in communities identified as urban, ranging from 94 per cent in Iceland to 33 per cent in the Canadian territory of Nunavut (Heleniak, 2014, p. 94). Communities too small to be considered "urban" further south are often significant demographic, economic, commercial, and administrative hubs for northern regions. Many Arctic regions have pluralities, or even majorities, of their populations concentrated in a single urban area, such as the 76 per cent of Yukoners who live in Whitehorse, the 45 per cent of people in the Northwest Territories who reside in Yellowknife, the 37 per cent of Icelanders who live in Reykjavik, and the 55 per cent of Alaskans who live in its two largest cities, Anchorage and Fairbanks. Even with a population of only 8,000, Iqaluit still represents more than 20 per cent of the population of Nunavut, while Nuuk's 18,000 residents likewise represent nearly a third of all Greenlanders. These Arctic cities anchor vast northern areas and are critical hubs with concentrated public services and amenities disproportionate to their size. By contrast, people in smaller Arctic communities must often travel to larger Arctic cities or far to the south to access amenities and essential services.

Climate change presents numerous challenges to Arctic communities, large and small. Warming temperatures are undermining the physical integrity of critical infrastructure built on ice and permafrost, such as roads, highways, bridges, airstrips, pipelines, sewage systems, homes, buildings, and mining facilities, including tailings ponds containing highly polluting contaminants (ACIA, 2004; Sohns, 2017). Given the concentration of critical infrastructure and services in larger Arctic communities, in case of failures there is limited redundancy or contingency available. If compromised, critical infrastructure takes considerable time and resources to repair. This occurred when the municipal water system in Iqaluit, Nunavut, was compromised in 2021–22 by thawing permafrost that ruptured a buried diesel tank and contaminated local drinking water. The water crisis took months to resolve and required the Canadian Armed Forces to deploy a special unit to provide purified water for residents. A permanent solution involving replacement and upgrades to the municipal water system is estimated to cost tens of millions of dollars and has yet to be funded by either the territorial or federal government (Little, 2022). This example demonstrates the importance of civilian infrastructure to maintaining conditions of human wellbeing and security in the Arctic region, as well as the important role of the military as an emergency responder for isolated and vulnerable northern communities (Greaves, 2024).

Despite the disruptive effects of climate change in the Arctic, some experts have predicted that as climate change makes northern regions increasingly habitable, states should both encourage and prepare for substantial population growth in Arctic and sub-Arctic cities (Coates & Poelzer, 2014; Smith, 2011; Studin, 2017). Cities are already experiencing the vast bulk of demographic growth in the Arctic, whose population has shrunk slightly since 2000 but is expected to grow by around 4 per cent by 2030 (Heleniak, 2014, p. 100). However, regional data mask considerable variation, since healthy rates of growth in the North American and European Arctic regions are balanced by continued steep declines in northern Russia that result in modest overall population growth across the region. A key obstacle to further growth in the Arctic remains the limited economic opportunities to support larger populations, yet, paradoxically, population growth is needed to maintain and expand Arctic economic sectors that require large pools of skilled labour, such as natural resource extraction, construction, and tourism industries (see Case Study 11.2). This suggests the need for governments to support the growth of Arctic populations through immigration and settlement programs while increasing public investments in infrastructure and core services to attract private capital to Arctic communities.

CASE STUDY 11.2. Last Chance Tourism: Whales, Bears, Tourists, and Tears

Few climate change images are more iconic than that of a lone polar bear stranded on a pathetically small piece of ice in a warming Arctic Ocean. Clearly the ice is disappearing; clearly the bear is in trouble. Polar bears rely on ice floes for travelling to hunting waters, as resting spots when hunting, and as safe places to raise and teach their young. The ongoing loss of ice from climate change has given rise to a new breed of tourist – the "last chance" tourist, who seeks out opportunities to enjoy a world that is rapidly disappearing.

Last chance tourism (or LCT) "is the concept by which tourists seek out regions and ecosystems under rapid change … in order to experience them in their classical setting before they are potentially, irrevocably changed" (Palma et al., 2019, s.3.1). In the Anthropocene, the "last chance" net can be cast widely: coral reefs, old growth forests, ocean mammals, and various habitats, species, communities, and cultures. While the world has always been changing, the drive to witness those aspects that are disappearing as a result of human action has opened up a new market based on a specific set of goals and an urgency that, ironically, speeds the losses that drive it.

The irony of LCT is well illustrated in the Arctic, where the climate-driven loss of summer ice opens up new opportunities for small and large boats to travel and explore. Yet as warming facilitates marine tourism, the tourism contributes to degrading the environment visitors come to see. Vehicles generate additional emissions and disturb ice and delicate habitats. Vehicles also generate smog, which dirties the ice and makes it darker; this lowers its albedo, which means it absorbs more heat and so melts more quickly. These emissions can arise from the transport of tourists but also through the delivery of the food they eat and the construction materials and machines needed to create the infrastructure they need, waste incineration, and heating and other energy use (Kerber, 2021).

Many people don't even associate their own tourism activities (even flying) with the changes they contribute to in delicate environments like the Arctic

(D'Souza et al., 2021). Yet sometimes the irony of LCT is thick: On Svalbard, a popular archipelago off Norway, a polar bear was shot when it attacked and injured a boat tour's mandatory "polar bear guard" in 2018; it was not hard to see that the bear was, in effect, "killed for acting like a wild animal" in its own wild home – the very wildness that humans have travelled to see (Associated Press, 2018).

Arctic tourism is not a new phenomenon, but the scale has grown, especially with the opening of the fabled Northwest Passage. In late summer 2016, the *Crystal Serenity*, with 13 decks, 600 crew, and 1,000 passengers on a vessel the length of three football fields, became the first large liner to transit the passage (Kassam, 2016). At times icebreakers and helicopters had to accompany the ship. Passengers on a ship like this can generate 8 litres of sewage per day, while the ships themselves often release thousands of litres of bilge water that can introduce pollutants (Connolly, 2019).

Communities can benefit from tourism revenue, but they are also experiencing the impacts of road and infrastructure changes that lead to food supply disruptions (like caribou declines), while warming degrades permafrost – damaging buildings, roads, and other infrastructure – and threatens transport routes like ice roads. Meanwhile, added shore services mean more shipping, which runs the risk of adding to the pollution and even introducing invasive species (Goldsmith et al., 2019). The added sea traffic can have unfortunate impacts on local fauna from engine noise and even direct collisions with animals (Halliday et al., 2018).

Governance reflects the institutional complexity within Arctic nation-states. In both Canada and Russia, for instance, over 30 different state agencies or authorities are involved in the regulation of cruise tourism (Pashkevich et al., 2015). Coordination among such a large number of entities might look to an intergovernmental body, and a key locus on this issue is the Arctic Council. One of the outcomes of Arctic Council activities was the establishment of the Sustainable Arctic Tourism Association (SATA), which was intended to build support for sustainable industry standards. SATA was unable to maintain momentum, however, and appears to have dissolved without notable impact. The impetus for any further action around Arctic tourism is currently in limbo even in the Arctic Council; as of March 4, 2022 (roughly coinciding with the beginning of Russia's "special military operation" in Ukraine), the council "is pausing all official meetings ... until further notice" (see Case Study 11.1 above for further discussion).

The complexities of Arctic governance mean the Arctic cruise industry can be characterized by "collective self-governance" in which industry actors, and especially associations, play a critical role in determining the culture and impact of "sustainable tourism" (Van Bets et al., 2017). The Association of Arctic Expedition Cruise Operators (AECO) is particularly important in the current context: It commits cruise operators to follow all laws and regulations as well as private policies on visitor, site-specific, operational, wildlife, and biosecurity guidelines. Yet success is a factor of industry uptake, and to date only a small fraction of Arctic cruise ship operators have joined. Thus "self-governance" is not always collective nor well integrated with local needs and concerns. "Overall, the complex and overlapping governance structures that regulate cruise tourism mean that local communities often feel disempowered and have little control over the development of Arctic cruise tourism" (Ren et al., 2021, p. 4).

Voluntary and market-driven measures have led to some improved practices, such as the growing popularity of participation in beach cleanups in hotspots like Svalbard. Here tourism in the wild runs headlong into the impacts of global streams of pollution, especially plastics. The cleanups often engage tour companies, locals, researchers, and tourists in a common endeavour and have become "an integral part of international cruise tourism practices," especially in Europe. These initiatives are tied to a broader global movement toward "citizen science" that can educate tourists while furthering the growth of knowledge (Bergmann et al., 2017).

Some argue these kinds of Arctic adventures are driven more by what tourists can handle of the Arctic wilderness than the wilderness itself. Kerber (2021) notes that the cruise industry relies on marketing an "Arctic" experience that reflects long-held myths and stories of the Arctic, but few visitors aspire to sharing the hardships of the Franklin Expedition or the lone Inuit hunter whose image is used to sell that experience. The tourist's journey also does little to reflect, or to reflect on, the massive lifestyle changes that northern peoples are experiencing from social and economic change – including the arrival of tourism – in the context of a warming climate.

Critical Thinking Questions

1. Do you think an increase in Arctic tourism will be a net benefit or net loss for environmental protection?
2. What are the novel risks of Arctic tourism, and will these risks ultimately lead to greater levels of awareness among tourists about the need to protect the Arctic from environmental harms?

INDIGENOUS GOVERNANCE

One of the defining features of the Arctic is the social role and formal institutionalization of the region's Indigenous Peoples within regional governance. Arctic Indigenous Peoples are diverse, and their historical experiences and current political situations differ greatly by national context (Greaves, 2020b). Indigenous Peoples number approximately 500,000 out of the total 4 million inhabitants across the circumpolar region, and they form an overlapping ring of transnational populations surrounding the Arctic Ocean. A majority live in Russia, which also has the greatest number of distinct peoples with over 41 different groups, including the more populous Chukchi, Evenki, Khaka, Khanty, Nenet, Tuvan, and Yakut peoples. Aleuts in the easternmost Russian region of Kamchatka also inhabit the islands off western Alaska. Alaska is also home to Athabaskan, Gwich'in, and Inuit (Alaskan Eskimo) peoples whose territories cross into northern Canada. Inuit form around half the total population of the Canadian Arctic and nearly 90 per cent in neighbouring Greenland. Sámi are the only recognized Indigenous Peoples in Europe, residing in Norway, Sweden, and Finland, with a small number on the Kola Peninsula in northwest Russia.

While they have become rooted in the social and political structures of their home countries, the sociological boundaries between Arctic Indigenous Peoples are not consistent with the colonial borders they live within. Indigenous Peoples serve as living reminders of pre-modern, pre-state patterns of habitation in the circumpolar region and reflect relationships and associations that transcend sovereign borders. This includes the distinct natural environments and non-human species that Indigenous Peoples co-exist with, maintain, and steward to this day (Arctic Council, 2023).

Since the 1960s, Indigenous Peoples had established representative organizations to lobby governments to speak on their people's behalf, which became a potent force for representation and decentralization across much of the circumpolar region. Some Arctic Indigenous Peoples have achieved different forms of autonomous self-government or devolved subnational governments, as is the case for Inuit in Greenland/Kalaallit Nunaat and Inuit and First Nations in the Canadian provinces and territories of Newfoundland and Labrador, Quebec, Nunavut, Northwest Territories, and Yukon (see Box 11.1). Others are represented by non-state or quasi-official bodies such as the Alaska Native Regional Corporation or the three Sámi parliaments in Finland, Sweden, and Norway. Indigenous Peoples and advocates were also central to the establishment of the Arctic Council and its institutional development ever since.

BOX 11.1. Inuit in Canada

Though not the only Indigenous People in the Canadian Arctic, Inuit are the most numerous and politically empowered and are central to the region's social fabric and political institutions. Approximately 65,000 Inuit live in 53 communities, forming around half the permanent population of northern Canada. Four self-governing Inuit regions – Nunavut, the Inuvialuit Settlement Region (Northwest Territories), Nunavik (Quebec), and Nunatsiavut (Newfoundland and Labrador) – comprise over 20 per cent of Canada's total area and are collectively known as *Inuit Nunangat*, which itself forms only part of the wider Inuit homeland of *Inuit Nunaat*, which includes territories in Alaska, Greenland, and Russia.

Inuit were one of the last Indigenous Peoples in the Americas to experience extensive contact with European settlers and their descendants. Today, as one of three constitutionally enshrined groups of Aboriginal people in Canada, Inuit are also sophisticated political actors represented through a national organization, Inuit Tapiriit Kanatami (ITK); the Inuit Circumpolar Council (ICC), a permanent participant on the Arctic Council; land claim corporations; and a range of local and regional organizations and governments, including the Government of Nunavut, where Inuit make up approximately 85 per cent of the population. The Constitution of Canada and modern treaties, called land claim agreements, grant Inuit legal title to large tracts of land, making Inuit the largest non-Crown landholders in Canada; they also have rights over how their traditional lands and waters are used. Recent decisions by the Supreme Court of Canada have further clarified the rights of Inuit to be consulted over land use decisions, making Inuit key stakeholders in the decisions over how Arctic lands and waters will be used, including with respect to new resource extraction projects.

When the Arctic states began to negotiate the creation of a permanent regional forum at the end of the Cold War, Canadian Inuit leader Mary Simon – later the first Indigenous person to serve as governor general of Canada – ensured Indigenous Peoples were included in the new council's design (English, 2013). Six non-governmental organizations represent Indigenous Peoples on the Council as permanent participants, alongside the eight states that govern them: the Arctic Athabaskan Council, Aleut International Association, Gwich'in Council International, Inuit Circumpolar Council, Russian Association of Indigenous Peoples of the North, and the Saami Council. They "sit at the same table with the Arctic states and may table proposals for decision. Even though final decisions [of the Arctic Council] are made by the Arctic states in consensus, the permanent participants must … be fully consulted, which is close to a *de facto* power of veto should they all reject a particular proposal" (Koivurova & Heinämäki, 2006, p. 104). As the first international intergovernmental body in the world to grant Indigenous Peoples status with rights to participation approximating that of the member-states, the Arctic Council marks the highest level of inclusion that Indigenous Peoples have achieved in any intergovernmental organization (Tennberg, 2010). To a significant extent, the Arctic region is defined by the political inclusion of Indigenous Peoples.

Although Arctic Indigenous Peoples are diverse in various ways, they are linked through similar comparable traditional knowledge systems and similar understandings of their relationships to their homelands. Indigenous Peoples continue to advocate for the protection of natural systems from human-caused degradation, including the protection of keystone species with important ecological and cultural functions, such as seal, whales, and reindeer/caribou. At the same time, Indigenous governments and organizations have become increasingly relevant actors for major investment decisions in the region, including natural resource extraction, implicating Indigenous Peoples in contemporary decision-making processes that struggle to reconcile Indigenous and non-Indigenous values. Faced with the prospect of continued poverty and material hardship, many communities feel they have no choice but to support new extractive projects. The trade-offs and dilemmas of having achieved a high-level of land ownership and land use rights through their successful efforts at self-determination will follow Indigenous Peoples as the Arctic region continues its transformation over the coming years.

CONCLUSION: THE ARCTIC AS AN ECOPOLITICAL FULCRUM

The Arctic is one of the key global ecopolitical regions for the twenty-first century. It is located at the geographic intersection of North America, Europe, and Asia; structured by international law and institutions that have helped govern the region effectively for decades but that have come under increasing strain from growing geopolitical tensions; and experiencing a fundamental ecological transformation because of human activities that affect all aspects of human and non-human life in the region as well as having implications for the stability of the global climate. It is clear, amid this uncertainty, that Arctic ecopolitics are uniquely positioned to have global impacts over the coming years. Long considered the "canary in the coalmine" of global climate change, the Arctic is experiencing warming three to four times higher than the global average, which is producing or exacerbating intersecting challenges and opportunities related to renewable and non-renewable resource extraction, the growth of sustainable economies, geopolitical competition among powerful states, and the lived realities for rural, remote, and Indigenous northern communities across the eight Arctic states. Where and how people across the Arctic live will continue to change because of the combination of these factors, with an emerging climate future shaping the existing realities of relatively disparate, isolated, and strained polar communities responding to forces beyond their control, which nonetheless profoundly alter their ways.

As one of the foremost Arctic countries, Canada is deeply connected to and impacted by developments across the circumpolar region. Canada has the second-largest Arctic area after Russia, and its Arctic population and economy are considerably larger than those of the Nordic states of the European Arctic. Canadian leadership and priorities have become deeply embedded in the fabric of Arctic governance, notably the establishment of the Arctic Council as a cooperative forum for pan-regional cooperation and the formal inclusion of Indigenous Peoples into transnational Arctic institutions. Given the centrality of Indigenous Peoples, notably Inuit, to the political and social fabric of northern Canada, ecopolitics in the Canadian Arctic requires reconciling local, territorial, and national interests and priorities with the inherent, constitutional, and Treaty rights of northern Indigenous Peoples. The modern history of the Arctic has been shaped through the contested interactions of national, subnational, and Indigenous political actors; as the region transforms because of climate change and other external forces, these struggles will continue to define ecopolitics in this region.

CHAPTER TWELVE

Assessing Canadian Ecopolitics

LEARNING OBJECTIVES

1. Synthesize the key themes, challenges, and future prospects for Canadian environmental politics and policy across multiple issue-areas.
2. Critically assess Canada's progress and shortcomings in addressing major environmental challenges like climate change, biodiversity loss, and pollution.
3. Analyze emerging governance approaches and ethical frameworks for advancing environmental sustainability and justice in Canada, including Indigenous rights and nature rights.

INTRODUCTION: THE PANORAMA OF CANADIAN ECOPOLITICS

After exploring the panorama of Canadian ecopolitics, we hope that you have come away with a new appreciation for the complexity of this multilayered subject and for its importance in shaping our everyday lives. It is clear that Canadian ecopolitics is best understood through the exploration of specific real-world examples that demonstrate how the various histories and forces interact to create a system with recognizable properties and features. As well, we hope that readers will begin to use a critical analysis and an ecopolitical lens to understand problems and to consider how to solve these equitably and sustainably, recognizing that our current circumstances speak to the need for some radical social, economic, and political transformations.

The most recent Intergovernmental Panel on Climate Change (IPCC) report notes that widespread and urgent changes are needed in industrial societies to keep warming below the 1.5-degree threshold and prevent the worst runaway effects of climate change. Despite technological advances and some policy incentives, it is clear the world is not moving forcefully enough in the right direction. However, as discussed in Chapter One, climate change is just one of a host of environmental problems that are reaching threshold levels for catastrophic tipping points (O'Neill et al., 2018). How might Canadian society grow in the face of increasingly destructive natural disasters and the collapse of ecosystems? How might Canadians protect access to health care, education and welfare programs even as the costs of adaptation to climate change mount? These questions confront the entirety of the Canadian system in its economic, political, social, and environmental dimensions, and so respective issue-areas inevitably infringe upon and interact with each other. These challenges call for an approach that reaches beyond environmental politics and policy to incorporate broader essential questions of Canadian governance for human wellbeing (Biermann, 2014, p. 25). In these concluding reflections, we will review the key issues of concern as touched on in the book and evaluate the prospects for Canadian ecopolitics in the future given the situation we face in the present day. Accordingly, this concluding chapter will revisit the themes discussed throughout this book, adding a brief discussion of the prospects for progress on each one and the implications for the future of Canadian ecopolitics. Following the pattern established in Chapter One, the discussion engages with each of the six recurrent themes of the book: Indigenous Peoples, climate change, biodiversity loss, pollution and product life cycles, security, and environmental ethics.

INDIGENOUS PEOPLES

We have endeavoured to ensure that this book reflects on Indigenous history and the longstanding connection Indigenous Peoples have to the lands and waters of Turtle Island. It highlights the encroachment upon Indigenous territories by colonialism and the ongoing struggle against systemic neglect, abuse, and assimilation efforts. Indigenous knowledge and contributions to biodiversity protection and ecological health are only recently being recognized and supported through government policies at both the provincial and federal levels. The province of British Columbia adopted legislation to align provincial laws with the UN Declaration on the Rights of Indigenous Peoples (UNDRIP), the first such jurisdiction to do so. Notably, this effort has borne fruit in the province's mining and environmental assessment processes, where the passage of the BC *UNDRIP Act* has strengthened legal respect for "ongoing government-to-government processes for joint decision making for all or part of Indigenous traditional territories" based on Indigenous-led processes of development approval or consent. Recently, the Ajax mine proposed on the Stk'emlupsemc te Secwépemc Nation (SSN) lands was rejected through a community-led assessment process that drew on traditional laws and cultural responsibilities, and the decision was subsequently supported by both the provincial and federal government environmental assessments (Allard & Curran, 2023, p. 10). These trends represent not just new processes for environmental assessment, but ongoing collaborative governance structures on a nation-to-nation basis.

However, many First Nations in Canada continue to oppose development projects and have been harassed and arrested by police and semi-police forces in the process. Heightened awareness of the historical and current impact of residential school abuses, as well as federal efforts to alleviate water-quality issues on reserves and court rulings recognizing the inequitable funding of Indigenous education on reserves have moved the dialogue forward in many ways. To that end, the passage of the federal *UNDRIP Act* on June 21, 2021, designed to help align Canadian law with the human rights considerations of the international declaration, is an important milestone. Symbolically, the appointment of Canada's first Indigenous governor general in 2021 was also an important moment. There is still much work to be done to align Canadian governance with Indigenous Peoples rights, to enable people to meet the needs of their communities, and to embrace cultural and traditional knowledge where appropriate. The 94 Calls to Action of the Truth and Reconciliation Commission were first published in 2015 (Truth and Reconciliation Commission, 2015) and are still far from being realized. Conflicts continue over land rights and resource development, pollution (see below), and continuing inequity in resource distribution and welfare and education spending.

CLIMATE CHANGE

Climate change, exemplified by the rapidly warming Arctic and oceans, severe floods, heatwaves, and forest fires, has shifted from a future threat to occupy a position of importance in the present. While environmental concerns have been ongoing, the scope of current challenges underscores the Anthropocene's gravity. All of these issues have been discussed through distinct lenses by various international bodies like the Intergovernmental Science-Policy Platform on Biodiversity and Ecosystem Services (IPBES), the IPCC, and the Group on Earth Observations (GEO). Despite improvements in some aspects the overall situation is deteriorating, as scientists warn about potential tipping points in earth's systems that could have catastrophic effects.

There are specific barriers to action that are institutional in nature and that call for change in the way environmental problems are addressed in the context of a settler-colonial administrative state structure. Federalism has its strengths, but for Canadian ecopolitics it has often been a source of lag. Despite the favourable ruling of Canada's Supreme Court in the 2021 carbon-pricing reference case, subsequent rulings have been less promising for a national carbon reduction plan (*References re Greenhouse Gas Pollution Pricing Act*, 2021). Recently, two federal court decisions, one on single-use plastics and one on the federal government's environmental impact assessment process, have underscored these difficulties (*Responsible Plastic Use Coalition v. Canada*, 2023; Dishakes, 2023; *Reference re Impact Assessment Act*, 2023). At the same time, the courts have recently granted permission for seven young people to sue the Government of Ontario for failing to protect their futures from the effects of climate change, and momentum is brewing to create a national Youth Climate Corps that would enable young people to work and study in environmental fields (EcoJustice, n.d.; Sarfraz, 2023). While there was consensus among the provinces and federal government at the start of the Liberal's tenure to tackle the climate issue, that has eroded as successive provincial governments have cooled to the federal role and moved support away from the use of federal policy instruments for emissions reductions. Pierre Poilievre, the leader of the federal Conservative Party, has made criticisms of the federal carbon tax a centrepiece of his campaign heading into a federal election in 2025. This opposition has gained some currency among the Canadian public, confronted with rising prices on everything from groceries to rent to home heating costs (see Case Study 12.1).

CASE STUDY 12.1. The Carbon Pricing Saga

As discussed in Chapter Nine, upon the election of the Liberal government under Justin Trudeau in 2015 the government pledged to introduce a "tax on pollution" as the centrepiece response to Canada's pledge to reduce greenhouse gas (GHG) emissions as part of its adoption of the Paris Agreement. The Pan-Canadian Framework included a series of measures that went beyond carbon prices to include policies to support industry reductions, climate adaptation, and green jobs. However, it was the focus on a national carbon price that became a lightning rod for controversy in the years that followed.

Carbon pricing can take different forms, whether it is through a direct levy or a cap-and-trade system in which provinces enforce a cap on emissions and encourage emitters to trade permits among themselves for a price. Both systems rely on market forces to reduce overall emissions, rather than direct governmental regulation. Under the *Greenhouse Gas Pollution Pricing Act*, which came into force in June 2018, provinces would be tasked with signing on to the federal government's carbon pricing benchmark system (used as a kind of "backstop") or developing their own plan that meets federal standards. Several provinces, including British Columbia and Quebec, had carbon prices in place that already met the standards, so those programs remained unchanged. Provinces that did not have carbon prices, or that had substandard plans, were required to agree to the federal plan. As well, under Canada's plan, the price per tonne would increase progressively each year, reaching $170/tonne of CO_2 by 2030 (Environment and Climate Change Canada, 2021d). Following court challenges by some provinces, the Supreme Court of Canada upheld the constitutionality of the Act in March 2021. By 2017 all provinces had some type of carbon levy in place (Office of the Commissioner of the Environment and Sustainable Development, 2021).

Canada's national carbon price plan allows for flexibility among the provinces in terms of what kind of plan they want to use and includes a carbon rebate plan that returns collected money to larger or rural households. Carbon prices are proven to reduce overall GHG emissions through built-in economic incentives to adjust to reduction targets either through technological innovation or changes in behaviour. As noted by the Government of Canada's Commissioner on the Environment and Sustainable Development, the use of carbon prices has become widespread among Organisation for Economic Cooperation and Development (OECD) countries (Office of the Commissioner of the Environment and Sustainable Development, 2021). As well, carbon prices are in alignment with important ethical principles, such as the polluter pays principle, and most experts have recommended a near-universal blanket approach to both meet efficiency goals and to ensure equity, transparency, and uniformity in the distribution of adjustment costs (see Snoddon & Van-Nijnatten, 2016).

Opposition to Canada's *Greenhouse Gas Pollution Pricing Act* emerged most strongly in Alberta, Saskatchewan, and Ontario. Saskatchewan never had its own carbon pricing mechanism, whereas conservative governments in Ontario and Alberta, elected in 2018 and 2019, respectively, abandoned the climate policies introduced by their predecessors, subjecting their provinces instead to the federal government's backstop carbon price. Although the federal government believed it had struck a balance between provincial and federal areas, these three provincial governments thought differently. Alberta's challenge rested on the federal division of powers under the *Constitution Act, 1867* and argued that the Act infringed on provincial jurisdiction over natural resources. Ontario and Saskatchewan also challenged the constitutionality of the Act, questioning the applicability of the "Peace, Order, and Good Government" (POGG) clause of Canada's Constitution. On March 25, 2021, the Supreme Court of Canada ruled that the federal government's carbon pricing law was constitutional, emphasizing that climate change is a matter of "national concern" that transcends provincial boundaries and therefore justifies federal intervention under the POGG clause (*References re Greenhouse Gas Pollution Pricing Act*, 2021).

As noted in this chapter, the consensus around the carbon tax has essentially disintegrated since 2015, at least at the government level. Ironically, a recent poll by Abacus Data (July 2024) suggests that eliminating the carbon tax is a "green line" (i.e., a vote winner) for Canadian voters: 37 per cent say they definitely would vote for a party that promised to "axe the tax." As stated by Abacus: "This data confirms that eliminating the carbon tax has become a vote winner for the Conservatives and a real liability for the Liberals" (Coletto, 2024). The situation has become so grave that a recent coalition of economists put forward a joint statement in support of carbon pricing: "As economists from across Canada, we are concerned about the significant threats from climate change. We encourage governments to use economically sensible policies to reduce emissions at a low cost, address Canadians' affordability concerns, maintain business competitiveness, and support Canada's transition to a low-carbon economy. Canada's carbon-pricing policies do all those things" (Ragan, 2024).

The case of Canada's carbon pricing policies demonstrates how Canadian ecopolitics can become highly contested, especially when an issue is linked with broader economic concerns such as rising costs of housing, inflation, and livelihoods. The point is perhaps not to "double down" on messages that oversimplify or distort the choices being faced in this moment, but to try to reach Canadians "where they are." This case starkly illustrates that, as we have proposed in this book, ecology and politics are sometimes strange but inextricable bedfellows.

Critical Thinking Questions

1. Why do you think Canadians have rejected the government's plan on carbon pricing? If you were in the government, how would you respond to criticisms of carbon pricing?
2. On what criteria should policies to reduce emissions be based: economic, ethical, or degree of popularity?

Economically, the situation is in many ways more encouraging. The Canadian economy remains relatively strong, with inflation and income measures fairly robust. Of course, there is a correspondence between economic swings and environmental impact. In particular, the global slowdown of activity in 2020 related to the COVID-19 pandemic actually improved air quality, lowered emissions, and made it easier for wildlife to thrive as human impacts decreased, even for a short time. As these impacts have roared back following the pandemic, the consequences on the environment have been increasing several fold. A recent report by the Commissioner on Sustainable Development on the federal government's *Net-Zero Emissions Accountability Act* finds that the government is not on track to reach its 2030 targets (Office of the Auditor General of Canada, 2023). Canadian emissions overall remain flat, however environmental science tells us that they need to fall – and urgently – to avoid the most catastrophic consequences of climate change.

The economic context for replacing fossil fuels with renewables is highly favourable. Indeed, one of the most influential factors in encouraging a switch from fossil fuels to renewable energy is the cost savings that consumers will accrue. As well, a series of federal government programs are rolling out in transportation, buildings, and industrial development that bode well for the

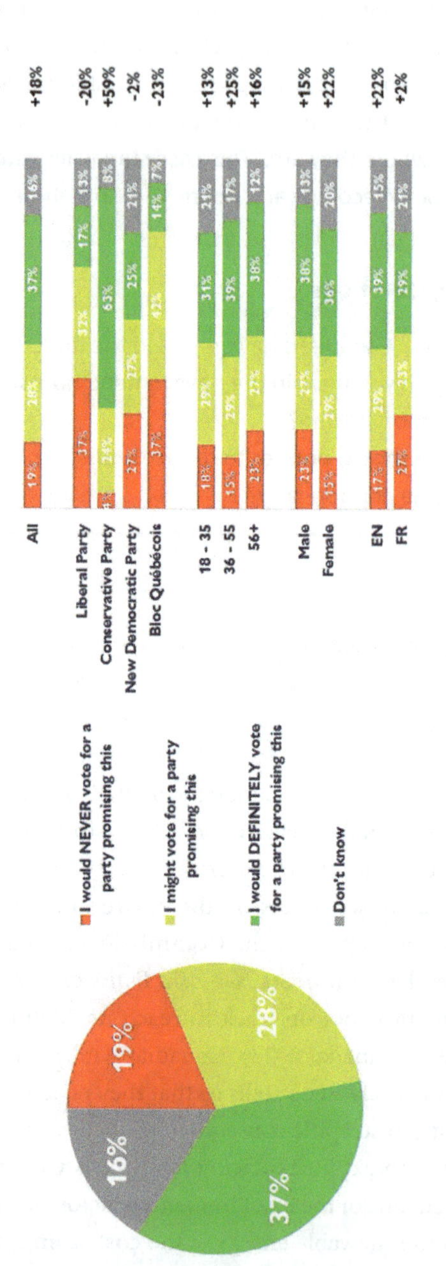

Source: Coletto, D. (2024). What policy ideas attract and repel Canadian voters? A look at the "third rails" of Canadian politics. *Abacus Data*. https://abacusdata.ca/policies-canadian-politics-attract-repell/. Reproduced with permission.

future of renewable energy. These measures include clean fuel and electricity standards, zero-emission vehicle sales mandates, an emission cap on the oil and gas sector, and a growing range of subsidies and expenditures (Winfield, 2023). For example, electrification remains a potent strategy for reducing emissions from energy use and transportation. Between 2016 and 2020, electricity from clean energy sources increased by 2 per cent to reach 83 per cent of the total electricity produced in Canada, including 68 per cent from renewables and 15 per cent from nuclear (Environment and Climate Change Canada, 2023b, p. 78). Nuclear energy, small modular reactors, and carbon capture removal storage and use (often shortened to CCRU) remain prominent features of the government's plan to enable an energy sector transition.

BIODIVERSITY LOSS

We noted the significant role of land and sea use changes, exploitation of organisms, climate change, pollution, and invasive alien species in biodiversity loss (IPBES, 2019). Throughout the book we have reflected on Canadian policies and regulatory efforts that are aimed at curbing the loss of biodiversity and ultimately restoring nature. Much of the public discussion and accompanying actions by governments are oriented toward the anthropocentric consideration of "ecosystem services" that nature provides for the benefit of humans (termed "nature's benefits for people" by IPBES). For example, in its discussion of the biodiversity outcomes framework, biodivcanada's website focuses on the role of biodiversity in creating "an insurance policy for life" that contributes to clean air and water, livelihoods, disaster resilience, climate regulation, and food security (Environment and Climate Change Canada, 2022a). The Government of Canada is developing a strategy to achieve the goals of the 2022 Montreal-Kunming Protocol for the Convention on Biodiversity at the time of writing. For example, Target 3 of the protocol calls for the conservation and management of 30 per cent of lands and waters by 2030 (Environment and Climate Change Canada, 2023a). The strategy, which will build upon a previous NBSAP (National Biodiversity Strategy and Action Plan), was presented in spring 2024, and Environment and Climate Change minister Steven Guilbeault introduced the final draft of the strategy and Bill C-73, the *Nature Accountability Act*, in June 2024; it has already been criticized as weak, not up to the task of achieving the Convention on Biodiversity (CBD) targets, and lacking in accountability to the Commissioner of the

Environment and Sustainable Development, who is tasked with independently evaluating the implementation of federal strategies. Whether or not this target can be met, there is little doubt that efforts to protect species and habitats will likely be hampered by compounding problems posed by climate change, economic adversity, and continuing economic growth and extraction, particularly in sensitive areas. The presentation of the imperative to achieve conservation will be very important moving forward: Despite their interlinkages, biodiversity loss is often overshadowed by climate change. While there is often public support for the conservation of select iconic species, the more difficult, encompassing task of preserving entire ecosystems receives less attention.

POLLUTION AND PRODUCT LIFE CYCLES

Pollution is addressed as a critical issue contributing to biodiversity loss and climate change. The product life cycle from raw resource extraction to waste disposal is examined at length in Chapters One and Six, where we emphasized the environmental costs of agricultural and industrial production processes, waste management challenges, and the urgency of responsible consumption. The outlines of a circular economy, which focuses on waste-free production, consumption, and extraction, have already been in place for decades but continue to occupy the margins of Canadian ecopolitical decision making. For example, from the Mount Polley mine disaster to the concerns over oil sands tailings ponds, mining as an activity inevitably produces large amounts of waste, yet there is a flurry of interest in reviving mining activities in northern Ontario and Quebec to unearth deposits of critical minerals for new renewable technologies. There is a real danger that the rush to decarbonize the global economy will lead to further problems associated with waste, colonialism, and human exploitation not just in Canada but elsewhere (see Stoett & Omrow, 2022).

Going beyond economic considerations, the calls for circular or "doughnut" economics are also, at their heart, issues of justice. Externalization and marginalization of people occurs alongside decisions about where and how to locate waste and how to distribute environmental risks. The prominent (and controversial) social ecologist Murray Bookchin (2005) argued that "all ecological problems are social problems" and that the stratification of society along the lines of ethnicity, race, gender, and class is always implicated in environmental decision making. Robert Bullard, considered by many to be the founder of the concept of environmental racism, defines **environmental justice** as "the fair treatment and meaningful involvement of all people regardless of race, color, national origin, or income with respect to the development, implementation, and enforcement of environmental laws, regulations, and policies" (Bullard & Johnson, 2000, p. 558).

While instances of environmental racism have led to legislative efforts to control chemical pollution and dump sites in the United States through the Environmental Protection Agency and other institutions, efforts in Canada have lagged behind. In Nova Scotia, descendants from Black Loyalist refugees from the American Revolutionary War, who were given land to settle in 1775 and 1812, found out only in the twenty-first century that they lacked title and found themselves displaced and their land degraded by local governments. In the 1960s, the thriving Black community of Africville outside Halifax, Nova Scotia, was declared an urban eyesore – after having been zoned as a location for a garbage dump, an infectious disease hospital, and an abattoir, by successive municipal plans. In 2015 Nova Scotia introduced an *Act to Prevent Environmental Racism*, noting the disproportionate number of Black Nova Scotian and Mi'kmaq communities living in close proximity to landfills, incinerators, and sewage treatment plants. The pattern is not uncommon and must be part of the discussion as we search for a less polluted living environment (See Case Study 10.1).

SECURITY

In this book, we explore the concept of security through different lenses: national security, human security, and environmental security. We have hopefully contributed to an ongoing dialogue concerning the origin, nature, scope, and prospects for various security issues. It is our goal to broaden the discussion beyond military defence to encompass ecological perspectives that include the political, economic, and social dimensions of security issues. There is little doubt today that this current **"polycrisis"** is confronting Canadian society with myriad severe threats to health, wellbeing, prosperity, and stability. City governments are on the frontlines of flooding, fires, severe storms, and drought, which are reshaping the way in which resources are distributed locally and globally. The traditional means of addressing security through national defence apparatuses seems increasingly inadequate in the face of these more complex threats and uncertainties. Recently, as with the COVID-19 crisis only a few short years ago, the fires of summer 2023 have provoked a national discussion about the role of militaries in responding to national emergencies, with calls for the formation of a national firefighting force capable of responding with the appropriate speed, personnel, and equipment to the challenge of large forest fires that threaten populated areas. However, the larger policy questions that environmental change provokes lie in the changed nature of security threats and the lack of fit with existing institutions of state sovereignty and the extractive settler-colonial model of development. Environmental security is not only a consideration of a wider range and scope of threats, but of different kinds of threats: ones that are longer term, global, intersectional, and potentially existential in nature.

Recently, the Canadian government published a comprehensive assessment of the implications of climate change for national security. In its *Defence Climate and Sustainability Strategy 2023–2027*, the Department of National Defence recognizes that climate change poses "significant environmental and security challenges, impacting all aspects of society." The strategy also recognizes that the effects of climate change extend beyond environmental concerns, influencing social, economic, and geopolitical tensions globally and contributing to resource scarcity, increased competition, and population displacement. Figure 12.2 summarizes these effects as described in the strategy (Department of National Defence, 2023).

ENVIRONMENTAL ETHICS

The above discussion of environmental justice brings to mind the questions raised in Chapter Two regarding the effects of environmental worldviews and social imaginaries. As the environmental movement has matured and become mainstream, the underlying message that motivates transformative change has shifted. The role of government in achieving social justice ends is both more accepted and more compromised. It seems clear after reading this book that the social imaginaries that accompany the Anthropocene represent transformational challenges to the prevailing dominant frames occupied by the sovereign state, established extractive capitalist development models, and the particularly Canadian process of regional and national nation building based on natural resources.

A shift in the representation of the relationships between human and non-human worlds constitutes an important potential axis of transformative change. The challenge of ecocentric and deep ecological worldviews to

Figure 12.2. National Security Implications of Climate Change

CLIMATE CHANGE EFFECTS

 Extreme Weather Events

 Fires

 Flooding

 Desertification

 Food & Water Insecurity

 Vector-Borne Disease

IMPACTS

 Population Movements

 Governance Disruptions

 Geopolitical Flashpoints

 Violent Extremists

 Hostile Activities by State Actors

 Economic Dissociation

RESPONSES

 Disaster Assistance

 Emergency Management

 Security & Intelligence

 International Military & Peace Support Missions

VULNERABLE GROUPS

 Habitants of small islands, low-lying regions, or other areas that may become uninhabitable due to extreme weather or rising sea levels

 Equity-seeking groups including women and children as well as Indigenous communities

 Developing and fragile nations especially in Africa and the Middle East

 Outdoor Occupations

Source: Department of National Defence. (2023). *Defence climate and sustainability strategy, 2023–2027*. www.canada.ca/en/department-national-defence/corporate/reports -publications/defence-climate-and-sustainability-strategy-2023–2027.html. Permission granted by the Privy Council Office. © His Majesty the King in Right of Canada, 2024.

prevailing anthropocentric values and systems is substantial (Adkin, 2009, p. 10). This book has tracked the origins and trajectory of this cultural shift as it has evolved in Canada, from a view of nature as an instrumental resource to a potential view of nature as a subject of law with inherent rights of its own (Lamalle & Stoett, 2023), reflecting its intrinsic value apart from the needs and interests of humans. This legal development has been spreading through Latin America and Asia and Europe, but there is stiff opposition to it from the extractive industry lobbies, which are quite well entrenched in policy circles. As discussed in our early chapters, the contemporary national narrative of the Canadian state was based largely on unbridled resource extraction.

The ethics of Canadian ecopolitics includes consideration of exciting but complex and evolving questions (see Case Study 12.2). For example, how might "business as usual" be transformed to improve the ecological sustainability, equity, and adaptability of Canada? How can we avoid the perennial oppressive error of imposing Eurocentric value systems on Indigenous communities? What obligations exist to compensate for the environmental and social problems created by past economic activities, such as fishery collapse, extinct species, orphaned oil wells, or employment dislocations as we move away from a fossil fuel–oriented economy? What kind of ethical basis is there to prompt policy changes, improve cooperation, and formulate innovative ways to solve ecological problems? In practical terms, if there is an urgent need, as illustrated in this book's case studies, to incorporate an ecological ethic that supersedes the short- to medium-term political context of policy decision making and to embrace a more holistic, longer-term, and system-based understanding of politics and policy, how do we get there?

CASE STUDY 12.2. Full Cost Accounting

While political debate on energy and climate often focuses on the current *costs* of moving away from an extractive model, it rarely takes into account the costs of the status quo. Political debates often point to the expenses of carbon taxes, technological innovation, retrofits for housing and transportation, and employment transitions, but it is rarer to focus on the current and ongoing costs being borne in Canada for the widespread extraction and consumption of fossil fuels. In many ways, Canadians have normalized and internalized the risks and real expenses associated with a fossil fuel–based system in our everyday lives. For example, Canadians tolerate gas leaks and explosions (both in homes and refineries), oil spills, polluted air, noise, volatile gas prices, repair costs, landscape blight from industrial facilities, and an accompanying overall decline in daily quality of life with little protest or awareness.

Cumulatively, these impacts take a huge toll on Canadians' health and wellbeing. While the rise in the immediate costs of addressing climate-related disasters and adapting to climate change are increasingly apparent, the cumulative effect of these plus the everyday impacts of our extractive economy are more hidden and more accepted. A recent piece published in *Inside Climate News* presents an interview with Kate Beaton, who wrote a graphic memoir titled *Ducks: Two Years in the Oil Sands* in which she recounts her experiences and the effects of the extractive economy in Canada. Her memoir about her journey from Cape Breton's declining coal mines and pulp mills to the Athabasca oil sands of Alberta recounts the many traumatic experiences she encountered in her work in the industry. These included sexual harassment, isolation, illness, fear of accidents and injuries, and damages to nature and the environment witnessed firsthand. The title of her memoir refers to an incident in 2008 when hundreds of ducks landed on a pond of mine tailings and died, an incident that she says was not unusual or out of the ordinary (Beaton, 2022).

As well as these measurable and real costs, and perhaps in part because they are so accepted, it is becoming even more apparent that a lot of loss and damage caused by fossil fuels goes unmeasured and unreported – and consequently unnoticed by the media and public. For example, a 2024 article in the journal *Science* reports that emissions from the oil sands of "total gas-phase organic carbon" may exceed estimates by as much as a factor of 64. In total, the authors report, these emissions exceed oil sands industry–reported values by 1,900 per cent to over 6,300 per cent, resulting in total organic carbon emissions equivalent to that from all other sources across Canada (He et al., 2024). If confirmed, these findings may well be so significant that we will have to substantially recalculate Canada's true carbon budget.

A full cost accounting of *future* expenses will also have to take a proper measure of the cost of climate change impacts relative to the costs (and also potential payoffs) of early action on emissions reduction. An article in *Maclean's* titled "Canada in the Year 2060" sets down in stark detail the ripple effect of these costs. For example, some studies have shown that children's exposure to wildfire smoke affects the functioning of a gene that regulates immune responses, leading to higher rates of bronchitis, laryngitis, and croup later in life. As well, full accounting needs to include the costs of impacts on Canada's disrupted food supply chain, care for displaced persons, higher rates of post-traumatic stress disorder, drug use, and effects on employment and productivity. The Canadian Climate Institute estimates that the costs of climate change will knock more than 5 per cent from the national GDP by 2095, compared to what it would have been in a world with a stable climate (Casselman, 2023).

Critical Thinking Questions

1. Why do you think we tend to discount the costs of the status quo and overestimate the costs of making changes?
2. Do you think a greater awareness of the costs of the status quo might encourage more action to address problems?

MULTILEVEL ADAPTIVE GOVERNANCE GAPS

Considering today's problems through the lens of the Anthropocene helps to identify governance gaps. In general, then, we can identify at least four governance gaps where we would anticipate a need for proactive, forward-thinking, and "enlightened" ecopolitics to coalesce in Canada.

Together, these gaps span legal, economic, and policy issues across the chapters. Let's consider each in turn.

Indigenous Self-Determination and Ways of Being

It seems highly unlikely that progress can be made on many ecopolitical issues without the direct involvement of Indigenous Peoples in decision making that affects their lives, and most decision making does, whether it emanates from Ottawa, provincial capitals, or local band councils. A parallel struggle for **self-governance** is impacting peoples across the country, as diverse bands look for ways to increase their independence and autonomy from the *Indian Act*, the primary legislative instrument that enables the federal government to control reserves. Solutions for self-government vary. For example, the small community of Sechelt has adopted a municipal-style government that enables them to control lands, taxation, and property collectively and democratically, but with delegated powers from the BC government. In northern Quebec, the Cree communities are self-governing under the Eeyou of Eeyou Istchee

(Grand Council of the Cree), which under the James Bay and Northern Quebec Agreement (discussed in Chapter Six) controls its own territories, resources, and also provides its own system of education, welfare, justice, and social services. The territory of Nunavut was established in 1999 and is one of four self-governing Inuit regions in Canada. While the commissioner of Nunavut nominally represents the Crown of Canada, the premier of Nunavut is elected by the population, and the territory elects one member to the Canadian House of Commons. Decisions made by the territorial assembly follow traditional Inuit cultural practices of governance by consensus, informed by *Inuit Qaujimajatuqangit* (the Inuit system of cultural and traditional knowledge). In 2024, self-governance took another step forward when the federal government devolved further authority over land use to the government of Nunavut, allowing it to fully control decisions over development on its lands and territories.

The patchwork of self-government arrangements across the country speaks to the inadequacy and lack of attention to the need for a national plan for Indigenous self-governance and the lack of options for replacing the *Indian Act*, which still governs life on reserves while "leaving out" Indigenous urban communities and bands that operate separately through Treaty and land claims agreements. Some areas under federal jurisdiction, such as parks and protected areas, natural resource management on federal or reserve lands, and some waterways and oceans, have explicitly incorporated co-management arrangements with Indigenous Peoples for specific areas and activities (see Houde, 2007), while other areas of environmental policy and governance leave them outside the legal framework, meaning they are sometimes marginalized in Canadian ecopolitics. For example, there appear to be few opportunities for Indigenous Peoples to impact policies on biodiversity, alternative and renewable energy, or chemical pollution that affects their health and well-being. There are even fewer possibilities for the incorporation and recognition of traditional Indigenous systems of knowledge into mainstream ecopolitics on an equal footing with western-based science and expertise, although many are working to make this a reality.

Accountability and Good Ecopolitical Citizenship

Another key theme of the text is shifting political analysis away from short- and medium-term thinking toward more holistic, systemic analyses of ecopolitics as a distinct realm or domain of conflict and cooperation. Local governments and municipalities enjoy a relatively high degree of public trust and have a substantial impact on people's everyday lives through their management of waste, land use planning, water, and transportation. However, local governments have few resources to tackle the most challenging aspects of environmental change, from climate adaptation to infrastructure development. Parliament, the prime minister, and the bureaucracy are responsible for generating, debating, and implementing policy decision making. The norms of democratic and liberal governance dictate that policy decisions should be checked, if not always completely aligned with, public opinion and the principles of fundamental justice, and checked also by judicial review.

The backdrop of the current unease with the federal role is an ongoing corrosion of Canadians' trust in and support for government actions across the board. The COVID-19 pandemic and some of the attendant response measures brought several populist narratives of opposition to the forefront. Though exercise of government powers to address the health emergency was relatively modest, the sensitivity of a small number of vocal publics to mask mandates, vaccine mandates, and other public health regulations increased substantially, reaching a high point with the "Freedom Convoy" protests by truckers in the winter of 2022. It is also likely that the heightened federal role triggered a provincial pushback to a potential rise in federal government actions in provincial areas of jurisdiction. In this atmosphere, the openness to government-led measures to address a range of ecopolitical issues has declined, along with a substantial degree of public trust. This mirrored the "MAGA" movement in the United States inspired largely by supporters of President Donald Trump.

While the meaning of "environmental" or ecological citizenship is hotly contested in the literature, the association between good governance principles and ecological sustainability is less controversial. This fact suggests, as Adkin (2009) argues, that "procedural democratic forms are also ends in themselves because civic self-determination and autonomy may be viewed as integral to a good life" (p. 13). In other words, there is considerable reinforcement between activism toward ecological health and toward human social wellbeing. Accountability, transparency, effectiveness, inclusivity, and equity are principles that are relevant to all forms of governmental institutional decision making, not just those around the environment or non-human elements.

ENVIRONMENTAL AND NON-HUMAN LEGAL RIGHTS AND REPRESENTATION

In addition to the above, the questions of ecological politics and governance are innovative in that they incorporate and recognize the non-human dimension of *planetary* wellbeing into the discussion (Dryzek, 1995; Smith, 2001). How might new governance forms be developed that might be "fit for purpose" in a world facing multiple ecological crises? The question speaks to the need to examine in more detail the changes to individual and state relationships that are fundamental issues of political philosophy. Adkin (2009) defines **ecological citizenship** as "the democratic, social, and environmental rights defended or demanded by social actors, along with the responsibilities for the well-being of other humans and other species that have emerged from political-ecological discourse" (p. 14). **Deliberative democracy** is defined by Adkin, following Gutman and Thompson, as "a form of government in which free and equal citizens (and their representatives) justify decisions in a process in which they give one another reasons that are mutually acceptable and reasonably accessible, with the aim of reaching conclusions that are binding in the present on all citizens but open to challenge in the future" (Gutmann & Thompson, 2009, p. 3).

How the non-human citizens of the planet might participate in a process of deliberative democracy remains an open question, but one which continues to be grappled with by legal scholars and thinkers worldwide (Lamalle & Stoett, 2023; Meijer, 2019). These discussions are at a rudimentary level in Canada, but as discussed in the book (see the Magpie River case in Case Study 7.2), there are some interesting legal innovations emerging that could potentially lead to more fundamental changes. The international campaign for nature rights has had global impact. ECOLEX lists some 216 countries that have incorporated environmental protection and conservation into their constitutions, as well as 5,200 or more legislative acts that incorporate environmental goals (IUCN, FAO, & UNEP, 2023). In July 2023 the *Canadian Environmental Protection Act* was amended to include recognition of Canadians' right to a healthy environment (Gordner, 2023). If this trend continues, it seems likely to affect Canadian ecopolitics through the work of organizations such as the West Coast Environmental Law Association, Ecojustice Canada, and Greenpeace, which have increasingly reached for litigation as a tool for policy change.

There is some precedent for using deliberative democracy in the form of citizens' assemblies, which have been established in the past to help inform government decision making on a variety of issues, especially electoral reform, at both provincial and federal levels. However, the possibility for Canada to be able to develop a model of deliberative democratic governance that fully incorporates the principles of earth system law or non-human rights remains remote.

Canada as a Global Citizen

The final theme embraced by this book is a shift beyond the analysis of the political context of Canadian environmental policy, including policy instruments, practices, and mechanisms, and toward questions of Canadian governance for human wellbeing, human security, and environmental ethics. In this text, we have stressed the ethical aspects of ecopolitics and their centrality in shaping conflicts and controversies. In general, we have advocated for an environmental ethic that embraces intergenerational justice and a shift in human perspectives toward the recognition and even entrenchment of the idea of the intrinsic value of nature. These ideas inevitably have implications for planetary wellbeing and for the governance of Canadian society. As well, this logically places Canada into a planetary frame, one that accounts for the position of the Canadian community within the natural world rather than simply being a territory or state member of an international system of states.

Some interesting initiatives present themselves at the global level that provide openings for states to move toward "green sovereignty." Canada has been an active participant in the voluntary national reviews for the United Nations Sustainable Development Goals, and Statistics Canada has developed a national portal for tracking progress on all 17 of the goals, which includes indicators for progress on key environmental targets such as reducing emissions and overfishing (Statistics Canada, n.d.). The federal government has also recently conducted a revision of Canada's Sustainable Development Strategy, which is being mainstreamed into ministries, agencies, and organizations governed by federal law. Activists are advocating that Canada follow the international precedents by fully incorporating non-human and nature rights into its National Biodiversity Strategy.

WHAT CAN YOU DO?

This book is about connections – between humans and nature, between local and global, and between ordinary people and the society in which we live.

An ecological worldview emphasizes the importance of connections for all life and for the future of the planet. To date, much of the focus of political systems is on the rights and responsibilities of national citizenship: in other words, the complex yet fundamental relationship of rights and duties between citizens and the state. In contrast, the concept of ecological citizenship asks us to consider not only our individual interests and our relationship with the state and with fellow citizens, but to radically reshape both our identity as citizens and how we live in the world. This demands not only sophisticated knowledge of the ecopolitical issues of our time but a fair amount of often-uncomfortable self-reflection.

Such a transformation toward ecological citizenship means an improved understanding of rights, roles, and obligations vis-à-vis the planet. Increasingly, politics is incorporating the rights and obligations that current generations hold toward future generations. It is also incorporating the consideration of the rights and responsibilities that inform our lives on Planet Earth. Connectedness brings more complex problems, and it is easy to get overwhelmed with the firehose of information out there. For that reason, we like to think that taking the forward step of reading this book and finding out more about the world of Canadian ecopolitics is a vital part of your journey toward understanding and appreciating your own role in making changes to the society that we will all inherit in the future. Simple slogans are appealing, but a deeper look at the situation involves tracing the root causes of environmental degradation, biodiversity loss, climate change, and the other problems we have discussed. It means critically examining the conditions that make life possible and that allow us to enjoy stability, security, health, prosperity, and freedom.

It is one of the goals of this book to improve your understanding of these root causes and to uncover ways of thinking and acting that will help us move toward a sustainable system of Canadian ecopolitics. Studies show that simple awareness of a problem is not sufficient to inspire changes in actions and behaviour, so those next steps are needed to institute more radical transformations. While it is important to have an awareness of yourself as an individual consumer, it is also vitally important to recognize that collective action is needed to move Canadian government and society toward a healthier and more sustainable path. Achieving that collective action requires vision, leadership, and organization. There is no single means or pathway forward. Rather, we as a society need to design solutions that draw on a diversity of viewpoints, skills, experiences, and knowledge to find the right combination of initiatives to address the daunting problems we face.

Solutions should also be based on the particular needs, interests, and circumstances that make up such a large and diverse country as Canada. Ecopolitics is not only a field in itself, it is also impacting a range of fields, including finance, economics, the sciences, tourism and travel, education, management, technology, agriculture, international development, human resources, communications, and even the arts. Canadian ecopolitics is in essence multidisciplinary, with avenues for the pursuit of new dialogues among scientists, engineers, activists, Indigenous Peoples, the private sector, and scholars regarding the complex adaptive challenges that persist and new ones that will emerge in the Anthropocene. Keep learning, keep voting according to your view of which politicians offer effective solutions, and keep acting in the marketplace as though your decisions matter – because they do.

References

Abbott, K.W. (2011). The transnational regime complex for climate change. *Environment and Planning C: Politics and Space*, 1813198. https://doi.org/10.2139/ssrn.1813198

Abramovitz, J. (1996). *Imperiled waters, impoverished future: The decline of freshwater ecosystems*. Worldwatch Paper 128.

ACIA. (2004). *Arctic climate impact assessment*. https://www.amap.no/documents/doc/arctic-arctic-climate-impact-assessment/796

Adkin, L.E. (Ed.). (2009). *Environmental conflict and democracy in Canada*. UBC Press. https://doi.org/10.59962/9780774816045

Aitken, H.G.J. (1958). The role of staple industries in Canada's economic development: Discussion. *Journal of Economic History, 18*(4), 451–452. https://doi.org/10.1017/S002205070010765X

Alberta Energy Regulator. (2023). *Alberta energy outlook 2023: Executive summary*. Calgary.

Allard, C., & Curran, D. (2023). Indigenous influence and engagement in mining permitting in British Columbia, Canada: Lessons for Sweden and Norway? *Environmental Management, 72*(1), 1–18. https://doi.org/10.1007/s00267-021-01536-0

Anderson, D. (2023, May 8). Documents reveal inside look as Alberta officials prepared for a "landslide" of orphan wells. *The Narwhal*. www.ctvnews.ca/business/documents-reveal-inside-look-as-alberta-officials-prepared-for-a-landslide-of-orphan-wells-1.6385515

Archambault, P., Snelgrove, P.V.R., Fisher, J.A.D., Gagnon, J.-M., Garbary, D.J., Harvey, M., Kenchington, E.L., Lesage, V., Levesque, M., Lovejoy, C., Mackas, D.L., McKindsey, C.W., Nelson, J.R., Pepin, P., Piché, L., & Poulin, M. (2010).

From sea to sea: Canada's three oceans of biodiversity. *PLoS ONE, 5*(8). https://doi.org/10.1371/journal.pone.0012182

Arctic Council. (2023). *Arctic peoples*. https://arctic-council.org/explore/topics/arctic-peoples

Armstrong, D.A., Lucas, J., & Taylor, Z. (2022). The urban-rural divide in Canadian federal elections, 1896–2019. *Canadian Journal of Political Science, 55*(1), 84–106. https://doi.org/10.1017/S0008423921000792

Asfaw, H.W., Sandy Lake First Nation, McGee, T.K., & Christianson, A.C. (2019). Evacuation preparedness and the challenges of emergency evacuation in Indigenous communities in Canada: The case of Sandy Lake First Nation, Northern Ontario. *International Journal of Disaster Risk Reduction, 34*, 55–63. https://doi.org/10.1016/J.IJDRR.2018.11.005

Ashford, O., Baines, J., Barbanell, M., & Wang, K. (2024, February 23). What we know about deep-sea mining – and what we don't. *World Resource Institute Insights*. www.wri.org/insights/deep-sea-mining-explained

Associated Press. (2018). Polar bear shot dead after attacking cruise ship guard in Norway. *The Guardian*. https://www.theguardian.com/world/2018/jul/29/polar-bear-shot-dead-after-attacking-cruise-ship-guard-in-norway

Awad, D., & Wiltse, K. (2022, May 25). *Reference re Impact Assessment Act*: Canada's federal impact assessment regime held to be unconstitutional by the Alberta court of appeal. *Canada Regulatory Review*. https://www.canadaregulatoryreview.com/reference-re-impact-assessment-act-canadas-federal-impact-assessment-regime-held-to-be-unconstitutional-by-the-alberta-court-of-appeal

Azar, C., Martin, J., Johansson, D., & Sterner, J. (2023). The social cost of methane. *Climatic Change, 176*(1), 1–17.

Bakx, K. (2023, October 14). How the Supreme Court dealt a blow to Trudeau's climate ambitions and what comes next. *CBC News*. https://www.cbc.ca/news/canada/calgary/bakx-scoc-ruling-1.6995962

Barbosa, L.C. (2000). *The Brazilian Amazon rainforest: Global ecopolitics, development, and democracy*. University Press of America.

Barclay, J., Lavoie, J., Macarthur, C., & Nallim, M. (2020, September 25). The impacts of climate change on North American defence and security. *Policy Primer*. NAADSN.

Barker, J. (2005). *Sovereignty matters: Locations of contestation and possibility in Indigenous struggles for self-determination*. University of Nebraska Press. https://doi.org/10.2307/j.ctt1dnncqc

Barlow, M. (2016). *Boiling point: Government neglect, corporate abuse, and Canada's water crisis*. ECW Press.

Barman, J. (2007). *The West beyond the West: A history of British Columbia* (3rd ed.). University of Toronto Press.

Barnsley, I. (2006). Dealing with change: Australia, Canada and the Kyoto Protocol to the Framework Convention on Climate Change. *Round Table, 95*(385), 399–410. https://doi.org/10.1080/00358530600748358

Barry, J. (2011). Ecopolitics. In J. Newman (Ed.), *Green ethics and philosophy: An A-to-Z guide* (Vol. 8, pp. 250–254). Routledge. https://doi.org/10.4135/9781412974608.n50

Barry, J. (2021, July 26). *Clean growth, green growth or beyond growth?* [Video]. YouTube.

Barton, J., & Rogerson, M. (2017). The importance of greenspace for mental health. *BJPsych International, 14*(4), 79–81. https://doi.org/10.1192/s2056474000002051.

Basdeo, M., & Bharadwaj, L. (2013). Beyond physical: Social dimensions of the water crisis on Canada's First Nations and considerations for governance. *Indigenous Policy Journal, 23*, 1–14.

BC Ministry of Forests. (2024). *Managing the health of our forests.* https://www2.gov.bc.ca/gov/content/environment/natural-resource-stewardship/laws-policies-standards-guidance/legislation-regulation/forest-range-practices-act

Beaton, K. (2022). *Ducks: Two years in the oil sands.* Drawn & Quarterly.

Beauchamp, B., & Huebert, R. (2008). Canadian sovereignty linked to energy development in the Arctic. *Arctic, 61*(3), 341–343. https://doi.org/10.14430/arctic62

Beaulieu, C.R. (2021). The historic and contemporary permanence of the doctrine of discovery in Canada. *USURJ: University of Saskatchewan Undergraduate Research Journal, 7*(1). https://doi.org/10.32396/usurj.v7i1.496

Beck, M., Rivers, N., & Yonezawa, H. (2015). A rural myth? The perceived unfairness of carbon taxes in rural communities. *SSRN Electronic Journal.* SSRN Scholarly Paper 2603565. https://doi.org/10.2139/ssrn.2603565

Beck, U. (1992). *The risk society: Towards a new modernity* (M. Ritter, Trans.). Sage Productions.

Bedeau, K. (2006). *Perceptions of health and environmental contamination on the Aamjiwnaang First Nation reserve (Ontario).* https://scholar.uwindsor.ca/etd/3035

Beisner, B., Ives, A.R., & Carpenter, S.R. (2003). The effects of an exotic fish invasion on the prey communities of two lakes. *Journal of Animal Ecology, 72*, 331–341. https://doi.org/10.1046/j.1365-2656.2003.00699.x

Bellrichard, C. (2019, January 7). Hereditary chiefs in B.C. stand opposed to Coastal GasLink pipeline despite injunction. *CBC News.* https://www.cbc.ca/news/indigenous/hereditary-chiefs-in-b-c-stand-opposed-to-coastal-gaslink-pipeline-despite-injunction-1.4968169

Belshaw, J.D., Nickel, S., & Horton, C. (2020). *Histories of Indigenous Peoples and Canada.* Creative Commons Attribution.

Bennett, N.J., Kaplan-Hallam, M., Augustine, G., Ban, N., Belhabib, D., Brueckner-Irwin, I., Charles, A., Couture, J., Eger, S., Fanning, L., Foley, P., Goodfellow, A.M., Greba, L., Gregr, E., Hall, D., Harper, S., Maloney, B., McIsaac, J., Ou, W., & Bailey, M. (2018). Coastal and Indigenous community access to marine resources and the ocean: A policy imperative for Canada. *Marine Policy, 87*, 186–193. https://doi.org/10.1016/j.marpol.2017.10.023

Bergmann, M., Lutz, B., Tekman, M.B., & Gutow, L. (2017). Citizen scientists reveal: Marine litter pollutes Arctic beaches and affects wildlife. *Marine Pollution Bulletin, 125*(1–2), 535–540. https://reader.elsevier.com/reader/sd/pii/S0025326X17307919

Berkes, F. (1990). Native subsistence fisheries: A synthesis of harvest studies in Canada. *Arctic, 43*(1), 35–42.

Berkes, F., Mahon, R., McConney, P., Pollnac, R., & Pomeroy, R. (2001). *Managing small-scale fisheries: Alternative directions and methods.* IDRC.

Berman, T. (1993). Towards an integrative ecofeminist praxis. *Canadian Woman Studies, 13*(3), 15–17.

Bernaldo de Quiros, Y., Fernandez, A., Baird, R.W., Brownell, R.L., Aguilar de Soto, N., Allen, D., Arbelo, M., Arregui, M., Costidis, A., Fahlman, A., Frantzis, A., Gulland, F.M.D., Iniguez, M., Johnson, M., Komnenou, A., Koopman, H., Pabst, D.A., Roe, W.D., Sierra, E., Tejedor, M., & Schorr, G. (2019). Advances in research on the impacts of anti-submarine sonar on beaked whales. *Proceedings of the Royal Society B: Biological Sciences, 286*(1895). https://doi.org/10.1098/rspb.2018.2533

Bernstein, S. (2002). International institutions and the framing of domestic policies: The Kyoto Protocol and Canada's response to climate change. *Policy Sciences, 35*(2), 203–237.

Bernstein, S. (2008). *A globally integrated climate policy for Canada.* University of Toronto Press. https://doi.org/10.3138/9781442683969

Bernstein, S., & Cashore, B. (2002). Globalization, internationalization, and liberal environmentalism: Exploring non-domestic sources of influence on Canadian environmental policy. In D. Vannijnatten & R. Boardman (Eds.), *Canadian environmental policy: Context and cases* (pp. 212–232). Oxford University Press.

Bezener, M., Bunge, S., Cannings, D., Holm, M., Lariviere, J., McFadyen, L., Meads, L., & Scoo, L. (2012). *Keeping nature in our future: A biodiversity conservation strategy for the South Okanagan Similkameen.* South Okanagan Similkameen Conservation Program.

Biermann, F. (2014). *Earth system governance: World politics in the Anthropocene.* MIT Press.

Biro, A. (2007). Half-empty or half-full? Water politics and the Canadian national imaginary. In K. Bakker (Ed.), *Eau Canada: The future of Canada's water* (pp. 321–333). UBC Press. https://doi.org/10.59962/9780774856201-022

Biro, A. (2015). The good life in the greenhouse? Autonomy, democracy, and citizenship in the Anthropocene. *Telos, 2015*(172), 15–37. https://doi.org/10.3817/0915172015

Blake, R.B. (1997). The international fishery off Canada's east coast in the 20th century. In J.E. Candow & C. Corbin (Eds.), *How deep is the ocean? Historical essays on Canada's Atlantic fishery.* University College of Cape Breton Press.

Blewitt, J. (2008). *Understanding sustainable development.* Earthscan Publications.

Block, N. (2017, March 3). Toronto's buried history: The dark story of how mining built a city. *The Guardian.*

Blunden, J., & Arndt, D.S. (2017). Special supplement to the state of the climate in 2016. *Bulletin of the American Meteorological Society, 98*(8). https://doi.org/10.117 5/2017BAMSStateoftheClimate.1

Boardman, R., & VanNijnatten, D. (2002). *Canadian environmental policy: Context and cases.* Oxford University Press.

Boardman, R., & VanNijnatten, D. (2009). *Canadian environmental policy and politics: Prospects for leadership and innovation.* Oxford University Press.

Bocking, S.A. (2000). *Biodiversity in Canada: Ecology, ideas, and action.* Broadview Press. https://doi.org/10.3138/9781442602373

Bocking, S.A. (2009). Making space for species: Local and global challenges of biodiversity. In P. Stoett & C. Gore (Eds.), *Environmental challenges and opportunities: Local-global perspectives on Canadian issues* (pp. 13–41). Emond Montgomery.

Bolvin-Rioux, A., Starr, M., Chassé, J., Scarratt, M., Perrie, W., Long, Z., & Lavoie, D. (2022). Harmful algae and climate change on the Canadian East Coast: Exploring occurrence predictions of *Dinophysis acuminata, D. norvegica,* and *Pseudo-nitzschia seriata. Harmful Algae, 112,* 102183. https://doi.org/10.1016 /j.hal.2022.102183

Bookchin, M. (1990). *Remaking society: Pathways to a green future.* South End Press.

Bookchin, M. (2005). *The ecology of freedom.* AK Press.

Borrows, J. (1997). Wampum at Niagara: The Royal Proclamation, Canadian legal history and self-government. In M. Asch (Ed.), *Aboriginal and treaty rights in Canada: Essays on law, equality and respect for difference* (pp. 169–172). UBC Press.

Borrows, J. (2010). *Canada's Indigenous constitution.* University of Toronto Press.

Bourgon, L. (2022). *Tree thieves: Crime and survival in North America's Woods.* Greystone Books.

Bown, S. (2020). *The company: The rise and fall of the Hudson's Bay empire.* Doubleday Canada.

Boyd, B. (2018). A province under pressure: Climate change policy in Alberta. *Canadian Journal of Political Science, 52*(1), 183–199. https://doi.org/10.1017 /s0008423918000410

Boyd, D.R. (2003). *Unnatural law: Rethinking Canadian environmental law and policy.* UBC Press.

Boyd, D.R. (2012). *The right to a healthy environment: Revitalizing Canada's constitution.* UBC Press. https://doi.org/10.59962/9780774824149

Boyd, D.R. (2015). *Cleaner, greener, healthier: A prescription for stronger Canadian environmental laws and policies.* UBC Press. https://doi.org/10.59962 /9780774830485

Boyd, D.R. (2017). *The rights of nature: A legal revolution that could save the world.* ECW Press.

Bradford, L., Bharadwaj, L., Okpalauwaekwe, U., & Waldner, C. (2016). Drinking water quality in Indigenous communities in Canada and health outcomes: A scoping review. *International Journal of Circumpolar Health, 75*(1). https:// doi.org/10.3402/ijch.v75.32336

Bratman, G., Anderson, C., Berman, M., Cochran, B., de Vries, S., Flanders, J., Folke, C., Frumkin, H., Gross, J.J., Hartig, T., Kahn, Jr., P.H., Kuo, M., Lawler, J.J., Levin, P.S., Lindahl, T., Meyer-Lindenberg, A., Mitchell, R., Ouyang, Z., Roe, H., & Daily, G.C. (2019). Nature and mental health: An ecosystem service perspective. *Science Advances, 5*, eaax0903. https://doi.org/10.1126/sciadv.aax0903

Breeze, H., Nolet, V., Thomson, D., Wright, A.J., Marotte, E., & Sanders, M. (2022). Efforts to advance underwater noise management in Canada. *Marine Pollution Bulletin, 178*, 113596.

Bright, C. (1998). *Life out of bounds: Bioinvasion in a borderless world.* Norton.

Brouhle, K., & Harrington, D.R. (2010). GHG registries: Participation and performance under the Canadian voluntary climate challenge program. *Environmental and Resource Economics, 47*(4), 521–548. https://doi.org/10.1007/s10640-010-9391-4

Brownsey, K. (2008). Enough for everyone: Policy fragmentation and water institutions in Alberta. In M. Sproule-Jones, C. Johns, & B. Timothy Heinmiller (Eds.), *Canadian water politics: Conflicts and institutions* (pp. 133–155). McGill-Queen's University Press. https://doi.org/10.1515/9780773575950-010

Brubaker, E. (2000). *Unnatural disaster: How politics destroyed Canada's Atlantic.* https://environment.probeinternational.org/2000/01/18/unnatural-disaster-how-politics-destroyed-canadas-atlantic-groundfisheries

Buckley, K. (1958). The role of staple industries in Canada's economic development. *Journal of Economic History, 18*(4), 439–450. https://doi.org/10.1017/S0022050700107648

Bullard, R.D. (1994). Overcoming racism in environmental decision making. *Environment, 36*(4), 10.

Bullard, R.D., & Johnson, G.S. (2000). Environmental justice: Grassroots activism and its impact on public policy decision making. *Journal of Social Issues, 56*(3), 555–578. https://doi.org/10.1111/0022-4537.00184

Burdon, R. (2003). *The suffering gene: Environmental threats to our health.* Zed Books.

Burney, D.H., & Hampson, F.O. (2012, June 21). How Obama lost Canada. *Foreign Affairs.* www.foreignaffairs.com/articles/canada/2012-06-21/how-obama-lost-canada

Burns, W. (Ed.). (2006). Special issue on the precautionary principle and its operationalisation in international environmental regimes and domestic policymaking. *International Journal of Global Environmental Issues, 5*(1–2).

Cahill, A.E., Aiello-Lammens, M.E., Fisher-Reid, M.C., Hua, X., Karanewsky, C.J., Ryu, H.Y., Sbeglia, G.C., Spagnolo, F., Waldron, J.B., Warsi, O., & Weins, J.J. (2013, January 7). How does climate change cause extinction? *Proceedings of the Royal Society B: Biological Sciences, 280*(1750). https://doi.org/10.1098/rspb.2012.1890

Cahn, M.A., & O'Brien, R. (1996). *Thinking about the environment: Readings on politics, property, and the physical world.* M.E. Sharpe.

Camacho, A.E. (2009). Assisted migration: Redefining nature and natural resource law under climate change. *Yale Journal on Regulation, 27*, 171.

Campanella, D. (2012). *Misplaced generosity: Update 2012 – Extraordinary profits in Alberta's oil and gas industry.* Parkland Institute.

Campbell, B. (2012). *Managing oil wealth: The Alberta/Canada model vs. the Norwegian model.* Canadian Centre for Policy Alternatives. https://www .policyalternatives.ca/publications/commentary/managing-oil-wealth

Campbell, K. (1998). From Rio to Kyoto: The use of voluntary agreements to implement the climate change convention. *Review of European, Comparative & International Environmental Law, 7*(2), 159–169. https://doi.org/10.1111 /1467-9388.00142

Campbell, M. (2022, February 1). South America's "lithium fields" reveal the dark side of our electric future. *Euronews.* https://www.euronews.com/green /2022/02/01/south-america-s-lithium-fields-reveal-the-dark-side-of-our -electric-future

Canada Energy Regulator. (2016, May 12). Impacts of the Fort McMurray wildfires on Canadian crude oil production. *Market Snapshots.* https://www.cer-rec.gc.ca /en/data-analysis/energy-markets/market-snapshots/2016/market-snapshot -impacts-fort-mcmurray-wildfires-canadian-crude-oil-production.html

Canada Energy Regulator. (2023). *Provincial and territorial energy profiles – Canada.* https://www.cer-rec.gc.ca/en/data-analysis/energy-markets/provincial-territorial -energy-profiles/provincial-territorial-energy-profiles-canada.html

Canadian Aquaculture Industry Alliance. (2023). *Welcome to Canadian aquaculture industry alliance.* https://aquaculture.ca/welcome-original-just-in-case

Canadian Endangered Species Conservation Council. (2022). *Wild species 2020: The general status of species in Canada.* www.wildspecies.ca/reports

Canadian Environmental Law Association. (2024). *Casework: Grassy Narrows first nation and environmental injustice.* https://cela.ca/casework-grassy-narrows -first-nation-and-environmental-injustice

Canadian Institute for Climate Choices. (2021). *Canada's net zero future: Finding our way in the global transition.* https://climatechoices.ca/reports/canadas-net -zero-future

Canadian Press. (2021, June 29). All new cars, light-duty trucks sold in Canada will be zero emissions by 2035, Liberals say. *CBC News.* https://www.cbc.ca/news /canada/calgary/canada-electric-cars-2035-1.6085540

Caranci, B., Francis, F., & El Baba, Y. (2021, April 6). *Don't let history repeat: Canada's energy sector transition and the potential impact on workers.* TD.

Cardinale, B.J., Duffy, J.E., Gonzalez, A., Hooper, D.U., Perrings, C., Venail, P., Narwani, A., Mace, G.M., Tilman, D., Wardle, D.A., Kinzig, A.P., Daily, G.C., Loreau, M., Grace, J.B., Larigauderie, A., Srivastava, D.S., & Naeem, S. (2012). Biodiversity loss and its impact on humanity. *Nature, 486*(7401), 59–67. https://doi.org/10.1038/NATURE11148

Carrington, D. (2021, January 22). Electric vehicles close to "tipping point" of mass adoption. *The Guardian.* https://www.theguardian.com/environment/2021 /jan/22/electric-vehicles-close-to-tipping-point-of-mass-adoption

Carrington, D. (2022, March 24). Microplastics found in human blood for first time. *The Guardian*. www.theguardian.com/environment/2022/mar/24/microplastics-found-in-human-blood-for-first-time

Carson, R. (1962). *Silent spring*. Random House.

Cashore, B.W. (2001). *In search of sustainability: British Columbia forest policy in the 1990s*. UBC Press.

Casselman, A. (2023, August 10). Canada in the year 2060. *Maclean's*. https://macleans.ca/society/environment/canada-in-the-year-2060

Castañeda, R.A., Burliuk, C.M.M., Casselman, J.M., Cooke, S.J., Dunmall, K.M., Forbes, L.S., Hasler, C.T., Howland, K.L., Hutchings, J.A., Klein, G.M., Nguyen, V.M., Price, M.H.H., Reid, A.J., Reist, J.D., Reynolds, J.D., Van Nynatten, A., & Mandrak, N.E. (2020). A brief history of fisheries in Canada. *Fisheries*, *45*(6), 303–318. https://doi.org/10.1002/fsh.10449

CBC News. (2008, November 29). Secret advice to politicians: Oilsands emissions hard to scrub. https://www.cbc.ca/news/canada/secret-advice-to-politicians-oilsands-emissions-hard-to-scrub-1.738803

CBC News. (2016, October 10). Idle no more call on Trudeau to keep promises on Indigenous, environmental issues. https://www.cbc.ca/news/canada/toronto/idle-no-more-trudeau-thanksgiving-1.3799110

CBC News. (2022, February 15). Newfoundland oil spill a major concern for wildlife, says seabird biologist. https://www.cbc.ca/news/canada/newfoundland-labrador/alaskaborg-oil-spill-sea-birds-1.6350766

CCME (Canadian Council of Ministers of the Environment). (2010, January 1). *Review and assessment of Canadian groundwater resources, management, current research mechanisms and priorities [PN 1441]*. https://open.alberta.ca/publications/review-and-assessment-of-canadian-groundwater-resources-management

CCME (Canadian Council of Ministers of the Environment). (2024). *Biodiv Canada*. https://www.biodivcanada.ca/national-biodiversity-strategy-and-action-plan

CEC (Commission for Environmental Cooperation). (2017). *Characteristics of management of food loss and waste in North America*. https://www.cec.org/files/documents/publications/11772-characterization-and-management-food-loss-and-waste-in-north-america-en.pdf

CEC (Commission for Environmental Cooperation). (2020). *Alberta tailings ponds II. Factual record regarding submission SEM-17-001*. Author.

Centre for Rupert's Land Studies. (2022). *What is "Rupert's Land"?* www.uwinnipeg.ca/rupertsland/about-us/what-is-rupertsland.html

CERES. (2013). *California's low carbon fuel standard: Compliance outlook for 2020*. Author.

Chastko, P. (2004). *Developing Alberta's oil sands: From Karl Clark to Kyoto*. University of Calgary Press. https://doi.org/10.1515/9781552383261

Chater, A. (2018). An examination of the framing of climate change by the government of Canada, 2006–2016. *Canadian Journal of Communication*, *43*(4), 583–600. https://doi.org/10.22230/cjc.2018v43n4a3300

Chater, A., Sarson, L., & Greaves, W. (2020). Assessing security governance in the Arctic. In G.H. Gjørv, M. Lanteigne, & H. Sam-Aggrey (Eds.), *Handbook on Arctic Security* (pp. 43–56). Routledge.

Chivian, E., & Bernstein, A. (2010). *How our health depends on biodiversity.* Harvard Center for Health and the Global Environment.

Christensen, R., & Lintner, A.M. (2007). Trading our common heritage? The debate over water rights transfers in Canada. In K. Bakker (Ed.), *Eau Canada: The future of Canada's water* (pp. 219–241). UBC Press. https://doi.org/10.59962 /9780774856201-017

Chuang, F., Manley, E., & Petersen, A. (2020). The role of worldviews in the governance of sustainable mobility. *Proceedings of the National Academy of Sciences of the United States of America, 117*(8), 4034–4042. https://doi.org /10.1073/pnas.1916936117

Chyba, C., & Greninger, A. (2004). Biotechnology and bioterrorism: An unprecedented world. *Survival, 46*(2), 143–161. https://doi.org/10.1093 /survival/46.2.143

Clapp, J., & Dauvergne, P. (2011). *Paths to a green world* (2nd ed.). MIT Press.

Clapperton, J. (2019). Environmental activism as anticonquest: The Nuu-chah-nulth and environmentalists in the contact zone of Clayoquot Sound. In J. Clapperton & L. Piper (Eds.), *Environmental activism on the ground: Small green and Indigenous organizing* (pp. 181–205). University of Calgary Press.

Clark, A., Hirji, Z., & Rathi, A. (2022, October 31). A methane cloud highlights cracks in Canada's climate ambitions. *Bloomberg BNN.* https://www .bnnbloomberg.ca/a-methane-cloud-highlights-cracks-in-canada-s-climate -ambitions-1.18394 94

Climate Action Network. (2011). *The tar sands' long shadow: Canada's campaign to kill climate policies outside our borders.* http://climateactionnetwork.ca/wp -content/uploads/2011/09/CAN_TarSands_report.pdf

Coad, L., Munro, D., Owusu, P., & Robins, A. (2016). *A changing tide: British Columbia's emerging liquefied natural gas industry.* Conference Board of Canada.

Coates, K., & Poelzer, G. (2014). The next northern challenge: The reality of the provincial north. Macdonald-Laurier Institute.

Cochran, K.A. (2020). *Tragedy of the commons: Books, media, articles, and more.* Salem Press.

Colautti, R., & MacIsaac, H. (2004). A neutral terminology to define "invasive" species. *Diversity and Distributions, 10*, 135–141. https://doi.org/10.1111 /j.1366-9516.2004.00061.x

Coletto, D. (2024). What policy ideas attract and repel Canadian voters? A look at the "third rails" of Canadian politics. Abacus Data. https://abacusdata.ca/policies -canadian-politics-attract-repell

Collier, M., & Bansal, S. (2023, March 2). A new USGS study has big implications for climate change mitigation plans to reduce greenhouse gases in the atmosphere. USGS. https://www.usgs.gov/news/featured-story/climate-warming-likely -cause-large-increases-wetland-methane-emissions

Collier, R. (1974). *The plague of the Spanish lady*. Allison and Busby.

Conniff, R. (2013). *Tracking the causes of sharp decline of the monarch butterfly*. Yale University. http://e360.yale.edu/feature/tracking_the_causes_of _sharpdecline_of_the_monarch_butterfly/2634

Connolly, K. (2019). Polar cruise boom harming the Arctic, explorer warns. *The Guardian*. https://www.theguardian.com/world/2019/aug/13/polar-cruise -increase-harming-the-arctic-explorer-arved-fuchs-warns

Conrad, M. (2011). *A concise history of Canada*. Cambridge University Press. https:// doi.org/10.1017/CBO9781139032407

Cook, R. (2006). Making a garden out of a wilderness. In D.F. Duke (Ed.), *Canadian environmental history* (pp. 155–172). Canadian Scholars' Press.

Cooke, S.J., & Gowx, I.G. (2004). The role of recreational fishing in global fisheries crises. *BioScience, 54*(9), 857–8559. https://doi.org/10.1641/0006-3568(2004) 054[0857:TRORFI]2.0.CO;2

Cousins, I.T., Johansson, J.H., Salter, M.E., Sha, B., & Scheringer, M. (2022). Outside the safe operating space of a new planetary boundary for per- and polyfluoroalkyl substances (PFAS). *Environmental Science & Technology, 56*(16), 11172–11179.

Cowie, R.H., Bouchet, P., & Fontaine, B. (2022). The sixth mass extinction: Fact, fiction or speculation? *Biological Reviews*. https://doi.org/10.1111/brv.12816

Cox, G. (1999). *Alien species in North America and Hawaii: Impacts on national ecosystems*. Island Press.

Crawford, A. (2017, July 26). Canada's endangered wild ginseng under threat from poachers. *CBC News*. https://www.cbc.ca/news/politics/wild-ginseng -poaching-endangered-plants-1.4212920

Crawford, S. (2001). *Salmonine introductions to the Laurentian great lakes: An historical review and evaluation of ecological effects*. NRC Press.

Crosby, A. (1986). *Ecological imperialism: The biological expansion of Europe*. Cambridge University Press.

Crosby, A.W. (1994). Ecological imperialism: The overseas migration of Western Europeans as a biological phenomenon. In *Germs, seeds and animals*. Routledge.

Cross, P. (2018, November 14). *LNG: Measuring its impact on the British Columbia economy*. https://www.resourceworks.com/highimpact-2018

Cunningham, N. (2024, September 5). Canadian LNG may not reach its potential, industry leaders warn. *Gas Outlook*. https://gasoutlook.com/analysis/canadian -lng-may-not-reach-its-potential-industry-leaders-warn

Daggett, C.N. (2019). *The birth of energy: Fossil fuels, thermodynamics, and the politics of work*. Duke University Press. https://doi.org/10.1215/9781478005346

Dalby, S. (2006). Environmental security: Ecology or international relations? In E. Laferriere & P. Stoett (Eds.), *International ecopolitical theory: Critical approaches* (pp. 17–33). UBC Press.

Dalby, S. (2019). Canadian geopolitical culture: Climate change and sustainability. *Canadian Geographer, 63*(1), 100–111. https://doi.org/10.1111/cag.12472

Daly, H.E., & Farley, J.C. (2004). *Ecological economics: Principles and applications.* Island Press.

Daoust, P.Y., Crook, A., Bollinger, T.K., Campbell, K.G., & Wong, J. (2002). Animal welfare and the harp seal hunt in Atlantic Canada. *Canadian Veterinary Journal, 43*(9), 687–694.

Davies, R.W.D., & Rangeley, R. (2010). Banking on cod: Exploring economic incentives for recovering Grand Banks and North Sea cod fisheries. *Marine Policy, 34*(1), 92–98. https://doi.org/10.1016/j.marpol.2009.04.019

De Coste, M., Saleem, S., Mian, H.R., Chhipi-Shrestha, G., Hewage, K., Mohseni, M., & Sadiq, R. (2024). Water security risks in small, remote, indigenous communities in Canada: A critical review on challenges and opportunities. *Cambridge Prisms: Water, 2*, e5. https://doi.org/10.1017/wat.2024.3

Dee, L.E., Cowles, J., Isbell, F., Pau, S., Gaines, S.D., & Reich, P.B. (2019). When do ecosystem services depend on rare species? *Trends in Ecology and Evolution, 34*(8), 746–758. https://doi.org/10.1016/j.tree.2019.03.010

Department of National Defence. (2023). *Defence climate and sustainability strategy 2023–2027.* https://www.canada.ca/en/department-national-defence/corporate /reports-publications/defence-climate-and-sustainability-strategy-2023–2027.html

Desert Research Institute. (2024). *What is cloud seeding?* www.dri.edu/cloud -seeding-program/what-is-cloud-seeding

De Souza, M., & Simmons, M. (2022, May 9). Emails reveal how the RCMP changed its story about arresting journalists in Wet'suwet'en raid. *The Narwhal.* https:// thenarwhal.ca/rcmp-emails-journalists-coastal-gaslink

Dewis, G. (2022, February 15). Repair or replace: What are Canadians doing with their old cell phones and computers? Statistics Canada. https://www150.statcan .gc.ca/n1/pub/16-002-x/2022001/article/00001-eng.htm

Dick, L. (2001). *Muskox land: Ellesmere Island in the age of contact.* University of Calgary Press.

Dillon, J. (2021). Current state of enteric methane and the carbon footprint of beef and dairy cattle in the United States. *Animal Frontiers, 11*(4), 57–68.

Dishakes. (2023, October 19). The Supreme Court ruling on the impact assessment act – climate change implications. *Canadian Environmental Law Association.* https://cela.ca/blog-the-supreme-court-ruling-on-the-impact-assessment -act-climate-change-implications

Doctors for Nuclear Energy. (2021). *Home page.* https://www.doctorsfor nuclearenergy.org

Doern, G.B., Auld, G., & Stoney, C. (2015). *Green-lite: Complexity in fifty years of Canadian environmental policy, governance, and democracy.* McGill-Queen's University Press. http://doi.org/10.1016/S0140-6736(21)01787-6

Downing, A., & Cuerrier, A. (2011, January). Synthesis of the impacts of climate change on the first nations and Inuit of Canada. *Indian Journal of Traditional Knowledge, 10.*

Drache, D. (1982). Harold Innis and Canadian capitalist development. *Canadian Journal of Political and Social Theory, 6*(1–2), 35–60.

Drexhage, J.R. (2010). *Climate change and foreign policy in Canada*. Canadian International Council.

Dryzek, J.S. (1995). Strategies of ecological democratization. In W. Lafferty & J. Meadowcroft (Eds.), *Democracy and the environment: Problems and prospects* (pp. 108–123). Edward Elger. https://doi.org/10.4337/9781035351886.00013

Dryzek, J.S. (2013). *The politics of the earth: Environmental discourses*. Oxford University Press.

D'Souza, J., Dawson, J., & Groulx, M. (2021). *Last chance tourism: A decade review of a case study on Churchill, Manitoba's polar bear viewing industry*. Taylor & Francis. www.tandfonline.com/doi/full/10.1080/09669582.2021.1910828?src=recsys

Duarte, C.M., Chapuis, L., Collin, S.P., Devassy, R.P., Eguiluz, V.M., Erbe, C., Gordon, T.A.C., Halpern, B.S., Harding, H.R., Havlik, M.N., Meekan, M., Merchant, N.D., Miksis-Olds, J., Parsons, M., Predragovic, M., Radford, A.N., Radford, C.A., Simpson, S.D., Slabbekoorn, H., … Juanes, F. (2021). The soundscape of the Anthropocene ocean. *Science, 371*(6529). https://doi.org/10.1126/science.aba4658

Duke, D.F. (2006). *Canadian environmental history: Essential readings*. Canadian Scholars' Press.

Dusyk, N., Turcotte, I., Gunton, T., Macnab, J., Mcbain, S., Penney, N., Pickrell-Barr, J., Pope, M., & Hands, A. (2021). *All hands on deck: An assessment of provincial, territorial and federal readiness to deliver a safe climate*. The Pembina Institute.

Dwivedi, O., Kyba, P., Stoett, P., & Tiesson, R. (2001). *Sustainable development and Canada: National and international perspectives*. Broadview Press.

Earle, T. (2023). *The liberty to take fish: Atlantic fisheries and federal power in nineteenth century America*. Cornell University Press. https://doi.org/10.7591/cornell/9781501768927.001.0001

EcoJustice. (n.d.). *#GenClimateAction*. https://ecojustice.ca/genclimateaction/

The Economist. (2023a, August 24). Climate change: World on fire. *The Economist, 452*(9411), 67–69.

The Economist. (2023b, May 28). *A new wave of mass migration has begun: What does it mean for rich-world economies?* www.economist.com/finance-and-economics/2023/05/28/a-new-wave-of-mass-migration-has-begun

Edmonds, A. (1965, November 1). Death of a great lake. *Maclean's*. https://archive.macleans.ca/article/1965/11/1/death-of-a-great-lake

Edwards, K. (1998). A critique of the general approach to invasive plant species. In U. Starfinger (Ed.), *Plant invasions: Ecological mechanisms and human responses* (pp. 85–94). Backhuys.

Eisen, M., & Brown, P. (2022). Rapid global phaseout of animal agriculture has the potential to stabilize greenhouse gas levels for 30 years and offset 68 percent of CO_2 emissions this century. *PLoS Clim 1*(2), e0000010. https://doi.org/10.1371/journal.pclm.0000010

Elliott, E.G., Trinh, P., Ma, X., Leaderer, B.P., Ward, M.H., & Deziel, N.C. (2017). Unconventional oil and gas development and risk of childhood leukemia: Assessing the evidence. *Science of the Total Environment, 576*, 138–147. https://doi.org/10.1016/j.scitotenv.2016.10.072

Energy Resources Conservation Board. (2012). *Production and reserves.* https://www
.ercb.ca/learn-about-energy/energy-in-alberta/production-reserves

Engler, Y. (2014). Canadian diplomatic efforts to sell the tar sands. In J. Kahn,
T. Black, S. D'Arcy, & T. Weis (Eds.), *Line in the tar sands: Struggles for
environmental justice.* PM Press.

English, J. (2013). *Ice and water: Politics, peoples, and the arctic council.* Allen Lane.

Environics. (2019). *Public opinion on marine protected areas.* https://wwf.ca
/wp-content/uploads/2020/09/Public-Opinion-on-Marine-Protected-Areas
_Environics_May-2019.pdf

Environment and Climate Change Canada. (2013). *Water resources: Groundwater.*
https://www.canada.ca/en/environment-climate-change/services/water-overview
/sources/groundwater.html

Environment and Climate Change Canada. (2016, October 3). *Pan-Canadian
approach to pricing carbon pollution.* https://www.canada.ca/en/environment
-climate-change/news/2016/10/canadian-approach-pricing-carbon-pollution.html

Environment and Climate Change Canada. (2017). *Groundwater contamination.*
https://www.canada.ca/en/environment-climate-change/services/water-overview
/pollution-causes-effects/groundwater-contamination.html

Environment and Climate Change Canada. (2018). *Ocean plastics charter.*
https://www.canada.ca/en/environment-climate-change/services/managing
-reducing-waste/international-commitments/ocean-plastics-charter.html

Environment and Climate Change Canada. (2019). *Summary of Canada's 6th national
report to the convention on biological diversity.* https://
www.biodivcanada.ca/s/EN_Summary-of-Canadas-6th-National-Report
_Final_2_compressed.pdf

Environment and Climate Change Canada. (2020). *A healthy environment and a
healthy economy: Canada's strengthened climate plan to create jobs and support
people, communities and the planet.* https://doi.org/10.1163/9789004322714
_cclc_2020-0173-0861

Environment and Climate Change Canada. (2021a, April 23). *Canada's enhanced
nationally determined contribution.* https://www.canada.ca/en/environment
-climate-change/news/2021/04/canadas-enhanced-nationally-determined
-contribution.html

Environment and Climate Change Canada. (2021b). *Canada's zero plastic waste
agenda.* https://www.canada.ca/en/environment-climate-change/services
/managing-reducing-waste/reduce-plastic-waste/canada-action.html

Environment and Climate Change Canada. (2021c, July 12). *Zero plastic waste: The
need for action.* https://www.canada.ca/en/environment-climate-change/services
/managing-reducing-waste/reduce-plastic-waste/need-action.html

Environment and Climate Change Canada. (2021d, August 5). *Update to the pan-
Canadian approach to carbon pollution pricing 2023–2030.* https://www
.canada.ca/en/environment-climate-change/services/climate-change/pricing
-pollution-how-it-will-work/carbon-pollution-pricing-federal-benchmark
-information/federal-benchmark-2023-2030.html

Environment and Climate Change Canada. (2022a). *2020 Biodiversity goals & targets for Canada*. www.biodivcanada.ca/

Environment and Climate Change Canada. (2022b). *Canada-US Great Lakes water quality agreement*. https://www.canada.ca/en/environment-climate-change/services /great-lakes-protection/canada-united-states-water-quality-agreement.html

Environment and Climate Change Canada. (2023a). *Achieving a sustainable future: Federal sustainable development strategy 2022–2026*. https://publications.gc.ca /site/eng/9.908526/publication.html

Environment and Climate Change Canada. (2023b). *Greenhouse gas emissions*. https://www.canada.ca/en/environment-climate-change/services/environmental -indicators/greenhouse-gas-emissions.html

Environment and Climate Change Canada. (2024, July 30). *Canada's 2030 nature strategy: Halting and reversing biodiversity loss in Canada*. https://www.canada .ca/en/environment-climate-change/services/biodiversity/canada-2030-nature -strategy.html

Ewald, P. (1994). *Evolution of infectious disease*. Oxford University Press. https:// doi.org/10.1093/oso/9780195060584.001.0001

Exner-Pirot, H. (2013). What is the Arctic a case of? The Arctic as a regional environmental security complex and the implications for policy. *Polar Journal, 3*(1), 120–135. https://doi.org/10.1080/2154896X.2013.766006

Exner-Pirot, H. (2021). Climate change will drive Arctic development, but not in the way you thought. Macdonald-Laurier Institute. https://macdonaldlaurier.ca /climate-change-will-drive-arctic-development-not-way-thought-heather-exner -pirot-inside-policy/

Fairbairn, K.J. (1980). Alberta and oil. *Yearbook of the Association of Pacific Coast Geographers, 42*, 89–99. https://doi.org/10.1353/pcg.1980.0008

FAO (Food and Agricultural Organization). (2022). *State of the world fisheries and aquaculture 2022: Towards blue transformation*. https://www.fao.org/documents /card/en/c/cc0461en

FAO (Food and Agriculture Organization). (2023). *The state of food security and nutrition in the world 2023: Urbanization, agrifood systems transformations and healthy diets across the rural-urban continuum*. https://www.fao.org/documents /card/en?details=cc3017en

FAO-IPPC (Food and Agriculture Organization–International Plant Protection Convention). (2018). *The fall army worm: An emerging food security global threat*. https://www.ippc.int/en/news/fall-armyworm-an-emerging-food-security -global-threat

Fauna & Flora International. (2020). *An assessment of the risks and impacts of seabed mining on marine ecosystems*. https://www.fauna-flora.org

FDA (Food and Drug Administration), USDA (United States Department of Agriculture), and Homeland Security. (2015). *Food and agriculture sector-specific plan*. https://www.cisa.gov/sites/default/files/publications/nipp-ssp -food-ag-2015-508.pdf

Feltmate, B. (2016, March 31). Alberta adapts to a changing climate. Adaptation Leaders Round Table Forum. https://www.eralberta.ca/wp-content/uploads /2017/05/CCEMC-Alberta-Adapts-Final-March-31-2016.pdf

Ferreira, B. (2022, February 2). There are more than 9,000 undiscovered tree species on earth, study says. *VICE.* www.vice.com/en/article/88gmjp/there-are-more -than-9000-undiscovered-tree-species-on-earth-study-says

First Nations Educational Steering Committee. (2024). *1906–1910: The Bryce report.* www.fnesc.ca

Fisheries and Oceans Canada. (2017, April 7). *Reducing disease risks.* https://www.dfo -mpo.gc.ca/aquaculture/protect-protege/reduce-disease-reduire-maladie-eng.html

Fisheries and Oceans Canada. (2024a). *Canada's ocean noise strategy.* https://www .dfo-mpo.gc.ca/oceans/publications/noise-bruit/strategy-strategie/index-eng.html

Fisheries and Oceans Canada. (2024b). *The Government of Canada outlines the next steps for Canada's blue economy.* https://www.canada.ca/en/fisheries-oceans/news /2024/06/the-government-of-canada-outlines-the-next-steps-for-canadas-blue -economy.html

Fisheries and Oceans Canada. (2024c, June 19). *Responsible, realistic, and achievable: The Government of Canada announces transition from open net-pen salmon aquaculture in coastal British Columbia.* https://www.canada.ca/en/fisheries -oceans/news/2024/06/responsible-realistic-and-achievable-the-government -of-canada-announces-transition-from-open-net-pen-salmon-aquaculture-in -coastal-british-columbia.html

Flanagan, E., Frappé-Sénéclauze, T.-P., Horne, M., & Zimmerman, D. (2016). *Race to the front: Tracking pan-Canadian climate progress and where we go from here.* Pembina Institute. https://www.pembina.org/pub/race-to-front

FLOW. (2020, December 16). New IJC report strengthens case for great lakes climate change framework. *For Love of Water.* https://forloveofwater.org/new-ijc-report -strengthens-case-for-great-lakes-climate-change-framework

Foster, J. (1998). *Working for wildlife: The beginning of preservation in Canada.* University of Toronto Press. https://doi.org/10.3138/9781442683662

Francis, D. (1984). *Arctic chase: A history of whaling in Canada's North.* Breakwater Books.

Froschauer, K. (1999). *White gold: Hydroelectric power in Canada.* UBC Press.

Gaard, G. (2011). Ecofeminism revisited: Rejecting essentialism and re-placing species in a material feminist environmentalism. *Feminist Formations, 23*(2), 26–53.

Gautier, D.L., Bird, K., Charpentier, R.R., & Grantz, A. (2009). Assessment of undiscovered oil and gas in the Arctic. *Science, 324*(5931), 1175–1179.

Gersony, L. (2022, September 20). Lake Erie's failed algae strategy hurts poor communities the most. *Circle of Blue.* https://www.circleofblue.org/2022/world /lake-eries-failed-algae-strategy-hurts-poor-communities-the-most

Gilchrist, E. (2018, June 21). "It's appalling": Greens, NDP oppose federal environmental assessment bill. *The Narwhal.* https://thenarwhal.ca /its-appalling-greens-ndp-oppose-federal-environmental-assessment-bill

Gillis, R.P. (2006). Rivers of sawdust: The battle over industrial pollution in Canada, 1865–1903. In D.F. Duke (Ed.), *Canadian environmental history* (pp. 265–283). Canadian Scholars' Press.

Gismondi, M. (2020, May 2). The untold story of the Hudson's Bay Company. *Canadian Geographic*. www.canadiangeographic.ca/article/untold-story -hudsons-bay-company

Glasser, R. (2004, July). We are not immune: Influenza, SARS, and the collapse of public health. *Harper's Magazine*, 35–42.

Global Affairs Canada. (2022). *State of trade 2022: The benefits of free trade agreements*. www.international.gc.ca/transparency-transparence/state-trade -commerce-international/2022.aspx?lang=eng

Global Affairs Canada. (2023). *Canada's position on seabed mining in areas beyond national jurisdiction*. https://www.canada.ca/en/global-affairs/news/2023/07 /canadas-position-on-seabed-mining-in-areas-beyond-national-jurisdiction.html

Global Affairs Canada. (2024a). *About CUSMA*. https://www.international.gc.ca /trade-commerce/trade-agreements-accords-commerciaux/agr-acc/cusma -aceum/about-cusma-a-propos-aceum.aspx?lang=eng

Global Affairs Canada. (2024b, August 13). *Statement by Minister Ng on U.S. Department of Commerce fifth review of duties on Canadian softwood lumber*. https://www.canada.ca/en/global-affairs/news/2024/08/statement-by-minister-ng -on-us-department-of-commerce-fifth-review-of-duties-on-canadian-softwood -lumber.html

Global Footprint Network. (2021). *Ecological footprint standards*. www.footprintnetwork.org/our-work/ecological-footprint

Global Footprint Network. (2024a). *Earth overshoot day – #MoveTheDate*. www.overshootday.org/

Global Footprint Network. (2024b). *Country overshoot days 2024*. https://overshoot .footprintnetwork.org/newsroom/country-overshoot-days/

Global News. (2024, April 23). Stratospheric aerosol injection: Climate scientists divided over controversial technology. https://globalnews.ca/video/10445793 /stratospheric-aerosol-injection-climate-scientists-divided-over-controversial -technology

Goldsmith, J., McKindsey, C., Archambault, P., & Howland, K.L. (2019). Ecological risk assessment of predicted marine invasions in the Canadian Arctic. *PLoS One, 14*(2), e0211815. www.ncbi.nlm.nih.gov/pmc/articles/PMC6366784

Gordner, T. (2023). *Canada recognizes the right to a healthy environment (and other amendments to the Canadian Environmental Protection Act, 1999)*. https:// mcmillan.ca/insights/canada-recognizes-the-right-to-a-healthy-environment-and -other-amendments-to-the-canadian-environmental-protection-act-1999/

Gore, C., & Stoett, P. (Eds.). (2009). *Environmental challenges and opportunities: Local-global perspectives on Canadian issues*. Emond Montgomery.

Gottlieb, N. (2024, August 28). Blockades and protests green new pipeline project. *The Tyee*. https://thetyee.ca/News/2024/08/28/Blockades-Protests-Greet -New-Pipeline-Project

Goulson, D. (2021). *Silent earth: Averting the insect apocalypse*. Harper Publishing.

Government of Alberta. (2023). *Oil sands*. www.alberta.ca/oil-sands.aspx

Government of British Columbia. (2014). *Mount Polley mine tailings breach: Environmental mitigation and remediation progress report*. https://www2.gov .bc.ca/gov/content/environment/air-land-water/spills-environmental -emergencies/spill-incidents/past-spill-incidents/mt-polley

Government of British Columbia. (2019). *CleanBC: Our nature, our power, our future*. https://cleanbc.gov.bc.ca/

Government of British Columbia. (2022). *Water licensing and rights*. https://www2 .gov.bc.ca/gov/content/environment/air-land-water/water/water-licensing-rights

Government of Canada. (1990). *Canada's Green Plan: Canada's Green Plan for a healthy environment*. Minister of Supply and Services Canada.

Government of Canada. (2000). *Action plan 2000 on climate change*.

Government of Canada. (2022). *Canada's fish and seafood trade in 2021: Overview*. https://waves-vagues.dfo-mpo.gc.ca/library-bibliotheque/41079486.pdf

Government of Canada. (2024). *Clean electricity regulations*. https://www.canada.ca /en/services/environment/weather/climatechange/climate-plan/clean-electricity -regulation.html

Government of Canada and the Provinces of British Columbia, Quebec, Newfoundland and Labrador, and Nova Scotia. (2008). *Statement of Canadian practice with respect to the mitigation of seismic sound in the marine environment*. https://www.dfo-mpo.gc. ca/oceans/publications/seismic-sismique/index-eng .html

Gray, A., Brodschneider, R., Adjlane, N., Ballis, A., Brusbardis, V., Charrière, J.-D., Chlebo, R., Coffey, M.F., Cornelissen, B., da Costa, C.M., Csáki, T., Dahle, B., Danihlík, J., Dražić, M.M., Evans, G., Fedoriak, M., Forsythe, I., de Graaf, D., Gregorc, A., & Soroker, V. (2019). Loss rates of honey bee colonies during winter 2017/18 in 36 countries participating in the COLOSS survey, including effects of forage sources. *Journal of Apicultural Research*, *58*(4), 479–485. https://doi.org /10.1080/00218839.2019.1615661

Greaves, W. (2017). Environmental security, energy security, and the Arctic in the Obama presidency. In P.W. Lackenbauer, H. Nicol, & W. Greaves (Eds.), *One Arctic: The Arctic council and circumpolar governance* (pp. 101–125). Canadian Arctic Resources Committee and Centre for Foreign Policy and Federalism.

Greaves, W. (2020a). Cities and human security in a warming arctic. In L. Heininen & H. Exner-Pirot (Eds.), *Climate change and security: Searching for a paradigm shift* (pp. 61–89). Palgrave Macmillan. https://doi.org/10.1007/978-3-030 -20230-9_5

Greaves, W. (2020b). Indigenous Peoples. In G.H. Gjørv, M. Lanteigne, & H. Sam-Aggrey (Eds.), *Handbook on Arctic security* (pp. 363–376). Routledge.

Greaves, W. (2021). Climate change and security in Canada. *International Journal*, *76*(2), 183–203. https://doi.org/10.1177/00207020211019325

Greaves, W. (2023). When great power fails: Russia, Ukraine, and the New Arctic geopolitics. In M. Lynch & H. Coombs (Eds.), *Kingston consortium for international security conference proceedings, 2022* (pp. 95–108). US Army War College Press.

Greaves, W. (2024). Human security, climate change, and the role of the Canadian Armed Forces: British Columbia, 2021. *Canadian Military Journal, 24*(1), 11–18.

Greaves, W., & Lackenbauer, P.W. (Eds.). (2021). *Breaking through: Understanding sovereignty and security in the circumpolar Arctic.* University of Toronto Press. https://doi.org/10.3138/9781487531041

Greenbaum, A.J., & Wellington, A. (2010). *Environmental law and policy in the Canadian context.* Captus Press.

Greer, A. (2012). Commons and enclosure in the colonization of North America. *American Historical Review, 117*(2), 365–386. https://doi.org/10.1086/ahr.117.2.365

Grigorovich, I., Colautti, R.I., Mills, E.L., Holeck, K., Ballert, A.G., & MacIsaac, H.J. (2003). Ballast-mediated animal introductions in the Laurentian Great Lakes: Retrospective and prospective analyses. *Canadian Journal of Fisheries and Aquatic Sciences, 60,* 740–756. https://doi.org/10.1139/f03-053

Grove, J.V. (2019). *Savage ecology: War and geopolitics at the end of the world.* Duke University Press.

Gudynas, E. (2017). Value, growth, development: South American lessons for a new ecopolitics. *Capitalism Nature Socialism, 30*(2), 1–10. https://doi.org/10.1080/10455752.2017.1372502

Guimarães, R.P. (1991). *The ecopolitics of development in the third world: Politics and environment in Brazil.* L. Rienner Publishers.

Gunn, B.L., & Fitzgerald, O.E. (2021). *UNDRIP implementation report subtitle: Comparative approaches, Indigenous voices from CANZUS Report.* www.cigionline.org/publications/undrip-implementation-comparative-approaches-indigenous-voices-canzus/

Gutmann, A., & Thompson, D.F. (2009). *Why deliberative democracy?* Princeton University Press. https://doi.org/10.4135/9781412979337.n37

Haines, A., & Frumkin, H. (2021). *Planetary health: Safeguarding human health and the environment in the Anthropocene.* Cambridge University Press.

Hall, A.J., Alberts, G., & McIntosh, A. (2019). Royal Proclamation of 1763. *The Canadian Encyclopedia.* www.thecanadianencyclopedia.ca/en/article/royal-proclamation-of-1763

Hall, S. (2023, January 19). Blueberry River First Nation, province reach an agreement. *Energetic City.* https://energeticcity.ca/2023/01/18/blueberry-river-first-nation-province-reach-an-agreement/

Hallegraeff, G.M. (1993). A review of harmful algal blooms and their apparent global increase. *Phycologia, 32*(2), 79–99. https://doi.org/10.2216/i0031-8884-32-2-79.1

Halliday, W.D., Barclay, D., Barkley, A.N., Cook, E., Dawson, J., Hilliard, R.C., Hussey, N.E., Jones, J.M., Juanes, F., Marcoux, M., Niemi, A., Nudds, S., Pine, M.K., Richards, C., Scharffenberg, K., Westdal, K., & Insley, S.J. (2021). Underwater sound levels in the Canadian Arctic, 2014–2019. *Marine Pollution Bulletin, 168.* https://doi.org/10.1016/j.marpolbul.2021.112437

Halliday, W.D., Têtu, P.-L., Dawson, J., Insley, S.J., & Hilliard, R.C. (2018). Tourist vessel traffic in important whale areas in the western Canadian Arctic: Risks and

possible management solutions. *Marine Policy*. https://doi.org/10.1016/j
.marpol.2018.08.035

Hamilton, C., Bonneuil, C., & Gemenne, F. (Eds.). (2015). *The Anthropocene and the global environmental crisis: Rethinking modernity in a new epoch*. Routledge.

Hammond, L. (2006). Marketing wildlife: The Hudson's Bay Company and the Pacific Northwest, 1821–1849. In D.F. Duke (Ed.), *Canadian environmental history* (pp. 203–222). Canadian Scholars' Press.

Harada, M., Hanada, M., Miyakita, T., Fujino, T., Tsuruta, K., Fukuhara, A., Orui, T., Nakachi, S., Araki, C., Tajiri, M., & Nagano, I. (2005). Long-term study on the effects of mercury contamination on two indigenous communities in Canada (1975–2004). *Research on Environmental Disruption, 34*(4). https://caid.ca/HarRep2005.pdf

Hardin, G. (1968). The tragedy of the commons. *Science, 162*(3859), 1243–1248. https://doi.org/10.1126/science.162.3859.1243

Hardt, J.N. (2017). *Environmental security in the Anthropocene: Assessing theory and practice*. Routledge.

Harrington, J. (2017). China, global ecopolitics and Antarctic governance: Converging paths? *Journal of Chinese Political Science, 22*(1), 37–56. https://doi.org/10.1007/s11366-016-9430-2

Harris, P.G. (2016). *Global ethics and climate change*. University of Edinburgh Press.

Harrison, D. (2009). Modern enclosure: Salmon aquaculture and First Nations resistance in British Columbia. In L.E. Adkin (Ed.), *Environmental conflict and democracy in Canada* (pp. 51–68). UBC Press.

Harrison, K. (2007). The road not taken: Climate change policy in Canada and the United States. *Global Environmental Politics, 7*(4), 92–117. https://doi.org/10.1162/glep.2007.7.4.92

Harrison, K. (2010). The struggle of ideas and self-interest in Canadian climate policy. In K. Harrison & L. McIntosh Sundstrom (Eds.), *Global commons, domestic decisions: The comparative politics of climate change*. MIT Press. https://doi.org/10.7551/mitpress/9780262014267.003.0006

Harter, J.H. (2004). Environmental justice for whom? Class, new social movements, and the environment: A case study of Greenpeace Canada, 1971–2000. *Labour, 54*, 83–119. https://doi.org/10.2307/25149506

Harvester, L., & Blenkinsop, S. (2010). Environmental education and ecofeminist pedagogy: Bridging the environmental and the social. *Canadian Journal of Environmental Education, 15*, 120–134.

Haskell, D.G. (2022, June 6). An ocean of noise: How sonic pollution is hurting marine life [Audio Podcast episode]. *The Guardian*. https://www.theguardian.com/news/audio/2022/jun/06/an-ocean-of-noise-how-sonic-pollution-is-hurting-marine-life-podcast

Hayden, A. (2014). *When green growth is not enough: Climate change, ecological modernization, and sufficiency*. McGill-Queen's University Press. https://doi.org/10.1515/9780773596337

He, M., Ditto, J.C., Gardner, L., Machesky, J., Hass-Mitchell, T.N., Chen, C., Khare, P., Sahin, B., Fortner, J.D., Plata, D.L., Drollette, B.D., Hayden, K.L., Wentzell, J.J.B.,

Mittermeier, R.L., Leithead, A., Lee, P., Darlington, A., Wren, S.N., Zhang, J., & Gentner, D.R. (2024). Total organic carbon measurements reveal major gaps in petrochemical emissions reporting. *Science, 383*(6681), 426–432. https://doi.org/10.1126/science.adj6233

Hebert, P., Ratnasingham, S., Zakharov, E.V., Telfer, A.C., Levesque-Beaudin, V., Milton, M.A., Pedersen, S., Jannetta, P., & deWaard, J.R. (2022). Counting animal species with DNA barcodes: Canadian insects. *Philosophical Transactions of the Royal Society B, 371*(1702). https://doi.org/10.1098/rstb.2015.0333

Heleniak, T. (2014). Arctic populations and migration. In J.N. Larsen & G. Fondahl (Eds.), *Arctic human development report: Regional processes and global linkages* (pp. 53–104). Steffanson Arctic Institute.

Hengeveld, R. (1989). *Dynamics of biological invasions*. Chapman and Hall.

Hessing, M., Howlett, M., Summerville, T., & Books, D. (2007). *Canadian natural resource and environmental policy*. UBC Press. https://doi.org/10.59962/9780774851459

Hild, C.M., & Stordahl, V. (2004). Human health and well-being. In AHDR (Ed.), *Arctic human development report* (pp. 155–168). Steffanson Arctic Institute.

Hill, S. (2017). *The clay we are made of: Haudenosaunee land tenure on the Grand River*. University of Manitoba Press. https://doi.org/10.1515/9780887554575

Hird, M.J. (2021). *Canada's waste flows*. McGill-Queen's University Press. https://doi.org/10.1515/9780228006459

Hoekstra, A.J.A., & Isaac, T. (2018, January 8). Implementing UNDRIP in Canada: Challenges with Bill C-262. *Our Insights*. https://cassels.com/insights/implementing-undrip-in-canada-challenges-with-bill-c-262/

Horbulyk, T. (2006). Liquid gold: Water markets in Canada. In K.J. Bakker (Ed.), *Eau Canada: The future of Canada's water* (pp. 205–218). Vancouver: UBC Press.

Houde, N. (2007). The six faces of traditional ecological knowledge: Challenges and opportunities for Canadian co-management arrangements. *Ecology and Society, 12*(2). https://doi.org/10.5751/ES-02270-120234

Huddart-Kennedy, E., Beckley, T.M., McFarlane, B.L., & Nadeau, S. (2009). Rural-urban differences in environmental concern in Canada. *Rural Sociology, 74*(3), 309–329. https://doi.org/10.1526/003601109789037268.

Hughes, D. (2015). *A clear look at BC LNG: Energy security, environmental implications and economic potential*. Centre for Policy Alternatives. https://policyalternatives.ca/sites/default/files/uploads/publications/BC%20Office/2015/05/CCPA-BC-Clear-Look-LNG-final_0_0.pdf

Hughes, L. (2000). Biological consequences of global warming: Is the signal already apparent? *Trends in Ecology and Evolution, 15*, 56–61. https://doi.org/10.1016/S0169-5347(99)01764-4

Humphries, M. (2008). *North American oil sands: History of development, prospects for the future*. Congressional Research Service.

IEA (Internameiol Energy Agency). (2022). *Global EV outlook 2022*. https://www.iea.org/reports/global-ev-outlook-2022

IFAW (International Fund for Animal Welfare). (2021). *Explore: Ocean noise pollution.* https://www.ifaw.org/explore/animal-welfare/ocean-noise-pollution

IJC (International Joint Commission). (2017). *First triennial assessment of progress on Great Lakes water quality.* https://www.ijc.org/en/first-triennial-assessment -progress-great-lakes-water-quality-tap

IJC (International Joint Commission). (2020). *Second triennial assessment of progress on Great Lakes water quality.* https://www.ijc.org/en/second-triennial -assessment-progress-great-lakes-water-quality-tap.

Ilyniak, N. (2014). Mercury poisoning in Grassy Narrows: Environmental injustice, colonialism, and capitalist expansion in Canada. *McGill Sociological Review, 4,* 43–66. www.mcgill.ca/msr/files/msr/ilyniak_2014.pdf

Inamine, H., Ellner, S.P., Springer, J.P., & Agrawal, A.A. (2016, April 7). Linking the continental migratory cycle of the monarch butterfly to understand its population decline. *Oikos, 125*(8), 1081–1091. https://onlinelibrary.wiley.com/doi/10.1111 /oik.03196

Indigenous Services Canada. (2024). *Remaining long-term drinking water advisories.* https://www.sac-isc.gc.ca/eng/1614387410146/1614387435325

Innis, H. (1930). *The fur trade in Canada: An introduction to Canadian economic history.* University of Toronto Press.

Innis, H. (1940). *The cod fisheries: The history of an international economy.* Ryerson Press.

Innis, H.A. (1949). The bias of communication. *Canadian Journal of Economics and Political Science, 15*(4), 457–476. https://doi.org/10.2307/211556

Innis, H.A., & Innis, M.Q. (1986). *Empire and communications.* Dundurn Press.

Institute for Catastrophic Loss Reduction. (2019). *Fort McMurray wildfire: Learning from Canada's costliest disaster.* https://www.iclr.org/wp-content /uploads/2019/10/Fort-McMurray-Wildfires_Canadian-Copright.FINAL-2 _One-Page.pdf

Insurance Board of Canada. (2024, January 8). *Severe weather in 2023 cost over $3.1 billion in insured damage.* https://www.ibc.ca/news-insights/news/ severe-weather-in-2023-caused-over-3-1-billion-in-insured-damage

Intergovernmental Panel on Climate Change. (2014). *Climate change 2014: Mitigation of climate change.* https://www.ipcc.ch/site/assets/uploads/2018/02/ipcc _wg3_ar5_full.pdf

International Consultants for Education and Fairs. (2024, January 24). *Canada hosted more than 1 million international students in 2023.* ICEF Monitor – Market Intelligence for International Student Recruitment. https://monitor.icef.com /2024/01/canada-hosted-more-than-1-million-international-students-in-2023/

IPBES (Intergovernmental Science-Policy Platform on Biodiversity and Ecosystem Services). (2016). *The assessment report of the Intergovernmental Science-Policy Platform on Biodiversity and Ecosystem Services on pollinators, pollination and food production.* https://doi.org/10.5281/zenodo.3402856

IPBES (Intergovernmental Science-Policy Platform on Biodiversity and Ecosystem Services). (2019). *Summary for policymakers of the global assessment report on*

biodiversity and ecosystem services. Zenodo. https://doi.org/10.5281
/ZENODO.3553579

IPBES (Intergovernmental Science-Policy Platform on Biodiversity and Ecosystem
Services). (2020). *Workshop report on biodiversity and pandemics of the
Intergovernmental Platform on Biodiversity and Ecosystem Services*. https://doi
.org/10.5281/zenodo.4147318

IRENA (International Renewable Energy Agency). (2021). *World energy transitions
outlook: 1.5°C pathway*. Author.

IUCN (International Union for Conservation). (2022, February). *IUCN red list of
threatened species*. www.iucnredlist.org

IUCN (International Union for Conservation), FAO (Food and Agriculture
Organization), & UNEP (United Nations Environment Programme). (2023).
ECOLEX: Gateway to environmental law. www.ecolex.org/result/?q
=&xdate_min=&xdate_max=&leg_type_of_document=Constitution

Iverson, K., Bio, R.P., & Haney, A. (2007). *Updated ecosystem mapping for the South
Okanagan valley*. Government of British Columbia.

Iverson, L., Schwartz, M.W., & Prasad, A.M. (2004). How fast and far might tree
species migrate in the eastern U.S. due to climate change? *Global Ecology and
Biogeography, 13*, 209–219. https://doi.org/10.1111/j.1466-822X.2004.00093.x

Jang, B. (2019a, February 26). Wet'suwet'en chiefs remove hereditary titles of three
women who support Coastal GasLink pipeline. *Globe and Mail*. https://www
.theglobeandmail.com/business/article-wetsuweten-chiefs-remove-hereditary
-titles-of-three-women-who

Jang, B. (2019b, June 9). Indigenous supporters of Coastal GasLink say majority
of Wet'suwet'en members back project. *Globe and Mail*. https://www
.theglobeandmail.com/business/article-indigenous-supporters-of-coastal
-gaslink-say-majority-of-wetsuweten

Jang, M. (2021, September 2). Rights of nature and Indigenous Peoples: Navigating a
new course. *University of British Columbia*. https://allard.ubc.ca/about-us
/blog/2021/rights-nature-and-indigenous-peoples-navigating-new-course

Jarvis, B. (2018). The insect apocalypse is here. *New York Times, 41*. https://www
.nytimes.com/2018/11/27/magazine/insect-apocalypse.html

Jarvis, C. (2021). Cancer-causing air pollution forecast at 44 times annual level in
Ont. First Nation, docs show. *Global News*. https://globalnews.ca/news/8369470
/ontario-first-nation-air-pollution-cancer-causing-chemicals-new-data

Jerez, B., Garcés, I., & Torres, R. (2021). Lithium extractivism and water injustices
in the Salar de Atacama, Chile: The colonial shadow of green electromobility.
Political Geography, 87. https://doi.org/10.1016/j.polgeo.2021.102382

Jessen, S. (2011). A review of Canada's implementation of the *Oceans Act* since
1997 – From leader to follower? *Coastal Management, 39*(1), 20–56. https://doi
.org/10.1080/08920753.2011.544537

Johns, C. (2008). Introduction. In M. Sproule-Jones, C. Johns, & B.T. Heinmiller
(Eds.), *Canadian water politics: Conflicts and institutions* (pp. 3–15). McGill-
Queen's University Press. https://doi.org/10.1515/9780773575950-005

Johns, C. (2009). Water pollution in the Great Lakes Basin: The global-local dynamic. In C. Gore & P. Stoett (Eds.), *Environmental challenges and opportunities: Local-global perspectives on Canadian issues*. Emond Montgomery.

Johns, C., Sproule-Jones, M., & Heinmiller, B.T. (2008). Water as a multiple-use resource and source of political conflict. In M. Sproule-Jones, C. Johns, & B.T. Heinmiller (Eds.), *Canadian water politics: Conflicts and institutions* (pp. 19–55). McGill-Queen's University Press. https://doi.org/10.1515/9780773575950-006

JWN Energy. (2022, March 30). *A brief history of Canada's climate plans*. https://www.jwnenergy.com/article/2022/3/30/a-brief-history-of-canadas-climate-plans/

Kahn, J., Black, T., D'Arcy, S., & Weis, T. (2014). *Line in the tar sands: Struggles for environmental justice*. PM Press.

Kamieniecki, S. (2000). Testing alternative theories of agenda setting: Forest policy change in British Columbia, Canada. *Policy Studies Journal, 28*(1), 176–189.

Karunananthan, M., & Willows, J. (2012). Canada's violations of the human right to water. United Nations Human Rights. https://www.ohchr.org/sites/default/files/lib-docs/HRBodies/UPR/Documents/Session16/CA/CC_UPR_CAN_S16_2013_CouncilofCanadiansBluePlanetProject_E.pdf

Kassam, A. (2016, October 4). Arctic cruise boom poses conundrum for Canada's indigenous communities. *The Guardian*. https://www.theguardian.com/world/2016/oct/04/arctic-cruise-boom-canada-inuit-indigenous-communities

Katwala, A. (2022). COVID-19's origins are more complicated than once thought. *WIRED*. https://www.wired.com/story/tracing-covid-pandemic-origins/

Kaufman, S. (2007, July). We come to bury carbon, not to praise it. *Globe and Mail*. https://www.theglobeandmail.com/servlet/story/RTGAM.20070723.wwcomment23/BNStory/Front

Keil, K. (2014). The Arctic: A new region of conflict? The case of oil and gas. *Cooperation and Conflict, 49*(2), 162–190. https://doi.org/10.1177/0010836713482555

Kelm, M.E. (2016). Idle no more. In D.B. Belshaw (Ed.), *Canadian history: Post confederation*. BC Campus.

Kenny, T.A., Archambault, P., Ayotte, P., Batal, M., Chan, H.M., Cheung, W., Eddy, T.D., Little, M., Ota, Y., Pétrin-Desrosiers, C., Plante, S., Poitras, J., Polanco, F., Singh, G., & Lemire, M. (2020). Oceans and human health – Navigating changes on Canada's coasts. *FACETS, 5*(1), 1037–1070. https://doi.org/10.1139/facets-2020-0035

Keohane, R.O. (1989). *International institutions and state power: Essays in international relations theory*. Westview Press.

Kerber, J. (2021). Tracing one warm line: Climate stories and silences in Northwest passage tourism. *Journal of Canadian Studies, 56*(2), 271–303.

Keyszer, L. (2021, June 19). Degrowth with Lorenz Keyszer (No. 125) [Audio podcast episode]. *Real progressives*. https://realprogressives.org/podcast_episode/episode-125-degrowth-with-lorenz-keyszer

Kheraj, S. (2020). A history of oil spills on long-distance pipelines in Canada. *Canadian Historical Review, 101*(2), 161–191. https://doi.org/10.3138/chr.2019-0005

Kikkert, P. (2021). In search of polar sovereignty, 1900–1959. In W. Greaves & P.W. Lackenbauer (Eds.), *Breaking through: Understanding sovereignty and security in the circumpolar Arctic* (pp. 26–44). University of Toronto Press. https://doi.org/10.3138/9781487531041-002

Kimbrough, L. (2021, January 25). Death by 1000 cuts: Are major insect losses imperiling life on Earth? *Mongabay News.* https://news.mongabay.com/2021/01/death-by-1000-cuts-are-major-insect-losses-imperiling-life-on-earth

Kimmerer, R.W. (2013). *Braiding sweetgrass: Indigenous wisdom, scientific knowledge and the teachings of plants.* Milkweed Editions.

Koivurova, T., & Heinämäki, L. (2006). The participation of Indigenous Peoples in international norm-making in the Arctic. *Polar Record, 42*(2), 101–109. https://doi.org/10.1017/S0032247406005080

Kolar, C., & Lodge, D. (2000). Freshwater nonindigenous species: Interactions with other global changes. In H. Mooney & R. Hobbs (Eds.), *Invasive species in a changing world* (pp. 3–30). Island Press.

Kolbert, E. (2014). *The sixth extinction: An unnatural history.* Henry Holt.

Kolbert, E. (2021). *Under a white sky: The nature of the future.* Crown.

Krasner, S.D. (1982). Structural causes and regime consequences: Regimes as intervening variables. *International Organization, 36*(2). https://doi.org/10.1017/S0020818300018920

Krasner, S.D. (1991). *International regimes.* Cornell University Press.

Kraushaar-Friesen, N., & Busch, H. (2020). Of pipe dreams and fossil fools: Advancing Canadian fossil fuel hegemony through the Trans Mountain Pipeline. *Energy Research and Social Science, 69.* https://doi.org/10.1016/j.erss.2020.101695

Krogh, N.M. (2020). *The impact of marine debris on oceans, the environment, wildlife, and human health.* Nova.

Kuehls, T. (2003). The environment of sovereignty. In W. Magnusson & K. Shaw (Eds.), *A political space: Reading the global through Clayoquot Sound* (pp. 179–198). University of Minnesota Press.

Kukucha, C.J. (2021). Canada's trade agenda. In R.W. Murray & P. Gecelovsky (Eds.), *The Palgrave handbook of Canada in international affairs* (pp. 393–411). Springer International. https://doi.org/10.1007/978-3-030-67770-1_18

Kunzig, R. (1995). Twilight of the cod. *Discover, 16*(4). https://www.discovermagazine.com/planet-earth/twilight-of-the-cod

Laferrière, E., & Stoett, P. (1999). *International relations theory and ecological thought: Towards synthesis.* Routledge.

Lamalle, S., & Stoett, P. (2023). *Representations and rights of the environment.* Cambridge University Press. https://doi.org/10.1017/9781108769327

Lamb, W.F., Wiedmann, T., Pongratz, J., Andrew, R., Crippa, M., Olivier, J.G.J., Wiedenhofer, D., Mattioli, G., Khourdajie, A.A., House, J., Pachauri, S., Figueroa, M., Saheb, Y., Slade, R., Hubacek, K., Sun, L., Ribeiro, S.K., Khennas, S., de la Rue du Can, S., … Minx, J. (2021). A review of trends and drivers of greenhouse gas emissions by sector from 1990 to 2018. *Environmental Research Letters, 16*(7), 073005. https://doi.org/10.1088/1748-9326/abee4e

Larsen, J.N. (2014). Polar regions. In V.R. Barros, C. Field, D.J. Dokken, M.D. Mastrandrea, K.J. Mach, T.E. Bilir, M. Chatterjee, K.L. Ebi, Y.O. Estrada, R.C. Genova, B. Girma, E.S. Kissel, A.N. Levy, S. MacCracken, P.R. Mastrandrea, & L.L. White (Eds.), *Climate change 2014: Impacts, adaptation, and vulnerability: Part B: Regional aspects*. Cambridge University Press.

Lasserre, F.L. (2007). Drawers of water: Water diversions in Canada and beyond. In K. Bakker (Ed.), *Eau Canada: The future of Canada's water* (pp. 143–162). UBC Press.

Lasserre, F.L., & Faury, O. (2020). *Arctic shipping: Climate change, commercial traffic and port development*. Routledge. https://doi.org/10.4324/9781351037464

Law, S. (2024a, June 4). Grassy Narrows first nation files lawsuit against Ontario, federal governments over mercury contamination. *CBC News*. https://www.cbc .ca/news/canada/thunder-bay/grassy-narrows-first-nation-lawsuit-1.7223442

Law, S. (2024b, July 10). Grassy Narrows first nation appeals to international human rights commission over mercury contamination. *CBC News*. https://www.cbc.ca/news/canada/thunder-bay/grassy-narrows -first-nation-human-rights-commission-1.7258531

Leahy, S. (2019, August 6). Insect "apocalypse" in U.S. driven by 50x increase in toxic pesticides. *National Geographic*.

Leakey, R.E., & Lewin, R. (1996). *The sixth extinction: Patterns of life and the future of humankind*. Anchor Books.

Lebuhn, M., Hanreich, A., Klocke, M., Schlüter, A., Bauer, C., & Perez, C.M. (2018). Towards molecular biomarkers for biogas production from lignocellulose-rich substrates. *Anaerobe, 29*, 10–21.

Ledger, P.M., Girdland-Flink, L., & Forbes, V. (2019). New horizons at L'Anse aux Meadows. *PNAS, 116*(31), 15341–15343.

Lee, M. (2021, January 7). It's 2021: Time to get serious about BC's carbon emissions. Policy Note. https://www.policynote.ca/carbon-emissions

Leiss, W. (2001). *In the chamber of risks: Understanding risk controversies*. McGill-Queen's University Press. https://doi.org/10.1515/9780773569515

Leiss, W., & Tyshekno, M. (2002). Some aspects of the "new biotechnology" and its regulation in Canada. In D. VanNijnatten & R. Boardman (Eds.), *Canadian environmental policy: Context and cases* (pp. 321–343). Oxford University Press.

Leitão, R.P., Zuanon, J., Villéger, S., Williams, S.E., Baraloto, C., Fortunel, C., Mendonça, F.P., & Mouillot, D. (2016). Rare species contribute disproportionately to the functional structure of species assemblages. *Proceedings of the Royal Society B: Biological Sciences, 283*(1828). https://doi.org/10.1098 /rspb.2016.0084

Lenton, T.M., Rockstrom, J., Gaffney, O., Rahmstorf, S., Richardson, K., Steffen, W., & Schellnhuber, H.J. (2019, November 27). Climate tipping points – Too risky to bet against. *Nature*. https://www.nature.com/articles/d41586-019-03595-0

Le Prestre, P. (2017). *Global ecopolitics revisited: Towards a complex governance of global environmental problems*. Routledge. https://doi.org/10.4324/9781315563695

Le Prestre, P., & Stoett, P. (Eds.). (2006). *Continental ecopolitics: Canadian-American relations and environmental policy*. Ashgate.

Le Prestre, P., & Stoett, P. (2007). *Bilateral ecopolitics: Continuity and change in Canadian-American environmental relations.* Taylor and Francis.

Lester, S., & Leitner, K. (1991). *WorldTradeLaw.net.* www.worldtradelaw.net/document.php

Levy, A. (2021). After COVID: Global pandemics and Canada's biosecurity strategy. Centre for International Governance and Innovation, Reimagining a Canadian National Security Strategy No. 5. https://www.cigionline.org/publications/after-covid-global-pandemics-and-canadas-biosecurity-strategy

Levy, D.L., & Newell, P.J. (2002). Business strategy and international environmental governance: Toward a neo-Gramscian synthesis. *Global Environmental Politics, 2*(4), 84–101. https://doi.org/10.1162/152638002320980632

Levy, M.A. (2009). *The Canadian oil sands: Energy security vs. climate change.* Council on Foreign Relations Special Report No. 47.

Liboiron, M. (2021). *Pollution is colonialism.* Duke University Press.

Lindsey, R. (2022, April 19). *Climate change: Global sea level.* National Atmospheric and Oceanic Administration. www.climate.gov/news-features/understanding-climate/climate-change-global-sea-level

Litfin, K.T. (1994). *Ozone discourses: Science and politics in global environmental cooperation.* Columbia University Press.

Little, K. (2022). Iqaluit's water crisis highlights deeper issues with Arctic infrastructure. Arctic Institute. https://www.thearcticinstitute.org/iqaluits-water-crisis-highlights-deeper-issues-arctic-infrastructure

LNG Canada. (2023). *LNG Canada – Province of British Columbia.* www.lngcanada.ca/

Locke, J. (1996). The Nature of Private Property. In M.A. Cahn & R. O'Brien (Eds.), *Thinking about the environment: Readings on politics, property, and the physical world.* M.E. Sharpe.

Logan, A., Berman, S., Berman, B., & Prescott, S.L. (2020). Project Earthrise: Inspiring creativity, kindness and imagination in planetary health. *Challenges, 11*(2), 19. https://doi.org/10.3390/challe11020019

Louv, R. (2008). *Last child in the woods: Saving our children from nature-deficit disorder.* Algonquin Books of Chapel Hill.

Lovell, W.G. (1992). "Heavy shadows and black night": Disease and depopulation in colonial Spanish America. *Annals of the Association of American Geographers, 82*(3), 426–443.

Lui, E. (2018, June 27). Trudeau fast-tracks new water and energy laws in Bill C-69. Council of Canadians. https://canadians.org/analysis/trudeau-fast-tracks-new-water-and-energy-laws-bill-c-69/

Luke, T.W. (1997). *Ecocritique: Contesting the politics of nature, economy, and culture.* University of Minnesota Press.

Lunney, D., Munn, D., & Meikle, W. (2008). *Too close for comfort: Contentious issues in human-wildlife encounters.* Royal Zoological Society of New South Wales.

Mabee, H.S., & Hoberg, G. (2004). Protecting culturally significant areas through watershed planning in Clayoquot Sound. *The Forestry Chronicle, 80*(2), 229–240.

Mabee, H.S., & Hoberg, G. (2006). Equal partners? Assessing comanagement of forest resources in Clayoquot Sound. *Society and Natural Resources, 19*(10), 875–888.

Macdonald, D. (2013). *Business and environmental politics in Canada*. University of Toronto Press. https://doi.org/10.3138/9781442603257

MacDougall, P. (2018, June 27). EVs can do more than just drive, they can help the grid too. *Natural Resources Defense Council Expert*. https://www.nrdc.org/experts/pamela-macdougall/evs-can-do-more-just-drive-they-can-help-grid-too

MacDowell, L.S. (2012). *An environmental history of Canada*. UBC Press. https://doi.org/10.59962/9780774821032

MacFarlene, D. (2017). Fluid relations: Hydro developments, the international joint commission, and Canada-U.S. border waters. In P. Stoett & O. Temby (Eds.), *Towards continental environmental policy? North American transnational environmental networks and governance*. SUNY Press. https://doi.org/10.1515/9781438467597-017

MacGregor, S. (2001). Fury for the Sound: The women at Clayoquot. *Women & Environments International Magazine, 52*, 49.

Machalaba, C., Romanelli, C., & Stoett, P. (2017). Global environmental change and emerging infectious diseases: Macrolevel drivers and policy responses. In M. Bouzid (Ed.), *Examining the role of environmental change on emerging infectious diseases and pandemics* (pp. 24–67). IGI Global. https://doi.org/10.4018/978-1-5225-0553-2.ch002

Machalaba, C., Romanelli, C., Stoett, P., Baum, S., Bouley, T., Daszak, P., & Karesh, W. (2015). Climate change and health: Transcending silos to find solutions. *Annals of Global Health, 81*(3), 445–458. https://doi.org/10.1016/j.aogh.2015.08.002

Maclean's. (2017, March 10). Justin Trudeau's speech in Houston: Read a full transcript. https://macleans.ca/economy/justin-trudeaus-speech-in-houston-read-a-full-transcript

Makhijani, A., & Gurney, K. (1995). *Mending the ozone hole: Science, technology, and policy*. MIT Press.

Mann, C.C. (2009). *Before Columbus: The Americas of 1491*. Atheneum Books.

Marketline. (2023). Marketline industry profile: Travel & tourism in Canada. *Travel & Tourism Industry Profile*, 1–92.

Marsden, W. (2007). *Stupid to the last drop: How Alberta is bringing environmental Armageddon to Canada (and doesn't seem to care)*. Vintage.

Marshall, J. (2019). Tailings dam collapses in the Americas: Lessons learned? *Canadian Dimension, 53*(1), 16–19.

Marvier, M. (2012). The value of nature revisited. *Frontiers in Ecology and the Environment, 10*(5), 227. https://doi.org/10.1890/i1540-9295-10-5-227

Mason, C.W. (2008). The construction of Banff as a "natural" environment: Sporting festivals, tourism, and representations of Aboriginal peoples. *Journal of Sport History, 35*(2), 221–239.

Mason, C.W. (2015). The Banff Indian days tourism festivals. *Annals of Tourism Research, 53*, 77–95. https://doi.org/10.1016/j.annals.2015.04.008

Mason, C.W., Carr, A., Vandermale, E., Snow, B., & Philipp, L. (2022). Rethinking the role of Indigenous knowledge in sustainable mountain development and protected area management in Canada and Aotearoa/New Zealand. *Mountain Research and Development, 42*(4), A1–A9. https://doi.org/10.1659/mrd.2022.00016

Mathews, D. (2020). *Trees in trouble: Wildfires, infestations, and climate change*. Counterpoint.

Matthews, L.P., & Parks, S.E. (2021). An overview of North Atlantic right whale acoustic behavior, hearing capabilities, and responses to sound. *Marine Pollution Bulletin, 173*. https://doi.org/10.1016/j.marpolbul.2021.113043

McAllister, M.L. (2016). Sustaining twenty-first-century Canadian communities in an era of complexity. In D. VanNijnatten (Ed.), *Canadian environmental policy and politics: The challenges of austerity and ambivalence* (pp. 146–161). Oxford University Press.

McBride, B. (2019, January 8). Most first nations in Northern B.C. support LNG pipeline, grqup says. *Kelowna Capital News*. https://www.kelownacapnews.com /news/most-first-nations-in-northern-b-c-support-lng-pipeline-group-says

McDiarmid, J. (2022, February 16). Environmental groups ask federal fisheries minister to intervene in Bradford bypass. *National Observer*. www.national observer.com/2022/02/16/news/environmental-groups-ask-federal-fisheries -minister-intervene-bradford-bypass

McDorman, T.L., & Chircop, A. (2012). Canada's oceans policy framework: An overview. *Coastal Management, 40*(2), 133–144. https://doi.org/10.1080/0892075 3.2012.652517

McGee, T.K. (2019). Preparedness and experiences of evacuees from the 2016 Fort McMurray Horse River wildfire. *Fire, 2*(1), 13. https://doi.org/10.3390 /FIRE2010013

McGregor, D., & Sritharan, M. (2023). Decolonising the dialogue on climate change: Indigenous knowledges, legal orders and ethics. In S. Lamalle & P. Stoett, *Representations and rights of the environment* (pp. 66–86). Cambridge University Press.

McKain, K., Down, A., Raciti, S.M., Budney, J., Hutyra, L.R., Floerchinger, C., Herndon, S.C., Nehrkorn, T., Zahniser, M.S., Jackson, R.B., Phillips, N., & Wofsy, S.C. (2015). Methane emissions from natural gas infrastructure and use in the urban region of Boston, Massachusetts. *Proceedings of the National Academy of Sciences of the United States of America, 112*(7), 1941–1946.

McKenzie, J. (2002). *Environmental politics in Canada: Managing the commons into the twenty-first century*. Oxford University Press.

McMichael, A., & Bouma, M. (2000). Global changes, invasive species, and human health. In H. Mooney & R. Hobbs (Eds.), *Invasive species in a changing world* (pp. 191–210). Island Press.

McMillan, L.J., & Prosper, K. (2016). Remobilizing *netukulimk*: Indigenous cultural and spiritual connections with resource stewardship and fisheries management in Atlantic Canada. *Reviews in Fish Biology and Fisheries, 26*, 629–647.

McNamee, K.A. (1909). *National parks of Canada*. Key Porter Books.

McNeely, J., Mooney, H.A., Neville, L.E., Schei, P.J., & Waage, J.K. (Eds.). (2001). *Global strategy on invasive species*. IUCN.

Meadows, D.H., Randers, J., & Meadows, D.L. (2005). *Limits to growth: The 30-year update*. Earthscan.

Meadows, D.H., Meadows, D.L., Randers, J., & Behrens III, W. (1972). *Limits to growth: Report of the Club of Rome*. Potomac Associates.

Meakin, S., & Kurvits, T. (2009). *Assessing the impacts of climate change on food security in the Canadian Arctic*. GRID-Arendal.

Meijer, E. (2019). *When animals speak: Toward an interspecies democracy. Animals in context*. New York University Press.

Merchant, N.D. (2019). Underwater noise abatement: Economic factors and policy options. *Environmental Science and Policy, 92*, 116–123. https://doi.org/10.1016/j.envsci.2018.11.014

Mezdour, A., Veronis, L., & McLeman, R. (2016). Environmental influences on Haitian migration to Canada and connections to social inequality: Evidence from Ottawa-Gatineau and Montreal. In R. McLeman, J. Schade, & T. Faist (Eds.), *Environmental migration and social inequality* (pp. 103–115). Springer International. https://doi.org/10.1007/978-3-319-25796-9_7

Miller, R.J. (2019). The Doctrine of Discovery: The international law of colonialism. *Indigenous Peoples' Journal of Law, Culture & Resistance, 5*(1). https://doi.org/10.5070/p651043048

Milman, O. (2022). *The insect crisis: The fall of the tiny empires that run the world*. W.W. Norton and Company.

Milstein, T. (2016). The performer metaphor: Mother Nature never gives us the same show twice. *Environmental Communication, 10*(2), 227–248. https://doi.org/10.1080/17524032.2015.1018295

Mitchell, T. (2011). *Carbon democracy: Political power in the age of oil*. Verso.

Molina, M.J., & Rowland, F.S. (1974). Stratospheric sink for chlorofluoromethanes: Chlorine atom-catalysed destruction of ozone. *Nature, 249*(5460), 810–812. https://doi.org/10.1038/249810a0

Montgomery, M. (2015, September 16). *History: September 15, 1971, the Canadian origins of Greenpeace*. Radio Canada International.

Moore, N. (2015). *The changing nature of eco/feminism: Telling stories from Clayoquot Sound*. UBC Press.

Muldoon, P., Lucas, A., Gibson, R., & Pickfield, P. (2009). *An introduction to environmental law and policy in Canada*. Emond Montgomery.

Mulligan, S. (2000). Biosafety, risk, and the global knowledge structure. *Peace Review, 14*(4), 571–577.

Murray, R.W., & Gecelovsky, P. (Eds.). (2021). *The Palgrave handbook of Canada in international affairs*. Springer International. https://doi.org/10.1007/978-3-030-67770-1

Myers, R.A., Hutchings, J.A., & Barrowman, N.J. (1997). Why do fish stocks collapse? The example of cod in Atlantic Canada. *Ecological Applications, 7*(1), 91–106.

Myers, R.A., & Worm, B. (2003). Rapid worldwide depletion of predatory fish communities. *Nature, 423*(6937), 280–283.

Naess, A. (2005). The shallow and the deep, long-range ecology movement: A summary. In A. Drengson (Ed.), *The selected works of Arne Naess* (pp. 2263–2269). Springer. https://doi.org/10.1007/978-1-4020-4519-6_85

National Energy Policy Group. (2001). *National energy policy: Reliable, affordable and environmentally-sound energy for America's future.* US Government Printing Office.

National Ocean and Atmospheric Administration. (2024, July). *Global climate report.* https://www.ncei.noaa.gov/access/monitoring/monthly-report /global/202407

National Research Council of Canada. (1999). *Canadian marine fisheries in a changing and uncertain world.* A report prepared for the Canadian Global Change Program of the Royal Society of Canada.

Natural Assets Initiative. (2023). *About NAI/our story.* https://mnai.ca/our-story/

Natural Resources Canada. (2013, October 25). *Mountain pine beetle.* https:// natural-resources.canada.ca/our-natural-resources/forests/insects-disturbances /top-forest-insects-and-diseases-canada/mountain-pine-beetle/13381

Neave, D.J., & Branch, C.F.S. (2002). *Canada's forest biodiversity: A decade of progress in sustainable management.* Natural Resources Canada.

Nellemann, C., Corcoran, E., Duarte, C.M., Valdes, L., DeYoung, C., Fonseca, L., & Grimsditch, G. (2009). *Blue carbon: The role of healthy oceans in binding carbon: A rapid response assessment.* UNEP.

Nienke, C., van Geel, F., Risch, D., & Wittich, A. (2022). A brief overview of current approaches for underwater sound analysis and reporting. *Marine Pollution Bulletin, 178.* Article 113610.

Nikiforuk, A. (2010). *Tar sands: Dirty oil and the future of a continent.* Greystone.

Nikiforuk, A. (2022, January 25). Are electric cars the solution? *The Tyee.* https:// thetyee.ca/Analysis/2022/01/25/Are-Electric-Cars-Solution

Nordman, E. (2021). *The uncommon knowledge of Elinor Ostrom: Essential lessons for collective action.* Island Press.

Nossal, K.R., Roussel, S., & Paquin, S. (2015). *The politics of Canadian foreign policy* (4th ed.). McGill-Queen's University Press.

Nowlan, L. (2007). Out of sight, out of mind? Taking Canada's groundwater for granted. In K. Bakker (Ed.), *Eau Canada: The future of Canada's water* (pp. 55–83). UBC Press.

NRG Research Group. (2019). *What we heard: Summary of public consultations on the proposed national park reserve in the South Okanagan-Similkameen.* https:// letstalksouthokanagansimilkameen.ca/7496/widgets/28644/documents/16201

OCCP (Okanagan Collaborative Conservation Program) and SOSCP (South Okanagan Similkameen Conservation Program). (2014). *Keeping nature in our future: A biodiversity conservation strategy for the Okanagan region.* http:// a100.gov.bc.ca/pub/acat/public/viewReport.do?reportId=42389

Office of the Auditor General of Canada. (2022). *Report 1 – Just transition to a low-carbon economy.* https://www.oag-bvg.gc.ca/internet/English/parl_cesd _202204_01_e_44021.html

Office of the Auditor General of Canada. (2023). *Report 6 – Canadian Net-Zero Emissions Accountability Act – 2030 emissions reduction plan.* https://www.oag -bvg.gc.ca/internet/English/parl_cesd_202311_06_e_44369.html

Office of the Commissioner of the Environment and Sustainable Development (2021, November 25). *Report 5 – Lessons learned from Canada's record on climate change.* https://www.oag-bvg.gc.ca/internet/English/parl_cesd _202111_05_e_43898.html

Old Growth Review Panel. (2020). *A new future for old forests: A strategic review of how British Columbia manages for old forests within its ancient ecosystems.* https:// www2.gov.bc.ca/assets/gov/farming-natural-resources-and-industry /forestry/stewardship/old-growth-forests/strategic-review-20200430.pdf

O'Lear, S., & Dalby, S. (Eds.). (2016). *Reframing climate change: Constructing ecological geopolitics.* Routledge.

Olive, A. (2014). *Land, stewardship, and legitimacy: Endangered species policy in Canada and the United States.* University of Toronto Press.

Olive, A. (2016). *The Canadian environment in political context.* University of Toronto Press.

Olive, A. (2019). *The Canadian environment in political context* (2nd ed.). University of Toronto Press.

Olszynski, M.Z.P. (2015). From "badly wrong" to worse: An empirical analysis of Canada's new approach to fish habitat protection laws. *Journal of Environmental Law & Practice, 28*(1).

Ommer, R.E., & Sinclair, P. (1999). Systemic crisis in rural newfoundland: Can the outports survive? In J.T. Pierce & A. Dale (Eds.), *Communities, development, and sustainability across Canada.* UBC Press.

O'Neill, D.W., Fanning, A.L., Lamb, W.F., & Steinberger, J.K. (2018). A good life for all within planetary boundaries. *Nature Sustainability, 1,* 88–95.

Ontario Ministry of Agriculture, Food and Agribusiness and Ministry of Rural Affairs. (2015, September 9). *Neonicotinoid regulations for growers.* http://omafra .gov.on.ca/english/crops/field/news/croptalk/2015/ct-0915a2.htm

Ortiz, J., & Jackson, R. (2022). Understanding Eunice Foote's 1856 experiments: Heat absorption by atmospheric gases. *Notes and Records, 76*(1), 67–84. https:// doi.org/10.1098/rsnr.2020.0031.

Osmundesen, T., & Olsen, M.S. (2017). The imperishable controversy over aquaculture. *Marine Policy, 76,* 136–142.

Ostrom, E. (1990). *Governing the commons: The evolution of institutions for collective action.* Cambridge University Press.

Ostry, A., Ogborn, M., Bassil, K.L., Takaro, T.K., & Allen, D.M. (2010). Climate change and health in British Columbia: Projected impacts and a proposed agenda for adaptation research and policy. *International Journal of Environmental Research and Public Health, 7*(3), 1018–1035.

Paehlke, R. (2000). Environmentalism in one country: Canadian environmental policy in an era of globalization. *Policy Studies Journal, 28*(1), 160–175. https:// doi.org/10.1111/j.1541-0072.2000.tb02021.x

Page, R., Bayley, S., Cook, J.D., Green, J.E., & Ritchie, J.R.B. (1996). *Banff-Bow Valley: At the crossroads. Summary report of the Banff-Bow Valley task force.* Minister of Canadian Heritage.

Palma, D., Varnajot, A., Dalen, K., Basaran, I.K., Brunette, C., Bystrowska, M., Korablina, A.D., Nowiciki, R.C., & Ronge, T.A. (2019). Cruising the marginal ice zone: Climate change and Arctic tourism. *Polar Geography, 42*(4), 215–235. https://doi.org/10.1080/1088937X.2019.1648585

Palmer, C., McShane, K., & Sandler, R. (2014). Environmental ethics. *Annual Review of Environment and Resources, 39*, 419–442.

Paquin, S. (2021). The role of Canada's provinces in Canadian foreign policy: Multilevel governance in the making. In R.W. Murray & P. Gecelovsky (Eds.), *The Palgrave handbook of Canada in international affairs* (pp. 141–157). Springer International. https://doi.org/10.1007/978-3-030-67770-1_7

Paris, M. (2012, May 29). *Fisheries Act* changes questioned by former ministers. *CBC News.* https://www.cbc.ca/news/politics/fisheries-act-changes-questioned -by-former-ministers-1.1208106

Parks Canada. (2019). *Proposed national park reserve in the South Okanagan-Similkameen – National parks.* https://www.pc.gc.ca/en/pn-np/cnpn-cnnp /okanagan

Parrique, T. (2022, April 7). *Degrowth in the IPCC AR6 WGIII.* https:// timotheeparrique.com/degrowth-in-the-ipcc-ar6-wgiii

Pashkevich, A., Dawson, J., & Stewart, E.J. (2015). Governance of expedition cruise ship tourism in the Arctic: A comparison of the Canadian and Russian Arctic. *Tourism in Marine Environments, 10*(3–4), 225–240. https://doi.org/10.3727 /154427315X14181438892883

Paterson, M. (2001). *Understanding global environmental politics: Domination, accumulation, resistance.* Palgrave.

Patomaki, H., & Steger, M.B. (2010). Social imaginaries and big history: Towards a new planetary consciousness? *Futures, 42*(10), 1056–1063. https://doi.org /10.1016/j.futures.2010.05.007

Patterson, B. (2016, December 19). Economist links site C dam to NAFTA and bulk water exports. Council of Canadians. https://canadians.org/analysis/economist -links-site-c-dam-nafta-and-bulk-water-exports

Pawson, C. (2023, August 29). 30 years after Clayoquot sound protests, old-growth logging continues unabated: B.C. conservation group. *CBC News.* https:// www.cbc.ca/news/canada/british-columbia/old-growth-logging-vancouver -island-clayoquot-sound-1.6951105

Payne, B. (2005). Fishing the North Atlantic border seas: American capital in a new environment, 1818–1854. *Acadiensis, 35*(1), 113–131.

Pearce, F. (2015, August 17). *Global extinction rates: Why do estimates vary so wildly?* Yale School of Environment. https://e360.yale.edu/features/global_extinction _rates_why_do_estimates_vary_so_wildly

Peloso, C. (2010). Crafting an international climate change protocol: Applying the lessons learned from the success of the Montreal Protocol and the ozone depletion problem. *Journal of Land Use & Environmental Law, 25*(2), 305–330.

Petit, R. (2004). Biological invasions at the gene level. *Diversity and Distributions, 10*, 159–165.

Phelps, J., Biggs, D., & Webb, E. (2016). Tools and terms for understanding illegal wildlife trade. *Frontiers in Ecology and the Environment, 186*(1), 479–489.

Pinchin, K. (2023). *Kings of their own ocean: Tuna, obsession, and the future of our seas.* Penguin Random House.

Pinder, M. (2021, July 30). *Yahey v British Columbia, 2021 BCSC 1287 (CanLII) – case summary.* Mandell Pinder LLP. www.mandellpinder.com/yahey-v-british -columbia-2021-bcsc-1287-canlii-case-summary/

Piper, L. (2011). Nutritional science, health, and changing Northern environments. In N. Klopfer & C. Mauch (Eds.), *Big country, big issues: Canada's environment, culture, and history* (Vol. 4, pp. 60–85). RCC Perspectives.

Pirages, D. (1978). *Global ecopolitics: The new context for international relations.* Duxbury.

Plumwood, V. (2003). *Feminism and the mastery of nature.* Routledge.

Pollon, Christopher. (2018, October 3). Blueberry River and the death by a thousand cuts. *The Narwhal.* https://thenarwhal.ca/blueberry-river-death-by-thousand-cuts/

Porter, J. (2017). Children of the poisoned river. *CBC News.* https://www.cbc.ca /news2/interactives/children-of-the-poisoned-river-mercury-poisoning-grassy -narrows-first-nation/

Pörtner, H.O., Scholes, R.J., Agard, J., Archer, E., Arneth, A., Bai, X., Barnes, D., Burrows, M., Chan, L., Cheung, W.L., Diamond, S., Donatti, C., Duarte, C., Eisenhauer, F., Foden, W., Gasalla, M.A., Handa, C., Hickler, T., Hoegh-Guldberg, O., & Ngo, H.T. (2021). *Scientific outcome of the IPBES-IPCC co-sponsored workshop on biodiversity and climate change.* IPBES Secretariat. https:// doi.org/10.5281/ZENODO.5101125

Pörtner, H.O., et al. (Eds.). (2022). *Climate change 2022: Impacts, adaptation, and vulnerability: Working group II contribution to the sixth assessment report of the Intergovernmental Panel on Climate Change.* Cambridge University Press.

Price-Smith, A. (2002). *The health of nations: Infectious disease, environmental change, and their effects on national security and development.* MIT Press.

Princen, T., Maniates, M., & Conca, K. (2002). *Confronting consumption.* MIT Press.

Quinn, G. (2018, March 14). Canada now has just four big towns that rely on forestry. *Bloomberg.* https://www.bloomberg.com/news/articles/2018-03-14 /canada-now-has-just-four-big-towns-that-rely-on-forestry-chart

Rabe, B. (2022). The politics of short-lived climate pollutants and North American methane policy. Ford School. https://fordschool.umich.edu/sites/default/files /2022-04/NACP_Rabe_final.pdf

Rabe, B. (2023, January 6). Methane comes front and center in climate change policy. Brookings Institution. https://www.brookings.edu/articles/methane-comes -front-and-center-in-climate-change-policy/

Rabone, M., Wiethase, J.H., Simon-Lledó, E., Emery, A.M., Jones, D.O.B., Dahlgren, T.G., Bribiesca-Contreras, G., Wiklund, H., Horton, T., & Glover, A.G. (2023). How many metazoan species live in the world's largest mineral exploration region? *Current Biology, 33*(12), 2382–2396.

Ragan, C. (2024). An open letter from economists on Canadian carbon pricing. *Canada's Ecofiscal Commission.* https://ecofiscal.ca/2024/03/26/open-letter-carbon-pricing

Rantanen, M., Karpechko, A.Y., Lipponen, A., Nordling, K., Hyvarinen, O., Ruosteenoja, K., Vihma, T., & Laaksonen, A. (2022). The Arctic has warmed nearly four times faster than the globe since 1979. *Communication Earth & Environment, 3*, article 168.

Raworth, K. (2012). *A safe and just space for humanity: Can we live within the doughnut?* (Oxfam Discussion Paper). Oxfam.

Rees, W.E. (2002). Globalization and sustainability: Conflict or convergence? *Bulletin of Science, Technology & Society, 22*(4), 249–268. https://doi.org/10.1177/0270467 602022004001.

Reference re Impact Assessment Act. (2023). 2023 SCC 23. https://decisions.scc-csc.ca /scc-csc/scc-csc/en/item/20102/index.do

References re Greenhouse Gas Pollution Pricing Act. (2021). 2021 SCC 11. https:// decisions.scc-csc.ca/scc-csc/scc-csc/en/item/18781/index.do

Remedios, S., & Ardanaz, J. (2021). Rights for rivers: Quebec river granted rights and legal personhood by Indigenous community and local municipality. *Canadian Bar Association, British Columbia Branch.* https://www.cbabc.org/Sections-and -Community/Business-Law/Business-Law-Quarterly/Q1-2021-Changing-Winds /Rights-for-Rivers

Ren, C., James, L., Pashkevich, A., & Hoarau-Heemstra, H. (2021). Cruise trouble: A practice-based approach to studying Arctic cruise tourism. *Tourism Management Perspectives, 40,* 100901. https://doi.org/10.1016/j.tmp.2021.100901

Responsible Plastic Use Coalition v. Canada (Environment and Climate Change). (2023). 2023 FC 1511.

Rezun, M. (1996). *Science, technology, and ecopolitics in the USSR.* Praeger.

Richmond, C.A.M., & Ross, N.A. (2009). The determinants of First Nation and Inuit health: A critical population health approach. *Health and Place, 15*(2), 403–411. https://doi.org/10.1016/j.healthplace.2008.07.004

Ricketts, P.J., & Harrison, P. (2007). Coastal and ocean management in Canada: Moving into the 21st century. *Coastal Zone Management Journal, 35*(1), 5–22.

Riddell-Dixon, E. (2017). *Breaking the ice: Canada, sovereignty, and the Arctic extended continental shelf.* Dundurn Press.

Rights of Rivers. (2020). *Rights of rivers: A global survey of the rapidly developing rights of nature jurisprudence pertaining to rivers.* https://www.internationalrivers. org/wp-content/uploads/sites/86/2020/09/Right-of-Rivers-Report-V3-Digital -compressed.pdf

Ritchie, H., & Roser, M. (2019). Land use. https://ourworldindata.org/land-use

Roberts, J. (2020). Political ecology. In F. Stein (Ed.), *The open encyclopedia of anthropology.* Cambridge University Press. http://doi.org/10.29164/20polieco

Roberts, M. (2019). Will action on short-lived climate forcers give the Arctic time to adapt? In E.B.W. Zubrow, E. Meidinger, & K.D. Connolly (Eds.), *The big thaw: Policy, governance, and climate change in the circumpolar north* (pp. 25–45). SUNY Press.

Robinson, J.M. , Aronson, J., Daniels, C.B., Goodwin, N., Liddicoat, C., Orlando, L., Phillips, D., Stanhope, J., Weinstein, P., Cross, A.T., & Breed, M.F. (2022). Ecosystem restoration is integral to humanity's recovery from COVID-19.

The Lancet Planetary Health, 6(9), E769–E773. https://doi.org/10.1016/S2542-5196(22)00171-1

Robinson, P.J. (2009). Urban sustainability in Canada: The global-local connection. In C.D. Gore & P. Stoett (Eds.), *Environmental challenges and opportunities: Local-global perspectives on Canadian issues.* Emond Montgomery.

Robock, A., & Toon, O.B. (2010). Local nuclear war, global suffering. *Scientific American, 302*(1), 74–81.

Rockström, J., Steffen, W., Noone, K., Persson, Å., Chapin III, F.S., Lambin, E., Lenton, T.M., Scheffer, M., Folke, C., Schellnhuber, H.J., Nykvist, B., de Wit, C.A., Hughes, T., van der Leeuw, S., Rodhe, H., Sörlin, S., Snyder, P.K., Costanza, R., Svedin, U., … Falkenmark, M. (2009). Planetary boundaries: Exploring the safe operating space for humanity. *Ecology and Society, 14*(2), 32.

Rogers, R.A. (1997). The aftermath of collapse: Ethical aspects in the regulatory failure of Canada's east coast fishery. In A. Wellington, A. Greenbaum, & W. Cragg (Eds.), *Canadian issues in environmental ethics.* Broadview Press.

Romanello, M. (2021). The 2021 report of the *Lancet* Countdown on health and climate change: Code red for a healthy future. *The Lancet, 398*(10311), 1619–1662.

Rothwell, D., & VanderZwaag, D.L. (2006). *Towards principled oceans governance: Australian and Canadian approaches and challenges.* Routledge. https://doi.org/10.4324/9780203967935

Roussopoulos, D. (2017). *The rise of cities.* Black Rose Books.

Roy, H.E., Pauchard, A., Stoett, P., Renard Truong, T., Bacher, S., Galil, B.S., Hulme, P.E., Ikeda, T., Sankaran, K.V., McGeoch, M.A., Meyerson, L.A., Nuñez, M.A., Ordonez, A., Rahlao, S.J., Schwindt, E., Seebens, H., Sheppard, A.W., and Vandvik, V. (Eds.). (2023). IPBES invasive alien species assessment: Summary for policymakers. https://doi.org/10.5281/zenodo.7430692

Royer, M.-J.S. (2016). *Climate, environment and Cree observations.* Springer.

Ryser, R. (2012). *Indigenous nations and modern states: The political emergence of nations challenging state power.* Routledge.

Sala, O., Meyerson, L., & Parmesan, C. (Eds.). (2009). *Biodiversity change and human health: From ecosystem services to spread of disease.* Island Press.

Saldanha, J., Haworth, J., & McKenna, C. (2020). *The Hudsons' Bay Company: Royal charters, rivalries and luxury hats in the North American fur trade.* Oxford Centre for Global History. https://globalcapitalism.history.ox.ac.uk/files/case10-thehudsonsbaycompanypdf

Sánchez-Bayo, F., & Wyckhuys, K.A.G. (2019). Worldwide decline of the entomofauna: A review of its drivers. *Biological Conservation, 232*, 8–27.

Sanders, J., & Stoett, P. (2006). Fighting extinction and invasion: Transborder conservation efforts. In P. LePrestre & P. Stoett (Eds.), *Continental ecopolitics: Canadian-American relations and environmental policy* (pp. 157–178). Ashgate.

Sandwell, R.W. (2016). *Powering up Canada: A history of power, fuel, and energy from 1600.* McGill-Queen's University Press.

Santese, A. (2020). Between pacifism and environmentalism: The history of Greenpeace. *USAbroad – Journal of American History and Politics, 3*(1S), 107–115. https://doi.org/10.6092/issn.2611-2752/11648

Sarfraz, A.M. (2023, December 5). NDP tables motion to create a climate-fighting youth corps. *Canada's National Observer*. https://www.nationalobserver.com/2023/12/05/news/ndp-tables-motion-create-climate-fighting-youth-corps

Saunders, J.O., & Wenig, M. (2007). Whose water? Canadian water management and the challenges of jurisdictional fragmentation. In K. Bakker (Ed.), *Eau Canada: The future of Canada's water* (pp. 119–141). UBC Press.

Saurin, J. (2001). Global capitalism as the "disaster triumphant": The private capture of public goods. *Global Environmental Politics, 10*(4).

Schindler, D. (2007). Foreword. In K. Bakker (Ed.), *Eau Canada: The future of Canada's water* (pp. xi–xiv). UBC Press.

Schmidt, C. (2023, Spring). Climate anxiety. *Harvard Medicine*. https://magazine.hms.harvard.edu/articles/climate-anxiety

Schrank, W. (1995). Extended fisheries jurisdiction: Origins of the current crisis in Atlantic Canada's fisheries. *Marine Policy, 19*(4), 285–299.

Schrijver, N., & Weiss, F. (Eds.). (2004). *International law and sustainable development: Principles and practice*. Martinus Nijhoff.

Schulte, P. (2012). The Great Lakes water agreements. In P.H. Gleick (Ed.), *The world's water*. Island Press. https://doi.org/10.5822/978-1-59726-228-6_9

Scientific Panel for Sustainable Forest Practices in Clayoquot Sound. (1995). *Sustainable ecosystem management in Clayoquot Sound: Planning and practices*. https://www.for.gov.bc.ca/hfd/library/documents/bib12571.pdf

Scoones, I. (2023). Livestock, methane, and climate change: The politics of global assessments. *WIREs Climate Change, 14*(1), e790.

Scott, J. (2022). *The climate crisis we already fixed (and what we can learn from it)* [Video]. YouTube.

Scott, K.N. (2004). International regulation of undersea noise. *ICLQ, 53*, 287–324.

Séguin, J. (Ed.). (2008). *Human health in a changing climate: A Canadian assessment of vulnerabilities and adaptive capacity*. Health Canada.

Seidel, J. (2022, August 27). Extreme China heatwave could lead to global chaos and food shortages. *New Zealand Herald*.

Service Canada. (2021, June 29). *Executive summary of the socio-economic and environmental study of the Canadian remanufacturing sector and other value-retention processes in the context of a circular economy*. https://www.canada.ca/en/services/environment/conservation/sustainability/circular-economy/summary-study-remanufacturing-sector-value-retention-processes.html

Shandro, J., Jokinen, L., Stockwell, A., & Mazzei, F. (2017). Risks and impacts to First Nation health and the Mount Polley mine tailings dam failure. *International Journal of Indigenous Health, 12*(2), 84.

Shaw, K. (2003). Encountering Clayoquot, reading the political. In W. Magnusson & K. Shaw (Eds.), *A political space: Reading the global through Clayoquot Sound* (pp. 25–66). McGill-Queen's University Press.

Smith, G. (2001). Taking deliberation seriously: Institutional design and green politics. *Environmental Politics, 10*(3), 72–93. https://doi.org/10.1080/714000562

Smith, H. (2002). Shades of grey in Canada's greening during the Mulroney era. In K.R. Nossal & N. Michaud (Eds.), *Diplomatic departures: The Conservative era in Canadian foreign policy, 1984–93* (pp. 71–83). UBC Press.

Smith, L.C. (2011). *The world in 2050: Four forces shaping civilization's northern future*. Penguin.

Snoddon, T., & VanNijnatten, D. (2016). Carbon pricing and intergovernmental relations in Canada. *IRPP Insight, 12*, 1.

SOGL (State of the Great Lakes Report). (2022, September 5). *EPA and government of Canada*. https://stateofgreatlakes.net

Sohns, A. (2017, June 7). Mining and lack of governance threaten Arctic freshwater supplies. *Fair Observer*. https://www.fairobserver.com/more/environment /mining-arctic-drilling-environmental-climate-change-global-warming-latest -news-today-54780

Sollund, R. (2019). *The crimes of wildlife trafficking: Issues of justice, legality and morality*. Routledge.

Solomon, S., Ivy, D.J., Kinnison, D., Mills, M.J., Neely, R.R., & Schmidt, A. (2016). Emergence of healing in the Antarctic ozone layer. *Science, 353*(6296), 269–274. https://doi.org/10.1126/science.aae0061

Soroye, P., Newbold, T., & Kerr, J. (2020). Climate change contributes to widespread declines among bumble bees across continents. *Science, 367*(6478), 685–688.

Southall, B.L., Scholik-Schlomer, A.R., Hatch, L., Bergmann, T., Jasny, M., Metcalf, K., Weilgart, L., & Wright, A.J. (2017). Underwater noise from large commercial ships – International collaboration for noise reduction. *Encyclopedia of Maritime and Offshore Engineering*. https://doi.org/10.1002/9781118476406.emoe056

Spears, T. (2004, October 3). Evolving superbugs threaten humans. *St. John's Telegram*, A16.

Sprout, H., & Sprout, M. (1971). *Toward a politics of the planet earth*. Van Nostrand Reinhold Company.

Stafford, K. (2021). Eavesdropping on a changing Arctic. *The Circle*. https://www .arcticwwf.org/the-circle/stories/eavesdropping-on-a-changing-arctic

Statista. (2022). *Provincial forestry and logging GDP Canada 2022*. https://www .statista.com/statistics/858270/provincial-forestry-and-logging-gdp-canada/

Statistics Canada. (n.d.). *Sustainable development goals data hub*. https://www144 .statcan.gc.ca/sdg-odd/index-eng.htm

Statistics Canada. (2006, September 4). Study: The Alberta economic juggernaut. *The Daily*. http://web.archive.org/web/20061012071646/www.statcan.ca/Daily /English/060914/d060914c.html

Statistics Canada. (2022a, June 15). Canada's 2021 census of agriculture: A closer look at farming across the regions. *The Daily*. https://www150.statcan.gc.ca/n1/daily -quotidien/220615/dq220615a-eng.htm

Statistics Canada. (2022b, July 13). Home alone: More persons living solo than ever before, but roomies the fastest growing household type. *The Daily*. https:// www150.statcan.gc.ca/n1/daily-quotidien/220713/dq220713a-eng.htm

Steeves, P. (2021). *The Indigenous paleolithic of the western hemisphere*. University of Nebraska Press.

Steffanson Arctic Institute. (2004). *Arctic human development report*. https://oaarchive.arctic-council.org/items/f6c63158-401c-4a14-a8d2-5bc9f10710bf

Steffen, W., Persson, Å., Deutsch, L., Zalasiewicz, J., Williams, M., Richardson, K., Crumley, C., Crutzen, P., Folke, C., Gordon, L., Molina, M., Ramanathan, V., Rockström, J., Scheffer, M., Schellnhuber, H.J., & Svedin, U. (2011). The Anthropocene: From global change to planetary stewardship. *Ambio, 40*(7), 739–761. https://doi.org/10.1007/S13280-011-0185-X

Steffen, W., Richardson, K., Rockström, J., Cornell, S.E., Fetzer, I., Bennett, E.M., Biggs, R., Carpenter, S.R., De Vries, W., De Wit, C.A., Folke, C., Gerten, D., Heinke, J., Mace, G.M., Persson, L.M., Ramanathan, V., Reyers, B., & Sörlin, S. (2015). Planetary boundaries: Guiding human development on a changing planet. *Science, 347*(6223). https://doi.org/10.1126/SCIENCE.1259855

Stelter, G., & Artibise, A. (2021). Resource towns in Canada. *Canadian Encyclopedia.* https://www.thecanadianencyclopedia.ca/en/article/resource-towns

Sterner, T., Barbier, E.B., Bateman, I., van den Bijgaart, I., Crepin, A.-S., Edenhofer, O., Fischer, C., Habla, W., Hassler, J., Johansson-Stenman, O., Lange, A., Polasky, S., Rockström, J., Smith, H.G., Steffen, W., Wagner, G., Wilen, J.E., Alpízar, F., Azar, C., … & Robinson, A. (2019). Policy design for the Anthropocene. *Nature Sustainability, 2*, 14–21. https://doi.org/10.1038/s41893-018-0194-x

Stevis, D. (2005). The globalization of the environment. *Globalizations, 2*(3), 323–333. https://doi.org/10.1080/14747730500367900

St-Hilaire, S., Ribble, C.S., Stephen, C., Anderson, E., Kurath, G., & Kent, M.L. (2002). Epidemiological investigation of infectious hematopoietic necrosis virus in salt water net-pen reared Atlantic salmon in B.C. Canada. *Aquaculture, 212*(1–4), 49–68.

Stiegman, M. (2009). Fisheries privatization versus community-based management in Nova Scotia: Emerging alliances between first nations and non-native fishers. In L.E. Adkin (Ed.), *Environmental conflict and democracy in Canada* (pp. 69–83). UBC Press.

Stilt, K. (2021). Rights of nature, rights of animals. *Harvard Law Review, 134*(5), 276–285.

Stoddart, M., & Tindall, D. (2010). Feminism and environmentalism: Perspectives on gender in the BC environmental movement during the 1990s. *BC Studies, 165*, 75–100.

Stoett, P.J. (1999). *Human and global security: An exploration of terms*. University of Toronto Press.

Stoett, P.J. (2001). Fishing for norms: Foreign policy and the turbot dispute of 1995. In R. Irwin (Ed.), *Ethics and security in Canadian foreign policy* (pp. 249–268). UBC Press.

Stoett, P.J. (2006). Biosecurity: The next public policy imperative for Canada and the world. *Policy Options Politiques, 26*(2), 24–30.

Stoett, P.J. (2010). Framing bioinvasion: Biodiversity, Climate Change, Security, Trade, and Global Governance. *Global Governance, 16*(1), 103.

Stoett, P.J. (2013). *Global ecopolitics: Crisis, governance, and justice.* University of Toronto Press.

Stoett, P.J. (2016). Review of earth system governance: World politics in the anthropocene. *Review of Policy Research, 33*(3), 342–343.

Stoett, P.J. (2019). *Global ecopolitics: Crisis, governance, and justice* (2nd ed.). University of Toronto Press.

Stoett, P.J. (2022). Plastic pollution: A global challenge in need of multi-level justice-centred solutions. *One Earth, 5*(6), 53–56.

Stoett, P.J., & Dalby, S. (2022). The Anthropocene: Rethinking humanity's role in international relations. In P.G. Harris (Ed.), *Routledge handbook of global environmental politics* (pp. 203–216). Routledge.

Stoett, P.J., & Laferrière, E. (2006). *International ecopolitical theory: Critical approaches.* UBC Press.

Stoett, P.J., & Omrow, D. (2022). *Spheres of transnational ecoviolence: Environmental crime, human security, and justice.* Palgrave Macmillan.

Stoett, P.J., & Temby, O. (2015). Bilateral and trilateral natural resource and biodiversity governance in North America: Organizations, networks, and inclusion. *Review of Policy Research, 32*(1), 1–18. https://doi.org/10.1111/ropr.12110

Stoett, P., & Vince, J. (2019). The plastic–climate nexus: Linking science, policy, and justice. In P.G. Harris (Ed.), *Climate change and ocean governance: Politics and policy for threatened seas* (pp. 345–361). Cambridge University Press. https://doi.org/10.1017/9781108502238.021

Stoett, P., & Vince, J. (2021). The marine debris nexus: Plastic, climate change, biodiversity and human health. In B. Siebenhuner & R. Djalante (Eds.), *Adaptiveness: Changing earth system governance* (pp. 83–101). Cambridge University Press.

Stone, C. (1972). Should trees have standing? Toward legal rights for natural objects. *Southern California Law Review, 45,* 450–501.

Strack, M., Davidson, S.J., Hirano, T., & Dunn, C. (2022). The potential of peatlands as nature-based climate solutions. *Current Climate Change Reports, 8,* 71–82. https://doi.org/10.1007/s40641-022-00183-9

Stuart-Ulin, C.R. (2021, February 24). Quebec's Magpie River becomes first in Canada to be granted legal personhood. *National Observer.* https://www.nationalobserver.com/2021/02/24/news/quebecs-magpie-river-first-in-canada-granted-legal-personhood

Studin, I. (2017, March 3). Canada: Population 100 million – part II. *Global Brief Magazine.* http://globalbrief.ca/blog/2017/03/03/canada-%E2%80%93-population-100-million-%E2%80%93-part-ii

Sunshine Project. (2002). *An introduction to biological weapons, their prohibition, and the relation to biosafety.* Jutaprint.

Sutherst, R. (2000). Climate change and invasive species: A conceptual framework. In A. Mooney & R. Hobbs (Eds.), *Invasive species in a changing world* (pp. 211–240). Island Press.

Suzuki, D., & Hanington, I. (2020, March 5). *The woman who discovered global warming – in 1856!* David Suzuki Foundation. https://davidsuzuki.org/story/the-woman-who-discovered-global-warming-in-1856

Swiaczny, F. (2019). *Demographic megatrends and global population growth.* UN-DESA. https://www.un.org/en/development/desa/population/events/pdf/expert/30/presentations/Monday/Session2/Frank_Swiaczny_UNDESA_PowerPoint_EGM%20CPD53.pdf

Tape, K.D., Clark, J.A., Jones, B.M., Wheeler, H.C., Marsh, P., & Rosell, F. (2021). *Beaver engineering: Tracking a new disturbance in the Arctic.* NOAA Arctic Report Card. https://doi.org/10.25923/0jtd-vv85

Taylor, R. (2014, March 10). *Recent changes to the Fisheries Act and what it means for biodiversity.* Beaty Biodiversity Museum. https://beatymuseum.ubc.ca/2014/03/10/recent-changes-to-the-fisheries-act-and-what-it-means-for-biodiversity

Temby, O., & Stoett, P. (Eds.). (2017). *Towards continental environmental policy: North American transnational networks and governance.* SUNY Press.

Tennberg, M. (2010). Indigenous Peoples as international political actors: A summary. *Polar Record, 46*(3), 264–270.

Theodoropoulas, D. (2003). *Invasion biology: Critique of a pseudoscience.* Avvar Books.

Theriault, S. (2013). Canadian Indigenous Peoples and climate change: The potential for Arctic land claims agreements to address changing environmental conditions. In *Climate change and Indigenous Peoples.* Edward Elgar Publishing. https://doi.org/10.4337/9781781001806.00025

Thomson, M.D.J.M., & Binder, C.M. (2021). Recalibrating the Department of National Defence approach to active sonar impact management. *Marine Pollution Bulletin, 173,* 113044.

Todd, Z. (2015). Indigenizing the Anthropocene. In H. Davies & E. Turpin (Eds.), *Art in the Anthropocene: Encounters among aesthetics, environment and epistemologies* (pp. 241–254). Open Humanities Press.

Toner, G., Meadowcroft, J., & Chernicak, D. (2016). The struggle of the Canadian federal government to institutionalize sustainable development. In D. VanNijnatten (Ed.), *Canadian environmental policy and politics: The challenges of austerity and ambivalence* (pp. 116–129). Oxford University Press.

Tough, F.J. (1992). Aboriginal rights versus the deed of surrender: The legal rights of native peoples and Canada's acquisition of the Hudson's Bay Company territory. *Prairie Forum, 17*(2), 225–250.

Trask, B. (2020). *Mega trends and families: The impact of demographic shifts, international migration and urbanization, climate change, and technological transformations.* United Nations. https://www.un.org/development/desa/family/wp-content/uploads/sites/23/2020/06/UN.MegaTrends.Final_.Trask_.2020.pdf

Truth and Reconciliation Commission. (2015). *Calls to action.* https://ehprnh2mwo3.exactdn.com/wp-content/uploads/2021/01/Calls_to_Action_English2.pdf

Turcheniuk, K., Bondarev, D., Singhal, V., & Yushin, G. (2018). Ten years left to redesign lithium-ion batteries. *Nature, 559*(7715), 467–470.

Turcotte, A., Kermany, N., Foster, S., Proctor, C.A., Gilmour, S.M., Doria, M., Sebes, J., Whitton, J., Cooke, S.J., & Bennett, J.R. (2021). Fixing the Canadian Species at Risk Act: Identifying major issues and recommendations for increasing accountability and efficiency. *FACETS, 6*, 1474–1494. https://doi.org/10.1139/facets-2020-0064

UNAIDS. (2022). *Global HIV & AIDS statistics: Full fact sheet*. https://www.unaids.org/sites/default/files/media_asset/UNAIDS_FactSheet_en.pdf

UNDP (United Nations Development Programme). (2006). *Human development report 2006: Beyond scarcity: Power, poverty, and the global water crisis*. https://hdr.undp.org/content/human-development-report-2006

UNEP (United Nations Environment Programme). (2002). *Global environmental outlook 3: Past, present, and future perspectives*. Earthscan.

UNEP (United Nations Environment Programme). (2016). *GEO-6: Global environmental outlook: Regional assessment for North America*. https://www.unep.org/resources/report/geo-6-global-environment-outlook-regional-assessment-north-america

UNEP (United Nations Environment Programme). (2021). *Global methane assessment: Benefits and costs of mitigating methane emissions*. https://www.ccacoalition.org/sites/default/files/resources//2021_Global-Methane_Assessment_full_0.pdf

UNGA (United Nations General Assembly). (2022, July 28). *UN General Assembly declares access to clean and healthy environment a universal human right*. https://news.un.org/en/story/2022/07/1123482

United Nations. (2017). *Goal 12: Responsible consumption and production*. www.un.org/sustainabledevelopment/sustainable-consumption-production/

United Nations. (2019). *State of the world's Indigenous Peoples: Implementing the United Nations Declaration on the Rights of Indigenous Peoples* (Vol. 4). https://social.un.org/unpfii/sowip-vol4-web.pdf

United Nations World Commission on Environment and Development (Ed.). (1987). *Our Common Future*. Oxford University Press.

University of Washington. (2024). *Marine cloud brightening program*. Department of Atmospheric and Climate Science. https://atmos.uw.edu/faculty-and-research/marine-cloud-brightening-program

Unrau, K. (2022, September 7). JFK Law files treaty claim on behalf of Duncan's First Nation to address the cumulative effects of development. *JFK Law*. https://jfklaw.ca/jfk-law-files-treaty-claim-on-behalf-of-duncans-first-nation-to-address-the-cumulative-effects-of-development/

UN Water. (2021, July). *Summary progress update 2021 – SDG 6 – water and sanitation for all*. https://www.unwater.org/sites/default/files/app/uploads/2021/12/SDG-6-Summary-Progress-Update-2021_Version-July-2021a.pdf

Urbina, I. (2019). *The outlaw ocean: Crime and survival in the last untamed frontier*. Vintage.

US EPA. (2006). *Extreme events: Climate change – Health and environmental effects*. http://www.epa.gov/climatechange/effects/extreme.html

US Trade Representative. (2023). *Canada*. http://ustr.gov/countries-regions/americas/canada

Van Bets, L.K.J., Lamers, M.A.J., & van Tatenhove, J.P.M. (2017). Collective self-governance in a marine community: Expedition cruise tourism at Svalbard. *Journal of Sustainable Tourism*, *25*(11), 1583–1599. https://doi.org/10.1080/09669582.2017.1291653

Van Driesche, J., & van Driesche, R. (2000). *Nature out of place: Biological invasions in the global age*. Island Press.

VanNijnatten, D.L. (2016). *Canadian environmental policy and politics: The challenges of austerity and ambivalence*. Oxford University Press.

VanNijnatten, D.L., & Boardman, R. (2009). Introduction. In D. VanNijnatten & R. Boardman (Eds.), *Canadian environmental policy and politics: Prospects for leadership and innovation* (pp. ix–xxvii). Oxford University Press.

VanNijnatten, D., & del Buey, E. (2021). Canada's international climate and environmental policy: Good intentions and staying the course – as things get ugly. In R.W. Murray & P. Gecelovsky (Eds.), *The Palgrave handbook of Canada in international affairs* (pp. 413–432). Springer International. https://doi.org/10.1007/978-3-030-67770-1_19

Vecsey, C. (1987). Grassy Narrows Reserve: Mercury pollution, social disruption, and natural resources: A question of autonomy. *American Indian Quarterly*, *11*(4), 287–314. https://www.jstor.org/stable/1184289?origin=JSTOR-pdf

Vogel, G. (2017). Where have all the insects gone? *Science, 356*(6338), 576–579.

Vogler, J. (2022). Mainstream theories: Realism, rationalism and revolutionism. In P.G. Harris (Ed.), *Routledge handbook of global environmental politics* (pp. 30–41). Routledge.

Wagner, D.L., Grames, E.M., Forister, M.L., Berenbaum, M.R., & Stopak, D. (2021). Insect decline in the Anthropocene: Death by a thousand cuts. *Proceedings of the National Academy of Sciences, 118*(2). https://doi.org/10.1073/pnas.2023989118

Waldron, I. (2018). *There's something in the water: Environmental racism in Indigenous and Black communities*. Fernwood Publishing.

Walkem, A. (2007). The land is dry: Indigenous peoples, water, and environmental justice. In K. Bakker (Ed.), *Eau Canada: The future of Canada's water* (pp. 303–319). UBC Press. https://doi.org/10.59962/9780774856201-021

Walks, R.A. (2005). The city-suburban cleavage in Canadian federal politics. *Canadian Journal of Political Science*, *38*(2), 383–413. https://doi.org/10.1017/S0008423905030842

Walter, P. (2007). Adult learning in new social movements: Environmental protest and the struggle for the Clayoquot Sound rainforest. *Adult Education Quarterly*, *57*(3), 248–263.

Wang, Q., Zhang, C., & Li, R. (2023). Plastic pollution induced by the COVID-19: Environmental challenges and outlook. *Environmental Science and Pollution Research*, *30*(14), 40405–40426. https://doi.org/10.1007/s11356-022-24901-w

Wang, X., Kinay, P., Augustine, P.J., & Augustine, M. (2023). Reporting evidence on the environmental and health impacts of climate change on Indigenous Peoples of Atlantic Canada: A systematic review. *Environmental Research: Climate, 2*(2), 1–23. doi:10.1088/2752-5295/accb01

Wapner, P.K. (1996). *Environmental activism and world civic politics: The cultural and political landscape of Anishinaabe anti-clearcutting activism*. State University of New York Press.

Warner, R. (2010). Ecological modernisation theory: Towards a critical ecopolitics of change? *Environmental Politics, 19*(4), 538–556. https://doi.org/10.1080/09644016.2010.489710

Warner, R. (2021). The ethical place of the non-human world in earth system law. In T. Cadman, M. Hurlbert, & A.C. Simonelli (Eds.), *Earth system law: Standing on the precipice of the anthropocene* (pp. 128–147). Routledge. https://doi.org/10.4324/9781003198437-8

Watkins, M.H. (1963). A staple theory of economic growth. *Canadian Journal of Economics and Political Science, 29*(2), 141–158. https://doi.org/10.2307/139461

Watson, B., Masterman, S., & Whitney, E. (2023). *Critical minerals in the Arctic: Forging the path forward*. Wilson Center. www.wilsoncenter.org/article/critical-minerals-arctic-forging-path-forward

Weber, B. (2022, February 15). *Climate change made B.C. floods at least twice as likely, environment Canada study suggests*. Canadian Press.

White, D. (1993). *Invasive plants of natural habitats in Canada*. Canadian Wildlife Service.

Whiteside, K. (2006). *Precautionary politics: Principle and practice in confronting environmental risk*. MIT Press.

WHO-CBD (World Health Organization–Convention on Biodiversity). (2015). *Connecting global priorities: Biodiversity and human health, a state of knowledge review*. C. Romanelli, lead author.

Wiebe, S.M. (2017). *Everyday exposure: Indigenous mobilization and environmental justice in Canada's chemical valley*. University of British Columbia Press.

Wilkins, B. (2022, May 11). "Terrifying": UK license plate "splatometer" survey finds 60% plunge in flying insect population. *Spirit of Change Magazine*. https://www.spiritofchange.org/terrifying-uk-license-plate-splatometer-survey-finds-60-plunge-in-flying-insect-population/

Williams, A.P., Cook, B.I., & Smerdon, J.E. (2022). Rapid intensification of the emerging southwestern North American megadrought in 2020–2021. *Nature Climate Change, 12*, 232–234. https://doi.org/10.1038/s41558-022-01290-z

Williams, J. (2012, March 12). Remembering the story of CFCs. *The Earthbound Report*. https://earthbound.report/2012/03/12/remembering-the-story-of-cfcs

Willms, I. (2011, March–April). Photo essay: Fort Chipewyan lives in the shadow of Alberta's oil sands. *This Magazine*.

Wilson, J. (1998). *Talk and log: Wilderness politics in British Columbia*. UBC Press.

Wilt, J. (2018, August 14). Are Albertans collecting a fair share of oilsands wealth? *The Narwhal*. https://thenarwhal.ca/are-albertans-collecting-a-fair-share-of-oilsands-wealth/

Winfield, M. (2023, November 19). Are freeloading premiers undermining Canada's climate strategy? *The Conversation*. http://theconversation.com/are-freeloading-premiers-undermining-canadas-climate-strategy-217638

Wood, S. (2024). Frustrated with Canada's spill response, Heiltsuk leaders take their fight international. *The Narwhal.* https://thenarwhal.ca/heiltsuk-nation-international-marine-organization

World Health Organization (WHO). (1946). *Constitution of the World Health Organization.* http://apps.who.int/gb/bd/PDF/bd47/EN/constitution-en.pdf?ua=1

World Tourism and Travel Council. (2023, May 15). *Strong signs of recovery for travel and tourism in Canada says WTTC.* PR Newswire. https://www.prnewswire.com/news-releases/strong-signs-of-recovery-for-travel-tourism-in-canada-says-wttc-301824594.html

World Wildlife Fund. (2022, July 14). *Canada's new offshore oil and gas regulations too weak to ensure safety and environmental protection.* https://wwf.ca/stories/canada-offshore-oil-and-gas-regulations-too-weak

Xing, L. (2019, June 15). Why electric vehicle owners are urging Ford government to fund charging stations. *CBC News.* https://www.cbc.ca/news/canada/toronto/electric-vehicle-charging-doug-ford-1.5174747

Yakabuski, K. (2011, August 24). Gary Doer sells oil sands from coast to U.S. coast. *Globe and Mail.* https://www.theglobeandmail.com/news/world/gary-doer-sells-oil-sands-from-coast-to-us-coast/article594249

Yergin, D. (2003). *The prize: The epic quest for oil, money, and power.* Free Press.

Young, N., & Matthews, R. (2010). *The aquaculture controversy in Canada: Activism, policy, and contested science.* UBC Press. https://doi.org/10.59962/9780774818124

Yousif, N., & Smith, M.D. (2020). What the Wet'suwet'en want. *Maclean's, 133*(4), 54–59.

Zelko, F. (2004). Making Greenpeace: The development of direct action environmentalism in British Columbia. *BC Studies,* 142–143.

Zubrow, E.B.W., Meidinger, E., & Connolly, K.D. (2019). *The big thaw: Policy, governance, and climate change in the circumpolar north.* SUNY Press.

Index